SRA Reading Mastery
Signature Edition

Presentation Book C
Grade 1

Siegfried Engelmann
Elaine C. Bruner

 McGraw Hill SRA

Columbus, OH

READING MASTERY® is a registered trademark of The McGraw-Hill Companies, Inc.

SRAonline.com

Printed in the United States of America.

Send all inquiries to this address:
SRA/McGraw-Hill
4400 Easton Commons
Columbus, OH 43219

ISBN: 978-0-07-612452-7
MHID: 0-07-612452-5

11 12 13 14 15 RMN 17 16 15 14

Table of Contents

Presentation Book A

Introductory pages . . . . iii-v
Planning Pages for Lessons 1–20 . . . . va
Lesson 1 1   Lesson 11 53
Lesson 2 7   Lesson 12 61
Lesson 3 13   Lesson 13 69
Lesson 4 17   Reading Hard
Reading Hard   Words Test 70
  Words Test 20   Lesson 14 72
Lesson 5* 22   Lesson 15* 78
Lesson 6 29   Lesson 16 84
Lesson 7 35   Lesson 17 90
Lesson 8 41   Lesson 18 96
Lesson 9 44   Lesson 19 99
Reading Hard   Lesson 20* 105
  Words Test 45   Group Accuracy
Lesson 10* 47   Test 109

Planning Pages for Lessons 21–40 . . . . 111a
Lesson 21 112   Lesson 31 172
Lesson 22 118   Lesson 32 178
Lesson 23 124   Lesson 33 181
Lesson 24 130   Lesson 34 187
Lesson 25* 136   Lesson 35* 194
Lesson 26 142   Lesson 36 201
Group Accuracy   Group Accuracy
  Test 145   Test 205
Lesson 27 148   Lesson 37 208
Lesson 28 154   Lesson 38 215
Lesson 29 160   Lesson 39 222
Lesson 30* 166   Lesson 40* 229

Planning Pages for Lessons 41–60 . . . . 234a
Lesson 41 235   Lesson 45* 257
Lesson 42 241   Lesson 46 263
Lesson 43 246   Lesson 47 269
Lesson 44 252   Lesson 48 273

Presentation Book B

Lesson 49 1   Lesson 55* 35
Lesson 50* 7   Lesson 56 41
Lesson 51 13   Lesson 57 47
Lesson 52 19   Lesson 58 52
Lesson 53 25   Lesson 59 57
Lesson 54 30   Lesson 60* 62

Planning Pages for Lessons 61–80 . . . . . 67a
Lesson 61 68   Lesson 71 123
Lesson 62 74   Lesson 72 127
Lesson 63 80   Lesson 73 132
Lesson 64 86   Lesson 74 137
Lesson 65* 92   Lesson 75* 142
Lesson 66 97   Lesson 76 147
Lesson 67 103   Lesson 77 152
Lesson 68 108   Lesson 78 157
Lesson 69 113   Lesson 79 162
Lesson 70* 118   Lesson 80* 167

Planning Pages for Lessons 81–100 . . . 171a
Lesson 81 172   Lesson 91 226
Lesson 82 177   Lesson 92 232
Lesson 83 182   Lesson 93 237
Lesson 84 188   Lesson 94 242
Lesson 85* 194   Lesson 95* 247
Lesson 86 200   Lesson 96 251
Lesson 87 205   Lesson 97 255
Lesson 88 210   Lesson 98 259
Lesson 89 215   Lesson 99 264
Lesson 90* 221   Lesson 100* 268

Planning Pages for Lessons 101–120 . 271a
Lesson 101 272   Lesson 103 280
Lesson 102 276   Lesson 104 284

Presentation Book C

Lesson 105* 1   Lesson 113 33
Lesson 106 5   Lesson 114 37
Lesson 107 9   Lesson 115* 41
Lesson 108 13   Lesson 116 45
Lesson 109 17   Lesson 117 49
Lesson 110* 21   Lesson 118 53
Lesson 111 25   Lesson 119 57
Lesson 112 29   Lesson 120* 61

Planning Pages for Lessons 121–140 . . 64a
Lesson 121 65   Lesson 131 113
Lesson 122 70   Lesson 132 117
Lesson 123 75   Lesson 133 122
Lesson 124 80   Lesson 134 126
Lesson 125* 85   Lesson 135* 130
Lesson 126 89   Lesson 136 134
Lesson 127 94   Lesson 137 138
Lesson 128 99   Lesson 138 142
Lesson 129 104   Lesson 139 146
Lesson 130* 109   Lesson 140* 150

Planning Pages for Lessons 141–160 . 153a
Lesson 141 154   Lesson 151 195
Lesson 142 158   Lesson 152 199
Lesson 143 162   Lesson 153 203
Lesson 144 166   Lesson 154 207
Lesson 145* 170   Lesson 155* 211
Lesson 146 174   Lesson 156 215
Lesson 147 178   Lesson 157 219
Lesson 148 182   Lesson 158 223
Lesson 149 186   Lesson 159 227
Lesson 150* 190   Lesson 160* 232

*Individual Checkout Lessons

Curriculum Map *at the back of the book*

READING VOCABULARY

EXERCISE 1

Teacher reads the words in red

a. I'll read each word in red. Then you'll spell each word.

b. (Touch the ball for **animal.**) My turn. (Slash as you say:) Animal. What word? (Signal.) *Animal.*

c. (Return to the ball.) Spell it. Get ready. (Tap under each letter as the children say:) *A-N-I-M-A-L.*

• What word did you spell? (Signal.) *Animal.*

d. (Repeat steps *b* and *c* for each word in red.)

e. Your turn to read all the words in this column.

f. (Touch the ball for **animal.** Pause.) Get ready. (Slash.) *Animal.*

g. (Repeat step *f* for each remaining word in the column.)

h. (Repeat steps *f* and *g* until firm.)

animal

tickle

roared

toad

howling

leave

turn

EXERCISE 2

Read the fast way

a. You're going to read all the words in this column the fast way.

b. (Touch the ball for **spell.** Pause.) Get ready. (Slash.) *Spell.*

c. (Repeat step *b* until firm.)

d. (Repeat steps *b* and *c* for each remaining word in the column.)

e. (Repeat the column until the children read all the words in order without making mistakes.)

spell

monster

magic

Castle

don't

stream

bead

EXERCISE 3

Words with underlined parts

a. First you're going to read the underlined part of each word in this column. Then you're going to read the whole word.

b. (Touch the ball for **stays.**) Read the underlined part. Get ready. (Tap the ball.) *Stays.*

• Read the whole word. (Pause.) Get ready. (Slash.) *Stays.*

c. (Repeat step *b* until firm.)

d. (Repeat steps *b* and *c* for each remaining word in the column.)

e. (Repeat the column until children read all the words in order without making a mistake.)

stays

meanest

turned

anybody

really

walls

holding

EXERCISE 4

Children spell, then read

a. First you're going to spell each word. Then you're going to read that word the fast way.

b. (Touch the ball for **Who.**) Spell it. Get ready. (Tap under each letter as the children say:) *W-H-O.*

• (Return to the ball.) Read it. Get ready. (Slash.) *Who.*

c. (Repeat step *b* for each remaining word in the column.)

d. (Repeat steps *b* and *c* until firm.)

Who

made

floated

watched

long

robed

robbed

Individual test

a. (Call on individual children to read one column of words from the lesson.)

b. (Praise children who read all words with no errors.)

STORY 105
EXERCISE 5

Reading—decoding

a. (Pass out Storybook 2.)

b. Everybody, open your reader to page 60.

c. Remember, if the group reads all the way to the red 5 without making more than five errors, we can go on.

d. Everybody, touch the title of the story. ✔

e. If you hear a mistake, raise your hand. Remember, children who do not have their place lose their turn. (Call on individual children to read two or three sentences. Do not ask comprehension questions. Tally all errors.)

To Correct

word-identification errors (**from,** for example)
1. That word is **from.** What word? *From.*
2. Go back to the beginning of the sentence and read the sentence again.

f. (If the children make more than five errors before they reach the red 5: when they reach the 5 return to the beginning of the story and have the children reread to the 5. Do not ask comprehension questions. Repeat step *f* until firm, and then go on to step *g*.)

g. (When the children read to the red 5 without making more than five errors: read the story to the children from the beginning to the 5. Ask the specified comprehension questions. When you reach the 5, call on individual children to continue reading the story. Have each child read two or three sentences.
Ask the specified comprehension questions.)

Boo Goes to the Castle[1]

The five mean ghosts had made Boo leave the old house. When Boo was walking to town, he found a talking frog. The frog was near a stream. But the frog was not really a frog. It was a king. <u>A monster had cast a spell on the king and turned him into a frog.</u>[2]

"I will help you," Boo said. "Just tell me where the monster stays."

The frog said, "The monster is in my castle. <u>That castle is on the other side of town.</u>"[3]

"You wait here," Boo said. "I will be back."

Boo floated up into the sky. He floated over the town like a bird. <u>Soon he came to the castle ★ on the other side of town.</u>[4] When he floated near the castle, the <u>hounds began to howl.</u>[5] Boo floated to the top of the wall that went around the castle. ⑤ The hounds were howling and howling.

Then the door to the castle opened and out came the meanest-looking monster Boo had ever seen. That monster roared, "Who is out here? <u>Who is making my hounds howl?</u>"[6]

---

[1] What's going to happen in this story? (Signal.) *Boo will go to the castle.*

[2] How did the king get to be a frog? (The children respond.) Yes, a monster cast a spell on the frog.

[3] Where does the monster stay? (The children respond.)

• Whose castle is it? (The children respond.)

• Where is that castle? (Signal.) *On the other side of town.*

[4] How did Boo get there? (The children respond.) Yes, he floated in the sky like a bird.

[5] Tell me how those hounds sounded. (The children respond.)

[6] Who is talking? (Signal.) *The monster.*

• Why are the hounds howling? (The children respond.)

Boo did not say a thing. He just watched the monster.

The monster roared, "If you don't leave, I'll get you. I'll turn you into a frog or a toad."[7]

When the monster went back into the castle, Boo floated from the wall. He found a window and went inside the castle. He could see the monster. Boo said to himself, "That monster is really mean."[8]

The monster was holding a gold rod. She was saying, "As long as I have this magic rod, I can cast a spell over anybody. I can turn anybody into a frog or a toad."[9]

Boo said to himself, "I must get that magic rod from the monster."[10]

Stop

[7] What did the monster say she would do? (Signal.) *Turn Boo into a frog or a toad.*

[8] Where is Boo? (Signal.) *Inside the castle.*

[9] What does the monster use to cast her spells? (Signal.) *A magic rod.*

[10] What does Boo want to get? (Signal.) *The magic rod.*

• Next time we'll see if he gets the magic rod.

EXERCISE 6

Picture comprehension

a. Look at the picture.

b. (Ask these questions:)

1. Who is that mean-looking thing? (Signal.) *The monster.*

   • That's the meanest monster I've ever seen. Are there really monsters like that? (The children respond.)

2. Does Boo look afraid? (Signal.) *Yes.*

3. What's that building the monster lives in? (Signal.) *A castle.*

4. What are the dogs doing? (Signal.) *Howling.*

5. Is it daytime or nighttime in this picture? (Signal.) *Nighttime.*

   • How do you know? (The children respond.)

INDEPENDENT ACTIVITIES
EXERCISE 7

Summary of independent activities

a. (Pass out Worksheet 105 to each child.)

b. Everybody, now you'll do your worksheet. Remember to do all parts of the worksheet and to read all the parts carefully.

INDIVIDUAL CHECKOUT
EXERCISE 8

2-minute individual fluency checkout: rate/accuracy

a. As you are doing your worksheet, I'll call on children one at a time to read to the star. Remember, you get two stars on the chart if you read to the star in less than two minutes and make no more than four errors.

b. (Call on each child. Tell the child:) Read to the star very carefully. Start with the title. Go. (Time the child. Tell the child any words the child misses. Stop the child as soon as the child makes the fifth error or exceeds the time limit.)

c. (If the child meets the rate-accuracy criterion, record two stars on your chart for lesson 105. Congratulate the child. Give children who do not earn two stars a chance to read to the star again before the next lesson is presented.)

120 words/**2 min** = 60 wpm **[4 errors]**

END OF LESSON 105

READING VOCABULARY

EXERCISE 1

Teacher reads the words in red

a. I'll read each word in red. Then you'll spell each word.

b. (Touch the ball for **dress.**) My turn. (Slash as you say:) Dress. What word? (Signal.) *Dress.*

c. (Return to the ball.) Spell it. Get ready. (Tap under each letter as the children say:) *D-R-E-S-S.*

• What word did you spell? (Signal.) *Dress.*

d. (Repeat steps *b* and *c* for each word in red.)

e. Your turn to read all the words in this column.

f. (Touch the ball for **dress.** Pause.) Get ready. (Slash.) *Dress.*

g. (Repeat step *f* for each remaining word in the column.)

h. (Repeat steps *f* and *g* until firm.)

dress

bod

bode

part

out

leaf

real

EXERCISE 2

Words with underlined parts

a. First you're going to read the underlined part of each word in this column. Then you're going to read the whole word.

b. (Touch the ball for **dresses.**) Read the underlined part. Get ready. (Tap the ball.) *Dress.*

• Read the whole word. (Pause.) Get ready. (Slash.) *Dresses.*

c. (Repeat step *b* until firm.)

d. (Repeat steps *b* and *c* for each remaining word in the column.)

e. (Repeat the column until children read all the words in order without making a mistake.)

dresses

wanted

needed

really

laughed

myself

himself

EXERCISE 3

Read the fast way

a. You're going to read all the words in this column the fast way.

b. (Touch the ball for **castle.** Pause.) Get ready. (Slash.) *Castle.*

c. (Repeat step *b* until firm.)

d. (Repeat steps *b* and *c* for each remaining word in the column.)

e. (Repeat the column until the children read all the words in order without making mistakes.)

castle

people

from

bead

didn't

long

fear

EXERCISE 4

Children spell, then read

a. First you're going to spell each word. Then you're going to read that word the fast way.

b. (Touch the ball for **moped.**) Spell it. Get ready. (Tap under each letter as the children say:) *M-O-P-E-D.*

• (Return to the ball.) Read it. Get ready. (Slash.) *Moped.*

c. (Repeat step *b* for each remaining word in the column.)

d. (Repeat steps *b* and *c* until firm.)

moped

once

canner

plan

scare

hope

work

Individual test

a. (Call on different children to read one column of words from the lesson.)

b. (Praise children who read all words with no errors.)

STORYBOOK

STORY 106
EXERCISE 5

Reading—decoding

a. (Pass out Storybook 2.)

b. Everybody, open your reader to page 63.

c. Remember, if the group reads all the way to the red 5 without making more than five errors, we can go on.

d. Everybody, touch the title of the story. ✔

e. If you hear a mistake, raise your hand. Remember, children who do not have their place lose their turn. (Call on individual children to read two or three sentences. Do not ask comprehension questions. Tally all errors.)

To Correct

word-identification errors (**from,** for example)
1. That word is **from.** What word? *From.*
2. Go back to the beginning of the sentence and read the sentence again.

f. (If the children make more than five errors before they reach the red 5: when they reach the 5 return to the beginning of the story and have the children reread to the 5. Do not ask comprehension questions. Repeat step *f* until firm, and then go on to step *g*.)

g. (When the children read to the red 5 without making more than five errors: read the story to the children from the beginning to the 5. Ask the specified comprehension questions. When you reach the 5, call on individual children to continue reading the story. Have each child read two or three sentences.

Ask the specified comprehension questions.)

Boo Gets a Fish Tail[1]

Boo was inside the monster's castle. The monster had a magic rod that was made of gold. The monster was saying that she could cast spells on people as long as she had the magic rod.[2]

Boo said to himself, "I must get that rod from the monster."

Boo said, "I will try to scare the monster." So Boo made himself as big and as mean as he could.[3] But he was still pretty small and he didn't really look mean.

He floated down at the monster. "Oooooow," he said.

The monster laughed.[4] "What's this?" she said. "A little ghost thinks he can fill me with fear. I'll show him some fear."

The monster held up the magic rod. "Bod bode, bed bead," she said.[5] All at once, Boo felt funny. He looked down and saw that he had the tail of a fish. ⑤ He had a big fin growing from his back.[6]

"That should hold you for a while," the monster said, and she began to laugh. "Now get out of here before I turn you into a leaf."

---

[1] What's going to happen in this story? (Signal.) *Boo will get a fish tail.*

[2] What did the monster use the magic rod for? (Signal.) *To cast spells on people.*

[3] Why did Boo do that? (The children respond.) Yes, he's trying to scare the monster and get the magic rod from her.

[4] Did Boo scare her? (Signal.) *No.*

[5] Let's read that together. (Signal. Teacher and children read:) *Bod bode, bed bead.* These are words she's using to cast her spell. I wonder if the spell will work.

[6] Did the spell work? (Signal.) *Yes.*

• What did Boo look like now? (The children respond.) Yes, he's part fish.

• How do you know? (The children respond.) Yes, he had a fish tail and a fin.

Boo really got out of there, because he was really scared. <u>When he was far from the castle, he stopped and looked at himself.</u>[7] <u>He was part fish and part ghost.</u>[8] He wanted to cry. But he didn't cry.

He said to himself, "I must think of some way to get that gold rod from the monster. If I get the rod, I could turn myself back into a real ghost. <u>But that gold rod is my only hope.</u>"[9]

Boo sat and began to think. He needed a plan. He sat for a long time. Then all at once, he said, "I have a plan now. <u>And I think it will work.</u>"[10]

Stop

---

[7] Why did Boo get out of the castle? (Signal.) *Because he was scared.*
- What's he going to look like? (The children respond.)

[8] What did Boo look like? (Signal.) *Part fish and part ghost.*

[9] Did Boo cry? (Signal.) *No.*
- What does he want to do? (Signal.) *Get that magic rod.*
- Why? (Signal.) *To turn himself back into a ghost.*

[10] What does he think will work? (Signal.) *His plan.*
- We'll find out next time what his plan is and if that plan works.

EXERCISE 6

Picture comprehension

a. Look at the picture.
b. (Ask these questions:)
  1. What is the monster doing? (The children respond.) Yes, she's casting a spell on Boo.
  2. What is she using to cast the spell? (Signal.) *The magic rod.*
  3. What is that thing on Boo's back? (Signal.) *A fin.*
  - What other part of a fish does Boo have? (Signal.) *A tail.*
  4. Does Boo look happy? (The children respond.)
  5. Do those hounds look mean? (The children respond.)

WORKSHEET 106

EXERCISE 7

Summary of independent activities

a. (Pass out Worksheet 106 to each child.)
b. Everybody, now you'll do your worksheet. Remember to do all parts of the worksheet and to read all the parts carefully.

END OF LESSON 106

READING VOCABULARY

EXERCISE 1

Teacher reads the word in red

a. I'll read the word in red. Then you'll spell the word.

b. (Touch the ball for **knock.**) My turn. (Slash as you say:) Knock. What word? (Signal.) *Knock.*

c. (Return to the ball.) Spell it. Get ready. (Tap under each letter as the children say:) *K-N-O-C-K.*

• What word did you spell? (Signal.) *Knock.*

d. Your turn to read all the words in this column.

e. (Touch the ball for **knock.** Pause.) Get ready. (Slash.) *Knock.*

f. (Repeat step e for each remaining word in the column.)

g. (Repeat steps e and f until firm.)

knock

table

tricks

Works

float

real

Yes

EXERCISE 2

Words with underlined parts

a. First you're going to read the underlined part of each word in this column. Then you're going to read the whole word.

b. (Touch the ball for **always.**) Read the underlined part. Get ready. (Tap the ball.) *All.*

• Read the whole word. (Pause.) Get ready. (Slash.) *Always.*

c. (Repeat step b until firm.)

d. (Repeat steps b and c for each remaining word in the column.)

e. (Repeat the column until children read all the words in order without making a mistake.)

always

found

meal

thousand

lead

eating

themselves

EXERCISE 3

Read the fast way

a. You're going to read all the words in this column the fast way.

b. (Touch the ball for **meaner.** Pause.) Get ready. (Slash.) *Meaner.*

c. (Repeat step *b* until firm.)

d. (Repeat steps *b* and *c* for each remaining word in the column.)

e. (Repeat the column until the children read all the words in order without making mistakes.)

meaner

stayed

nobody

anybody

everybody

getting

themselves

EXERCISE 4

Children spell, then read

a. First you're going to spell each word. Then you're going to read that word the fast way.

b. (Touch the ball for **caped.**) Spell it. Get ready. (Tap under each letter as the children say:) *C-A-P-E-D.*

• (Return to the ball.) Read it. Get ready. (Slash.) *Caped.*

c. (Repeat step *b* for each remaining word in the column.)

d. (Repeat steps *b* and *c* until firm.)

caped

capped

What

scare

bod

bode

dress

Individual test

a. (Call on individual children to read one column of words from the lesson.)

b. (Praise children who read all words with no errors.)

"He's your puppy," her mom said.[9] Jean hugged the puppy harder. The puppy licked her face again.

Jean's mom said, "Somebody left this puppy for you. There was a note with him."[10]

Jean's dad handed the note to Jean. The note said: "This dog is for Jean. His name is Wizard.[11] And here is the rule about Wizard: If you love him and play with him, he will grow up to be the best dog in the land."[12]

Jean was so happy that tears were running down her cheeks. She said, "Thank you, Wizard.[13] Thank you very much."

She followed the rule, and her dog Wizard did become the very best dog in the land.

This is the end.

[9] Can Jean keep the puppy? (Signal.) *Yes.*

[10] How did the dog get there? (Signal.) *Somebody left him.*

• I wonder what the note says.

[11] What is the dog's name? (Signal.) *Wizard.*

• How about that.

[12] What will that puppy grow up to be? (Signal.) *The best dog in the land.*

[13] Why do you suppose she said that? (The children respond.)

EXERCISE 7

Picture comprehension

a. Look at the picture.

b. (Ask these questions:)

1. Where is Jean now? (The children respond.)
2. What is on the bed with her? (Signal.) *A puppy.*
3. What's the puppy's name? (Signal.) *Wizard.*

• How do you know? (The children respond.)

4. How do you think Jean feels about that puppy? (The children respond.)

WORKSHEET 160

INDEPENDENT ACTIVITIES
EXERCISE 8

Reading comprehension

a. (Pass out Worksheet 160 to each child.)

b. Everybody, turn to side 2 of your worksheet. ✔

c. (Point to the story on side 2 of your worksheet.) Everybody, find this story on your worksheet. ✔

d. Today you're going to read a passage that tells about the first people.

e. Everybody, look at the picture. (Pause.) This picture shows some people who lived a long time ago. They are hungry, so they are hunting for food. But they don't have guns, or even bows and arrows. What are they going to use to try to kill the animal? (The children respond.)

• Do you think it will work? (The children respond.)

f. When you do your independent work, read the story carefully to yourself. Then answer the questions.

EXERCISE 9

Summary of independent activities

Everybody, now you'll do your worksheet. Remember to do all parts of the worksheet and to read all the parts carefully.

INDIVIDUAL CHECKOUT
EXERCISE 10

2-minute individual fluency checkout: rate/accuracy

a. As you are doing your worksheet, I'll call on children one at a time to read to the star. Remember, you get two stars on the chart if you read to the star in less than two minutes and make no more than five errors.

b. (Call on each child. Tell the child:) Read to the star very carefully. Start with the title. Go. (Time the child. Tell the child any words the child misses. Stop the child as soon as the child makes the sixth error or exceeds the time limit.)

c. (If the child meets the rate-accuracy criterion, record two stars on your chart for lesson 160. Congratulate the child. Give children who do not earn two stars a chance to read to the star again.)

184 words/**2 min** = 92 wpm **[5 errors]**

END OF LESSON 160

STORYBOOK

STORY 107
EXERCISE 5

Reading—decoding

a. (Pass out Storybook 2.)

b. Everybody, open your reader to page 66.

c. Remember, if the group reads all the way to the red 5 without making more than five errors, we can go on.

d. Everybody, touch the title of the story. ✔

e. If you hear a mistake, raise your hand. Remember, children who do not have their place lose their turn. (Call on individual children to read two or three sentences. Do not ask comprehension questions. Tally all errors.)

To Correct

word-identification errors (**from,** for example)
1. That word is **from.** What word? *From.*
2. Go back to the beginning of the sentence and read the sentence again.

f. (If the children make more than five errors before they reach the red 5: when they reach the 5 return to the beginning of the story and have the children reread to the 5. Do not ask comprehension questions. Repeat step *f* until firm, and then go on to step *g*.)

g. (When the children read to the red 5 without making more than five errors: read the story to the children from the beginning to the 5. Ask the specified comprehension questions. When you reach the 5, call on individual children to continue reading the story. Have each child read two or three sentences. Ask the specified comprehension questions.)

Boo's Plan Works[1]

Boo had a plan for getting the gold rod from the monster.[2] Boo floated back to the old house where the other ghosts stayed. He floated inside the house. The other five ghosts were eating their big meal. They always ate a big meal before they went out to do mean things.[3]

When the ghosts saw Boo, they stopped eating and said, "What are you doing here? We made you leave this house. So get out."

Boo said, "I am here because I have found somebody you can't scare."[4]

The five ghosts jumped up from the table. The biggest ghost made himself as big as a horse. Then he made himself look meaner than the monster. "I can scare anybody," he shouted.

The other ghosts made themselves look big and mean, too. "We can scare anybody," they said.[5]

"No, you can't," Boo said. ⑤"There is a monster near here who is so mean that you can't scare her. And she can do magic things. Look at what she did to me."

The five ghosts looked at Boo's fish tail and his fin. They started to laugh.[6]

"That monster can play magic tricks on you," the biggest ghost said. "But you are not much of a ghost. Her magic won't work on us. We are real ghosts."[7]

"No," Boo said. "She will turn you into a log or into a frog."

"Come on," one of the ghosts said. "Let's go get that monster. Let's see her try to play tricks on us."[8]

The other ghosts said, "Yes, let's go. Lead us to her."

Had Boo's plan worked?[9]

Stop

[1] Will Boo's plan work in this story? (Signal.) *Yes.*
- How do you know? (Signal.) *Because the title says Boo's plan works.*

[2] What was Boo's plan for? (Signal.) *Getting the gold rod from the monster.*

[3] Where did Boo go? (Signal.) *Back to the old house.*
- Were the other ghosts there? (Signal.) *Yes.*
- What were they doing? (Signal.) *Eating.*

[4] Who can't they scare? (Signal.) *The monster.*

[5] Do you know what Boo's plan is? (The children respond.) Yes, I think he wants those mean ghosts to scare the monster.

[6] Why are those ghosts laughing at Boo? (The children respond.)
- He sure must look a sight.

[7] Does the biggest ghost think the monster can play magic tricks on them? (Signal.) *No.*
- Why not? (Signal.) *They are real ghosts.*

[8] Where are the ghosts going? (The children respond.)

[9] Say that question. (Signal.) *Had Boo's plan worked?*
- What's the answer? (Signal.) *Yes.*

RULE REVIEW
EXERCISE 5

Rule Review

a. Everybody, you have learned rules in the earlier Jean stories.

b. You learned a rule about flying. Say that rule. Get ready. (Signal.) *If you tap your foot three times, you will fly.*

• (Repeat until firm.)

c. You learned a rule about the man who can become letters. Say that rule. Get ready. (Signal.) *If you tell him to become a dog, he becomes the letters D-O-G.*

• (Repeat until firm.)

d. You learned a rule about making the wizard disappear. Say that rule. Get ready. (Signal.) *If you want the wizard to disappear, say, "But what and when."*

• (Repeat until firm.)

e. (If the children missed any rules, repeat steps *b* through *d*.)

STORY 160
EXERCISE 6

Reading—decoding

a. (Pass out Storybook 2.)

b. Everybody, open your reader to page 236.

c. Remember, if the group reads all the way to the red 5 without making more than five errors, we can go on.

d. Everybody, touch the title of the story. ✔

e. If you hear a mistake, raise your hand. Remember, children who do not have their place lose their turn. (Call on individual children to read two or three sentences. Do not ask comprehension questions. Tally all errors.)

Leaving the Land of Peevish Pets[1]

Jean had found out fifteen rules.[2] The last rule she found out told about making the wizard disappear. She needed only one more rule. So she sat down and began to think. Suddenly, she jumped up. She said, "I've got it. Every time I needed help, the wizard appeared. I think that's the rule.[3] I'll find out." She stood up and yelled, "I need help."[4]

Suddenly, the wizard appeared.[5] Jean said, "I think I know all of the rules. I know how to make you appear. Here's the rule: If you want the wizard to appear, call for help."

"Good," the wizard said.

Then Jean said, "So now I can leave this land of peevish pets."

"That is right," the wizard said. "You have found out all the rules. So you may leave. Just close your eyes."[6]

Jean closed her eyes. Suddenly, she felt something licking her face.⑤[7]

She opened her eyes. She was in bed. Her mom and dad were standing near the bed, and there was a puppy on the bed.[8] He ★ was licking Jean's face. He was black and brown and white. And he had a long tail. He was very pretty. Jean hugged him.

"Can I keep him?" she asked. "Can I, please?"

To Correct

word-identification errors (**from**, for example)

1. That word is **from.** What word? *From.*
2. Go back to the beginning of the sentence and read the sentence again.

f. (If the children make more than five errors before they reach the red 5: when they reach the 5 return to the beginning of the story and have the children reread to the 5. Do not ask comprehension questions. Repeat step *f* until firm, and then go on to step *g*.)

g. (When the children read to the red 5 without making more than five errors: read the story to the children from the beginning to the 5. Ask the specified comprehension questions. When you reach the 5, call on individual children to continue reading the story. Have each child read two or three sentences. Ask the specified comprehension questions.)

[1] What will Jean do in this story? (Signal.) *Leave the land of peevish pets.*

[2] How many more does she need? (Signal.) *One.*

[3] What is this rule about? (The children respond.)

• Let's read and see if you're right.

[4] What did she say? (Signal.) *I need help.*

[5] Did the wizard appear? (Signal.) *Yes.*

• She figured out that rule for herself.

[6] What did she have to do to go home? (Signal.) *Close her eyes.*

[7] What could it be? (The children respond.)

[8] Where was she? (The children respond.)

• Tell me everything she saw. (The children respond.)

EXERCISE 6

Picture comprehension

a. What do you think you'll **see** in the picture? (The children respond.)

b. Turn the page and look at the picture.

c. (Ask these questions:)

1. What are the ghosts in this picture doing? (Signal.) *Eating.*

2. Why is that big ghost pointing to Boo? (The children respond.)

3. What do you think he is saying to Boo? (The children respond.)

4. Which ghost do you think looks the meanest? (The children respond.)

EXERCISE 7

Summary of independent activities

a. (Pass out Worksheet 107 to each child.)

b. Everybody, now you'll do your worksheet. Remember to do all parts of the worksheet and to read all the parts carefully.

END OF LESSON 107

EXERCISE 3

Read the fast way

a. You're going to read all the words in this column the fast way.

b. (Touch the ball for **brown.** Pause.) Get ready. (Slash.) *Brown.*

c. (Repeat step *b* until firm.)

d. (Repeat steps *b* and *c* for each remaining word in the column.)

e. (Repeat the column until the children read all the words in order without making mistakes.)

brown

tail

become

became

ever

every

EXERCISE 4

Children spell, then read

a. First you're going to spell each word. Then you're going to read that word the fast way.

b. (Touch the ball for **nap.**) Spell it. Get ready. (Tap under each letter as the children say:) *N-A-P.*

• (Return to the ball.) Read it. Get ready. (Slash.) *Nap.*

c. (Repeat step *b* for each remaining word in the column.)

d. (Repeat steps *b* and *c* until firm.)

nap

diner

timer

pinned

pined

closed

note

Individual test

a. (Call on individual children to read one column of words from the lesson.)

b. (Praise children who read all words with no errors.)

READING VOCABULARY

EXERCISE 1

Teacher reads the words in red

a. I'll read each word in red. Then you'll spell each word.

b. (Touch the ball for **along**.) My turn. (Slash as you say:) Along. What word? (Signal.) *Along.*

c. (Return to the ball.) Spell it. Get ready. (Tap under each letter as the children say:) *A-L-O-N-G.*

• What word did you spell? (Signal.) *Along.*

d. (Repeat steps *b* and *c* for each word in red.)

e. Your turn to read all the words in this column.

f. (Touch the ball for **along**. Pause.) Get ready. (Slash.) *Along.*

g. (Repeat step *f* for each remaining word in the column.)

h. (Repeat steps *f* and *g* until firm.)

along

Plop

plate

flew

leaf

thousand

mean

EXERCISE 2

Words with underlined parts

a. First you're going to read the underlined part of each word in the column. Then you're going to read the whole word.

b. (Touch the ball for **flash**.) Read the underlined part. Get ready. (Tap the ball.) *sh.*

• Read the whole word. (Pause.) Get ready. (Slash.) *Flash.*

c. (Repeat step *b* until firm.)

d. (Repeat steps *b* and *c* for each remaining word in the column.)

e. (Repeat the column until children read all the words in order without making a mistake.)

flash

hounds

telling

dart

really

Another

he'll

LESSON 160

READING VOCABULARY

EXERCISE 1

Teacher reads the words in red

a. I'll read each word in red. Then you'll spell each word.

b. (Touch the ball for **U.S.**) My turn. (Slash as you say:) U-S. What word? (Signal.) *U-S.*

c. (Return to the ball.) Spell it. Get ready. (Tap under each letter and period as the children say:) *U-period-S-period.*

- What word did you spell? (Signal.) *U-S.*

d. (Touch the ball for **arrows**.) My turn. (Slash as you say:) Arrows. What word? (Signal.) *Arrows.*

e. (Return to the ball.) Spell it. Get ready. (Tap under each letter as the children say:) *A-R-R-O-W-S.*

- What word did you spell? (Signal.) *Arrows.*

f. (Repeat steps *d* and *e* for each word in red.)

g. Your turn to read all the words in this column.

h. (Touch the ball for **U.S.** Pause.) Get ready. (Slash.) *U-S.*

i. (Repeat step *h* for each remaining word in the column.)

j. (Repeat steps *h* and *i* until firm.)

U.S.

arrows

hey

push

motor

puppy

squeak

letter

EXERCISE 2

Words with underlined parts

a. First you're going to read the underlined part of each word in this column. Then you're going to read the whole word.

b. (Touch the ball for **liked**.) Read the underlined part. Get ready. (Tap the ball.) *Like.*

- Read the whole word. (Pause.) Get ready. (Slash.) *Liked.*

c. (Repeat step *b* until firm.)

d. (Repeat steps *b* and *c* for each remaining word in the column.)

e. (Repeat the column until children read all the words in order without making a mistake.)

liked

licked

darted

morning

finally

hugged

breathe

EXERCISE 3

Words with underlined parts

a. First you're going to read the underlined part of each word in this column. Then you're going to read the whole word.

b. (Touch the ball for **rammed.**) Read the underlined part. Get ready. (Tap the ball.) *Ramm.*

• Read the whole word. (Pause.) Get ready. (Slash.) *Rammed.*

c. (Repeat step *b* until firm.)

d. (Repeat steps *b* and *c* for each remaining word in the column.)

e. (Repeat the column until children read all the words in order without making a mistake.)

rammed

knocked

themselves

spells

behind

floating

heaved

EXERCISE 4

Children spell, then read

a. First you're going to spell each word. Then you're going to read that word the fast way.

b. (Touch the ball for **bit.**) Spell it. Get ready. (Tap under each letter as the children say:) *B-I-T.*

• (Return to the ball.) Read it. Get ready. (Slash.) *Bit.*

c. (Repeat step *b* for each remaining word in the column.)

d. (Repeat steps *b* and *c* until firm.)

bit

bite

bites

broke

turned

grew

near

Individual test

a. (Call on individual children to read one column of words from the lesson.)

b. (Praise children who read all words with no errors.)

"I wish that old wizard was here," Jean said. "I want to find out more rules so I can get out of here."

Just then the wizard appeared. He said, "You have found out a rule about the man who can become letters."

"Yes," Jean said. "If you tell him to become a dog, he becomes the letters d-o-g."[12]

"Very good," the wizard said. "Remember that rule, because I cannot tell you any more rules. You have to find out the last two rules by yourself."[13]

Jean said, "But what and when . . . ." The wizard disappeared.

She said, "Darn that wizard. Every time I say 'But what and when,' he disappears."[14]

Suddenly, Jean jumped up. She said, "That's the rule for making the wizard disappear. If you want the wizard to disappear, you say, 'But what and when.'"[15] Say that rule with Jean.[16]

Jean needed only one more rule to leave the land of peevish pets.

This is almost the end.[17]

---

[12] Everybody, say that rule with me. (Signal. Teacher and children say:) *If you tell him to become a dog, he becomes the letters D-O-G.*
- (Repeat until firm.)
- All by yourselves. Get ready. (Signal. The children repeat the rule until firm.)

[13] Jean knows fourteen rules. How is she going to find out the last two? (The children respond.)

[14] What happens every time Jean says, "But what and when"? (Signal.) *The wizard disappears.*
- That sounds like a rule.

[15] Everybody, say that rule with me. (Signal. Teacher and children say:) *If you want the wizard to disappear, you say, "But what and when."*
- (Repeat until firm.)

[16] Now say it one more time with Jean. (Signal.) Get ready. (Signal.) *If you want the wizard to disappear, you say, "But what and when."*

[17] We'll finish the story of Jean next time.

EXERCISE 7

Picture comprehension

a. Look at the picture.

b. (Ask these questions:)
1. Is there a real dog in this picture? (Signal.) *No.*
2. (Point to the letters **D-O-G.**) What word do these letters spell? (Signal.) *Dog.*
- Would you want a pet like that? (The children respond.)
3. Why does Jean look angry? (The children respond.)
4. What would the wizard be saying? (The children respond.)

WORKSHEET 159

INDEPENDENT ACTIVITIES
EXERCISE 8

Reading comprehension

a. (Pass out Worksheet 159 to each child.)

b. Everybody, turn to side 2 of your worksheet. ✔

c. (Point to the story on side 2 of your worksheet.) Everybody, find this story on your worksheet. ✔

d. Everybody, tell me the largest animal in the world. Get ready. (Signal.) *The whale.*

e. Today, you're going to learn about whales and how they breathe.

f. Everybody, show me how you breathe. (The children respond.)
- What are you breathing? (Signal.) *Air.*

g. (Repeat step *f* until firm.)

h. Everybody, touch the top of the whale's head. ✔
- Do you see the whale's breath coming from the top of its head? (The children respond.)
- The whale breathes through a hole in the top of its head.

i. When you do your independent work, read the story carefully to yourself. Then answer the questions.

EXERCISE 9

Summary of independent activities

Everybody, now you'll do your worksheet. Remember to do all parts of the worksheet and to read all the parts carefully.

END OF LESSON 159

STORY 108
EXERCISE 5

Reading—decoding

a. (Pass out Storybook 2.)

b. Everybody, open your reader to page 69.

c. Remember, if the group reads all the way to the red 5 without making more than five errors, we can go on.

d. Everybody, touch the title of the story. ✔

e. If you hear a mistake, raise your hand. Remember, children who do not have their place lose their turn. (Call on individual children to read two or three sentences. Do not ask comprehension questions. Tally all errors.)

To Correct

word-identification errors (**from,** for example)
1. That word is **from.** What word? *From.*
2. Go back to the beginning of the sentence and read the sentence again.

f. (If the children make more than five errors before they reach the red 5: when they reach the 5 return to the beginning of the story and have the children reread to the 5. Do not ask comprehension questions. Repeat step *f* until firm, and then go on to step *g*.)

g. (When the children read to the red 5 without making more than five errors: read the story to the children from the beginning to the 5. Ask the specified comprehension questions. When you reach the 5, call on individual children to continue reading the story. Have each child read two or three sentences. Ask the specified comprehension questions.)

The Ghosts Meet the Monster[1]

Boo was leading the way to the monster's castle. The biggest ghost said, "I'll scare her so much she'll turn into a mouse."[2] Another ghost said, "I'll scare her so much she'll turn into a bug."[3]

Soon, Boo and the other ghosts came to the castle. The hounds began to howl. One of the ghosts floated down near the hounds. He made himself as big as a horse. Then he said, "Eeeeeeeeeee." The hounds ran away like a flash.[4]

Then the ghosts floated into the castle. The monster was sitting at one end of a long table. The gold rod was at the other end.[5] One of the ghosts rammed into the table and broke the table into a thousand bits.[6] Another ghost picked up the monster's plate and heaved it at the monster. "Plop." It hit her in the nose.

Another ghost got behind the monster and made a loud sound. ⑤ "Rrrrr." When the monster turned around, the biggest ghost flew at the monster and knocked her down. All of the ghosts were howling and making themselves look as mean as they could.[7]

---

[1] What's this story going to be about? (Signal.) *The ghosts meet the monster.*

[2] What did the biggest ghost say? (Signal.) *I'll scare her so much she'll turn into a mouse.*

• Who is he going to scare? (Signal.) *The monster.*

[3] What did that ghost say? (Signal.) *I'll scare her so much she'll turn into a bug.*

[4] Why did they do that? (The children respond.)

• I guess I'd run away if I saw a ghost that big.

[5] Was the gold rod near the monster? (Signal.) *No.*

[6] What happened to the table? (The children respond.)

[7] Why were they doing that? (Signal.) *To scare the monster.*

• Do you think they'll scare her enough to make her leave? (The children respond.)

• Let's read and find out.

EXERCISE 6

Reading—decoding

a. (Pass out Storybook 2.)

b. Everybody, open your reader to page 233.

c. Remember, if the group reads all the way to the red 5 without making more than five errors, we can go on.

d. Everybody, touch the title of the story. ✔

e. If you hear a mistake, raise your hand. Remember, children who do not have their place lose their turn. (Call on individual children to read two or three sentences. Do not ask comprehension questions. Tally all errors.)

To Correct

word-identification errors (**from,** for example)
1. That word is **from.** What word? *From.*
2. Go back to the beginning of the sentence and read the sentence again.

f. (If the children make more than five errors before they reach the red 5: when they reach the 5 return to the beginning of the story and have the children reread to the 5. Do not ask comprehension questions. Repeat step *f* until firm, and then go on to step *g*.)

g. (When the children read to the red 5 without making more than five errors: read the story to the children from the beginning to the 5. Ask the specified comprehension questions. When you reach the 5, call on individual children to continue reading the story. Have each child read two or three sentences. Ask the specified comprehension questions.)

The Strange-Looking Man[1]

What did Jean do so that she could fly?[2]

What's the rule?[3]

Who did she see when she was flying?[4]

What did the strange-looking man say to her?[5]

Jean said, "Can't you say anything but 'bark, bark'?"

The man said, "Squeak, squeak."[6]

"I hate this place," Jean said. "I'm sorry that I ever wanted to dream about pets. I haven't seen a good pet in this place.[7] I want to go home."

The man handed Jean a note. The note said, "This man is a pet. He is any kind of pet you want. He can be a cat, or a dog, or a horse, or a pig. Just tell him what kind of pet you want."[8]

Jean looked at the man and said, "Let's see you be a dog."[9] And the man became the word dog. The man became three letters, d-o-g. ⑤[10]

"This is too much," Jean said. She began to walk away. The letters d-o-g said, "Bark, bark."[11]

"Oh, be quiet," Jean said. "Dogs don't say, 'Bark, bark.' They say, 'Woof, woof.'"

"Bark, bark," the letters said.

---

[1] What's the title of this story? (Signal.) *The strange-looking man.*

[2] What's the answer? (Signal.) *Tapped her foot three times.*

[3] Say the rule. (Signal.) *If you tap your foot three times, you will fly.*

[4] What's the answer? (Signal.) *A strange-looking man.*

[5] What's the answer? (Signal.) *Bark, bark.*

[6] What else did the man say? (Signal.) *Squeak, squeak.*

[7] Do you remember what Jean wanted to dream about? (Signal.) *Pets.*

[8] Could the man be a cat? (Signal.) *Yes.*
• Could he be a dog? (Signal.) *Yes.* Right. He is any kind of pet you want.

[9] What kind of pet did Jean want? (Signal.) *A dog.*

[10] Did he become a real dog? (Signal.) *No.* Right. He became the word **dog.**
• And how do you spell the word **dog**? (Signal.) *D-o-g.* Yes, the man became the letters, **D-O-G.**

[11] What did the letters D-O-G say? (Signal.) *Bark, bark.*

The monster got up. "What's going on here?" she shouted.

Then all five ghosts flew at her.

"I'm leaving," the monster said. And she ran away from the castle as fast as she could go.[8]

The biggest ghost flew over and grabbed the gold rod.[9]

"This must be a magic rod," he said. "We can have a lot of fun with this rod. We can turn Boo into a leaf."[10]

"That's a fine plan," the other ghosts said.

Stop

---

[8] Did the monster leave the castle? (Signal.) *Yes.*

[9] Did the monster take the magic rod with her? (Signal.) *No.*

- Did Boo get the rod? (Signal.) *No.*
- What happened to it? (Signal.) *The biggest ghost grabbed it.*

[10] What do these mean ghosts want to do to Boo? (Signal.) *Turn him into a leaf.*

- Do you think they can? (The children respond.)
- We'll find out if their plan works next time.

EXERCISE 6

Picture comprehension

a. Look at the picture.

b. (Ask these questions:)

1. What are those ghosts doing? (Signal.) *Scaring the monster.*
2. Does the monster look scared? (Signal.) *Yes.*
3. Where is the monster going? (The children respond.)
4. Did the monster take the magic rod with her? (Signal.) *No.*
- Where is it? (The children respond.)
5. What is Boo doing? (The children respond.) Yes, he's hiding and watching.
6. What would you do if you were the monster? (The children respond.)

WORKSHEET 108

EXERCISE 7

Summary of independent activities

a. (Pass out Worksheet 108 to each child.)

b. Everybody, now you'll do your worksheet. Remember to do all parts of the worksheet and to read all the parts carefully.

END OF LESSON 108

EXERCISE 4

Children spell, then read

a. First you're going to spell each word. Then you're going to read that word the fast way.

b. (Touch the ball for **diner**.) Spell it. Get ready. (Tap under each letter as the children say:) *D-I-N-E-R.*

• (Return to the ball.) Read it. Get ready. (Slash.) *Diner.*

c. (Repeat step *b* for each remaining word in the column.)

d. (Repeat steps *b* and *c* until firm.)

diner

dinner

noted

Woof

last

sorry

RULE REVIEW
EXERCISE 5

Rule review

a. Everybody, you have learned rules in the earlier Jean stories.

b. You learned a rule about how to be cold. Say that rule. Get ready. (Signal.) *If you want to be cold, say, "Side, slide."*

• (Repeat until firm.)

c. You learned a rule about talking animals. Say that rule. Get ready. (Signal.) *Talking animals lie.*

• (Repeat until firm.)

d. You learned a rule about flying. Say that rule. Get ready. (Signal.) *If you tap your foot three times, you will fly.*

• (Repeat until firm.)

e. (If the children missed any rules, repeat steps *b* through *d*.)

Individual test

a. (Call on individual children to read one column of words from the lesson.)

b. (Praise children who read all words with no errors.)

READING VOCABULARY

EXERCISE 1

Teacher reads the words in red

a. I'll read each word in red. Then you'll spell each word.

b. (Touch the ball for **Nothing.**) My turn. (Slash as you say:) Nothing. What word? (Signal.) *Nothing.*

c. (Return to the ball.) Spell it. Get ready. (Tap under each letter as the children say:) *N-O-T-H-I-N-G.*

• What word did you spell? (Signal.) *Nothing.*

d. (Repeat steps *b* and *c* for each word in red.)

e. Your turn to read all the words in this column.

f. (Touch the ball for **Nothing.** Pause.) Get ready. (Slash.) *Nothing.*

g. (Repeat step *f* for each remaining word in the column.)

h. (Repeat steps *f* and *g* until firm.)

Nothing

Bine

Bin

flower

anyhow

magic

scream

EXERCISE 2

Words with underlined parts

a. First you're going to read the underlined part of each word in this column. Then you're going to read the whole word.

b. (Touch the ball for **saying.**) Read the underlined part. Get ready. (Tap the ball.) *ing.*

• Read the whole word. (Pause.) Get ready. (Slash.) *Saying.*

c. (Repeat step *b* until firm.)

d. (Repeat steps *b* and *c* for each remaining word in the column.)

e. (Repeat the column until children read all the words in order without making a mistake.)

saying

holding

picked

spells

You're

biggest

can't

EXERCISE 3

Teacher reads the words in red

a. I'll read each word in red. Then you'll spell each word.

b. (Touch the ball for **contest.**) My turn. (Slash as you say:) Contest. What word? (Signal.) *Contest.*

c. A **contest** is a kind of test to see who is better at doing things. A race is a **contest.** You could have a **contest** to see who can jump the highest or who can do the dishes the fastest.

d. (Return to ball.) Spell it. Get ready. (Tap under each letter as the children say:) *C-O-N-T-E-S-T.* What word did you spell? (Signal.) *Contest.*

e. (Touch the ball for **finally.**) My turn. (Slash as you say:) Finally. What word? (Signal.) *Finally.*

f. Something that **finally** happens takes a long time to happen. If somebody **finally** gets to school, it takes them a long time. If the children **finally** stop talking, the children have talked for a long time.

g. (Return to the ball.) Spell it. Get ready. (Tap under each letter as the children say:) *F-I-N-A-L-L-Y.* What word did you spell? (Signal.) *Finally.*

h. (Touch the ball for **dock.**) My turn. (Slash as you say:) Dock. What word? (Signal.) *Dock.*

i. A **dock** is a place to park boats. What's a **dock?** (Signal.) *A place to park boats.*

j. (Return to the ball.) Spell it. Get ready. (Tap under each letter as the children say:) *D-O-C-K.* What word did you spell? (Signal.) *Dock.*

k. (Touch the ball for **bay.**) My turn. (Slash as you say:) Bay. What word? (Signal.) *Bay.*

l. A **bay** is a large place along the shore of an ocean. A **bay** does not usually have large waves. So it's a good place for boat docks.

m. (Return to the **ball.**) Spell it. Get ready. (Tap under each letter as the children say:) *B-A-Y.* What word did you spell? (Signal.) Bay.

n. Your turn to read all the words in this column.

o. (Touch the ball for **contest.** Pause.) Get ready. (Slash.) *Contest.*

p. (Repeat steps *o* for each remaining word in the column.)

q. (Repeat steps *o* and *p* until firm.)

contest ⟶

finally ⟶

dock ⟶

bay ⟶

morning ⟶

EXERCISE 3

Read the fast way

a. You're going to read all the words in this column the fast way.

b. (Touch the ball for **salt.** Pause.) Get ready. (Slash.) *Salt.*

c. (Repeat step *b* until firm.)

d. (Repeat steps *b* and *c* for each remaining word in the column.)

e. (Repeat the column until the children read all the words in order without making mistakes.)

salt

doesn't

read

meal

well

right

held

EXERCISE 4

Children spell, then read

a. First you're going to spell each word. Then you're going to read that word the fast way.

b. (Touch the ball for **cloud.**) Spell it. Get ready. (Tap under each letter as the children say:) *C-L-O-U-D.*

• (Return to the ball.) Read it. Get ready. (Slash.) *Cloud.*

c. (Repeat step *b* for each remaining word in the column.)

d. (Repeat steps *b* and *c* until firm.)

cloud

cope

side

hopper

hoper

fine

fin

Individual test

a. (Call on individual children to read one column of words from the lesson.)

b. (Praise children who read all words with no errors.)

READING VOCABULARY

EXERCISE 1

Teacher reads the words in red

a. I'll read each word in red. Then you'll spell each word.

b. (Touch the ball for **Darn.**) My turn. (Slash as you say:) Darn. What word? (Signal.) *Darn.*

c. (Return to the ball.) Spell it. Get ready. (Tap under each letter as the children say:) *D-A-R-N.*

• What word did you spell? (Signal.) *Darn.*

d. (Repeat steps *b* and *c* for each word in red.)

e. Your turn to read all the words in this column.

f. (Touch the ball for **Darn.** Pause.) Get ready. (Slash.) *Darn.*

g. (Repeat step *f* for each remaining word in the column.)

h. (Repeat steps *f* and *g* until firm.)

Darn

Squeak

breathe

letter

they

flying

idea

EXERCISE 2

Words with underlined parts

a. First you're going to read the underlined part of each word in this column. Then you're going to read the whole word.

b. (Touch the ball for **needed.**) Read the underlined part. Get ready. (Tap the ball.) *Need.*

• Read the whole word. (Pause.) Get ready. (Slash.) *Needed.*

c. (Repeat step *b* until firm.)

d. (Repeat steps *b* and *c* for each remaining word in the column.)

e. (Repeat the column until children read all the words in order without making a mistake.)

needed

almost

leave

winter

strange

became

quickly

STORY 109
EXERCISE 5

Reading—decoding

a. (Pass out Storybook 2.)

b. Everybody, open your reader to page 72.

c. Remember, if the group reads all the way to the red 5 without making more than five errors, we can go on.

d. Everybody, touch the title of the story. ✔

e. If you hear a mistake, raise your hand. Remember, children who do not have their place lose their turn. (Call on individual children to read two or three sentences. Do not ask comprehension questions. Tally all errors.)

To Correct
word-identification errors (**from,** for example)
1. That word is **from.** What word? *From.*
2. Go back to the beginning of the sentence and read the sentence again.

f. (If the children make more than five errors before they reach the red 5: when they reach the 5 return to the beginning of the story and have the children reread to the 5. Do not ask comprehension questions. Repeat step *f* until firm, and then go on to step *g*.)

g. (When the children read to the red 5 without making more than five errors: read the story to the children from the beginning to the 5. Ask the specified comprehension questions. When you reach the 5, call on individual children to continue reading the story. Have each child read two or three sentences. Ask the specified comprehension questions.)

The Ghosts Turn on Boo[1]

The biggest ghost had the magic rod. He was going to turn Boo into a leaf. He held the rod and said, "Turn Boo into a leaf." But nothing happened.[2]

"This thing doesn't work," the biggest ghost said.

Another ghost looked at the rod and said, "You're not saying the right words.[3] You have to say funny words if you want to cast a spell. Say something funny."

The biggest ghost said, "Bine bin, fine fin."[4] Nothing happened to Boo. But the biggest ghost turned into a big red flower.[5] The other ghosts laughed. "That was a good trick," they said.

One of the other ghosts grabbed the rod. He said, "I never did like that big ghost anyhow. Now I'm the biggest ghost and I will make this magic rod work for me."

He held the rod and said, "Tim time, cop cope."⑤[6] Nothing happened to Boo, but the ghost who was holding the rod turned into a leaf.[7]

The other mean ghosts laughed and laughed. Then one of them picked up the rod and said, "Now I am the biggest ghost. And I will find a way to make that rod work."

He held the rod and looked at it for a long time. Then he said, "I see words on the side of this rod. Those words tell how to cast spells."

The other mean ghosts said, "Well, read the words."[8]

The ghost who was holding the rod said, "I can't read."[9]

Stop

[1] What's the title of this story? (Signal.) *The Ghosts Turn on Boo.*
- What does it mean to "turn on Boo"? (The children respond.) Yes, they'll try to get him.
[2] Did the biggest ghost turn Boo into a leaf? (Signal.) *No.*
[3] Why didn't it work? (The children respond.) Yes, you've got to say the right magic words.
[4] Let's read the funny words together. (Signal. Teacher and children read:) *Bine bin, fine fin.*
[5] Did anything happen to Boo? (Signal.) *No.*
- What happened to the biggest ghost? (Signal.) *He turned into a big red flower.*

[6] Let's read the funny words together. (Signal. Teacher and children read:) *Tim time, cop cope.*
[7] Did anything happen to Boo? (Signal.) *No.*
- What happened to the ghost that said, "Tim time, cop cope"? (Signal.) *He turned into a leaf.*
[8] What did they say? (Signal.) *Well, read the words.*
- Who were they talking to? (The children respond.)
- What did the words on the rod tell? (Signal.) *How to cast spells.*
[9] Can that ghost read? (Signal.) *No.*
- We'll see what happens in the next story.

"Thank you," Jean said. "You are a talking animal and I tricked you. I will tap my foot three times and see what happens."

"Don't do that," the bug cried. "You will be sad. You will be a snake. Don't do it."[6]

Jean tapped her foot three times. Suddenly, she was flying like a bird.[7] The wind was blowing her striped hair. She went down. Then she went up. "Wow," she said. Then she did a loop. "Wow," she said again. "This is more fun than anything."

She began to fly faster. Then she said, "I hope I remember the rule about flying."

What do you do if you want to fly?[8] Tell Jean the rule.[9]

Jean was flying over a town now. She looked down and saw a man that looked like the wizard. So she dropped down to the ground. But the man was not the wizard.[10] He was very strange-looking. He stared at Jean and she stared at him.[11] Then she said, "Hello, my name is Jean."

He said, "Bark, bark."[12]

More to come[13]

---

[6] Do you think she'll turn into a snake? **(The children respond.)**
- Read some more.

[7] Did she turn into a snake? **(Signal.)** *No.*
- What did happen? **(Signal.)** *She was flying like a bird.*

[8] What do you think? **(The children respond.)** Yes, tap your foot three times.

[9] Say the rule with me. **(Signal. Teacher and children say:)** *If you tap your foot three times, you will fly.*
- **(Repeat until firm.)** All by yourselves. Get ready. **(Signal.) (The children repeat the rule until firm.)**

[10] Did she see the wizard when she was flying? **(Signal.)** *No.*

[11] What did they do? **(Signal.)** **Stared at each other.)**

[12] Who is talking? **(Signal.)** *The strange man.*
- He sure must be strange. Who usually says, "Bark, bark"? **(Signal.)** *A dog.*

[13] We'll find out more about the strange man next time.

EXERCISE 7

Picture comprehension

a. Look at the picture.
b. (Ask these questions:)

1. What is Jean doing? **(Signal.)** *Flying.*
- How do you know she's flying? **(The children respond.)**
2. Do you think she's having fun? **(Signal.)** *Yes.*
- How can you tell? **(The children respond.)**
3. Why does the bug have his fist like that? **(The children respond.)**
4. What do you think the bug is saying to her? **(The children respond.)**

INDEPENDENT ACTIVITIES
EXERCISE 8

Reading comprehension

a. (Pass out Worksheet 158 to each child.)
b. Everybody, turn to side 2 of your worksheet. ✔
c. (Point to the story on side 2 of your worksheet.) Everybody, find this story on your worksheet. ✔
d. Today you're going to read a passage that tells about mountains.
e. Everybody, touch the first picture. ✔
- That picture shows a very tall mountain. The line on the mountain shows how tall the mountain is. That mountain is nearly four miles tall. How tall is that mountain? **(Signal.)** *Nearly four miles tall.*
f. Everybody, touch the second picture. ✔
- That mountain is more than five miles tall. How tall is that mountain? **(Signal.)** *More than five miles tall.*
- That's the tallest mountain in the world. It is called Everest. What's it called? **(Signal.)** *Everest.*
- That mountain is in a land called Tibet. Where is Everest? **(Signal.)** *In Tibet.*
g. (Repeat steps e and f until firm.)
h. When you do your independent work, read the story carefully to yourself. Then answer the questions.

EXERCISE 9

Summary of independent activities

Everybody, now you'll do your worksheet. Remember to do all parts of the worksheet and to read all the parts carefully.

END OF LESSON 158

EXERCISE 6

Picture comprehension

a. What do you think you'll see in the picture? **(The children respond.)**

b. Turn the page and look at the picture.

c. (Ask these questions:)

1. Is that really a flower in that pot? **(Signal.)** *No.*

- What is it? **(The children respond.)** Yes, the biggest ghost.
- How did the ghost turn into a flower? **(The children respond.)**

2. Look at the big leaf. Is it really a leaf? **(Signal.)** *No.*

- What is it? **(The children respond.)** Yes, another ghost.

3. Look at the ghost holding the rod. Does he look happy? **(Signal.)** *No.*

- Why not? **(Signal.)** *He can't read.*

4. Does the ghost behind him look happy? **(Signal.)** *No.*

5. Do you think he can read? **(Signal.)** *No.*

6. Touch Boo. ✔

7. What do you think Boo is thinking? **(The children respond.)**

EXERCISE 7

Summary of independent activities

a. (Pass out Worksheet 109 to each child.)

b. Everybody, now you'll do your worksheet. Remember to do all parts of the worksheet and to read all the parts carefully.

END OF LESSON 109

STORYBOOK

RULE REVIEW
EXERCISE 5

Rule review

a. Everybody, you have learned rules in the earlier Jean stories.

b. You learned a rule about how to be warm again. Say that rule. Get ready. (Signal.) *If you want to be warm again, say, "I want to be warm again."*

- (Repeat until firm.)

c. You learned a rule about how to be cold. Say that rule. Get ready. (Signal.) *If you want to be cold, say, "Side, slide."*

- (Repeat until firm.)

d. You learned a rule about talking animals. Say that rule. Get ready. (Signal.) *Talking animals lie.*

- (Repeat until firm.)

e. (If the children missed any rules, repeat steps *b* through *d*.)

STORY 158
EXERCISE 6

Reading—decoding

a. (Pass out Storybook 2.)

b. Everybody, open your reader to page 230.

c. Remember, if the group reads all the way to the red 5 without making more than five errors, we can go on.

d. Everybody, touch the title of the story. ✔

e. If you hear a mistake, raise your hand. Remember, children who do not have their place lose their turn. (Call on individual children to read two or three sentences. Do not ask comprehension questions. Tally all errors.)

She Tricks a Talking Animal[1]

Jean had met a talking bug. She said to herself, "This is a talking animal. There is a rule about talking animals, but I can't remember it." <u>Tell Jean the rule about talking animals.</u>[2]

The bug said, "I will help you get out of here. I know all the rules, and I will tell you the best rules."

Jean had an idea about how to trick the talking animal. She said to herself, "If this animal says that something is fun, it won't be fun. If he tells me that something is good, it won't be good. <u>If he tells me that something is bad, it won't be bad.</u>"[3]

Jean smiled to herself. "I will ask him to tell me a rule about something that is really bad. But he won't tell me a rule about something that is bad. He will lie.⑤ He will tell me a rule about something that is good. <u>I will trick him.</u>"[4]

Jean said, "I have to find out more about the bad things in this place. Tell me a rule about something that is very, very bad."

The bug smiled and said, "Here's a rule about something that is really bad. <u>If you tap your foot three times, you will turn into a snake.</u>"[5]

To Correct

word-identification errors (**from**, for example)
1. That word is **from**. What word? *From.*
2. Go back to the beginning of the sentence and read the sentence again.

f. (If the children make more than five errors before they reach the red 5: when they reach the 5 return to the beginning of the story and have the children reread to the 5. Do not ask comprehension questions. Repeat step *f* until firm, and then go on to step *g*.)

g. (When the children read to the red 5 without making more than five errors: read the story to the children from the beginning to the 5. Ask the specified comprehension questions. When you reach the 5, call on individual children to continue reading the story. Have each child read two or three sentences. Ask the specified comprehension questions.)

[1] Who will trick a talking animal? (Signal.) *Jean.*

[2] What's the rule? (Signal.) *Talking animals lie.*

[3] Doesn't that animal tell the truth? (Signal.) *No.*

- What does that animal do? (Signal.) *He lies.*

[4] Her trick is to ask for something bad when she really wants something. . . . (Signal.) *Good.*

[5] What did the bug say will happen if you tap your foot three times? (Signal.) *You will turn into a snake.*

READING VOCABULARY

EXERCISE 1

Teacher reads the words in red

a. I'll read each word in red. Then you'll spell each word.

b. (Touch the ball for **snake**.) My turn. (Slash as you say:) Snake. What word? (Signal.) *Snake.*

c. (Return to the ball.) Spell it. Get ready. (Tap under each letter as the children say:) *S-N-A-K-E.*

• What word did you spell? (Signal.) *Snake.*

d. (Repeat steps *b* and *c* for each word in red.)

e. Your turn to read all the words in this column.

f. (Touch the ball for **snake**. Pause.) Get ready. (Slash.) *Snake.*

g. (Repeat step *f* for each remaining word in the column.)

h. (Repeat steps *f* and *g* until firm.)

snake

shy

smiling

dup

might

smile

stream

EXERCISE 2

Words with underlined parts

a. First you're going to read the underlined part of each word in this column. Then you're going to read the whole word.

b. (Touch the ball for **farmer**.) Read the underlined part. Get ready. (Tap the ball.) *ar.*

• Read the whole word. (Pause.) Get ready. (Slash.) *Farmer.*

c. (Repeat step *b* until firm.)

d. (Repeat steps *b* and *c* for each remaining word in the column.)

e. (Repeat the column until children read all the words in order without making a mistake.)

farmer

also

seem

feel

green

bean

cloud

EXERCISE 3

Teacher reads the words in red

a. I'll read each word in red. Then you'll spell each word.

b. (Touch the ball for **sleek.**) My turn. (Slash as you say:) Sleek. What word? (Signal.) *Sleek.*

c. (Return to the ball.) Spell it. Get ready. (Tap under each letter as the children say:) *S-L-E-E-K.* What word did you spell? (Signal.) *Sleek.*

• Yes. Things that are **sleek** are smooth and pretty.

d. (Touch the ball for **brag.**) My turn. (Slash as you say:) Brag. What word? (Signal.) *Brag.*

e. (Return to the ball.) Spell it. Get ready. (Tap under each letter as the children say:) *B-R-A-G.* What word did you spell? (Signal.) *Brag.*

• Yes. When you **brag,** you tell how good you are. It's not fun to listen to people who **brag** a lot.

f. Your turn to read all the words in this column.

g. (Touch the ball for **sleek.** Pause.) Get ready. (Slash.) *Sleek.*

h. (Repeat step *g* for each remaining word in the column.)

i. (Repeat steps *g* and *h* until firm.)

sleek

brag

wonder

figure

eight

easiest

EXERCISE 4

Children spell, then read

a. First you're going to spell each word. Then you're going to read that word the fast way.

b. (Touch the ball for **taper.**) Spell it. Get ready. (Tap under each letter as the children say:) *T-A-P-E-R.*

• (Return to the ball.) Read it. Get ready. (Slash.) *Taper.*

c. (Repeat step *b* for each remaining word in the column.)

d. (Repeat steps *b* and *c* until firm.)

taper

tapper

loop

stare

stared

Individual test

a. (Call on individual children to read one column of words from the lesson.)

b. (Praise children who read all words with no errors.)

EXERCISE 3

Read the fast way

a. You're going to read all the words in this column the fast way.

b. (Touch the ball for **make.** Pause.) Get ready. (Slash.) *Make.*

c. (Repeat step *b* until firm.)

d. (Repeat steps *b* and *c* for each remaining word in the column.)

e. (Repeat the column until the children read all the words in order without making mistakes.)

make

making

we

king

handed

laugh

Casts

EXERCISE 4

Children spell, then read

a. First you're going to spell each word. Then you're going to read that word the fast way.

b. (Touch the ball for **bite.**) Spell it. Get ready. (Tap under each letter as the children say:) *B-I-T-E.*

• (Return to the ball.) Read it. Get ready. (Slash.) *Bite.*

c. (Repeat step *b* for each remaining word in the column.)

d. (Repeat steps *b* and *c* until firm.)

bite

panes

pans

flew

sip

would

who

Individual test

a. (Call on individual children to read one column of words from the lesson.)

b. (Praise children who read all words with no errors.)

LESSON 158

READING VOCABULARY

EXERCISE 1

Teacher reads the word in red

a. I'll read each word in red. Then you'll spell each word.

b. (Touch the ball for **U.S.**) My turn. (Slash as you say:) U-S. What word? (Signal.) *U-S.*

c. The full word for **U-S** is **United States.** What does **U-S** stand for? (Signal.) *United States.*

d. (Return to the ball.) **U-period-S-period** is an abbreviation for **United States.** Spell the abbreviation for **United States.** Get ready. (Tap under each letter and period as the children say:) *U-period-S-period.*

e. (Touch the ball for **barge.**) My turn. (Slash as you say:) Barge. What word? (Signal.) *Barge.*

f. (Repeat step e for **large.**)

g. Your turn to read all the words in this column.

h. (Touch the ball for **U.S.** Pause.) Get ready. (Slash.) *U-S.*

i. (Repeat step h for each remaining word in the column.)

h. (Repeat steps h and i until firm.)

U.S.

barge

large

idea

town

babies

EXERCISE 2

Words with underlined parts

a. First you're going to read the underlined part of each word in this column. Then you're going to read the whole word.

b. (Touch the ball for **Everest.**) Read the underlined part. Get ready. (Tap the ball.) *Ever.*

• Read the whole word. (Pause.) Get ready. (Slash.) *Everest.*

c. (Repeat step *b* until firm.)

d. (Repeat steps *b* and *c* for each remaining word in the column.)

e. (Repeat the column until children read all the words in order without making a mistake.)

Everest

she'll

spring

steering

quietly

223 Lesson 158

STORYBOOK

STORY 110
EXERCISE 5

Reading—decoding

a. (Pass out Storybook 2.)

b. Everybody, open your reader to page 75.

c. Remember, if the group reads all the way to the red 5 without making more than five errors, we can go on.

d. Everybody, touch the title of the story. ✔

e. If you hear a mistake, raise your hand. Remember, children who do not have their place lose their turn. (Call on individual children to read two or three sentences. Do not ask comprehension questions. Tally all errors.)

To Correct

word-identification errors (**from,** for example)
1. That word is **from.** What word? *From.*
2. Go back to the beginning of the sentence and read the sentence again.

f. (If the children make more than five errors before they reach the red 5: when they reach the 5 return to the beginning of the story and have the children reread to the 5. Do not ask comprehension questions. Repeat step *f* until firm, and then go on to step *g*.)

g. (When the children read to the red 5 without making more than five errors: read the story to the children from the beginning to the 5. Ask the specified comprehension questions. When you reach the 5, call on individual children to continue reading the story. Have each child read two or three sentences. Ask the specified comprehension questions.)

Boo Casts Some Spells[1]

The ghosts had found words on the side of the rod. The ghost who was holding the rod said, "I can't read." Then he looked at the other mean ghosts. "Who can read these words?" he asked.

"Not me," they all said.[2] Then the three ghosts looked at Boo.

"You can read," one ghost said. "So read these words and tell us how to turn you into a leaf."[3]

Boo said, "Hand me the rod and I will do the best I can."

So the ghost handed the rod to Boo, and Boo looked at the words on the rod. Then Boo held the rod and said, "Bit bite, ben bean."[4]

Nothing happened to Boo, but the other ghosts began to smile.[5] One ghost said, "I don't feel mean anymore."

Another ghost said, "I feel ★ like playing games with the boys and girls in town." ⑤

Another ghost said, "Not me. I feel like going out and helping a farmer milk cows."[6]

Before they left, they turned to Boo and said, "Thank you for making us feel so good."[7]

After they left, Boo held up the rod and said, "Sip dim, dime dup." The flower turned back into a smiling ghost. And the leaf turned back into a smiling ghost. They both gave Boo a kiss and they left for school.

"We want to read books," they said.[8]

Boo said some magic words to make his fins and tail go away. Then he said, "Now I will go find the frog and turn him back into a king."[9]

More to come

[1] What's the title? (Signal.) *Boo Casts Some Spells.*

[2] Who is speaking? (Signal.) *The mean ghosts.*
• What can't they do? (Signal.) *Read.*

[3] Why do they want Boo to read the words? (Signal.) *So they can turn him into a leaf.*
• Do you think Boo will tell them how to do that? (The children respond.)

[4] Let's read what Boo said together. (Signal. Teacher and children read:) *Bit bite, ben bean.*

[5] Did anything happen to Boo? (Signal.) *No.*
• What happened to the other ghosts? (Signal.) *They began to smile.*

[6] Were those ghosts still mean? (Signal.) *No.*

[7] What did they say to Boo? (Signal.) *Thank you for making us feel so good.*

[8] Did the ghosts turn back into ghosts? (Signal.) *Yes.*
• Now what did they want to do? (Signal.) *Read books.*

[9] What's Boo going to do? (The children respond.)

"That's right," the wizard said. "Now you know a rule about talking animals. Talking animals lie.⁹ Don't do what they tell you to do, or you will get in a mess."

"I will remember that," Jean said. "If a talking animal tells me to do something, I will not do it."

Jean ran her hand across her striped hair. Then she began to ask the wizard a question. "But what and when . . . ." she said.

But the wizard had disappeared. Jean said to herself, "That's strange. Every time I say, 'But what and when . . . .' the wizard disappears."¹⁰

Just then somebody said, "Hello." Jean looked around, but she did not see anybody.

"I am down here. I am a little bug."¹¹ Jean bent down and looked at the bug. She said, "Are you a talking animal?"¹²

"No," the bug said. "I never talk."¹³

More next time

---

⁹ What do talking animals do? (Signal.) *Lie.*

¹⁰ When does the wizard disappear? (Signal.) *Every time Jean says, "But what and when . . ."* I wonder if that's a rule.

¹¹ Who is talking? (Signal.) *A little bug.*

¹² Is the bug an animal? (Signal.) *Yes.*

• And is he talking? (Signal.) *Yes.*

• What do we know about talking animals? (Signal.) *They lie.*

¹³ What did he say? *(Signal.) I never talk.*

• Is that bug talking? (Signal.) *Yes.*

• That talking animal sure can lie.

EXERCISE 7

Picture comprehension

a. Look at the picture.

b. (Ask these questions:)

　1. (Point to the bug.) What is that? (Signal.) *A bug.*

　2. What is the bug sitting on? (Signal.) *A flower.*

　3. Why is Jean bending down like that? (The children respond.)

　4. What do you think the bug is saying? (The children respond.)

WORKSHEET 157

INDEPENDENT ACTIVITIES

EXERCISE 8

Reading comprehension

a. (Pass out Worksheet 157 to each child.)

b. Everybody, turn to side 2 of your worksheet. ✔

c. (Point to the story on side 2 of your worksheet.) Everybody, find this story on your worksheet. ✔

d. Today you're going to read a passage that tells about when trees start growing in the spring.

e. The picture shows a large tree, a middle-sized tree, and a small tree when they start growing in early spring. Everybody, what season does the picture show? (Signal.) *Spring.*

f. Everybody, which tree has grown the most leaves? (Signal.) *The small tree.*

g. Everybody, which tree hasn't even started to grow new leaves yet? (Signal.) *The large tree.*

h. (Repeat steps *f* and *g* until firm.)

i. The story that you'll read tells why the smaller trees start growing first in the spring. When you do your independent work, read the story carefully to yourself. Then answer the questions.

EXERCISE 9

Summary of independent activities

Everybody, now you'll do your worksheet. Remember to do all parts of the worksheet and to read all the parts carefully.

END OF LESSON 157

WORKSHEET 110

EXERCISE 6

Picture comprehension

a. Look at the picture.

b. (Ask these questions:)

1. What is the big ghost doing to Boo? *Kissing him.*

2. Is Boo still part fish in this picture? (Signal.) *Yes.*

3. Why are those ghosts smiling? (Signal.) *They are happy.*

4. Which ghost looks the happiest? (The children respond.)

5. Which ghost do you think was the leaf? (The children respond.)

6. Which ghosts do you think are going to read books? **(The children respond.)** Yes, all of them.

INDEPENDENT ACTIVITIES
EXERCISE 7

Summary of independent activities

a. (Pass out Worksheet 110 to each child.)

b. Everybody, now you'll do your worksheet. Remember to do all parts of the worksheet and to read all the parts carefully.

INDIVIDUAL CHECKOUT
EXERCISE 8

2-minute individual fluency checkout: rate/accuracy

a. As you are doing your worksheet, I'll call on children one at a time to read to the star. Remember, you get two stars on the chart if you read to the star in less than two minutes and make no more than five errors.

b. (Call on each child. Tell the child:) Read to the star very carefully. Start with the title. Go. (Time the child. Tell the child any words the child misses. Stop the child as soon as the child makes the sixth error or exceeds the time limit.)

c. (If the child meets the rate-accuracy criterion, record two stars on your chart for lesson 110. Congratulate the child. Give children who do not earn two stars a chance to read to the star again before the next lesson is presented.)

139 words/**2 min** = 70 wpm [**5 errors**]

END OF LESSON 110

RULE REVIEW
EXERCISE 5

Rule review

a. Everybody, you have learned rules in the earlier Jean stories.

b. You learned a rule about getting hair back. Say that rule. Get ready. (Signal.) *If you want your hair back, clap your hands.*
- (Repeat until firm.)

c. You learned a rule about how to be warm again. Say that rule. Get ready. (Signal.) *If you want to be warm again, say, "I want to be warm again."*
- (Repeat until firm.)

d. You learned a rule about how to be cold. Say that rule. Get ready. (Signal.) *If you want to be cold, say, "Side, slide."*
- (Repeat until firm.)

e. (If the children missed any rules, repeat steps *b* through *d*.)

STORY 157
EXERCISE 6

Reading—decoding

a. (Pass out Storybook 2.)

b. Everybody, open your reader to page 226.

c. Remember, if the group reads all the way to the red 5 without making more than five errors, we can go on.

d. Everybody, touch the title of the story. ✔

e. If you hear a mistake, raise your hand. Remember, children who do not have their place lose their turn. (Call on individual children to read two or three sentences. Do not ask comprehension questions. Tally all errors.)

Jean Figures Out a Rule[1]

The talking animal had told Jean a rule about how to be cold. But he had told her that it was a rule for how to have fun.

What is the rule about how to be cold?[2]

Then Jean had found out a rule for how to be warm again. Tell Jean that rule.[3] If you don't remember it, turn the page around and read the rule.[4]

want to be warm again."

I," 'yes, 'niege mrew eq oq quem

Now Jean was trying to figure out a rule about talking animals.[5] She said to herself, "That talking animal lied to me when he told me the rule about the dusty path. He lied when he told me the rule about jumping in the lake. And he lied about what would happen if I said, 'Side, slide.'[6] I think I know the rule about talking animals." ⑤

She turned to the wizard. "Here's the rule," she said. "Talking animals lie."[7]

"That's right," the wizard said.[8] "Never believe what a talking animal tells you. If he tells you that pink ice cream is good to eat, you know that pink ice cream is not good to eat. If he tells you that big crumps are very mean, you know that big crumps are not mean."

Jean said, "And if he tells you to eat three green apples, you know you shouldn't eat three green apples."

> **To Correct**
>
> word-identification errors (**from**, for example)
> 1. That word is **from**. What word? *From.*
> 2. Go back to the beginning of the sentence and read the sentence again.

f. (If the children make more than five errors before they reach the red 5: when they reach the 5 return to the beginning of the story and have the children reread to the 5. Do not ask comprehension questions. Repeat step *f* until firm, and then go on to step *g*.)

g. (When the children read to the red 5 without making more than five errors: read the story to the children from the beginning to the 5. Ask the specified comprehension questions. When you reach the 5, call on individual children to continue reading the story. Have each child read two or three sentences. Ask the specified comprehension questions.)

[1] What's the title? (Signal.) *Jean figures out a rule.*
- Let's see which rule she figures out.

[2] Everybody, say the rule. (Signal.) *If you want to be cold, say, "Side, slide."*

[3] Try that rule for how to be warm again. (Signal.) *If you want to be warm again, say, "I want to be warm again."*

[4] Go ahead and read the rule to yourself.

[5] What was she trying to figure out? (Signal.) *A rule about talking animals.*

[6] Did the talking animal lie to Jean? (Signal.) *Yes.*

[7] Do you think she's found out another rule? (Signal.) *Yes.*
- Everybody, say that rule. (Signal.) *Talking animals lie.*

[8] Was Jean right? (Signal.) *Yes.*
- Were you right? (The children respond.)

READING VOCABULARY

EXERCISE 1

Teacher reads the words
in red

a. I'll read each word in red.
Then you'll spell each word.

b. (Touch the ball for
bumpy.) My turn. (Slash
as you say:) Bumpy. What
word? (Signal.) *Bumpy.*

c. (Return to the ball.) Spell it.
Get ready. (Tap under each
letter as the children say:)
B-U-M-P-Y. What word did
you spell? (Signal.) *Bumpy.*

d. (Repeat steps *b* and *c* for
each word in red.)

e. Your turn to read all the
words in this column.

f. (Touch the ball for **bumpy.**
Pause.) Get ready. (Slash.)
Bumpy.

g. (Repeat step *f* for each
remaining word in the
column.)

h. (Repeat steps *f* and *g* until
firm.)

bumpy

genie

master

rolled

shore

storm

know

EXERCISE 2

Words with underlined parts

a. First you're going to read
the underlined part of each
word in this column. Then
you're going to read the
whole word.

b. (Touch the ball for **every.**)
Read the underlined part.
Get ready. (Tap the ball.)
er. Read the whole word.
(Pause.) Get ready. (Slash.)
Every.

c. (Repeat step *b* until firm.)

d. (Repeat steps *b* and *c* for
each remaining word in
the column.)

e. (Repeat the column until
children read all the words
in order without making a
mistake.)

every

around

feel

year

appear

peek

wishes

EXERCISE 3

Teacher reads the words in red

a. I'll read the word in red. Then you'll spell the word.

b. (Touch the ball for **steer.**) My turn. (Slash as you say:) Steer. What word? (Signal.) *Steer.*

c. (Return to the ball.) Spell it. Get ready. (Tap under each letter as the children say:) *S-T-E-E-R.*

• What word did you spell? (Signal.) *Steer.* Yes. When you **steer** a bike, you make it go where you want it to go.

d. Your turn to read all the words in this column.

e. (Touch the ball for **steer.** Pause.) Get ready. (Slash.) *Steer.*

f. (Repeat step *e* for each remaining word in the column.)

g. (Repeat steps *e* and *f* until firm.)

steer

figure

believe

lied

mess

strange

easiest

EXERCISE 4

Words with underlined parts

a. First you're going to read the underlined part of each word in this column. Then you're going to read the whole word.

b. (Touch the ball for **wheels.**) Read the underlined part. Get ready. (Tap the ball.) *wh.*

• Read the whole word. (Pause.) Get ready. (Slash.) *Wheels.*

c. (Repeat step *b* until firm.)

d. (Repeat steps *b* and *c* for each remaining word in the column.)

e. (Repeat the column until children read all the words in order without making a mistake.)

wheels

cream

Never

disappears

Individual test

a. (Call on individual children to read one column of words from the lesson.)

b. (Praise children who read all words with no errors.)

EXERCISE 3

Read the fast way

a. You're going to read all the words in this column the fast way.

b. (Touch the ball for **very.** Pause.) Get ready. (Slash.) *Very.*

c. (Repeat step *b* until firm.)

d. (Repeat steps *b* and *c* for each remaining word in the column.)

e. (Repeat the column until the children read all the words in order without making mistakes.)

very

couldn't

wouldn't

won't

don't

didn't

Let's

EXERCISE 4

Children spell, then read

a. First you're going to spell each word. Then you're going to read that word the fast way.

b. (Touch the ball for **canned.**) Spell it. Get ready. (Tap under each letter as the children say:) *C-A-N-N-E-D.*

• (Return to the ball.) Read it. Get ready. (Slash.) *Canned.*

c. (Repeat step *b* for each remaining word in the column.)

d. (Repeat steps *b* and *c* until firm.)

canned

caned

wishes

Maybe

games

Everybody

night

Individual test

a. (Call on individual children to read one column of words from the lesson.)

b. (Praise children who read all words with no errors.)

READING VOCABULARY

EXERCISE 1

Teacher reads the words in red

a. I'll read each word in red. Then you'll spell each word.

b. (Touch the ball for **mind.**) My turn. (Slash as you say:) Mind. What word? (Signal.) *Mind.*

c. (Return to the ball.) Spell it. Get ready. (Tap under each letter as the children say:) *M-I-N-D.*

• What word did you spell? (Signal.) *Mind.* Yes. If you don't **mind** something, it doesn't bother you.

d. (Touch the ball for **spring.**) My turn. (Slash as you say:) Spring. What word? (Signal.) *Spring.*

e. (Return to the ball.) Spell it. Get ready. (Tap under each letter as the children say:) *S-P-R-I-N-G.*

• What word did you spell? (Signal.) *Spring.*

f. (Repeat steps *d* and *e* for each word in red.)

g. Your turn to read all the words in this column.

h. (Touch the ball for **mind.**) (Pause.) Get ready. (Slash.) *Mind.*

i. (Repeat step *h* for each remaining word in the column.)

j. (Repeat steps *h* and *i* until firm.)

mind

spring

quiet

quick

idea

winter

whale

EXERCISE 2

Words with underlined parts

a. First you're going to read the underlined part of each word in this column. Then you're going to read the whole word.

b. (Touch the ball for **tapped.**) Read the underlined part. Get ready. (Tap the ball.) *Tapp.*

• Read the whole word. (Pause.) Get ready. (Slash.) *Tapped.*

c. (Repeat step *b* until firm.)

d. (Repeat steps *b* and *c* for each remaining word in the column.)

e. (Repeat the column until children read all the words in order without making a mistake.)

tapped

warmer

trapper

anybody

somebody

tallest

taped

STORYBOOK

STORY 111
EXERCISE 5

Reading—decoding

a. (Pass out Storybook 2.)

b. Everybody, open your reader to page 78.

c. Remember, if the group reads all the way to the red 5 without making more than five errors, we can go on.

d. Everybody, touch the title of the story. ✔

e. If you hear a mistake, raise your hand. Remember, children who do not have their place lose their turn. (Call on individual children to read two or three sentences. Do not ask comprehension questions. Tally all errors.)

To Correct

word-identification errors (**from,** for example)
1. That word is **from.** What word? *From.*
2. Go back to the beginning of the sentence and read the sentence again.

f. (If the children make more than five errors before they reach the red 5: when they reach the 5 return to the beginning of the story and have the children reread to the 5. Do not ask comprehension questions. Repeat step *f* until firm, and then go on to step *g.*)

g. (When the children read to the red 5 without making more than five errors: read the story to the children from the beginning to the 5. Ask the specified comprehension questions. When you reach the 5, call on individual children to continue reading the story. Have each child read two or three sentences. Ask the specified comprehension questions.)

Everybody Is Happy [1]

Boo had turned the mean ghosts into smiling ghosts. Then Boo had made his tail and fins go away. [2] Now Boo was on his way to turn the frog back into a king.

Boo found the frog on a log in the stream. [3] Boo held up the magic rod. "Come to the shore," Boo said, "and I will turn you into a king."

"Hot dog," the frog said. He jumped from the log and swam to shore in a flash.

Then Boo said, "Hog, sog, bumpy log," and the frog turned into a king. The king said, "Hot dog, I'm a king again. [4] Hot dog."

The king ran around, and yelled, and shouted, and laughed, and rolled around in the sand. When the king was tired out, Boo told him how the ghosts had scared the monster into leaving the castle. ⑤

Then the king said, "Boo, you must come and live with me in the castle."

"No, no," Boo said, "I couldn't do that."

"Why not?" the king asked.

Boo said, "I, well . . . I, well . . . ." Boo was shy. [5]

The king said, "You must come and live with me. As king of this land, I'm telling you to come and live with me in my fine castle."

So Boo went to live with the king. And he lived with the king for years and years and years.

Things were very good in the land. The people had a good king. The king had a good friend. And all of the ghosts in the land were very good ghosts. The people didn't say, "Let's not go out at night." They said, "Let's go out at night. [6] Maybe we can find a ghost and play games with him. Ghosts are fun." [7]

The end

---

[1] What's the title of this story? (Signal.) *Everybody is happy.*

[2] What had Boo done after he made the ghosts happy? (Signal.) *Made his tail and fins go away.*

[3] Where was the frog? (Signal.) *On a log in the stream.*

[4] What did he say? (Signal.) *Hot dog, I'm a king again.* Does he sound happy? (Signal.) *Yes.*

[5] Do you think Boo wanted to live with the king? (The children respond.)

[6] Why did they like to go out at night? (The children respond.)

[7] Do you think you would like to live in that land? (The children respond.)

The old wizard laughed. Then he said, "That talking animal told you the rule for cold.[7] Here's the rule: If you want to be cold, say, 'Side, slide.'"[8]

Jean said, "There are so many new rules that I mix them up. Let's see if I know the right rule. If you want to be cold, say, 'Side, slide.'"[9]

"That is right," the wizard said.

Jean said, "And if you want to be warm again, you say, 'I want to be warm again.'"

"That is right," the wizard said.

Jean said both of those rules to herself a few times. Then she said, "But why did that talking animal tell me a rule that didn't work? Doesn't he know the rules?"

"He knows them," the wizard said. "But there is a rule about talking animals. I'll ask you some questions. See if you can find out the rule."[10]

The wizard asked, "Did that talking animal tell you the right rule about dusty paths?"[11]

Then he asked, "Did he tell you the right rule about what would happen if you jumped in the lake?"[12]

Then he asked, "Did he tell you the right rule about what would happen if you said, 'Side, slide'?"[13]

Jean said, "I think I know the rule about talking animals."[14]

More to come

---

[7] That's why she was cold when she said, "Side, slide."

[8] Read that rule with me. Get ready. (Signal. Teacher and children read:) *If you want to be cold, say, "Side, slide."*

• Once more. (Signal. Teacher and children read:) *If you want to be cold, say, "Side, slide."*

[9] Did Jean say the rule right? (Signal.) *Yes.*

• Get ready to say the rule about being cold. (Signal.) *If you want to be cold, say, "Side, slide."*

[10] Let's see if Jean can figure it out.

[11] What's the answer? (Signal.) *No.*

[12] What's the answer? (Signal.) *No.*

[13] What's the answer? (Signal.) *No.*

[14] What do you think the rule is? (The children respond.)

• Next time we'll read and see if you're right.

EXERCISE 7

Picture comprehension

a. Look at the picture.

b. (Ask these questions:)
1. Where is Jean standing? (Signal.) *In the snow.*
2. Is she cold? (Signal.) *Yes.* How do you know? (The children respond.)
3. What's the wizard wearing? (The children respond.)

INDEPENDENT ACTIVITIES
EXERCISE 8

Reading comprehension

a. (Pass out Worksheet 156 to each child.)

b. Everybody, turn to side 2 of your worksheet. ✔

c. (Point to the story on side 2 of your worksheet.) Everybody, find this story on your worksheet. ✔

d. Today you're going to read a passage that tells about large animals.

e. Everybody, touch the first picture. ✔

• What animal is that? (Signal.) *An elephant.*

f. Everybody, touch the second picture. ✔

• That picture shows the largest animal in the world. It is a whale. What kind of animal is it? (Signal.) *A whale.*

g. When you do your independent work, read the story carefully to yourself. Then answer the questions.

EXERCISE 9

Summary of independent activities

Everybody, now you'll do your worksheet. Remember to do all parts of the worksheet and to read all the parts carefully.

END OF LESSON 156

WORKSHEET 111

EXERCISE 6

Picture comprehension

a. Look at the picture.

b. (Ask these questions:)

1. Is Boo part fish in this picture? *(Signal.) No.*

2. What is the king doing? (The children respond.)

3. Is it night or day in this picture? (Signal.) *Night.* How do you know? (The children respond.)

4. Do you think that the king likes Boo? (The children respond.)

EXERCISE 7

Summary of independent activities

a. (Pass out Worksheet 111 to each child.)

b. Everybody, now you'll do your worksheet. Remember to do all parts of the worksheet and to read all the parts carefully.

END OF LESSON 111

RULE REVIEW
EXERCISE 5

Rule review

a. Everybody, you have learned rules in the earlier Jean stories.

b. You learned a rule about getting rid of white hair. Say that rule. Get ready. (Signal.) *If you stand on one foot, the white hair will disappear.*

• (Repeat until firm.)

c. You learned a rule about getting hair back. Say that rule. Get ready. (Signal.) *If you want your hair back, clap your hands.*

• (Repeat until firm.)

d. The talking animal told Jean a rule about having fun. Say that rule. Get ready. (Signal.) *If you want to have fun, say, "Side, slide."*

• (Repeat until firm.)

e. (If the children missed any rules, repeat steps *b* through *d*.)

STORY 156
EXERCISE 6

Reading—decoding

a. (Pass out Storybook 2.)

b. Everybody, open your reader to page 222.

c. Remember, if the group reads all the way to the red 5 without making more than five errors, we can go on.

d. Everybody, touch the title of the story. ✔

e. If you hear a mistake, raise your hand. Remember, children who do not have their place lose their turn. (Call on individual children to read two or three sentences. Do not ask comprehension questions. Tally all errors.)

Jean Says, "Side, Slide."[1]

What rule did the talking animal tell Jean?[2]

Jean wanted to have some fun, so she said, "Side, slide." But she didn't have fun. All at once, she found herself up to her nose in snow. She was very cold. Snow was falling. The wind was howling. She shouted, "This is no fun.[3] Wizard, where are you?"

The wizard popped out of a pile of snow. "Here I am," he said.

"Get me out of here," she shouted. "I'm cold. I want to be warm again."

Suddenly, the snow disappeared and Jean was warm again. She said, "What happened? I said, 'I want to be warm again,' and I was warm again."

The wizard smiled. He said, "That is the easiest rule in the land of peevish pets.[4] If you want to be warm again, you say, 'I want to be warm again.'"⑤[5]

Jean said the rule to herself five times. Say it with her.[6]

Then Jean sat down and said to the wizard, "I don't understand something. That talking animal told me a rule about having fun. But the rule didn't work. He said, 'If you want to have fun, say, "Side, slide."' But I said those words, and I didn't have fun."

To Correct

word-identification errors (**from,** for example)
1. That word is **from.** What word? *From.*
2. Go back to the beginning of the sentence and read the sentence again.

f. (If the children make more than five errors before they reach the red 5: when they reach the 5 return to the beginning of the story and have the children reread to the 5. Do not ask comprehension questions. Repeat step *f* until firm, and then go on to step *g*.)

g. (When the children read to the red 5 without making more than five errors: read the story to the children from the beginning to the 5. Ask the specified comprehension questions. When you reach the 5, call on individual children to continue reading the story. Have each child read two or three sentences. Ask the specified comprehension questions.)

[1] Everybody, say the title. (Signal.) *Jean says, "Side, slide."*

[2] Say that rule. (Signal.) *If you want to have fun, say, "Side, slide."*

[3] Was she having fun? (Signal.) *No.*

• Why not? (The children respond.)

[4] Here comes that easy rule.

[5] Let's say that rule together. (Signal. Teacher and children say:) *If you want to be warm again, you say, "I want to be warm again."*

• (Repeat until firm.) All by yourselves. Get ready. (Signal.) (Children repeat the rule until firm.)

[6] Say the rule with Jean one more time. (Signal.) *If you want to be warm again, you say, "I want to be warm again."*

READING VOCABULARY
EXERCISE 1

Teacher reads the words in red

a. I'll read each word in red. Then you'll spell each word.

b. (Touch the ball for **puff**.) My turn. (Slash as you say:) Puff. What word? (Signal.) *Puff.*

c. (Return to the ball.) Spell it. Get ready. (Tap under each letter as the children say:) *P-U-F-F.*
- What word did you spell? (Signal.) *Puff.*

d. (Repeat steps *b* and *c* for each word in red.)

e. Your turn to read all the words in this column.

f. (Touch the ball for **puff**. Pause.) Get ready. (Slash.) *Puff.*

g. (Repeat step *f* for each remaining word in the column.)

h. (Repeat steps *f* and *g* until firm.)

puff

Ott

alligator

strange

apple

disappear

bottles

EXERCISE 2

Words with underlined parts

a. First you're going to read the underlined part of each word in this column. Then you're going to read the whole word.

b. (Touch the ball for **green**.) Read the underlined part. Get ready. (Tap the ball.) *Eee.*
- Read the whole word. (Pause.) Get ready. (Slash.) *Green.*

c. (Repeat step *b* until firm.)

d. (Repeat steps *b* and *c* for each remaining word in the column.)

e. (Repeat the column until children read all the words in order without making a mistake.)

green

wishes

Every

what

shouted

why

teacher

EXERCISE 3

Read the fast way

a. You're going to read all the words in this column the fast way.

b. (Touch the ball for **old.** Pause.) Get ready. (Slash.) *Old.*

c. (Repeat step *b* until firm.)

d. (Repeat steps *b* and *c* for each remaining word in the column.)

e. (Repeat the column until the children read all the words in order without making mistakes.)

old

rather

wonder

monkey

won't

metal

angry

EXERCISE 4

Children spell, then read

a. First you're going to spell each word. Then you're going to read that word the fast way.

b. (Touch the ball for **talking.**) Spell it. Get ready. (Tap under each letter as the children say:) *T-A-L-K-I-N-G.*

• (Return to the ball.) Read it. Get ready. (Slash.) *Talking.*

c. (Repeat step *b* for each remaining word in the column.)

d. (Repeat steps *b* and *c* until firm.)

talking

taking

flew

few

warm

Side

anywhere

Individual test

a. (Call on individual children to read one column of words from the lesson.)

b. (Praise children who read all words with no errors.)

EXERCISE 3

Read the fast way

a. You're going to read all the words in this column the fast way.

b. (Touch the ball for **were.** Pause.) Get ready. (Slash.) *Were.*

c. (Repeat step *b* until firm.)

d. (Repeat steps *b* and *c* for each remaining word in the column.)

e. (Repeat the column until the children read all the words in order without making mistakes.)

were

where

people

Genie

says

school

rubs

EXERCISE 4

Children spell, then read

a. First you're going to spell each word. Then you're going to read that word the fast way.

b. (Touch the ball for **right.**) Spell it. Get ready. (Tap under each letter as the children say:) *R-I-G-H-T.*

• (Return to the ball.) Read it. Get ready. (Slash.) *Right.*

c. (Repeat step *b* for each remaining word in the column.)

d. (Repeat steps *b* and *c* until firm.)

right

night

year

know

notes

noted

smoke

Individual test

a. (Call on individual children to read one column of words from the lesson.)

b. (Praise children who read all words with no errors.)

READING VOCABULARY

EXERCISE 1

Teacher reads the words in red

a. I'll read each word in red. Then you'll spell each word.

b. (Touch the ball for **figure**.) My turn. (Slash as you say:) Figure. What word? (Signal.) *Figure*.

c. (Return to the ball.) Spell it. Get ready. (Tap under each letter as the children say:) *F-I-G-U-R-E*.

• What word did you spell? (Signal.) *Figure*.

d. (Repeat steps *b* and *c* for each word in red.)

e. Your turn to read all the words in this column.

f. (Touch the ball for **figure**. Pause.) Get ready. (Slash.) *Figure*.

g. (Repeat step *f* for each remaining word in the column.)

h. (Repeat steps *f* and *g* until firm.)

figure

whale

easiest

winter

cold

nobody

broken

EXERCISE 2

Words with underlined parts

a. First you're going to read the underlined part of each word in this column. Then you're going to read the whole word.

b. (Touch the ball for **slider**.) Read the underlined part. Get ready. (Tap the ball.) *Slide*.

• Read the whole word. (Pause.) Get ready. (Slash.) *Slider*.

c. (Repeat step *b* until firm.)

d. (Repeat steps *b* and *c* for each remaining word in the column.)

e. (Repeat the column until children read all the words in order without making a mistake.)

slider

understand

wouldn't

we've

you've

they'll

someday

STORYBOOK

STORY 112
EXERCISE 5

Reading—decoding

a. (Pass out Storybook 2.)

b. Everybody, open your reader to page 81.

c. Remember, if the group reads all the way to the red 5 without making more than five errors, we can go on.

d. Everybody, touch the title of the story. ✔

e. If you hear a mistake, raise your hand. Remember, children who do not have their place lose their turn. (Call on individual children to read two or three sentences. Do not ask comprehension questions. Tally all errors.)

To Correct

word-identification errors (**from,** for example)
1. That word is **from.** What word? *From.*
2. Go back to the beginning of the sentence and read the sentence again.

f. (If the children make more than five errors before they reach the red 5: when they reach the 5 return to the beginning of the story and have the children reread to the 5. Do not ask comprehension questions. Repeat step *f* until firm, and then go on to step *g*.)

g. (When the children read to the red 5 without making more than five errors: read the story to the children from the beginning to the 5. Ask the specified comprehension questions. When you reach the 5, call on individual children to continue reading the story. Have each child read two or three sentences. Ask the specified comprehension questions.)

Ott Is in Genie School[1]

Ott was going to school. He was trying to be a genie, but he did not know many genie tricks.

Genies live in bottles.[2] When somebody rubs the bottle, the genie comes out in a puff of smoke.[3] Then the genie says, "Yes, master, what can I do for you?"[4]

The master tells what he wants, and the genie gets him what he wants. If the master wishes for an elephant, the genie makes an elephant appear.[5] If the master wishes for a bag of gold, the genie makes a bag of gold appear.

But Ott could not do these tricks. That is why he was still going to school. And he was not the best of those who were in school. When their teacher told the genies to make an apple appear on the table, Ott made an alligator appear on the table. ⑤[6] When the teacher told Ott to make gold appear on the floor, Ott made a pot of beans appear on the floor.[7]

---

[1] Who is this story about? (Signal.) *Ott.*

[2] Where do genies live? (Signal.) *In bottles.*

[3] What happens when somebody rubs the bottle? (Signal.) *The genie comes out.* Genies must be magic.

[4] Everybody, say that. (Signal.) *Yes, master, what can I do for you?*

• Who is the genie talking to? (Signal.) *The master.*

• Who is the master? (The children respond.) Yes, the person who rubs the bottle.

[5] What does the genie do if the master wishes for an elephant? (Signal.) *Makes the elephant appear.*

• What does it mean to make something appear? (The children respond.)

• Yes, all at once there it is.

[6] What was Ott supposed to make appear on the table? (Signal.) *An apple.*

• Did he make an apple appear? (Signal.) *No.*

• What did he make appear? (Signal.) *An alligator.*

[7] What did the teacher tell Ott to make appear this time? (Signal.) *Gold.*

• Did he make gold appear? (Signal.) *No.*

• What did he make appear? (Signal.) *A pot of beans.*

The talking animal said, "Here is another good rule: If you jump in the lake, you will get red stripes."[7]

"No," Jean said. "If you jump in the lake, the stripes will disappear."

The talking animal looked very angry. "Do not say that I lie. Talking animals never lie.[8] If you don't want to know the rules, I will not tell you any new rules."

Jean said, "Please tell me a new rule. I must know the rules so that I can leave this strange place."

"All right," the talking animal said. "Here is a good rule: If you want to have fun, say, 'Side, slide.'"[9]

Help Jean say that rule.[10]

"Thank you," Jean said. "I think I will have some fun right now."

What can Jean say to have fun?[11]

More next time[12]

[7] Is he telling the truth? (Signal.) *No.*
We know that if you jump in the lake the stripes will disappear.

[8] Who is saying that? (The children respond.)
• He sounds like he's been lying to me.

[9] Everybody, say that rule with me. (Signal. Teacher and children say:) *If you want to have fun, say, "Side, slide."*
• (Repeat until firm.)

[10] Your turn to help Jean. (Signal.) *If you want to have fun, say, "Side, slide."*
• Watch out, Jean. I wouldn't trust that talking animal.

[11] What's the answer? (Signal.) *Side, slide.*

[12] We'll find out next time if Jean really has fun after she says, "Side, slide."

EXERCISE 7

Picture comprehension

a. Look at the picture.
b. (Ask these questions:)
1. Tell me about that funny-looking animal. (The children respond.)
• Which part of that funny-looking animal is like a monkey? (The children respond.)
• Which part is like a horse? (The children respond.)
2. Where did he appear from? (Signal.) *The lake.*
• How do you know? (The children respond.)
3. What do you think he's saying? (The children respond.)
4. Does Jean look like she trusts him? (Signal.) *No.*

INDEPENDENT ACTIVITIES
EXERCISE 8

Summary of independent activities

a. (Pass out Worksheet 155 to each child.)
b. Everybody, now you'll do your worksheet. Remember to do all parts of the worksheet and to read all the parts carefully.

INDIVIDUAL CHECKOUT
EXERCISE 9

2-minute individual fluency checkout: rate/accuracy

a. As you are doing your worksheet, I'll call on children one at a time to read to the star. Remember, you get two stars on the chart if you read to the star in less than two minutes and make no more than five errors.
b. (Call on each child. Tell the child:) Read to the star very carefully. Start with the title. Go. (Time the child. Tell the child any words the child misses. Stop the child as soon as the child makes the sixth error or exceeds the time limit.)
c. (If the child meets the rate-accuracy criterion, record two stars on your chart for lesson 155. Congratulate the child. Give children who do not earn two stars a chance to read to the star again before the next lesson is presented.)
179 words/**2 min** = 90 wpm **[5 errors]**

END OF LESSON 155

Then one day, something strange happened. Ott and the other genies were working at getting into a little bottle. All at once, an old woman ran into the school and ran up to the teacher. The old woman said, "We need more genies.[8] Somebody has found an old yellow bottle that should have a genie in it.[9] But we have not had a genie in that bottle for years and years."

"What about all of our other genies?" the teacher asked. "Why can't we send one of them to the yellow bottle?"

"They are all working," the old woman said. "This is a big year for genies. People have been finding old genie bottles all year. Every one of our genies is working, so we will have to send one of the children from your school to the yellow bottle."[10]

More to come

---

[8] What did she say? (Signal.) *We need more genies.*

[9] Why do they need a genie? (The children respond.)

[10] Why can't they use some of the genies who have graduated from genie school? (Signal.) *They're all working.*

• Next time we'll see if they pick Ott for the bottle.

EXERCISE 6

Picture comprehension

a. Look at the picture.
b. (Ask these questions:)
   1. Where are the genies in this picture? (Signal.) *In school.* Yes, in genie school.
   2. Show me which genie is Ott. (The children respond.)
   • Why doesn't he look happy? (The children respond.)
   3. How many apples are on the table? (Signal.) *Three.*
   4. What's that thing that's eating the apples? (Signal.) *An alligator.*
   5. What do you think the woman is saying to the teacher? (The children respond.)

WORKSHEET 112

EXERCISE 7

Summary of independent activities

a. (Pass out Worksheet 112 to each child.)
b. Everybody, now you'll do your worksheet. Remember to do all parts of the worksheet and to read all the parts carefully.

END OF LESSON 112

STORYBOOK

RULE REVIEW
EXERCISE 5

Rule review

a. Everybody, you have learned rules in the earlier Jean stories.

b. You learned a rule about getting rid of red stripes. Say that rule. Get ready. **(Signal.)** *If you jump in the lake, the stripes will disappear.*

* (Repeat until firm.)

c. You learned a rule about getting rid of white hair. Say that rule, Get ready. **(Signal.)** *If you stand on one foot, the white hair will disappear.*

* (Repeat until firm.)

d. You learned a rule about getting hair back. Say that rule. Get ready. **(Signal.)** *If you want your hair back, clap your hands.*

* (Repeat until firm.)

e. (If the children missed any rules, repeat steps *b* through *d*.)

STORY 155
EXERCISE 6

Reading—decoding

a. (Pass out Storybook 2.)

b. Everybody, open your reader to page 219.

c. Remember, if the group reads all the way to the red 5 without making more than five errors, we can go on.

d. Everybody, touch the title of the story. ✔

e. If you hear a mistake, raise your hand. Remember, children who do not have their place lose their turn. (Call on individual children to read two or three sentences. Do not ask comprehension questions. Tally all errors.)

A Funny Animal Appears[1]

The wizard told Jean a rule for getting her hair back. Tell Jean that rule.[2]

Jean started to ask the wizard, "But what and when . . . ."

But the wizard disappeared before she could ask the question. Jean said, "I think I'll get my hair back." Jean clapped her hands. So did she get her hair back?[3]

Jean felt her head. Her hair was back. She ran to the lake and looked at herself in the water. Her hair was back, but it was striped again.[4]

She said, "Oh, well. I would rather have striped hair than be bald."

Just then a big, funny-looking animal came out of the lake. Part of that animal looked like a horse, and part of that animal looked like a monkey.[5] The animal walked up to Jean and said, "I can help you get out of this place. I know all sixteen rules."⑤

"Good," Jean said, "Teach me the rules I don't know."

The funny animal said, "Here's a good rule: All dusty paths lead to the mountain."[6]

"No," Jean said. ★ "That's not right. Dusty paths do not lead to the mountain."

The animal looked very angry. He said, "Are you saying that I would tell a lie?"

"No," Jean said.

To Correct

word-identification errors (**from,** for example)
1. That word is **from.** What word? *From.*
2. Go back to the beginning of the sentence and read the sentence again.

f. (If the children make more than five errors before they reach the red 5: when they reach the 5 return to the beginning of the story and have the children reread to the 5. Do not ask comprehension questions. Repeat step *f* until firm, and then go on to step *g*.)

g. (When the children read to the red 5 without making more than five errors: read the story to the children from the beginning to the 5. Ask the specified comprehension questions. When you reach the 5, call on individual children to continue reading the story. Have each child read two or three sentences. Ask the specified comprehension questions.)

[1] What's going to happen in this story? (Signal.) *A funny animal will appear.*

[2] Tell her the rule for getting her hair back. (Signal.) *If you want your hair back, clap your hands.*

[3] Do you think she'll get her hair back? (Signal.) *Yes.*

* Why? (Signal.) *Because she clapped her hands.*

[4] Did she get her hair back? (Signal.) *Yes.*

* But what was it like now? (Signal.) *It was striped again.*

[5] What did that funny animal look like? (The children respond.)

[6] Is he saying the rule right? (Signal.) *No.* Right. We know that every dusty path leads to the lake.

READING VOCABULARY

EXERCISE 1

Teacher reads the words in red

a. I'll read each word in red. Then you'll spell each word.

b. (Touch the ball for **Test.**) My turn. (Slash as you say:) Test. What word? (Signal.) *Test.*

c. (Return to the ball.) Spell it. Get ready. (Tap under each letter as the children say:) *T-E-S-T.*

• What word did you spell? (Signal.) *Test.*

d. (Repeat steps *b* and *c* for each word in red.)

e. Your turn to read all the words in this column.

f. (Touch the ball for **Test.** Pause.) Get ready. (Slash.) *Test.*

g. (Repeat step *f* for each remaining word in the column.)

h. (Repeat steps *f* and *g* until firm.)

Test

suddenly

beach

peach

peaches

heel

hear

EXERCISE 2

Words with underlined parts

a. First you're going to read the underlined part of each word in this column. Then you're going to read the whole word.

b. (Touch the ball for **himself.**) Read the underlined part. Get ready. (Tap the ball.) *Self.*

• Read the whole word. (Pause.) Get ready. (Slash.) *Himself.*

c. (Repeat step *b* until firm.)

d. (Repeat steps *b* and *c* for each remaining word in the column.)

e. (Repeat the column until children read all the words in order without making a mistake.)

himself

themselves

genies

dimes

dimmer

asked

answered

EXERCISE 3

Read the fast way

a. You're going to read all the words in this column the fast way.

b. (Touch the ball for **third**. Pause.) Get ready. (Slash.) *Third.*

c. (Repeat step *b* until firm.)

d. (Repeat steps *b* and *c* for each remaining word in the column.)

e. (Repeat the column until the children read all the words in order without making mistakes.)

EXERCISE 4

Children spell, then read

a. First you're going to spell each word. Then you're going to read that word the fast way.

b. (Touch the ball for **Side**.) Spell it. Get ready. (Tap under each letter as the children say:) *S-I-D-E.*
  • (Return to the ball.) Read it. Get ready. (Slash.) *Side.*

c. (Repeat step *b* for each remaining word in the column.)

d. (Repeat steps *b* and *c* until firm.)

third

turn

first

jerk

babies

Appears

which

Side

slide

dim

three

there

striped

Part

Individual test

a. (Call on individual children to read one column of words from the lesson.)

b. (Praise children who read all words with no errors.)

EXERCISE 3

Read the fast way

a. You're going to read all the words in this column the fast way.

b. (Touch the ball for **didn't.** Pause.) Get ready. (Slash.) *Didn't.*

c. (Repeat step *b* until firm.)

d. (Repeat steps *b* and *c* for each remaining word in the column.)

e. (Repeat the column until the children read all the words in order without making mistakes.)

didn't

appear

right

disappear

rubs

falling

know

EXERCISE 4

Children spell, then read

a. First you're going to spell each word. Then you're going to read that word the fast way.

b. (Touch the ball for **piles.**) Spell it. Get ready. (Tap under each letter as the children say:) P-I-L-E-S.

• (Return to the ball.) Read it. Get ready. (Slash.) *Piles.*

c. (Repeat step *b* for each remaining word in the column.)

d. (Repeat steps *b* and *c* until firm.)

piles

Takes

None

smoke

would

dim

dimmed

Individual test

a. (Call on individual children to read one column of words from the lesson.)

b. (Praise children who read all words with no errors.)

READING VOCABULARY

EXERCISE 1

Teacher reads the words in red

a. I'll read each word in red. Then you'll spell each word.

b. (Touch the ball for **metal.**) My turn. (Slash as you say:) Metal. What word? (Signal.) *Metal.*

c. (Return to the ball.) Spell it. Get ready. (Tap under each letter as the children say:) *M-E-T-A-L.*
- What word did you spell? (Signal.) *Metal.*

d. (Repeat steps *b* and *c* for each word in red.)

e. Your turn to read all the words in this column.

f. (Touch the ball for **metal.** Pause.) Get ready. (Slash.) *Metal.*

g. (Repeat step *f* for each remaining word in the column.)

h. (Repeat steps *f* and *g* until firm.)

metal

monkey

rather

warm

angry

few

blew

EXERCISE 2

Words with underlined parts

a. First you're going to read the underlined part of each word in this column. Then you're going to read the whole word.

b. (Touch the ball for **calling.**) Read the underlined part. Get ready. (Tap the ball.) *Call.*
- Read the whole word. (Pause.) Get ready. (Slash.) *Calling.*

c. (Repeat step *b* until firm.)

d. (Repeat steps *b* and *c* for each remaining word in the column.)

e. (Repeat the column until children read all the words in order without making a mistake.)

calling

herself

himself

you've

I'm

saying

looking

STORY 113
EXERCISE 5

Reading—decoding

a. (Pass out Storybook 2.)

b. Everybody, open your reader to page 84.

c. Remember, if the group reads all the way to the red 5 without making more than five errors, we can go on.

d. Everybody, touch the title of the story. ✓

e. If you hear a mistake, raise your hand. Remember, children who do not have their place lose their turn. (Call on individual children to read two or three sentences. Do not ask comprehension questions. Tally all errors.)

To Correct

word-identification errors (**from,** for example)
1. That word is **from.** What word? *From.*
2. Go back to the beginning of the sentence and read the sentence again.

f. (If the children make more than five errors before they reach the red 5: when they reach the 5 return to the beginning of the story and have the children reread to the 5. Do not ask comprehension questions. Repeat step *f* until firm, and then go on to step *g*.)

g. (When the children read to the red 5 without making more than five errors: read the story to the children from the beginning to the 5. Ask the specified comprehension questions. When you reach the 5, call on individual children to continue reading the story. Have each child read two or three sentences. Ask the specified comprehension questions.)

Ott Takes a Test [1]

Ott was going to genie school. One day an old woman came in and told Ott's teacher, "We need more genies. We must send one of the children from your school to the yellow bottle."

"No, no," the teacher said. "These children cannot go to work as genies. [2] They are not that smart."

The old woman said, "We cannot wait. The girl who found the yellow bottle may rub it any time, and when she rubs it, a genie must come out of that bottle." [3]

The teacher looked at the children who were working to be genies. The teacher said, "I don't know which of these children to pick. None of them would be a good genie."

The old woman said, "I will give the children a test. The child who does the best on the test will go and work in the yellow bottle." (5) [4]

The old woman walked over to the children. "Here is what I want you to do. Make a peach appear on the floor." [5]

All of the children began to say things to themselves. Then peaches began to appear on the floor—one peach, two peaches, three peaches, and then . . . all of the peaches disappeared under a pile of sand. Ott didn't make a peach appear. He made a beach appear. [6]

---

[1] What is the title of this story? (Signal.) *Ott takes a test.*

[2] Everybody, say that. (Signal.) *These children cannot go to work as genies.*

• Why do you think the teacher said that? (The children respond.)

[3] What was supposed to happen when the girl rubbed the bottle? (The children respond.)

[4] Why was the old woman going to give a test to the children? (The children respond.)

[5] What were the children supposed to do on the test? (Signal.) *Make a peach appear on the floor.*

[6] What did Ott do? (Signal.) *Made a beach appear.*

• Was that what he was supposed to do? (Signal.) *No.*

• What was he supposed to make appear? (Signal.) *A peach.*
Right. A peach.

Here are the questions the wizard asked:[9]

1. What do you know about all little crumps?[10]

2. How do you make mean crumps go away?[11]

3. What do you know about every dusty path?[12]

4. What do you know about every rocky path?[13]

5. What do you know about red food?[14]

6. What happens if you eat three red bananas?[15]

7. How do you get rid of the red stripes?[16]

8. How do you make white hair disappear?[17]

The wizard said, "You already know eight rules."

Jean said, "I don't care. I want to know how to make my hair come back. I don't like to be bald."

The wizard said, "Here's the rule: If you want your hair back, clap your hands."[18]

Help Jean say that rule.[19]

More of this story next time

---

9 Soon you can answer all of them. Let's read.

10 (1.) Everybody, what's the answer? (Signal.) *They are mean.*

11 (2.) What's the answer? (Signal.) *Say, "Away, away."*

• Wow, you are smart!

12 (3.) What's the answer? (Signal.) *It leads to the lake.*

13 (4.) What's the answer? (Signal.) *It leads to the mountain.*

14 (5.) What's the answer? (Signal.) *It is good to eat.*

15 (6.) What happens? (Signal.) *You get red stripes.*

16 (7.) What's the answer? (Signal.) *Jump in the lake.*

17 (8.) What do you do? (Signal.) *Stand on one foot.*

18 Everybody, say that with me. (Signal. **Teacher and children say:)** *If you want your hair back, clap your hands.*

• **(Repeat until firm.) All by yourselves. Get ready. (Signal.) (The children repeat the rule until firm.)**

19 Let's hear you tell her in a nice loud voice. **(Signal.)** *If you want your hair back, clap your hands.*

EXERCISE 6

Picture comprehension

a. What do you think you'll see in the picture? **(The children respond.)**

b. Turn the page and look at the picture.

c. (Ask these questions:)
1. Tell me about Jean's hair. **(The children respond.)**
   • What happened to it? **(The children respond.)**
2. Who is she looking at? **(Signal.)** *Herself.*
3. How can she see herself without a mirror? **(The children respond.)** Right. She sees her reflection in the lake.
4. How would you feel if you were bald like that? **(The children respond.)**

INDEPENDENT ACTIVITIES
EXERCISE 7

Reading comprehension

a. (Pass out Worksheet 154 to each child.)

b. Everybody, turn to side 2 of your worksheet. ✔

c. (Point to the story on side 2 of your worksheet.) Everybody, find this story on your worksheet. ✔

d. In the last lesson, you learned a rule about all living things. Everybody, say the rule. (Signal.) *All living things grow, and all living things need water.*

• (Repeat until firm.)

e. Today, you're going to learn about something else that all living things do. When you do your independent work, read the story carefully to yourself. Then answer the questions.

EXERCISE 8

Summary of independent activities

Everybody, now you'll do your worksheet. Remember to do all parts of the worksheet and to read all the parts carefully.

END OF LESSON 154

"Who did that?" the old woman shouted.

Ott didn't say anything because he didn't know that he had made the beach appear.

The old woman said, "We can't wait anymore. I'll just have to pick one of the children." She looked at each of the children. She stopped in front of Ott.

"You," she said to Ott. "You go to the yellow bottle.[7] Do it now."

Ott smiled and made himself disappear in a puff of smoke. He could not hear his teacher yelling, "No, no, not that one. He never does anything the right way."[8]

More next time[9]

[7] Who was the old woman talking to? (Signal.) *Ott.* Why did she choose Ott? (The children respond.)
- Did Ott do well on the test? (Signal.) *No.* I think that was a bad choice.
[8] Everybody, say that. (Signal.) *He never does anything the right way.*
- What did Ott do wrong in this story? (The children respond.)
[9] Next time we'll see if Ott gets out of the bottle.

EXERCISE 6

Picture comprehension

a. Look at the picture.
b. (Ask these questions:)
 1. Show me which genie is Ott. (The children respond.)
 2. Look at the floor. What's that great big pile? (Signal.) *Sand.*
 3. What do you think that old woman is thinking? (The children respond.)
 4. Show me what the other children made appear. (The children respond.)
 - What are those? (Signal.) *Peaches.*
 5. Do those other children look happy? (Signal.) *Yes.*
 6. What would you do if you were the old woman? (The children respond.)

WORKSHEET 113

EXERCISE 7

Summary of independent activities

a. (Pass out Worksheet 113 to each child.)
b. Everybody, now you'll do your worksheet. Remember to do all parts of the worksheet and to read all the parts carefully.

END OF LESSON 113

STORY 154
EXERCISE 5
Reading—decoding

a. (Pass out Storybook 2.)

b. Everybody, open your reader to page 215.

c. Remember, if the group reads all the way to the red 5 without making more than five errors, we can go on.

d. Everybody, touch the title of the story. ✔

e. If you hear a mistake, raise your hand. Remember, children who do not have their place lose their turn. (Call on individual children to read two or three sentences. Do not ask comprehension questions. Tally all errors.)

To Correct

word-identification errors (**from,** for example)
1. That word is **from.** What word? *From.*
2. Go back to the beginning of the sentence and read the sentence again.

f. (If the children make more than five errors before they reach the red 5: when they reach the 5 return to the beginning of the story and have the children reread to the 5. Do not ask comprehension questions. Repeat step *f* until firm, and then go on to step *g.*)

g. (When the children read to the red 5 without making more than five errors: read the story to the children from the beginning to the 5. Ask the specified comprehension questions. When you reach the 5, call on individual children to continue reading the story. Have each child read two or three sentences. Ask the specified comprehension questions.)

Jean Makes Her White Hair Go Away [1]

Jean's hair had turned white. The wizard had told her what she had to do to make the white hair go away. <u>What did she have to do?</u>[2]

<u>Tell Jean the rule.</u>[3] See if you were right. <u>Turn the page around and read the rule.</u>[4]

will disappear.

If you stand on one foot, the white hair

Jean stood on one foot. <u>Did her white hair go away?</u>[5]

<u>Tell Jean the rule again.</u>[6]

Jean ran over to the lake. She bent down and looked at herself in the water. Then she said, "Oh, no." The white hair had gone away. But now Jean did not have any hair at all. <u>She was bald.</u>[7] She felt the top of her head.

"Oh, no," she said. "<u>I hate this place.</u>[8] I wish the wizard was here so that he could tell me what to do." ⑤

Just then the wizard appeared. The wizard laughed when he looked at Jean. She said, "Don't laugh at me. I'm just trying to get out of this place."

The wizard said, "And you are doing a good job, my dear. You must know sixteen rules before you can leave the land of peevish pets. And look at all the rules you know. See if you can answer all of these questions."

---

[1] What will Jean do in today's story? (Signal.) *Make her white hair go away.*

[2] Say that question. (Signal.) *What did she have to do?*

• What's the answer? (Signal.) *Stand on one foot.*

[3] Tell her. (Signal.) *If you stand on one foot, the white hair will disappear.*

[4] Read it out loud. Get ready. (Signal.) *If you stand on one foot, the white hair will disappear.*

[5] Did it? (Signal.) *Yes.* Why? (Signal.) *Because she stood on one foot.*

[6] Everybody, say the rule again. (Signal.) *If you stand on one foot, the white hair will disappear.*

[7] Did the white hair disappear? (Signal.) *Yes.*

• All her white hair went away. Poor Jean was bald.

[8] Was Jean happy in the land of peevish pets? (Signal.) *No.*

READING VOCABULARY

EXERCISE 1

Teacher reads the words in red

a. I'll read each word in red. Then you'll spell each word.

b. (Touch the ball for **bust**.) My turn. (Slash as you say:) Bust. What word? (Signal.) *Bust.*

c. (Return to the ball.) Spell it. Get ready. (Tap under each letter as the children say:) *B-U-S-T.*

• What word did you spell? (Signal.) *Bust.*

d. (Repeat steps b and c for each word in red.)

e. Your turn to read all the words in this column.

f. (Touch the ball for **bust**. Pause.) Get ready. (Slash.) *Bust.*

g. (Repeat step f for each remaining word in the column.)

h. (Repeat steps f and g until firm.)

bust

bunch

junk

melt

Carla

step

smoke

EXERCISE 2

Words with underlined parts

a. First you're going to read the underlined part of each word in this column. Then you're going to read the whole word.

b. (Touch the ball for **lies**.) Read the underlined part. Get ready. (Tap the ball.) *Lie.*

• Read the whole word. (Pause.) Get ready. (Slash.) *Lies.*

c. (Repeat step b until firm.)

d. (Repeat steps b and c for each remaining word in the column.)

e. (Repeat the column until children read all the words in order without making a mistake.)

lies

alone

hanging

icebox

watched

didn't

Suddenly

EXERCISE 3

Words with underlined parts

a. First you're going to read the underlined part of each word in this column. Then you're going to read the whole word.

b. (Touch the ball for **bald**.) Read the underlined part. Get ready. (Tap the ball.) *All.*

- Read the whole word. (Pause.) Get ready. (Slash.) *Bald.*

c. (Repeat step *b* until firm.)

d. (Repeat steps *b* and *c* for each remaining word in the column.)

e. (Repeat the column until children read all the words in order without making a mistake.)

b<u>al</u>d

w<u>i</u>sh

wh<u>en</u>

wh<u>ile</u>

wh<u>ich</u>

s<u>ixtee</u>n

t<u>rapper</u>

Individual test

a. (Call on individual children to read one column of words from the lesson.)

b. (Praise children who read all words with no errors.)

STORYBOOK

RULE REVIEW
EXERCISE 4

Rule review

a. Everybody, you have learned rules in the earlier Jean stories.

b. You learned a rule about if you eat three red bananas. Say that rule. Get ready. (Signal.) *If you eat three red bananas, you get red stripes.*

- (Repeat until firm.)

c. You learned a rule about getting rid of red stripes. Say that rule. Get ready. (Signal.) *If you jump in the lake, the stripes will disappear.*

- (Repeat until firm.)

d. You learned a rule about getting rid of white hair. Say that rule. Get ready. (Signal.) *If you stand on one foot, the white hair will disappear.*

- (Repeat until firm.)

e. (If the children missed any rules, repeat steps *b* through *d*.)

EXERCISE 3

Words with underlined parts

a. First you're going to read the underlined part of each word in this column. Then you're going to read the whole word.

b. (Touch the ball for **beat**.) Read the underlined part. Get ready. (Tap the ball.) *eee.*

• Read the whole word. (Pause.) Get ready. (Slash.) *Beat.*

c. (Repeat step *b* until firm.)

d. (Repeat steps *b* and *c* for each remaining word in the column.)

e. (Repeat the column until children read all the words in order without making a mistake.)

beat

smash

fool

leave

reached

I'm

I'll

EXERCISE 4

Children spell, then read

a. First you're going to spell each word. Then you're going to read that word the fast way.

b. (Touch the ball for **Bide**.) Spell it. Get ready. (Tap under each letter as the children say:) *B-I-D-E.*

• (Return to the ball.) Read it. Get ready. (Slash.) *Bide.*

c. (Repeat step *b* for each remaining word in the column.)

d. (Repeat steps *b* and *c* until firm.)

Bide

coned

conned

kept

Nothing

flies

scare

Individual test

a. (Call on individual children to read one column of words from the lesson.)

b. (Praise children who read all words with no errors.)

READING VOCABULARY

EXERCISE 1

Teacher reads the word in red

a. I'll read the word in red. Then you'll spell the word.

b. (Touch the ball for **babies**.) My turn. (Slash as you say:) Babies. What word? (Signal.) *Babies.*

c. (Return to the ball.) Spell it. Get ready. (Tap under each letter as the children say:) *B-A-B-I-E-S.*

• What word did you spell? (Signal.) *Babies.*

d. Your turn to read all the words in this column.

e. (Touch the ball for **babies**. Pause.) Get ready. (Slash.) *Babies.*

f. (Repeat step *e* for each remaining word in the column.)

g. (Repeat steps *e* and *f* until firm.)

babies

bent

Hair

baby

right

head

eight

EXERCISE 2

Words with underlined parts

a. First you're going to read the underlined part of each word in this column. Then you're going to read the whole word.

b. (Touch the ball for **become**.) Read the underlined part. Get ready. (Tap the ball.) *Come.*

• Read the whole word. (Pause.) Get ready. (Slash.) *Become.*

c. (Repeat step *b* until firm.)

d. (Repeat steps *b* and *c* for each remaining word in the column.)

e. (Repeat the column until children read all the words in order without making a mistake.)

become

became

turned

you've

we've

you'll

doing

STORY 114
EXERCISE 5

Reading—decoding

a. (Pass out Storybook 2.)

b. Everybody, open your reader to page 87.

c. Remember, if the group reads all the way to the red 5 without making more than five errors, we can go on.

d. Everybody, touch the title of the story. ✔

e. If you hear a mistake, raise your hand. Remember, children who do not have their place lose their turn. (Call on individual children to read two or three sentences. Do not ask comprehension questions. Tally all errors.)

To Correct

word-identification errors (**from**, for example)
1. That word is **from**. What word? *From.*
2. Go back to the beginning of the sentence and read the sentence again.

f. (If the children make more than five errors before they reach the red 5: when they reach the 5 return to the beginning of the story and have the children reread to the 5. Do not ask comprehension questions. Repeat step *f* until firm, and then go on to step *g*.)

g. (When the children read to the red 5 without making more than five errors: read the story to the children from the beginning to the 5. Ask the specified comprehension questions. When you reach the 5, call on individual children to continue reading the story. Have each child read two or three sentences. Ask the specified comprehension questions.)

Ott Comes Out of the Bottle[1]

Ott was very happy. He was picked to go into the yellow bottle. It was dark inside that bottle, but Ott didn't care. He was waiting for the girl to rub the bottle.[2] That girl's name was Carla.[3] She had found the bottle in a pile of junk.[4] When she found it, she said, "I like that bottle. I will take it home with me."

So now she was on her way home. She was going down Bide Street. She wasn't thinking about what she was doing.

A bunch of bad boys were always hanging around on Bide Street. Suddenly, Carla saw that three mean boys were following her. One of them said, "What do you have in that bottle?"

"Nothing," Carla said, and she kept on walking.

One of the boys said to the other boys, "Let's take that bottle and bust it."⑤[5]

The boys all went, "Ho, ho, ho."

Carla stopped and looked at the boys. "You better leave me alone," she said. "Or I'll rub this bottle and a genie will come out and beat you up."

"Ho, ho," the boys said. "That girl can really tell lies.[6] Do you think you can fool us with that silly story about the genie?"

Carla didn't know what to do. She didn't really think that there was a genie in the bottle, but she wanted to scare the mean boys.[7] "If you take one more step, I'll rub the bottle."

"I'm going to take that bottle and smash it," one of the boys said. He reached for the bottle. Carla rubbed the bottle. There was a puff of smoke.[8] The boys stopped. They watched as the smoke became a genie.[9]

More to come[10]

---

[1] What's the title of this story? (Signal.) *Ott comes out of the bottle.*

• What's going to happen today? (Signal.) *Ott will come out of the bottle.*

[2] Why didn't Ott care if it was dark inside that bottle? (The children respond.)

[3] What's her name? (Signal.) *Carla.*

[4] Where did Carla find the bottle? (Signal.) *In a pile of junk.*

[5] Everybody, say that. (Signal.) *Let's take that bottle and bust it.*

• Why would they do such a thing? (Signal.) *They are mean.*

[6] What did Carla tell them? (The children respond.) Right. She's going to rub the bottle. A genie will come out and beat them up.

[7] Did she really think there was a genie in the bottle? (Signal.) *No.*

• So why did she say that there was? (Signal.) *She wanted to scare the mean boys.*

[8] What happened to the bottle when Carla rubbed it? (Signal.) *There was a puff of smoke.*

[9] Did the boys run away? (Signal.) *No.*

• What did they do? (The children respond.)

[10] We'll find out next time what Ott does to those mean boys.

What's the rule?[12]

The red stripes disappeared, but now her hair had turned white.[13]

She said, "Oh, my. Oh, dear. I wish the old wizard was here."

Suddenly, the wizard appeared. He said, "Listen, my dear, and I will tell you the rule for getting rid of your white hair. If you stand on one foot, the white hair will disappear."[14]

Jean tried to say the rule five times. But she couldn't do it. Help her out. Say that rule for her.[15]

At last, Jean said the rule. Then she said, "But what and when . . . ."

The wizard disappeared.

To be continued

---

[12] Say that rule. Get ready. (Signal.) *If you jump in the lake, the stripes will disappear.* Yes, Jean jumped in the lake. So the stripes must have disappeared.

[13] What happened to her hair? (Signal.) *It turned white.*

• She needs another rule.

[14] Say that rule with me. (Signal. Teacher and children say:) *If you stand on one foot, the white hair will disappear.*

• (Repeat until firm.) All by yourselves. Get ready. (Signal.) (Children repeat the rule until firm.)

[15] Everybody, say it. (Signal.) *If you stand on one foot, the white hair will disappear.*

EXERCISE 7

Picture comprehension

a. What do you think you'll see in the picture? (The children respond.)

b. Turn the page and look at the picture.

c. (Ask these questions:)
  1. Is Jean striped in this picture? (Signal.) *No.*
  2. What color is her hair? (Signal.) *White.*
  3. Where is she? (Signal.) *In the lake.*
  4. Does she look happy? (Signal.) *Yes.*
  5. Do you think she knows her hair is white? (The children respond.)

INDEPENDENT ACTIVITIES

EXERCISE 8

Reading comprehension

a. (Pass out Worksheet 153 to each child.)

b. Everybody, turn to side 2 of your worksheet. ✔

c. (Point to the story on side 2 of your worksheet.) Everybody, find this story on your worksheet. ✔

d. Today you're going to read a passage that tells about living things.

e. I'll name some living things: a person, a cat, an insect, and a tree. Your turn. When I call on you, name some other living things. (Call on individual children. Praise appropriate responses.)

f. Today's passage gives a rule about all living things: All living things grow, and all living things need water. Everybody, say that rule. (Signal.) *All living things grow, and all living things need water.*

• (Repeat until firm.)

g. When you do your independent work, read the story carefully to yourself. Then answer the questions.

EXERCISE 9

Summary of independent activities

Everybody, now you'll do your worksheet. Remember to do all parts of the worksheet and to read all the parts carefully.

END OF LESSON 153

EXERCISE 6

Picture comprehension

a. Look at the picture.

b. (Ask these questions:)

1. What's Carla carrying? (Signal.) *A bottle.*
2. Does she look happy? (Signal.) *No.*
- Why not? (The children respond.)
3. What does it say on that street sign? (Signal.) *Bide Street.*
4. Do those boys look friendly? (The children respond.)
5. What do you think they are saying to her? (The children respond.)

EXERCISE 7

Summary of independent activities

a. (Pass out Worksheet 114 to each child.)

b. Everybody, now you'll do your worksheet. Remember to do all parts of the worksheet and to read all the parts carefully.

END OF LESSON 114

STORYBOOK

RULE REVIEW

EXERCISE 5

Rule review

a. Everybody, you have learned rules in the earlier Jean stories.

b. You learned a rule about red food. Say that rule. Get ready. **(Signal.)** *Red food is good to eat.*

• (Repeat until firm.)

c. You learned a rule about if you eat three red bananas. Say that rule. Get ready. **(Signal.)** *If you eat three red bananas, you get red stripes.*

• (Repeat until firm.)

d. You learned a rule about getting rid of red stripes. Say that rule. Get ready. **(Signal.)** *If you jump in the lake, the stripes will disappear.*

• (Repeat until firm.)

e. (If the children missed any rules, repeat steps *b* through *d*.)

STORY 153

EXERCISE 6

Reading—decoding

a. (Pass out Storybook 2.)

b. Everybody, open your reader to page 212.

c. Remember, if the group reads all the way to the red 5 without making more than five errors, we can go on.

d. Everybody, touch the title of the story. ✔

e. If you hear a mistake, raise your hand. Remember, children who do not have their place lose their turn. (Call on individual children to read two or three sentences. Do not ask comprehension questions. Tally all errors.)

Jean Makes the Red Stripes Disappear[1]

Why did Jean have red stripes all over?[2]

What could she do to make the red stripes disappear?[3]

So which path was she taking?[4]

Jean ran down the dusty path. Did the path lead to the mountain?[5]

What's the rule about every dusty path?[6]

Soon Jean came to the lake. But there were five little crumps on the path in front of her. Jean said, "I wonder if those little crumps are mean."

Tell Jean the rule about all little crumps.[7]

The crumps began to run after Jean. Jean said, "Oh, my. Oh, dear. Oh, oh. I forgot what to say to make these mean crumps go away."

Tell Jean what to say.[8]

Jean said, "Away, away." And what did the mean crumps do?[9]

What's the rule about making mean crumps go away?[10]

After the mean crumps went away, Jean jumped into the lake. ⑤

Did the red stripes disappear?[11]

To Correct

word-identification errors (**from,** for example)

1. That word is **from.** What word? *From.*
2. Go back to the beginning of the sentence and read the sentence again.

f. (If the children make more than five errors before they reach the red 5: when they reach the 5 return to the beginning of the story and have the children reread to the 5. Do not ask comprehension questions. Repeat step *f* until firm, and then go on to step *g*.)

g. (When the children read to the red 5 without making more than five errors: read the story to the children from the beginning to the 5. Ask the specified comprehension questions. When you reach the 5, call on individual children to continue reading the story. Have each child read two or three sentences. Ask the specified comprehension questions.)

[1] Will Jean get rid of the red stripes in this story? (Signal.) *Yes.*

[2] Say that question. (Signal.) *Why did Jean have red stripes all over?*

• What's the answer? (Signal.) *She ate three red bananas.*

[3] What's the answer? (Signal.) *Jump in the lake.*

[4] Say that question. (Signal.) *So which path was she taking?*

• What's the answer? (Signal.) *The dusty path.*

[5] Did it? (Signal.) *No.*

[6] Say the rule. Get ready. (Signal.) *Every dusty path leads to the lake.*

[7] Let's hear you tell her. (Signal.) *All little crumps are mean.*

[8] Tell her quick. (Signal.) *Away, away.*

[9] What do you think they did? (Signal.) *They went away.*

[10] What is that rule? (Signal.) *If you say, "Away, away," a mean crump will go away.*

[11] What's the answer? (Signal.) *Yes.*

READING VOCABULARY

EXERCISE 1

Teacher reads the words in red

a. I'll read each word in red. Then you'll spell each word.

b. (Touch the ball for **remember.**) My turn. (Slash as you say:) Remember. What word? (Signal.) *Remember.*

c. (Return to the ball.) Spell it. Get ready. (Tap under each letter as the children say:) *R-E-M-E-M-B-E-R.*

• What word did you spell? (Signal.) *Remember.*

d. (Repeat steps *b* and *c* for each word in red.)

e. Your turn to read all the words in this column.

f. (Touch the ball for **remember.** Pause.) Get ready. (Slash.) *Remember.*

g. (Repeat step *f* for each remaining word in the column.)

h. (Repeat steps *f* and *g* until firm.)

remember

forget

city

Rome

middle

banking

kind

EXERCISE 2

Words with underlined parts

a. First you're going to read the underlined part of each word in this column. Then you're going to read the whole word.

b. (Touch the ball for **spanking.**) Read the underlined part. Get ready. (Tap the ball.) *ing.*

• Read the whole word. (Pause.) Get ready. (Slash.) *Spanking.*

c. (Repeat step *b* until firm.)

d. (Repeat steps *b* and *c* for each remaining word in the column.)

e. (Repeat the column until children read all the words in order without making a mistake.)

spanking

easy

Boop

sounded

watched

years

thousands

EXERCISE 3

Read the fast way

a. You're going to read all the words in this column the fast way.

b. (Touch the ball for **were.** Pause.) Get ready. (Slash.) *Were.*

c. (Repeat step *b* until firm.)

d. (Repeat steps *b* and *c* for each remaining word in the column.)

e. (Repeat the column until the children read all the words in order without making mistakes.)

were →

become →

became →

white →

dear →

disappeared →

sounded →

EXERCISE 4

Children spell, then read

a. First you're going to spell each word. Then you're going to read that word the fast way.

b. (Touch the ball for **mountain.**) Spell it. Get ready. (Tap under each letter as the children say:) *M-O-U-N-T-A-I-N.*

• (Return to the ball.) Read it. Get ready. (Slash.) *Mountain.*

c. (Repeat step *b* for each remaining word in the column.)

d. (Repeat steps *b* and *c* until firm.)

mountain →

happened →

handle →

four →

forget →

forgot →

stripes →

Individual test

a. (Call on individual children to read one column of words from the lesson.)

b. (Praise children who read all words with no errors.)

EXERCISE 3

Read the fast way

a. You're going to read all the words in this column the fast way.

b. (Touch the ball for **hoped.** Pause.) Get ready. (Slash.) *Hoped.*

c. (Repeat step *b* until firm.)

d. (Repeat steps *b* and *c* for each remaining word in the column.)

e. (Repeat the column until the children read all the words in order without making mistakes.)

hoped

very

rubbed

folded

mean

should

lies

EXERCISE 4

Children spell, then read

a. First you're going to spell each word. Then you're going to read that word the fast way.

b. (Touch the ball for **sitting.**) Spell it. Get ready. (Tap under each letter as the children say:) *S-I-T-T-I-N-G.*

• (Return to the ball.) Read it. Get ready. (Slash.) *Sitting.*

c. (Repeat step *b* for each remaining word in the column.)

d. (Repeat steps *b* and *c* until firm.)

sitting

lived

miles

Suddenly

waved

appears

able

Individual test

a. (Call on individual children to read one column of words from the lesson.)

b. (Praise children who read all words with no errors.)

READING VOCABULARY

EXERCISE 1

Teacher reads the word in red

a. I'll read the word in red. Then you'll spell the word.

b. (Touch the ball for **eight**.) My turn. (Slash as you say:) Eight. What word? (Signal.) *Eight.*

c. (Return to the ball.) Spell it. Get ready. (Tap under each letter as the children say:) *E-I-G-H-T.*

• What word did you spell? (Signal.) *Eight.*

d. Your turn to read all the words in this column.

e. (Touch the ball for **eight**. Pause.) Get ready. (Slash.) *Eight.*

f. (Repeat step *e* for each remaining word in the column.)

g. (Repeat steps *e* and *f* until firm.)

EXERCISE 2

Words with underlined parts

a. First you're going to read the underlined part of each word in this column. Then you're going to read the whole word.

b. (Touch the ball for **mopper**.) Read the underlined part. Get ready. (Tap the ball.) *Mopp.*

• Read the whole word. (Pause.) Get ready. (Slash.) *Mopper.*

c. (Repeat step *b* until firm.)

d. (Repeat steps *b* and *c* for each remaining word in the column.)

e. (Repeat the column until children read all the words in order without making a mistake.)

eight

wonder

stairs

hair

thank

think

thing

mopper

moped

hated

Makes

you're

you'll

shouldn't

STORY 115

EXERCISE 5

Reading—decoding

a. (Pass out Storybook 2.)

b. Everybody, open your reader to page 90.

c. Remember, if the group reads all the way to the red five without making more than five errors, we can go on.

d. Everybody, touch the title of the story. ✓

e. If you hear a mistake, raise your hand. Remember, children who do not have their place lose their turn. (Call on individual children to read two or three sentences. Do not ask comprehension questions. Tally all errors.)

To Correct

> word-identification errors (**from,** for example)
> 1. That word is **from.** What word? *From.*
> 2. Go back to the beginning of the sentence and read the sentence again.

f. (If the children make more than five errors before they reach the red 5: when they reach the 5 return to the beginning of the story and have the children reread to the 5. Do not ask comprehension questions. Repeat step *f* until firm, and then go on to step *g*.)

g. (When the children read to the red 5 without making more than five errors: read the story to the children from the beginning to the 5. Ask the specified comprehension questions. When you reach the 5, call on individual children to continue reading the story. Have each child read two or three sentences. Ask the specified comprehension questions.)

Ott Tells Lies[1]

When the mean boys tried to take the bottle from Carla, she rubbed the bottle and Ott appeared.

Ott said, "Oh, master Carla, what can I do for you?"

Carla said, "Give those boys a spanking."[2]

"Yes, master," Ott said. He sounded smart, but he didn't know how to give the boys a spanking. He could only remember the word banking.[3]

"Well," Carla said at last, "are you going to give them a spanking?"

"Yes," Ott said. "A spanking it will be."

Ott waved his hands. Suddenly, Carla, Ott, and the three boys were in a bank. They were banking.

Carla said, "What kind of a genie are you?"

The boys said, "Let's get out of here," and they began to run from the bank as fast as they could go.

Ott was very sad. He said, ★ "Carla, I am a very old genie.(5)[4] I have been in the bottle for thousands of years.[5] I have not done tricks for thousands of years."

---

[1] What's the title of this story? (Signal.) *Ott tells lies.*

● What will Ott do in this story? (Signal.) *Ott will tell lies.*

[2] Everybody, say that. (Signal.) *Give those boys a spanking.*

● Who is Carla talking to? (Signal.) *Ott.*

[3] Did he remember the word spanking? (Signal.) *No.*

● What word could he remember? (Signal.) *Banking.*

[4] What did he say? (Signal.) *Carla, I am a very old genie.*

● Is that true? (Signal.) *No.* Right. He's telling a lie.

[5] Has he been in the bottle for thousands of years? (Signal.) *No.* Right. He's telling another lie.

The wizard disappeared.[10]

Jean said, "Well, I had better go to the lake."

Jean saw a rocky path. She ran down it as fast as she could go.⑤ Where did the rocky path lead?[11]

Tell Jean the rule about every rocky path.[12]

When Jean came back to the mountain, she remembered the rule about rocky paths. She saw two more paths. One path was muddy. One path was dusty. Tell Jean which path leads to the lake.[13]

"Thank you," Jean said, and ran down the dusty path. Her striped legs were going very fast, and her striped hair was flying in the wind.

To be continued

[10] What happened when Jean said, "But what and when . . . ." (Signal.)
The wizard disappeared.
• I wonder if that's a rule.
[11] What's the answer? (Signal.)
To the mountain.
[12] Tell her. (Signal.) *Every rocky path leads to the mountain.*
[13] Tell her which path to take. (Signal.)
The dusty path.

EXERCISE 7

Picture comprehension

a. Look at the picture.
b. (Ask these questions:)
  1. Is Jean still striped? (Signal.) *Yes.*
  2. What is she doing?
     (The children respond.)
  3. Where is she running? (Signal.)
     To the lake.
  • Yes, every dusty path leads to the lake.
  4. Why does she want to get to the lake?
     (The children respond.)

WORKSHEET 152

INDEPENDENT ACTIVITIES
EXERCISE 8

Reading comprehension

a. (Pass out Worksheet 152 to each child.)
b. Everybody, turn to side 2 of your worksheet. ✔
c. (Point to the story on side 2 of your worksheet.) Everybody, find this story on your worksheet. ✔
d. Today you're going to read a passage that tells about a man named Isaac Newton. Find his name in the first sentence of the story. ✔
e. Everybody, look at the picture. (Pause.) What is falling from the tree? (Signal.) *An apple.*
• In which direction is that apple going? (Signal.) *Down.*
f. Everybody, what would happen to a ball if you threw it up in the air very far? (The children respond.)
g. You'll read about the rule that Isaac Newton figured out: **What goes up must come down.** Everybody, say that rule. (Signal.) *What goes up must come down.*
• (Repeat until firm.)
h. When you do your independent work, read the passage to yourself. Then answer the questions.

EXERCISE 9

Summary of independent activities

Everybody, now you'll do your worksheet. Remember to do all parts of the worksheet and to read all the parts carefully.

END OF LESSON 152

Ott was telling some big lies. He was not a very old genie. He had not lived in the bottle for thousands of years, and he didn't forget how to do genie tricks. He never was able to do them.[6]

Carla said, "Well, can you get us out of this bank and take us home?"

"Yes, master Carla," Ott said. "That should be easy."

Ott folded his arms. He said some words. Boop.

Suddenly, Ott and Carla were standing in the middle of a big city.[7]Carla looked around. Then she said, "This is not home. This is Rome.[8]Rome is thousands of miles from my home."[9]

More next time[10]

[6] What wasn't he able to do? (Signal.) *Tricks.*
Right. He told a lie about doing tricks too.
[7] How did Ott and Carla get there?
(The children respond.)
Right. Ott said some words.
[8] Did he take Carla home? (Signal.) *No.* Right.
• Where did he take her? (Signal.) *To Rome.*
• What is Rome? (The children respond.) Yes, Rome is a city.
[9] Everybody, say that. (Signal.) *Rome is thousands of miles from my home.*
[10] Everybody, tell me what you think will happen. (The children respond.)

EXERCISE 6
Picture comprehension

a. Look at the picture.
b. (Ask these questions:)
1. What city are Carla and Ott in?
(Signal.) *Rome.*
• How do you know that this is a picture of Rome? (The children respond.)
2. What do you think Carla is saying?
(The children respond.)
• She sure is unhappy.
3. What do you think Ott is saying?
(The children respond.)
• He has told lots of lies.

WORKSHEET 115
INDEPENDENT ACTIVITIES
EXERCISE 7
Summary of independent activities

a. (Pass out Worksheet 115 to each child.)
b. Everybody, now you'll do your worksheet. Remember to do all parts of the worksheet and to read all the parts carefully.

INDIVIDUAL CHECKOUT
EXERCISE 8
2-minute individual fluency checkout: rate/accuracy

a. As you are doing your worksheet, I'll call on children one at a time to read to the star. Remember, you get two stars on the chart if you read to the star in less than two minutes and make no more than five errors.
b. (Call on each child. Tell the child:) Read to the star very carefully. Start with the title. Go. (Time the child. Tell the child any words the child misses. Stop the child as soon as the child makes the sixth error or exceeds the time limit.)
c. (If the child meets the rate-accuracy criterion, record two stars on your chart for lesson 115. Congratulate the child. Give children who do not earn two stars a chance to read to the star again before the next lesson is presented.)
140 words/**2 min** = 70 wpm [**5 errors**]

END OF LESSON 115

STORYBOOK

RULE REVIEW
EXERCISE 5

Rule review

a. Everybody, you have learned rules in the earlier Jean stories.

b. You learned a rule about every rocky path. Say that rule. Get ready. (Signal.) *Every rocky path leads to the mountain.*
- (Repeat until firm.)

c. You learned a rule about red food. Say that rule. Get ready. (Signal.) *Red food is good to eat.*
- (Repeat until firm.)

d. You learned a rule about if you eat three red bananas. Say that rule. Get ready. (Signal.) *If you eat three red bananas, you get red stripes.*
- (Repeat until firm.)

e. (If the children missed any rules, repeat steps *b* through *d*.)

STORY 152
EXERCISE 6

Reading—decoding

a. (Pass out Storybook 2.)

b. Everybody, open your reader to page 209.

c. Remember, if the group reads all the way to the red 5 without making more than five errors, we can go on.

d. Everybody, touch the title of the story. ✔

e. If you hear a mistake, raise your hand. Remember, children who do not have their place lose their turn. (Call on individual children to read two or three sentences. Do not ask comprehension questions. Tally all errors.)

Jean Wants to Get Rid of the Red Stripes[1]

Jean was having a dream. What was the name of the land in her dream?[2]

Was Jean having a good time?[3]

Why did Jean have red stripes all over herself?[4]

What's the rule about three red bananas?[5]

She said, "Oh, I wish the wizard was here." Just as she said the words, the wizard appeared. Then Jean said, "What's the rule about getting rid of all these red stripes?"[6]

The wizard said, "Here's the rule: If you jump in the lake, the stripes will disappear.[7] Can you say that rule?"[8]

Jean tried to say the rule, but she got mixed up. Help her say the rule.[9]

After Jean said the rule, she said, "But what and when . . . ."

To Correct

word-identification errors (**from**, for example)
1. That word is **from**. What word? *From.*
2. Go back to the beginning of the sentence and read the sentence again.

f. (If the children make more than five errors before they reach the red 5: when they reach the 5 return to the beginning of the story and have the children reread to the 5. Do not ask comprehension questions. Repeat step *f* until firm, and then go on to step *g*.)

g. (When the children read to the red 5 without making more than five errors: read the story to the children from the beginning to the 5. Ask the specified comprehension questions. When you reach the 5, call on individual children to continue reading the story. Have each child read two or three sentences. Ask the specified comprehension questions.)

[1] What does Jean want to do? (Signal.) *Get rid of the red stripes.*

[2] What's the answer? (Signal.) *The land of peevish pets.*

[3] What's the answer? (Signal.) *No.*

[4] What's the answer? (Signal.) *She ate three red bananas.*

[5] Everybody, say that rule. (Signal.) *If you eat three red bananas, you get red stripes.*

[6] What does Jean want a rule about? (Signal.) *Getting rid of the red stripes.*

[7] Everybody, say the rule with me. (Signal. Teacher and children say:) *If you jump in the lake, the stripes will disappear.*
- (Repeat until firm.)

[8] Let's hear you. (Signal.) *If you jump in the lake, the stripes will disappear.*

[9] Everybody, help her in a nice loud voice. (Signal.) *If you jump in the lake, the stripes will disappear.*
- I think she heard that.

READING VOCABULARY

EXERCISE 1

Teacher reads the words in red

a. I'll read each word in red. Then you'll spell each word.

b. (Touch the ball for **air**.) My turn. (Slash as you say:) Air. What word? (Signal.) *Air.*

c. (Return to the ball.) Spell it. Get ready. (Tap under each letter as the children say:) *A-I-R.*

• What word did you spell? (Signal.) *Air.*

d. (Repeat steps *b* and *c* for each word in red.)

e. Your turn to read all the words in this column.

f. (Touch the ball for **air**. Pause.) Get ready. (Slash.) *Air.*

g. (Repeat step *f* for each remaining word in the column.)

h. (Repeat steps *f* and *g* until firm.)

air

face

blushed

spin

poorest

bank

middle

EXERCISE 2

Words with underlined parts

a. First you're going to read the underlined part of each word in this column. Then you're going to read the whole word.

b. (Touch the ball for **forest**.) Read the underlined part. Get ready. (Tap the ball.) *For.*

• Read the whole word. (Pause.) Get ready. (Slash.) *Forest.*

c. (Repeat step *b* until firm.)

d. (Repeat steps *b* and *c* for each remaining word in the column.)

e. (Repeat the column until children read all the words in order without making a mistake.)

forest

waited

remember

being

laughing

forget

hatter

EXERCISE 3

Read the fast way

a. You're going to read all the words in this column the fast way.

b. (Touch the ball for **found.** Pause.) Get ready. (Slash.) *Found.*

c. (Repeat step *b* until firm.)

d. (Repeat steps *b* and *c* for each remaining word in the column.)

e. (Repeat the column until the children read all the words in order without making mistakes.)

found

where

here

there

Rid

Red

buying

EXERCISE 4

Children spell, then read

a. First you're going to spell each word. Then you're going to read that word the fast way.

b. (Touch the ball for **filed.**) Spell it. Get ready. (Tap under each letter as the children say:) *F-I-L-E-D.*

• (Return to the ball.) Read it. Get ready. (Slash.) *Filed.*

c. (Repeat step *b* for each remaining word in the column.)

d. (Repeat steps *b* and *c* until firm.)

filed

filled

mopped

having

third

moped

striped

Individual test

a. (Call on individual children to read one column of words from the lesson.)

b. (Praise children who read all words with no errors.)

EXERCISE 3

Read the fast way

a. You're going to read all the words in this column the fast way.

b. (Touch the ball for **hater.** Pause.) Get ready. (Slash.) *Hater.*

c. (Repeat step *b* until firm.)

d. (Repeat steps *b* and *c* for each remaining word in the column.)

e. (Repeat the column until the children read all the words in order without making mistakes.)

hater

alligator

Poof

city

beach

peach

Please

EXERCISE 4

Children spell, then read

a. First you're going to spell each word. Then you're going to read that word the fast way.

b. (Touch the ball for **words.**) Spell it. Get ready. (Tap under each letter as the children say:) *W-O-R-D-S.*

• (Return to the ball.) Read it. Get ready. (Slash.) *Words.*

c. (Repeat step *b* for each remaining word in the column.)

d. (Repeat steps *b* and *c* until firm.)

words

Could

best

pile

laugh

kind

Rome

Individual test

a. (Call on individual children to read one column of words from the lesson.)

b. (Praise children who read all words with no errors.)

READING VOCABULARY
EXERCISE 1

Teacher reads the words in red

a. I'll read each word in red. Then you'll spell each word.

b. (Touch the ball for **wonder.**) My turn. (Slash as you say:) Wonder. What word? (Signal.) *Wonder.*

c. (Return to the ball.) Spell it. Get ready. (Tap under each letter as the children say:) *W-O-N-D-E-R.*

- What word did you spell? (Signal.) *Wonder.*

d. (Repeat steps *b* and *c* for each word in red.)

e. Your turn to read all the words in this column.

f. (Touch the ball for **wonder.** Pause.) Get ready. (Slash.) *Wonder.*

g. (Repeat step *f* for each remaining word in the column.)

h. (Repeat steps *f* and *g* until firm.)

EXERCISE 2

Words with underlined parts

a. First you're going to read the underlined part of each word in this column. Then you're going to read the whole word.

b. (Touch the ball for **dusty.**) Read the underlined part. Get ready. (Tap the ball.) *Dust.*

- Read the whole word. (Pause.) Get ready. (Slash.) *Dusty.*

c. (Repeat step *b* until firm.)

d. (Repeat steps *b* and *c* for each remaining word in the column.)

e. (Repeat the column until children read all the words in order without making a mistake.)

wonder

handle

soft

mixed

disappeared

help

two

dusty

muddy

rocky

jumped

something

anybody

anyhow

STORY 116
EXERCISE 5

Reading—decoding

a. (Pass out Storybook 2.)

b. Everybody, open your reader to page 93.

c. Remember, if the group reads all the way to the red 5 without making more than five errors, we can go on.

d. Everybody, touch the title of the story. ✔

e. If you hear a mistake, raise your hand. Remember, children who do not have their place lose their turn. (Call on individual children to read two or three sentences. Do not ask comprehension questions. Tally all errors.)

> **To Correct**
> word-identification errors (**from,** for example)
> 1. That word is **from.** What word? *From.*
> 2. Go back to the beginning of the sentence and read the sentence again.

f. (If the children make more than five errors before they reach the red 5: when they reach the 5 return to the beginning of the story and have the children reread to the 5. Do not ask comprehension questions. Repeat step *f* until firm, and then go on to step *g.*)

g. (When the children read to the red 5 without making more than five errors: read the story to the children from the beginning to the 5. Ask the specified comprehension questions. When you reach the 5, call on individual children to continue reading the story. Have each child read two or three sentences. Ask the specified comprehension questions.)

Ott Is a Very Sad Genie[1]

Carla had told Ott to take her home, but Ott didn't take Carla home. He took her to Rome.[2] Carla was getting mad. She was also getting a little scared. She said, "Please get us home this time."

"I will do my best trick," Ott said.[3] He began to spin around. As he was spinning, he said things to himself. Poof. Suddenly, Carla and Ott were standing in the middle of a forest.[4] Carla said, "You must be the poorest genie there is. Where are we now?"

"I don't know," Ott said. "I will have to read my trick book to see what I did to bring us here."[5]

So Ott began to read his trick book and Carla waited and waited. At last, she said, "Could you bring me something to eat while I'm waiting?"[6]

"Yes," Ott said. "What do you want?" ⑤
Carla said, "I would like an apple or a peach."[7]

"An apple and a peach you will have," Ott said. He said some words and what do you think appeared for an apple? An alligator. And what do you think appeared for a peach? A beach.[8]

---

[1] What's the title of this story? (Signal.) *Ott is a very sad genie.*

• Why do you think he's sad? (The children respond.)

[2] What happened when Carla told Ott to send her home? (Signal.) *He took her to Rome.*

[3] What did Ott say? (Signal.) *I will do my best trick.*

• Do you think it will work? (The children respond.)

• Let's read and find out.

[4] Where were they now? (Signal.) *In the middle of a forest.*

• How did they get there? (The children respond.)

• Ott said the wrong words again.

[5] What's he going to do? (Signal.) *Read his trick book.*

• Why is he going to do that? (The children respond.) Right. He wants to find out what he did to bring them there.

[6] Everybody, say that. (Signal.) *Could you bring me something to eat while I'm waiting?*

[7] What did Carla want? (Signal.) *An apple or a peach.*

• Do you think Ott can make an apple or a peach appear? (The children respond.)

[8] What appeared for an apple? (Signal.) *An alligator.*

• And for a peach? (Signal.) *A beach.*

• He did it wrong again.

The wizard answered, "There is a rule about red bananas. <u>If you eat three red bananas, you get red stripes.</u>"[12]

Jean said, "Why didn't you tell me that rule before? Look at me. I have red stripes all over. I don't want to have red stripes."

"But now you know another rule," the wizard said. <u>"That is good."</u>[13]

Jean said, "But what and when . . . ." Suddenly, the wizard disappeared. Jean was all alone again. She began to rub her arm to get rid of the red stripes. <u>But they wouldn't rub off.</u>[14]

She was very sad. Suddenly something said, "Crump, crump." She turned around and saw a little crump coming after her. <u>Tell Jean how to make that crump go away.</u>[15]

Jean said, "Away, away." And the crump went away. But Jean still had red stripes.

She said, "I hope I remember that rule about eating three red bananas." <u>Help Jean say the rule.</u>[16]

<u>More about Jean's stripes next time</u>[17]

---

[12] Everybody, say that rule with me. **(Signal. Teacher and children say:)** *If you eat three red bananas, you get red stripes.*

- **(Repeat until firm.)** All by yourselves. Get ready. **(Signal.) (The children repeat the rule until firm.)**

[13] What's the rule Jean just learned? **(Signal.)** *If you eat three red bananas, you get red stripes.*

[14] Could she get rid of the stripes? **(Signal.)** *No.*

[15] Tell her. **(Signal.)** *Say, "Away, away."*

[16] Everybody, help her say the rule. **(Signal.)** *If you eat three red bananas, you get red stripes.*

[17] Do you think she'll get rid of the red stripes? **(The children respond.)**

- We'll read more next time.

EXERCISE 7

Picture comprehension

a. Look at the picture.

b. (Ask these questions:)
  1. What does Jean have all over herself? **(Signal.)** *Red stripes.*
  2. Show me what she ate. **(The children respond.)**
  - What were they? **(Signal.)** *Three red bananas.*
  3. How do you think Jean feels? **(The children respond.)**
  4. What could that funny animal be thinking? **(The children respond.)**

WORSHEET 151

INDEPENDENT ACTIVITIES
EXERCISE 8

Reading comprehension

a. (Pass out Worksheet 151 to each child.)

b. Everybody, turn to side 2 of your worksheet. ✔

c. (Point to the story on side 2 of your worksheet.) Everybody, find this story on your worksheet. ✔

d. Today you're going to read a passage that tells about melting glass.

e. Everybody, touch the first picture. ✔
- What object does that picture show? **(Signal.)** *A bottle.* That's how a glass bottle looks when it is not hot.

f. Everybody, touch the second picture. ✔
- What's happening to the bottle? **(The children respond.)** That's what happens to it when it gets very hot.

g. Everybody, touch the third picture. ✔
- That shows what happens to glass when it is so hot that it flows like water.

h. I'm not going to read the passage. When you do your independent work, read the passage to yourself. Then answer the questions.

EXERCISE 9

Summary of independent activities

Everybody, now you'll do your worksheet. Remember to do all parts of the worksheet and to read all the parts carefully.

END OF LESSON 151

Carla said, "You are a mess of a genie. I asked for an apple or a peach. All I see is an alligator and a pile of sand."

"I will try again," Ott said. "This time, I will try to get you a hot dog."

Ott said some words to himself. Suddenly, a log appeared. The log was on fire.⁹ Carla began to laugh.

"That is not a hot dog," she said. "That's a hot log."¹⁰

Ott was not laughing. He was very sad. He was very poor at being a genie.¹¹

More about Ott and Carla next time¹²

⁹ What was Ott trying to get? (Signal.) *A hot dog.*
• Did he get a hot dog? (Signal.) *No.*
¹⁰ What did he get? (Signal.) *A hot log.*
¹¹ Why was Ott sad? (The children respond.)
¹² Do you think they'll get home? (The children respond.)
• We'll read more next time.

EXERCISE 6

Picture comprehension

a. Look at the picture.
b. (Ask these questions:)
 1. Where are Carla and Ott in this picture? (Signal.) *In a forest.*
 2. Why is Carla laughing? (The children respond.)
 3. Why does Ott look sad? (The children respond.)
 4. Show me what Ott made instead of a peach. (The children respond.)
 • What is that? (Signal.) *A beach.*
 5. Show me what Ott made instead of an apple. (The children respond.)
 • What is that? (Signal.) *An alligator.*

WORKSHEET 116

EXERCISE 7

Summary of independent activities

a. (Pass out Worksheet 116 to each child.)
b. Everybody, now you'll do your worksheet. Remember to do all parts of the worksheet and to read all the parts carefully.

END OF LESSON 116

RULE REVIEW
EXERCISE 5

Rule review

a. Everybody, you have learned rules in the earlier Jean stories.

b. You learned a rule about every dusty path. Say that rule. Get ready. (Signal.) *Every dusty path leads to the lake.*

- (Repeat until firm.)

c. You learned a rule about every rocky path. Say that rule. Get ready. (Signal.) *Every rocky path leads to the mountain.*

- (Repeat until firm.)

d. You learned a rule about red food. Say that rule. Get ready. (Signal.) *Red food is good to eat.*

- (Repeat until firm.)

e. (If the children missed any rules, repeat steps *b* through *d*.)

STORY 151
EXERCISE 6

Reading—decoding

a. (Pass out Storybook 2.)

b. Everybody, open your reader to page 206.

c. Remember, if the group reads all the way to the red 5 without making more than five errors, we can go on.

d. Everybody, touch the title of the story. ✔

e. If you hear a mistake, raise your hand. Remember, children who do not have their place lose their turn. (Call on individual children to read two or three sentences. Do not ask comprehension questions. Tally all errors.)

Jean Eats Red Bananas[1]

Let's see how much you remember.

What is the name of the land that Jean was dreaming about?[2]

How many rules did she have to know before she could leave this land?[3]

She knew a rule about little crumps. What did she know about all little crumps?[4]

What do you do to make a mean crump go away?[5]

What kind of path would you take if you wanted to go to the lake?[6]

What kind of path would you take if you wanted to go to the mountain?[7]

What kind of food is good to eat?[8]

Jean had eaten a red banana, and it was very good. She picked up another red banana and ate it. Then she ate another red banana. When she had eaten the third red banana, she looked at her hand. It had red stripes on it.[9] Her other hand had red stripes, too. ⑤

She said, "What is happening to me?" She looked at her legs. They had red stripes. Her feet had red stripes. She had red stripes all over herself.[10]

She shouted, "Where is that wizard?"

"Here I am," the wizard said, and stepped out from behind a tree.

Jean asked, "Why do I have red stripes all over myself?"[11]

To Correct

word-identification errors (**from**, for example)
1. That word is **from.** What word? *From.*
2. Go back to the beginning of the sentence and read the sentence again.

f. (If the children make more than five errors before they reach the red 5: when they reach the 5 return to the beginning of the story and have the children reread to the 5. Do not ask comprehension questions. Repeat step *f* until firm, and then go on to step *g*.)

g. (When the children read to the red 5 without making more than five errors: read the story to the children from the beginning to the 5. Ask the specified comprehension questions. When you reach the 5, call on individual children to continue reading the story. Have each child read two or three sentences. Ask the specified comprehension questions.)

[1] What will Jean eat in this story? (Signal.) *Red bananas.*

[2] Say that question. (Signal.) *What is the name of the land that Jean was dreaming about?*
- What's the answer? (Signal.) *The land of peevish pets.*

[3] What's the answer? (Signal.) *Sixteen.*

[4] What's the answer? (Signal.) *They are mean.*

[5] What's the answer? (Signal.) *Say, "Away, away."*

[6] What's the answer? (Signal.) *A dusty path.*

[7] What's the answer? (Signal.) *A rocky path.*

[8] What's the answer? (Signal.) *Red food.*

[9] What happened to her hand after she had eaten the third red banana? (Signal.) *It had red stripes on it.*

[10] What happened to Jean? (The children respond.) Yes, she had red stripes.

[11] What did Jean ask? (Signal.) *Why do I have red stripes all over myself?*

- I think there's a rule about getting red stripes.

READING VOCABULARY

EXERCISE 1

Teacher reads the word in red

a. I'll read the word in red. Then you'll spell the word.

b. (Touch the ball for **filled.**) My turn. (Slash as you say:) Filled. What word? (Signal.) *Filled.*

c. (Return to the ball.) Spell it. Get ready. (Tap under each letter as the children say:) *F-I-L-L-E-D.*
 • What word did you spell? (Signal.) *Filled.*

d. Your turn to read all the words in this column.

e. (Touch the ball for **filled.** Pause.) Get ready. (Slash.) *Filled.*

f. (Repeat step *e* for each remaining word in the column.)

g. (Repeat steps *e* and *f* until firm.)

filled

we're

spin

never

haven't

flying

forest

EXERCISE 2

Word with underlined parts

a. First you're going to read the underlined part of each word in this column. Then you're going to read the whole word.

b. (Touch the ball for **which.**) Read the underlined part. Get ready. (Tap the ball.) *wh.*
 • Read the whole word. (Pause.) Get ready. (Slash.) *Which.*

c. (Repeat step *b* until firm.)

d. (Repeat steps *b* and *c* for each remaining word in the column.)

e. (Repeat the column until children read all the words in order without making a mistake.)

which

each

sounded

blushed

streaming

wished

laughing

EXERCISE 3

Read the fast way

a. You're going to read all the words in this column the fast way.

b. (Touch the ball for **stepped**. Pause.) Get ready. (Slash.) *Stepped.*

c. (Repeat step *b* until firm.)

d. (Repeat steps *b* and *c* for each remaining word in the column.)

e. (Repeat the column until the children read all the words in order without making mistakes.)

stepped

grape

bananas

grabbed

fine

vine

rules

EXERCISE 4

Words with underlined parts

a. First you're going to read the underlined part of each word in this column. Then you're going to read the whole word.

b. (Touch the ball for **filled**.) Read the underlined part. Get ready. (Tap the ball.) *Fill.*

• Read the whole word. (Pause.) Get ready. (Slash.) *Filled.*

c. (Repeat step *b* until firm.)

d. (Repeat steps *b* and *c* for each remaining word in the column.)

e. (Repeat the column until children read all the words in order without making a mistake.)

filled

filed

disappear

striped

paths

myself

more

Individual test

a. (Call on individual children to read one column of words from the lesson.)

b. (Praise children who read all words with no errors.)

EXERCISE 3

Words with underlined parts

a. First you're going to read the underlined part of each word in this column. Then you're going to read the whole word.

b. (Touch the ball for **someone.**) Read the underlined part. Get ready. (Tap the ball.) *One.*

• Read the whole word. (Pause.) Get ready. (Slash.) *Someone.*

c. (Repeat step *b* until firm.)

d. (Repeat steps *b* and *c* for each remaining word in the column.)

e. (Repeat the column until children read all the words in order without making a mistake.)

someone

somebody

Maybe

folded

poorest

appeared

hears

EXERCISE 4

Children spell, then read

a. First you're going to spell each word. Then you're going to read that word the fast way.

b. (Touch the ball for **hopping.**) Spell it. Get ready. (Tap under each letter as the children say:) *H-O-P-P-I-N-G.*

• (Return to the ball.) Read it. Get ready. (Slash.) *Hopping.*

c. (Repeat step *b* for each remaining word in the column.)

d. (Repeat steps *b* and *c* until firm.)

hopping

hoping

Again

words

laughed

face

air

Individual test

a. (Call on indiviual children to read one column of words from the lesson.)

b. (Praise children who read all words with no errors.)

READING VOCABULARY

EXERCISE 1

Teacher reads the words in red

a. I'll read each word in red. Then you'll spell each word.

b. (Touch the ball for **soft.**) My turn. (Slash as you say:) Soft. What word? (Signal.) *Soft.*

c. (Return to the ball.) Spell it. Get ready. (Tap under each letter as the children say:) *S-O-F-T.*

• What word did you spell? (Signal.) *Soft.*

d. (Repeat steps *b* and *c* for each word in red.)

e. Your turn to read all the words in this column.

f. (Touch the ball for **soft.** Pause.) Get ready. (Slash.) *Soft.*

g. (Repeat step *f* for each remaining word in the column.)

h. (Repeat steps *f* and *g* until firm.)

soft

third

first

cried

tried

could

Thud

EXERCISE 2

Words with underlined parts

a. First you're going to read the underlined part of each word in this column. Then you're going to read the whole word.

b. (Touch the ball for **mountain.**) Read the underlined part. Get ready. (Tap the ball.) *ou.*

• Read the whole word. (Pause.) Get ready. (Slash.) *Mountain.*

c. (Repeat step *b* until firm.)

d. (Repeat steps *b* and *c* for each remaining word in the column.)

e. (Repeat the column until children read all the words in order without making a mistake.)

mountain

eaten

cloud

chop

shouted

eating

around

STORY 117
EXERCISE 5

Reading—decoding

a. (Pass out Storybook 2.)

b. Everybody, open your reader to page 96.

c. Remember, if the group reads all the way to the red five without making more than 5 errors, we can go on.

d. Everybody, touch the title of the story. ✔

e. If you hear a mistake, raise your hand. Remember, children who do not have their place lose their turn. (Call on individual children to read two or three sentences. Do not ask comprehension questions. Tally all errors.)

To Correct

word-identification errors (from, for example)
1. That word is **from.** What word? *From.*
2. Go back to the beginning of the sentence and read the sentence again.

f. (If the children make more than five errors before they reach the red 5: when they reach the 5 return to the beginning of the story and have the children reread to the 5. Do not ask comprehension questions. Repeat step *f* until firm, and then go on to step *g*.)

g. (When the children read to the red 5 without making more than five errors: read the story to the children from the beginning to the 5. Ask the specified comprehension questions. When you reach the 5, call on individual children to continue reading the story. Have each child read two or three sentences. Ask the specified comprehension questions.)

Carla and Ott Can't Get Home[1]

Ott and Carla were in a forest. When Ott tried to get a hot dog for Carla, a hot log appeared. Carla laughed, but Ott felt very sad. Carla said, "Can you call for help? If someone hears us, they can tell us which way to go."

"Yes," Ott said. "I will make a sound that is very loud—very loud."[2] Ott said some words to himself. But there was no loud sound. There was a cloud.[3] Again Carla laughed.

She said, "You tried to make something that was loud, but you made a cloud.[4] So why don't you try to make a cloud? Maybe then you'll make a sound that is loud."

"Yes, master," Ott said. He folded his arms and said some words. Suddenly a loud sound filled the air.[5] "Help, help."

Ott said, "It worked. When I tried to make the cloud, I made a sound that is loud."⑤

Then Ott jumped up and down. He shouted and laughed. Then he said, "I've got it. I've got it. I know how to get us home."

"How?" Carla asked. "How?"

"Well," Ott said, still hopping up and down a bit. "When I wished us to go home, we went to Rome. So if I wish us to go to Rome . . . ."[6]

---

[1] What's their problem? (Signal.) *They can't get home.* Right.
- Where did Ott take them first? (Signal.) *To Rome.*
- Then where did he take them? (Signal.) *To a forest.*

[2] What is Ott trying to do? (The children respond.) Yes, make a sound that is loud.

[3] Did he make a sound that was loud? (Signal.) *No.*
- What did happen? (The children respond.) You're right. He made a cloud.
- Poor Ott.

[4] Everybody, say that. (Signal.) *You tried to make something that was loud, but you made a cloud.*

[5] When he tried to make a cloud, what happened? (The children respond.) Yes, he made something loud.

[6] What does Ott hope will happen? (The children respond.) Yes, he'll wish for Rome and maybe they'll get home.

5. (Call on a child.) Read the next sentence. *Sid has a tin cup.*
- Everybody, does Sid have a tin cup? (Signal.) *Yes.*
- And where are the frogs? (Signal.) *In every tin cup.*
- So does Sid have a frog? (Signal.) *Yes.* Yes, Sid has a frog.

6. (Call on child.) Read the next sentence. *Spot does not have a tin cup.*
- Everybody, does Spot have a tin cup? (Signal.) *No.*
- And where are the frogs? (Signal.) *In every tin cup.*
- So we don't know if Spot has a frog.

7. (Call on a child.) Read the next sentence. *Boo has a tin cup.*
- Everybody, does Boo have a tin cup? (Signal.) *Yes.*
- And where are the frogs? (Signal.) *In every tin cup.*
- So does Boo have a frog? (Signal.) *Yes.* Yes, Boo has a frog.

8. (Call on a child.) Read the last sentence. *Who has frogs?*
- Everybody, what do you have to tell? (Signal.) *Who has frogs.*
- Write in the blanks the names of everyone who has frogs. ✔

INDEPENDENT ACTIVITIES
EXERCISE 9
Reading comprehension

a. Everybody, turn to side 2 of your worksheet. ✔

b. (Point to the story on side 2 of your worksheet.) Everybody, find this story on your worksheet. ✔

c. Today you're going to read a passage that tells about how wood is used.

d. Everybody, touch the first picture. ✔
- You can see the inside of the tree. That part is made of wood. What's it made of? (Signal.) *Wood.*

e. Everybody, touch the second picture. ✔
- That picture shows something that is made from the wood of a tree. What object is in the picture? (Signal.) *A table.*

f. Everybody, touch the third picture. ✔
- That picture shows something else that is made from wood. What object is in the picture? (Signal.) *Paper.*

g. I'll read the passage. Everybody, follow along. (Read the passage to the children. Check that they are following along as you read.)

h. When you do your independent work, read the passage to yourself. Then answer the questions.

EXERCISE 10
Summary of independent activities

Everybody, now you'll do your worksheet. Remember to do all parts of the worksheet and to read all the parts carefully.

INDIVIDUAL CHECKOUT
EXERCISE 11
2-minute individual fluency checkout: rate/accuracy

a. As you are doing your worksheet, I'll call on children one at a time to read to the star. Remember, you get two stars on the chart if you read to the star in less than two minutes and make no more than five errors.

b. (Call on each child. Tell the child:) Read to the star very carefully. Start with the title. Go. (Time the child. Tell the child any words the child misses. Stop the child as soon as the child makes the sixth error or exceeds the time limit.)

c. (If the child meets the rate-accuracy criterion, record two stars on your chart for lesson 150. Congratulate the child. Give children who do not earn two stars a chance to read to the star again before the next lesson is presented.)
181 words/**2 min** = 90 wpm **[5 errors]**

END OF LESSON 150

"We will go home," Carla said. She ran over and gave Ott a kiss.

Ott blushed.[7] Then he folded his arms and said some words. Suddenly, Carla seemed to be flying in the air.[8] And then she stopped and looked around.

"Oh nuts," she said. "We're not at home. We are back in Rome."[9]

Ott said, "I don't know how I do that."

More of this story next time[10]

[7] What happens when you blush? **(The children respond.)**

[8] How did they get there? **(The children respond.)** Yes, Ott said some words.

[9] Did they get home? **(Signal.)** *No.*

- Where are they? **(Signal.)** *In Rome.*
- Did his trick work? **(Signal.)** *No.*

[10] I sure hope Carla gets home.

EXERCISE 6

Picture comprehension

a. What do you think you'll see in the picture? **(The children respond.)**

b. Turn the page and look at the picture.

c. (Ask these questions:)

1. Where are Ott and Carla in this picture? **(Signal.)** *In a forest.*

2. What is Carla doing? **(Signal.)** *Kissing Ott.*

- Why is she doing that? **(The children respond.)** Yes, she thinks this time he'll get her home.

3. What is Carla holding? **(Signal.)** *The bottle.*

4. What is that alligator doing? **(The children respond.)**

EXERCISE 7

Summary of independent activities

a. (Pass out Worksheet 117 to each child.)

b. Everybody, now you'll do your worksheet. Remember to do all parts of the worksheet and to read all the parts carefully.

END OF LESSON 117

Red food is good to eat.

Jean saw big white grapes on a vine. Should she eat those white grapes?[9]

How do you know?[10]

Tell Jean the rule before she tries to eat them.[11]

Jean saw a red banana. Should she eat that red banana?[12]

How do you know?[13]

Tell Jean the rule.[14]

Jean did not think that the banana looked very good, but she took a bite out of it.

"Wow," she said. "This is the best banana I have ever had."[15] She ate that banana.

Then she found another banana. That banana was yellow. Should she eat that banana?[16]

How do you know?[17]

Tell Jean the rule.[18]

Jean dropped the yellow banana and picked up a red banana. She began eating it.

This is not the end.[19]

---

[9] What's the answer? (Signal.) *No.*

[10] What's the answer? (The children respond.)

[11] Everybody, say the rule. (Signal.)
Red food is good to eat.

[12] What's the answer? (Signal.) *Yes.*

[13] What's the answer? (Signal.)
Because it is red.

[14] Tell her in a nice soft voice. (Signal.)
Red food is good to eat.

[15] Did she like the banana? (Signal.) *Yes.*

[16] What's the answer? (Signal.) *No.*

[17] How do you know? (Signal.)
Because it's not red.

[18] Tell her in a loud voice. (Signal.)
Red food is good to eat.

[19] You'll be surprised next time at what happens to Jean.

EXERCISE 7

Picture comprehension

a. Look at the picture.

b. (Ask these questions:)

1. What is Jean doing? (Signal.)
Eating the red banana.

• What do you know about the banana? (The children respond.)

2. What other food do you see? (The children respond.)

3. That bowl has yellow ice cream in it. Why didn't Jean eat it? (Signal.)
Because it is not red.

4. Is she eating those white grapes? (Signal.) *No.* Why not? (The children respond.)

DEDUCTIONS

The children will need pencils.

EXERCISE 8

Written deductions

a. (Pass out Worksheet 150 to each child.)

b. (Hold up side 1 of your worksheet and touch the sentence above the box in the deductions exercise.)

c. Everybody, touch this sentence on your worksheet. ✔

d. I'm going to call on individual children to read a sentence. Everybody, follow along.

1. (Call on a child.) Read the sentence above the box. *Find out who has frogs.*

• Everybody, what do you have to find out? (Signal.) *Who has frogs.*

2. (Call on a child.) Read the sentence in the box. (Rule:)
There are frogs in every tin cup.

• Everybody, what's the rule? (Signal.)
There are frogs in every tin cup.

• You need that rule to find out where the frogs are.

3. (Call on a child.) Read the first sentence under the box. *Ellen has a tin cup.*

• Everybody, does Ellen have a tin cup? (Signal.) *Yes.*

• And where are the frogs? (Signal.)
In every tin cup.

• So does Ellen have a frog? *Yes.* Yes, Ellen has a frog.

4. (Call on a child.) Read the next sentence. *Ott does not have a tin cup.*

• Everybody, does Ott have a tin cup? (Signal.) *No.*

• And where are the frogs? (Signal.)
In every tin cup.

• So we don't know if Ott has a frog.

READING VOCABULARY
EXERCISE 1
Teacher reads the words in red

a. I'll read each word in red. Then you'll spell each word.

b. (Touch the ball for **through**.) My turn. (Slash as you say:) Through.

• What word? (Signal.) *Through.*

c. (Return to the ball.) Spell it. Get ready. (Tap under each letter as the children say:) *T-H-R-O-U-G-H.*

• What word did you spell? (Signal.) *Through.*

d. (Repeat steps *b* and *c* for each word in red.)

e. Your turn to read all the words in this column.

f. (Touch the ball for **through**. Pause.) Get ready. (Slash.) *Through.*

g. (Repeat step *f* for each remaining word in the column.)

h. (Repeat steps *f* and *g* until firm.)

through

fact

wise

woman

across

sorry

face

EXERCISE 2
Words with underlined parts

a. First you're going to read the underlined part of each word in this column. Then you're going to read the whole word.

b. (Touch the ball for **picked**.) Read the underlined part. Get ready. (Tap the ball.) *Pick.*

• Read the whole word. (Pause.) Get ready. (Slash.) *Picked.*

c. (Repeat step *b* until firm.)

d. (Repeat steps *b* and *c* for each remaining word in the column.)

e. (Repeat the column until children read all the words in order without making a mistake.)

picked

tossed

streaming

haven't

closer

resting

tear

RULE REVIEW
EXERCISE 5

Rule review

a. Everybody, you have learned rules in the earlier Jean stories.

b. You learned a rule about if you say, "Away, away." Say that rule. Get ready. (Signal.) *If you say, "Away, away," a mean crump will go away.*

• (Repeat until firm.)

c. You learned a rule about dusty paths. Say that rule. Get ready. (Signal.) *Every dusty path leads to the lake.*

• (Repeat until firm.)

d. You learned a rule about rocky paths. Say that rule. Get ready. (Signal.) *Every rocky path leads to the mountain.*

• (Repeat until firm.)

e. (If the children missed any rules, repeat steps *b* through *d*.)

STORY 150
EXERCISE 6

Reading—decoding

a. (Pass out Storybook 2.)

b. Everybody, open your reader to page 203.

c. Remember, if the group reads all the way to the red 5 without making more than five errors, we can go on.

d. Everybody, touch the title of the story. ✔

e. If you hear a mistake, raise your hand. Remember, children who do not have their place lose their turn. (Call on individual children to read two or three sentences. Do not ask comprehension questions. Tally all errors.)

Jean Looks for Food[1]

Jean was dreaming about a strange place. She was at the mountain in the land of peevish pets. And she was very hungry. She said, "I wish I had something to eat, and I wish the wizard was here."[2]

Just then the wizard appeared. He said, "You may eat all you want, but remember this rule: Red food is good to eat.[3] See if you can say that rule."

Jean said, "Red food is good to eat."[4]

The wizard said, "Good remembering."

Jean said, "I will remember that rule. But what and when . . . ."

The wizard was gone again. Jean said to herself, "That is strange. Every time I say 'But what and when,' the wizard goes away."[5]

Jean looked around and found lots of food. There was food on the ground. There was food on the side of the mountain. There was a bowl of yellow ice cream right in front of her. ⑤ Should she eat that yellow ice cream?[6]

How do you know?[7]

Tell Jean the rule before she tries to eat that ice cream. ★[8]

To Correct

word-identification errors (**from**, for example)
1. That word is **from**. What word? *From.*
2. Go back to the beginning of the sentence and read the sentence again.

f. (If the children make more than five errors before they reach the red 5: when they reach the 5 return to the beginning of the story and have the children reread to the 5. Do not ask comprehension questions. Repeat step *f* until firm, and then go on to step *g*.)

g. (When the children read to the red 5 without making more than five errors: read the story to the children from the beginning to the 5. Ask the specified comprehension questions. When you reach the 5, call on individual children to continue reading the story. Have each child read two or three sentences. Ask the specified comprehension questions.)

[1] What will Jean look for in this story? (Signal.) *Food.*

[2] What two things did she wish for? (The children respond.)

• Let's read and see if he gives her a rule about food.

[3] Everybody, say that rule. (Signal.) *Red food is good to eat.*

• (Repeat until firm.)

[4] What did Jean say? (Signal.) *Red food is good to eat.*

• Did she say the rule right? (Signal.) *Yes.*

• Can you say the rule right? (Signal.) *Yes.*

• Let's hear you. (Signal.) *Red food is good to eat.*

[5] When does the wizard go away? (Signal.) *Every time Jean says, "But what and when."*

• I wonder if that's a rule.

[6] What's the answer? (Signal.) *No.*

[7] What's the answer? (The children respond.) Right. She knows about red food.

[8] Tell her the rule. Get ready. (Signal.)

EXERCISE 3

Read the fast way

a. You're going to read all the words in this column the fast way.

b. (Touch the ball for **never.** Pause.) Get ready. (Slash.) *Never.*

c. (Repeat step *b* until firm.)

d. (Repeat steps *b* and *c* for each remaining word in the column.)

e. (Repeat the column until the children read all the words in order without making mistakes.)

never

ever

cheek

Crash

Disappears

we're

were

EXERCISE 4

Teacher reads the words in red

a. I'll read each word in red. Then you'll spell each word.

b. (Touch the ball for **Splat.**) My turn. (Slash as you say:) Splat. What word? (Signal.) *Splat.*

c. (Return to the ball.) Spell it. Get ready. (Tap under each letter as the children say:) *S-P-L-A-T.*

• What word did you spell? (Signal.) *Splat.*

d. (Repeat steps *b* and *c* for each word in red.)

e. Your turn to read all the words in this column.

f. (Touch the ball for **Splat.** Pause.) Get ready. (Slash.) *Splat.*

g. (Repeat step *f* for each remaining word in the column.)

h. (Repeat steps *f* and *g* until firm.)

Splat

formed

flow

believe

dinner

diner

copper

Individual test

a. (Call on individual children to read one column of words from the lesson.)

b. (Praise children who read all words with no errors.)

EXERCISE 3

Read the fast way

a. You're going to read all the words in this column the fast way.

b. (Touch the ball for **apple.** Pause.) Get ready. (Slash.) *Apple.*

c. (Repeat step *b* until firm.)

d. (Repeat steps *b* and *c* for each remaining word in the column.)

e. (Repeat the column until the children read all the words in order without making mistakes.)

apple

ground

green

banana

tries

How

know

EXERCISE 4

Children spell, then read

a. First, you're going to spell each word. Then you're going to read that word the fast way.

b. (Touch the ball for **using.**) Spell it. Get ready. (Tap under each letter as the children say:) *U-S-I-N-G.*

• (Return to the ball.) Read it. Get ready. (Slash.) *Using.*

c. (Repeat step *b* for each remaining word in the column.)

d. (Repeat steps *b* and *c* until firm.)

using

hoper

hopper

these

those

always

pink

Individual test

a. (Call on individual children to read one column of words from the lesson.)

b. (Praise children who read all words with no errors.)

STORYBOOK

STORY 118
EXERCISE 5

Reading—decoding

a. (Pass out Storybook 2.)

b. Everybody, open your reader to page 99.

c. Remember, if the group reads all the way to the red 5 without making more than five errors, we can go on.

d. Everybody, touch the title of the story. ✔

e. If you hear a mistake, raise your hand. Remember, children who do not have their place lose their turn. (Call on individual children to read two or three sentences. Do not ask comprehension questions. Tally all errors.)

To Correct

word-identification errors (**from,** for example)
1. That word is **from.** What word? *From.*
2. Go back to the beginning of the sentence and read the sentence again.

f. (If the children make more than five errors before they reach the red 5: when they reach the 5 return to the beginning of the story and have the children reread to the 5. Do not ask comprehension questions. Repeat step *f* until firm, and then go on to step *g*.)

g. (When the children read to the red 5 without making more than five errors: read the story to the children from the beginning to the 5. Ask the specified comprehension questions. When you reach the 5, call on individual children to continue reading the story. Have each child read two or three sentences. Ask the specified comprehension questions.)

Ott Disappears[1]

Carla was sad. She felt a tear streaming down her cheek.[2] She said, "You are not a very funny genie. Can't you see that I want to go home? I don't want to stay in forests and get logs that are on fire. I don't want to be standing in the middle of Rome. I just want to go home. Do you hear me?"

Ott said, "I'm really very sorry, master." Now a tear was streaming down Ott's cheek. "I must tell you something," he said. "I told you a lie. I am not a very old genie.[3] I have not been resting in that bottle for thousands of years.[4] I am not old and wise. I am still going to genie school."

Carla said, "Well, isn't there some way to get out of this mess? Can you call for help?"

"Yes," Ott said. "That is one of the things I can do."⑤[5]

Ott folded his arms and said some things to himself. Then Carla could see something flying across the sky. Suddenly it began to dive down to Ott. It came closer and closer. Now Carla could see that it was a big, wet fish.[6] Splat. It hit Ott in the face.

Carla said, "You can't even call for help. You're not much help as a genie at all. In fact, I wish you would get out of here."[7]

"Yes, master," Ott said with a tear running down his cheek. Slowly a puff of smoke formed, and slowly Ott disappeared into the smoke. Then the smoke began to flow into the yellow bottle.[8]

Carla picked up the bottle and tossed it as hard as she could. Crash. It went through the window of a house.[9]

More to come

---

[1] What will Ott do in this story? (Signal.) *Disappear.*

[2] What was Carla doing? (Signal.) *Crying.*
• Why was she crying? (The children respond.)

[3] What was one lie Ott told Carla? (Signal.) *That he was a very old genie.*

[4] What was another lie he told? (Signal.) *That he had been in the bottle for thousands of years.*

[5] What is one of the things Ott can do? (Signal.) *Call for help.*

[6] What did Carla see flying across the sky? (Signal.) *A fish.*
• Was Ott calling for a fish? (Signal.) *No.*
• What was Ott calling for? (Signal.) *Help.*

• He said the wrong words again.

[7] What did Carla want Ott to do? (The children respond.)

[8] Where did Ott go? (The children respond.)
• Did Ott disappear? (Signal.) *Yes.*

[9] What did Carla do with the bottle? (The children respond.)
• Do you think she meant to throw it through the window? (The children respond.)
• I wonder if Ott will ever appear again. We'll read more next time.

READING VOCABULARY

EXERCISE 1

Teacher reads the words in red

a. I'll read each word in red. Then you'll spell each word.

b. (Touch the ball for **vine**.) My turn. (Slash as you say:) Vine. What word? (Signal.) *Vine.*

c. (Return to the ball.) Spell it. Get ready. (Tap under each letter as the children say:) *V-I-N-E.*

• What word did you spell? (Signal.) *Vine.*

d. (Repeat steps *b* and *c* for each word in red.)

e. Your turn to read all the words in this column.

f. (Touch the ball for **vine**. Pause.) Get ready. (Slash.) *Vine.*

g. (Repeat step *f* for each remaining word in the column.)

h. (Repeat steps *f* and *g* until firm.)

vine

grape

Chop

sleepy

melt

yellow

passed

EXERCISE 2

Words with underlined parts

a. First you're going to read the underlined part of each word in this column. Then you're going to read the whole word.

b. (Touch the ball for **couldn't**.) Read the underlined part. Get ready. (Tap the ball.) *Could.*

• Read the whole word. (Pause.) Get ready. (Slash.) *Couldn't.*

c. (Repeat step *b* until firm.)

d. (Repeat steps *b* and *c* for each remaining word in the column.)

e. (Repeat the column until children read all the words in order without making a mistake.)

couldn't

shouldn't

tallest

longest

hadn't

hasn't

wooden

WORSHEET 118

EXERCISE 6

Picture comprehension

a. Look at the picture.

b. (Ask these questions:)

1. Where are Ott and Carla in this picture?
   (Signal.) *In Rome.*
2. What's happening to Ott in this story?
   (The children respond.)
3. Where did that fish come from?
   (The children respond.) Yes, out of the sky.
4. Look at Carla. How do you think she is
   feeling? **(The children respond.)**
5. Does Ott look happy?
   (The children respond.)
6. What would you do if you were Carla?
   (The children respond.)

EXERCISE 7

Summary of independent activities

a. (Pass out Worksheet 118 to each child.)

b. Everybody, now you'll do your worksheet.
   Remember to do all parts of the worksheet
   and to read all the parts carefully.

END OF LESSON 118

WORKSHEET 149

Jean said, "Go away." Did the crumps go away?¹³ Why not?¹⁴

Jean said, "Away, away." Did the crumps go away.¹⁵ Why?¹⁶ What's the rule?¹⁷ After you say the rule, turn this page around and read the rule.¹⁸

will go away.

If you say, "Away, away," a mean crump

More in the next story¹⁹

¹³ Say that question. (Signal.) *Did the crumps go away?*
- What's the answer? (Signal.) *No.*
¹⁴ What's the answer? (Signal.) *She didn't say, "Away, away."*
¹⁵ What's the answer? (Signal.) *Yes.*
¹⁶ What's the answer? (Signal.) *Because she said, "Away, away."*
¹⁷ Say the rule. (Signal.) *If you say, "Away, away," a mean crump will go away.*
¹⁸ Everybody, read the rule to yourself. Good work.
¹⁹ Wait till you read what happens in the next story when Jean gets hungry.

EXERCISE 6

Picture comprehension
a. Look at the picture.
b. (Ask these questions:)
   1. What kind of path is Jean on? (Signal.) *A rocky path.*
   2. And where does that path lead? (Signal.) *To the mountain.* Yes, she's at the mountain now.
   3. Show me some **mean** little crumps. (The children respond.)
   - Do they look friendly? (Signal.) *No.* They're mean.
   4. If you were there, what would you say to make the mean crumps go away? (Signal.) *Away, away.*

DEDUCTIONS

The children will need pencils.

EXERCISE 7

Written deductions

a. (Pass out Worksheet 149 to each child.)
b. (Hold up side 1 of your worksheet and touch the sentence above the box in the deductions exercise.)
c. Everybody, touch this sentence on your worksheet. ✔
d. I'm going to call on individual children to read a sentence. Everybody, follow along.
   1. (Call on a child.) Read the sentence above the box. *Find out who will go to Japan.*
   - Everybody, what do you have to find out? (Signal). *Who will go to Japan.*
   2. (Call on a child.) Read the sentence in the box. *Here is the rule: The people who are running will go to Japan.*
   - Everybody, what's the rule? (Signal.) *The people who are running will go to Japan.*
   - You need that rule to find out who will go to Japan.
   3. (Call on a child.) Read the first sentence below the box. *The boss is running.*
   - Everybody, is the boss running? (Signal.) *Yes.*
   - And who will go to Japan? (Signal.) *The people who are running.*
   - So will the boss go to Japan? (Signal.) *Yes.* Yes, the boss will go to Japan.
   4. (Call on a child.) Read the next sentence. *Ellen is running.*
   - Everybody, is Ellen running? (Signal.) *Yes.*
   - And who will go to Japan? (Signal.) *The people who are running.*
   - So will Ellen go to Japan? (Signal.) *Yes.* Yes, Ellen will go to Japan.

   5. (Call on a child.) Read the next sentence. *Boo is sitting.*
   - Everybody, is Boo running? (Signal.) *No.*
   - And who will go to Japan. (Signal.) *The people who are running.*
   - So we don't know if Boo will go to Japan.
   6. (Call on a child.) Read the next sentence. *Jean is standing.*
   - Everybody, is Jean running? (Signal.) *No.*
   - And who will go to Japan? (Signal.) *The people who are running.*
   - So we don't know if Jean will go to Japan.
   7. (Call on a child.) Read the next sentence. *The turtle is not running.*
   - Everybody, is the turtle running? (Signal.) *No.*
   - And who will go to Japan? (Signal.) *The people who are running.*
   - So we don't know if the turtle will go to Japan.
   8. (Call on a child.) Read the last sentence. *Who will go to Japan?*
   - What do you have to tell? (Signal.) *Who will go to Japan.*
   - Write in the blanks the names of everyone who will go to Japan. ✔

EXERCISE 8

Summary of independent activities

Everybody, now you'll do your worksheet. Remember to do all parts of the worksheet and to read all the parts carefully.

END OF LESSON 149

READING VOCABULARY

EXERCISE 1

Children spell, then read

a. First you're going to spell each word. Then you're going to read that word the fast way.

b. (Touch the ball for **broken.**) Spell it. Get ready. (Tap under each letter as the children say:) *B-R-O-K-E-N.*

• (Return to the ball.) Read it. Get ready. (Slash.) *Broken.*

c. (Repeat step *b* for each remaining word in the column.)

d. (Repeat steps *b* and *c* until firm.)

broken

cans

canes

pane

bent

through

believed

EXERCISE 2

Words with underlined parts

a. First you're going to read the underlined part of each word in this column. Then you're going to read the whole word.

b. (Touch the ball for **hard.**) Read the underlined part. Get ready. (Tap the ball.) *ar.*

• Read the whole word. (Pause.) Get ready. (Slash.) *Hard.*

c. (Repeat step *b* until firm.)

d. (Repeat steps *b* and *c* for each remaining word in the column.)

e. (Repeat the column until children read all the words in order without making a mistake.)

hard

longer

each

being

screamed

Then

After

149

STORY 149
EXERCISE 5

Reading—decoding

a. (Pass out Storybook 2.)

b. Everybody, open your reader to page 200.

c. Remember, if the group reads all the way to the red 5 without making more than five errors, we can go on.

d. Everybody, touch the title of the story. ✔

e. If you hear a mistake, raise your hand. Remember, children who do not have their place lose their turn. (Call on individual children to read two or three sentences. Do not ask comprehension questions. Tally all errors.)

To Correct

word-identification errors (from, for example)

1. That word is **from.** What word? *From.*
2. Go back to the beginning of the sentence and read the sentence again.

f. (If the children make more than five errors before they reach the red 5: when they reach the 5 return to the beginning of the story and have the children reread to the 5. Do not ask comprehension questions. Repeat step *f* until firm, and then go on to step *g*.)

g. (When the children read to the red 5 without making more than five errors: read the story to the children from the beginning to the 5. Ask the specified comprehension questions. When you reach the 5, call on individual children to continue reading the story. Have each child read two or three sentences. Ask the specified comprehension questions.)

Jean Follows a Rocky Path[1]

Jean was mad. And she was tired. She was trying to leave the lake. She walked down dusty paths, but they led right back to the lake.

Tell Jean the rule about dusty paths.[2] After you say the rule, turn this page around and read it.[3]

Every dusty path leads to the lake.

Jean said, "I wish that wizard was around here."

Just then the wizard appeared. He said, "I see that you know the rule about the dusty paths. Now I will tell you the rule about the rocky paths.[4] Every rocky path leads to the mountain."[5]

"I can remember that rule," Jean said. "Every rocky path leads to the mountain."[6]

"Very good remembering," the wizard said. "Soon you will know all sixteen rules."

Jean said, "But what and when . . . ."

Again the wizard was gone. Jean said, "I want to go to the mountain.⑤ But I can't remember which path to take."[7]

Tell Jean the rule about the paths that go to the mountain.[8]

"Oh, thank you," Jean said. She took a rocky path and soon she came to a big mountain. But there were crumps all around the mountain. And some of them were little. What do you know about little crumps?[9]

Jean said, "Oh, dear. There's a rule about how to get rid of mean crumps, but I can't remember that rule."

The mean crumps were starting to run after Jean. Help Jean out. Tell her what to do to make the mean crumps go away.[10]

Jean said, "Away." Did the crumps go away?[11] Why not?[12]

---

[1] What will Jean do in this story? (Signal.) *Follow a rocky path.*

[2] Everybody, tell Jean that rule. Get ready. (Signal.) *Every dusty path leads to the lake.*

[3] Turn the page around and read the rule to yourself.

[4] Is the wizard going to tell Jean a new rule? (Signal.) *Yes.*

• About what? (Signal.) *Rocky paths.* Yes, rocky paths.

[5] Everybody, say that rule with me. (Signal. Teacher and children say:) *Every rocky path leads to the mountain.*

• (Repeat until firm.) All by yourselves. Get ready. (Signal.) *The children repeat the rule until firm.*

[6] What did Jean say? (Signal.) *Every rocky path leads to the mountain.* Is she right? (Signal.) *Yes.* Good for her. She really remembered that rule.

[7] Oh, oh. She forgot the rule.

[8] Tell her. Get ready. (Signal.) *Every rocky path leads to the mountain.*

[9] What do you know about them? (Signal.) *They are mean.*

[10] Tell her what to do. (Signal.) *Say, "Away, away."*

[11] What's the answer? (Signal.) *No.*

[12] What's the answer? (Signal.) *She didn't say, "Away, away."*

EXERCISE 3

Read the fast way

a. You're going to read all the words in this column the fast way.

b. (Touch the ball for **woman.** Pause.) Get ready. (Slash.) *Woman.*

c. (Repeat step *b* until firm.)

d. (Repeat steps *b* and *c* for each remaining word in the column.)

e. (Repeat the column until the children read all the words in order without making mistakes.)

woman

happen

were

spank

we're

stick

glass

EXERCISE 4

Words with underlined parts

a. First you're going to read the underlined part of each word in this column. Then you're going to read the whole word.

b. (Touch the ball for **grabbed.**) Read the underlined part. Get ready. (Tap the ball.) *Grabb.*
- Read the whole word. (Pause.) Get ready. (Slash.) *Grabbed.*

c. (Repeat step *b* until firm.)

d. (Repeat steps *b* and *c* for each remaining word in the column.)

e. (Repeat the column until children read all the words in order without making a mistake.)

grabbed

suddenly

smiled

didn't

windows

tossed

looked

EXERCISE 3

Words with underlined parts

a. First you're going to read the underlined part of each word in this column. Then you're going to read the whole word.

b. (Touch the ball for **paths.**) Read the underlined part. Get ready. (Tap the ball.) *Path.*

• Read the whole word. (Pause.) Get ready. (Slash.) *Paths.*

c. (Repeat step *b* until firm.)

d. (Repeat steps *b* and *c* for each remaining word in the column.)

e. (Repeat the column until children read all the words in order without making a mistake.)

paths

hoped

hopped

couldn't

haven't

hasn't

hadn't

Individual test

a. (Call on individual children to read one column of words from the lesson.)

b. (Praise children who read all words with no errors.)

RULE REVIEW
EXERCISE 4

Rule review

a. Everybody, you have learned rules in the earlier Jean stories.

b. You learned a rule about all little crumps. Say that rule. Get ready. (Signal.) *All little crumps are mean.*

• (Repeat until firm.)

c. You learned a rule about if you say, "Away, away." Say that rule. Get ready. (Signal.) *If you say, "Away, away," a mean crump will go away.*

• (Repeat until firm.)

d. You learned a rule about dusty paths. Say that rule. Get ready. (Signal.) *Every dusty path leads to the lake.*

• (Repeat until firm.)

e. (If the children missed any rules, repeat steps *b* through *d*.)

EXERCISE 5

Read the fast way

a. You're going to read all the words in this column the fast way.

b. (Touch the ball for **fact**. Pause.) Get ready. (Slash.) *Fact.*

c. (Repeat step *b* until firm.)

d. (Repeat steps *b* and *c* for each remaining word in the column.)

e. (Repeat the column until the children read all the words in order without making mistakes.)

fact

wise

across

splat

formed

flow

Poof

Individual test

a. (Call on individual children to read one column of words from the lesson.)

b. (Praise children who read all words with no errors.)

STORY 119
EXERCISE 6

Reading—decoding

a. (Pass out Storybook 2.)

b. Everybody, open your reader to page 102.

c. Remember, if the group reads all the way to the red 5 without making more than five errors, we can go on.

d. Everybody, touch the title of the story. ✔

e. If you hear a mistake, raise your hand. Remember, children who do not have their place lose their turn. (Call on individual children to read two or three sentences. Do not ask comprehension questions. Tally all errors.)

To Correct

word-identification errors (from, for example)

1. That word is **from.** What word? *From.*
2. Go back to the beginning of the sentence and read the sentence again.

f. (If the children make more than five errors before they reach the red 5: when they reach the 5 return to the beginning of the story and have the children reread to the 5. Do not ask comprehension questions. Repeat step *f* until firm, and then go on to step *g*.)

g. (When the children read to the red 5 without making more than five errors: read the story to the children from the beginning to the 5. Ask the specified comprehension questions. When you reach the 5, call on individual children to continue reading the story. Have each child read two or three sentences. Ask the specified comprehension questions.)

READING VOCABULARY
EXERCISE 1

Teacher reads the words in red

a. I'll read each word in red. Then you'll spell each word.

b. (Touch the ball for **banana.**) My turn. (Slash as you say:) Banana. What word? (Signal.) *Banana.*

c. (Return the ball.) Spell it. Get ready. (Tap under each letter as the children say:) *B-A-N-A-N-A.*

• What word did you spell? (Signal.) *Banana.*

d. (Repeat steps *b* and *c* for each word in red.)

e. Your turn to read all the words in this column.

f. (Touch the ball for **banana.** Pause.) Get ready. (Slash.) *Banana.*

g. (Repeat step *f* for each remaining word in the column.)

h. (Repeat steps *f* and *g* until firm.)

banana

mammal

tickled

gone

page

rocky

forward

EXERCISE 2

Words with underlined parts

a. First you're going to read the underlined part of each word in this column. Then you're going to read the whole word.

b. (Touch the ball for **appear.**) Read the underlined part. Get ready. (Tap the ball.) *eee.*

• Read the whole word. (Pause.) Get ready. (Slash.) *Appear.*

c. (Repeat step *b* until firm.)

d. (Repeat steps *b* and *c* for each remaining word in the column.)

e. (Repeat the column until children read all the words in order without making a mistake.)

appear

mountain

starting

chunk

dusty

sounded

remembering

Ott Helps Carla [1]

Carla picked up the bottle and tossed it through the window of a house.[2] Then a big woman came out, holding the bottle. "Who tossed this bottle through my window?" she screamed.

She ran over and grabbed Carla. "You did it, didn't you? You are the one who tossed that bottle through my window."

"Yes, I did," Carla said. "But I didn't mean to. I didn't . . . ."

"I'll show you," the woman said. She put the bottle down. Then she picked up a broom. She was going to spank Carla with the broom.[3]

Carla bent over and rubbed the bottle. Poof. Ott was back.[4]

He said, "I will try to get you out of this, master." Ott said some words. Suddenly the pane of glass in the window was not broken.

"Stop," Carla said. "Look at your window. It is no longer broken."[5]

The woman looked at her window. (5) "I don't believe it," she said to herself. "I saw the glass go flying this way and that way. Now the glass is back in the window."

The woman dropped the broom and went back into her house. After she left, Carla gave Ott a big hug. "You did it," she said. "You wanted the window to have a pane of glass and you made it happen."

Ott smiled. "I think I'm getting better at being a genie."[6]

Carla said, "Maybe you can get us out of here now."

"I will try very hard," Ott said. "And please, master, don't hate me if I don't do well."[7]

Carla looked at Ott and smiled. "Okay," she said.

More to come

[1] What will Ott do in this story? (Signal.) *He will help Carla.*

[2] What did she do? (Signal.) *Picked up the bottle and tossed it through the window of a house.*
• Why did she do that? (The children respond.)

[3] What does the woman want the broom for? (Signal.) *To spank Carla.*
• Carla sure needs Ott's help.

[4] Why did Ott come back? (Signal.) *Carla rubbed the bottle.*

[5] How did the window get fixed? (The children respond.)
• Yes, did Ott say the right words this time? (Signal.) *Yes.*

[6] Everybody, say that. (Signal.) *I think I'm getting better at being a genie.*

[7] Why did Ott say that? (The children respond.) Right. He wants to do well.
• Next time we'll see if he does well.

EXERCISE 7
Picture comprehension

a. What do you think you'll see in the picture? (The children respond.)
b. Turn the page and look at the picture.
c. (Ask these questions:)
 1. What's that woman doing? (The children respond.)
 2. What does she want to do with the broom? (Signal.) *Spank Carla.*
 • Why? (The children respond.)
 3. Look at the window. Has Ott fixed it yet? (Signal.) *No.*
 • How do you know? (The children respond.)

WORKSHEET 119

EXERCISE 8
Summary of independent activities

a. (Pass out Worksheet 119 to each child.)
b. Everybody, now you'll do your worksheet. Remember to do all parts of the worksheet and to read all the parts carefully.

END OF LESSON 119

Worksheet 148

What's the rule?[12]

The path led right back to the lake. Why?[13]

Yes, the rule says that every dusty path leads to the lake.

Jean tried to leave the lake by taking another dusty path. Where do you think that path led?[14] Why?[15]

Yes, the rule says that every dusty path leads to the lake. That path was dusty, so it led right back to the lake.

To be continued[16]

12 Everybody, say the rule. **(Signal.)** ***Every dusty path leads to the lake.***

13 What's the answer? **(Signal.)** ***Because every dusty path leads to the lake.***

14 What's the answer? **(Signal.)** ***To the lake.***

15 What's the answer? **(Signal.)** ***Because every dusty path leads to the lake.***

16 Jean will meet some more crumps next time.

EXERCISE 6

Picture comprehension

a. Look at the picture.

b. **(Ask these questions:)**

1. What kind of path is Jean walking on? **(Signal.)** ***A dusty path.***
2. And where does that path lead? **(Signal.)** ***To the lake.***
3. What does she see in the lake? **(The children respond.)**
4. Do you think Jean likes what she sees? **(Signal.)** ***No.***
   - How do you know? **(The children respond.)**

DEDUCTIONS

The children will need pencils.

EXERCISE 7

Written deductions

a. **(Pass out Worksheet 148 to each child.)**

b. **(Hold up side 1 of your worksheet and touch the sentence above the box in the deductions exercise.)**

c. Everybody, touch this sentence on your worksheet. ✔

d. I'm going to call on individual children to read a sentence. Everybody, follow along.

1. **(Call on a child.)** Read the sentence above the box. ***Find out where the bugs are.***
   - Everybody, what do you have to find out? **(Signal.)** ***Where the bugs are.***
2. **(Call on a child.)** Read the sentence in the box. ***Here is the rule: Every white house has bugs.***
   - Everybody, what's the rule? **(Signal.)** ***Every white house has bugs.***
   - You need that rule to find out where the bugs are.
3. **(Call on a child.)** Read the first sentence below the box. ***Kim's house is brown.***
   - Everybody, is Kim's house white? **(Signal.)** ***No.***
   - And where are the bugs? **(Signal.)** ***In every white house.***
   - So we don't know if Kim's house has bugs.
4. **(Call on a child.)** Read the next sentence. ***Spot's house is white.***
   - Everybody, is Spot's house white? **(Signal.)** ***Yes.***
   - And where are the bugs? **(Signal.)** ***In every white house.***
   - So does Spot's house have bugs? **(Signal.)** ***Yes.*** Yes, Spot's house has bugs.
5. **(Call on a child.)** Read the next sentence. ***Ott's house is white.***
   - Everybody, is Ott's house white? ***Yes.*** And where are the bugs? **(Signal.)** ***In every white house.***
   - So does Ott's house have bugs? **(Signal.)** ***Yes.*** Yes, Ott's house has bugs.
6. **(Call on a child.)** Read the next sentence. ***Tim's house is red.***
   - Everybody, is Tim's house white? **(Signal.)** ***No.***
   - And where are the bugs? **(Signal.)** ***In every white house.***
   - So we don't know if Tim's house has bugs.
7. **(Call on a child.)** Read the next sentence. ***Mom's house is black.***
   - Everybody, is Mom's house white? **(Signal.)** ***No.***
   - And where are the bugs? **(Signal.)** ***In every white house.***
   - So we don't know if Mom's house has bugs.
8. **(Call on a child.)** Read the last sentence. ***Who has a house with bugs?***
   - Everybody, what do you have to tell? **(Signal.)** ***Who has a house with bugs.***
   - Write in the blanks the names of everyone who has a house with bugs. ✔

INDEPENDENT ACTIVITIES

EXERCISE 8

Summary of independent activities

Everybody, now you'll do your worksheet. Remember to do all parts of the worksheet and to read all the parts carefully.

END OF LESSON 148

READING VOCABULARY
EXERCISE 1

Teacher reads the words in red

a. I'll read each word in red. Then you'll spell each word.

b. (Touch the ball for **few.**) My turn. (Slash as you say:) Few. What word? (Signal.) *Few.*

c. (Return to the ball.) Spell it. Get ready. (Tap under each letter as the children say:) *F-E-W.*
- What word did you spell? (Signal.) *Few.*

d. (Repeat steps *b* and *c* for each word in red.)

e. Your turn to read all the words in this column.

f. (Touch the ball for **few.** Pause.) Get ready. (Slash.) *Few.*

g. (Repeat step *f* for each remaining word in the column.)

h. (Repeat steps *f* and *g* until firm.)

few

blanks

wonderful

through

were

we're

flip

EXERCISE 2

Words with underlined parts

a. First you're going to read the underlined part of each word in this column. Then you're going to read the whole word.

b. (Touch the ball for **flipped.**) Read the underlined part. Get ready. (Tap the ball.) *Flipp.*
- Read the whole word. (Pause.) Get ready. (Slash.) *Flipped.*

c. (Repeat step *b* until firm.)

d. (Repeat steps *b* and *c* for each remaining word in the column.)

e. (Repeat the column until children read all the words in order without making a mistake.)

flipped

times

folded

worked

wished

cheered

parting

STORY 148
EXERCISE 5

Reading—decoding

a. (Pass out Storybook 2.)
b. Everybody, open your reader to page 196.
c. Remember, if the group reads all the way to the red 5 without making more than five errors, we can go on.
d. Everybody, touch the title of the story. ✔
e. If you hear a mistake, raise your hand. Remember, children who do not have their place lose their turn. (Call on individual children to read two or three sentences. Do not ask comprehension questions. Tally all errors.)
f. (If the children make more than five errors before they reach the red 5: when they reach the 5 return to the beginning of the story and have the children reread to the 5. Do not ask comprehension questions. Repeat step *f* until firm, and then go on to step *g*.)
g. (When the children read to the red 5 without making more than five errors: read the story to the children from the beginning to the 5. Ask the specified comprehension questions. When you reach the 5, call on individual children to continue reading the story. Have each child read two or three sentences. Ask the specified comprehension questions.)

¹ What will Jean do in this story? (Signal.) *Follow a dusty path.*
² Is Jean dreaming? (Signal.) *Yes.* How many rules does she have to know before she can leave? (Signal.) *Sixteen.*
³ What's the rule? (Signal.) *If you say, "Away, away," a mean crump will go away.*

Jean Follows a Dusty Path[1]

Jean was having a strange dream. In her dream, a wizard told her that she must know sixteen rules before she could leave the place in her dream.[2] She already knew a rule about little crumps: All little crumps are mean. She also knew a rule about getting rid of mean crumps.[3] After you say that rule, you can turn this page around and read it.[4]

If you say, "Away, away," a mean crump will go away.

Jean said to herself, "I will walk and walk until I find a way out of this silly place. I wish that wizard was here."

Just then, the wizard popped out from behind a tree.[5] He said, "If you are going to walk around, remember this rule: Every dusty path leads to the lake."[6]

Jean said, "Thank you. I can remember that rule. Every path leads to the lake."⑤[7]

"No," the wizard said. "Every dusty path leads to the lake."

Jean said the rule to herself. Then she turned to the wizard and said, "But what and when . . . ."

The wizard was gone.

Jean said, "I think I will go to the lake. What was the rule about going to the lake?"

Tell Jean the rule. Say it loud so that she can hear it.[8]

"Thank you," Jean said. "Every dusty path leads to the lake."

So Jean went down a dusty path.[9] Soon she came to the lake. But she didn't like the lake.[10] The water was pink and there were funny animals all around the lake. She said, "I will leave this lake." So she started to walk back down a dusty path.

Do you think that dusty path led away from the lake?[11]

⁴ You said the rule. Now turn the page around and read it. Get ready. (Signal.) (The children respond.)
⁵ Where did the wizard come from this time? (Signal.) *Behind a tree.*
⁶ Everybody, say that rule with me. (Signal. Teacher and children say:) *Every dusty path leads to the lake.*
• (Repeat until firm.) All by yourselves. Get ready. (Signal. The children repeat the rule until firm.)
⁷ What did Jean say? (Signal.) *Every path leads to the lake.*
• Is that right? (Signal.) *No.*
• What's the rule? (Signal.) *Every dusty path leads to the lake.*
⁸ Tell Jean the rule about going to the lake. Get ready. (Signal.) *Every dusty path leads to the lake.*
⁹ Is she going to come to the lake? (Signal.) *Yes.*
• How do you know? (Signal.) *Because every dusty path leads to the lake.*
¹⁰ Did she like the lake? (Signal.) *No.*
¹¹ Did it lead away from the lake? (Signal.) *No.*

EXERCISE 3

Read the fast way

a. You're going to read all the words in this column the fast way.

b. (Touch the ball for **night.** Pause.) Get ready. (Slash.) *Night.*

c. (Repeat step *b* until firm.)

d. (Repeat steps *b* and *c* for each remaining word in the column.)

e. (Repeat the column until the children read all the words in order without making mistakes.)

night

again

remember

stuck

right

splat

yet

EXERCISE 4

Children spell, then read

a. First you're going to spell each word. Then you're going to read that word the fast way.

b. (Touch the ball for **plan.**) Spell it. Get ready. (Tap under each letter as the children say:) *P-L-A-N.*

• (Return to the ball.) Read it. Get ready. (Slash.) *Plan.*

c. (Repeat step *b* for each remaining word in the column.)

d. (Repeat steps *b* and *c* until firm.)

plan

plane

shade

planned

planed

across

woman

Individual test

a. (Call on individual children to read one column of words from the lesson.)

b. (Praise children who read all words with no errors.)

EXERCISE 3

Children spell, then read

a. First you're going to spell each word. Then you're going to read that word the fast way.

b. (Touch the ball for **dance**.) Spell it. Get ready. (Tap under each letter as the children say:) *D-A-N-C-E.*

• (Return to the ball.) Read it. Get ready. (Slash.) *Dance.*

c. (Repeat step *b* for each remaining word in the column.)

d. (Repeat steps *b* and *c* until firm.)

dance →

dancing →

thing →

think →

pink →

lake →

last →

Individual test

a. (Call on individual children to read one column of words from the lesson.)

b. (Praise children who read all words with no errors.)

RULE REVIEW
EXERCISE 4

Rule review

a. Everybody, you have learned rules in the earlier Jean stories.

b. You learned a rule about all little crumps. Say that rule. Get ready. (Signal.)
All little crumps are mean.

• (Repeat until firm.)

c. You learned a rule about if you say, "Away, away." Say that rule. Get ready. (Signal.)
If you say, "Away, away," a mean crump will go away.

• (Repeat until firm.)

d. (If the children missed any rules, repeat steps *b* and *c*.)

STORYBOOK

STORY 120
EXERCISE 5

Reading—decoding

a. (Pass out Storybook 2.)

b. Everybody, open your reader to page 105.

c. Remember, if the group reads all the way to the red 5 without making more than five errors, we can go on.

d. Everybody, touch the title of the story. ✔

e. If you hear a mistake, raise your hand. Remember, children who do not have their place lose their turn. (Call on individual children to read two or three sentences. Do not ask comprehension questions. Tally all errors.)

> **To Correct**
> word-identification errors (**from,** for example)
> 1. That word is **from.** What word? *From.*
> 2. Go back to the beginning of the sentence and read the sentence again.

f. (If the children make more than five errors before they reach the red 5: when they reach the 5 return to the beginning of the story and have the children reread to the 5. Do not ask comprehension questions. Repeat step *f* until firm, and then go on to step *g*.)

g. (When the children read to the red 5 without making more than five errors: read the story to the children from the beginning to the 5. Ask the specified comprehension questions. When you reach the 5, call on individual children to continue reading the story. Have each child read two or three sentences. Ask the specified comprehension questions.)

Carla Reads the Genie Book[1]

Carla and Ott were in Rome. Ott had just made something happen the right way. He had wished for a window pane, and the pane came.

"I think I can get us out of here," Ott said. "But maybe I should call for help. I think I can do that now."

"All right," Carla said. "Call for help." Ott folded his arms and began to say things to himself. Then something began to fly across the sky. It began to dive at Ott. "Splat." It was a big wet, fat fish.[2]

Carla began to laugh. Then she said, "I don't think you're a genie yet."[3]

"You are right," Ott said. Then he held up a big book. "This is my school book," he said. "It tells you how to do things like a genie.[4] Maybe we can read the book and find out how to ★ go home." ⑤[5]

"Good plan," Carla said. "Let's go to a park and sit down in the shade."

So Ott and Carla went to a park. They sat near a little stream.[6]

Carla said, "Let's flip to the back of the book. That part will tell how to do the hard tricks."

So Carla flipped to the back of the book.[7] She stopped at the part that said, "How to Go Home."

"This is what we want," Carla said. She began to read the part out loud.[8]

More next time

---

[1] What will Carla do in this story? (Signal.) *Read the genie book.*
- Why do you suppose she wants to do that? (The children respond.)

[2] Where did that fish come from? (Signal.) *Out of the sky.*
- Was Ott calling for a fish? (Signal.) *No.*
- What was he calling for? (Signal.) *Help.*
- He said the wrong words again.

[3] What did she say? (Signal.) *I don't think you're a genie yet.*
- Why did she say that? (The children respond.) Yes, he said the wrong words again.

[4] What does Ott's book tell you? (Signal.) *How to do things like a genie.*

[5] What are they going to look for in the book? (The children respond.) Yes, how to go home.
- Where are they now? (Signal.) *In Rome.*

[6] Where is that stream? (Signal.) *In the park.*

[7] Where are the hard tricks? (Signal.) *In the back of the book.*

[8] What part is she reading? (The children respond.) Right. The part on how to go home. I hope she gets home.

READING VOCABULARY

EXERCISE 1

Teacher reads the words in red

a. I'll read each word in red. Then you'll spell each word.

b. (Touch the ball for **page**.) My turn. (Slash as you say:) Page. What word? (Signal.) *Page.*

c. (Return to the ball.) Spell it. Get ready. (Tap under each letter as the children say:) *P-A-G-E.*

• What word did you spell? (Signal.) *Page.*

d. (Repeat steps *b* and *c* for each word in red.)

e. Your turn to read all the words in this column.

f. (Touch the ball for **page**. Pause.) Get ready. (Slash.) *Page.*

g. (Repeat step *f* for each remaining word in the column.)

h. (Repeat steps *f* and *g* until firm.)

page

Dusty

forward

path

tent

rule

knew

EXERCISE 2

Words with underlined parts

a. First you're going to read the underlined part of each word in this column. Then you're going to read the whole word.

b. (Touch the ball for **lead**.) Read the underlined part. Get ready. (Tap the ball.) *eee.*

• Read the whole word. (Pause.) Get ready. (Slash.) *Lead.*

c. (Repeat step *b* until firm.)

d. (Repeat steps *b* and *c* for each remaining word in the column.)

e. (Repeat the column until children read all the words in order without making a mistake.)

lead

also

beach

chunk

really

always

popped

WORKSHEET 120

EXERCISE 6

Picture comprehension

a. Look at the picture.

b. (Ask these questions:)

1. Ott and Carla are in the park. What are they sitting on? **(The children respond.)** Yes, a bench.

2. What are they doing? **(Signal.)** *Reading the genie book.*

3. Do they look happy? **(The children respond.)**

INDEPENDENT ACTIVITIES
EXERCISE 7

Summary of independent activities

a. (Pass out Worksheet 120 to each child.)

b. Everybody, now you'll do your worksheet. Remember to do all parts of the worksheet and to read all the parts carefully.

INDIVIDUAL CHECKOUT
EXERCISE 8

2-minute individual fluency checkout: rate/accuracy

a. As you are doing your worksheet, I'll call on children one at a time to read to the star. Remember, you get two stars on the chart if you read to the star in less than two minutes and make no more than five errors.

b. (Call on each child. Tell the child:) Read to the star very carefully. Start with the title. Go. (Time the child. Tell the child any words the child misses. Stop the child as soon as the child makes the sixth error or exceeds the time limit.)

c. (If the child meets the rate-accuracy criterion, record two stars on your chart for lesson 120. Congratulate the child. Give children who do not earn two stars a chance to read to the star again before the next lesson is presented.)

150 words/**2 min** = 75 wpm **[5 errors]**

END OF LESSON 120

The wizard laughed. He said, "You can't leave this place until you know sixteen rules.[13] You already know one rule. Here is the next rule: If you say, 'Away, away,' a mean crump will go away."[14]

Jean said, "I think I have that rule. If you say, 'Away, away,' a crump will go away."[15]

"No," the wizard yelled. "A mean crump will go away."

Jean said, "But what and when . . . ."

The wizard was gone again. The little crump was sneaking up behind Jean. She turned around and tried to remember what to do, but she couldn't remember the rule.

Tell Jean how to make the mean crump go away.[16]

Jean yelled, "Away, away." What do you think happened?[17] That's right. The little mean crump went away.

More next time

---

[13] What does she have to know before she can leave? (Signal.) *Sixteen rules.*

[14] Everybody, say that rule with me. (Signal. Teacher and children say:) *If you say, "Away, away," a mean crump will go away.*

- (Repeat until firm.) All by yourselves. Get ready. (Signal. Children repeat the rule until firm.)

[15] What did Jean say? (Signal.) *If you say, "Away, away," a crump will go away.*

- Is that right? (Signal.) *No.*
- What's the rule? (Signal.) *If you say, "Away, away," a mean crump will go away.*

[16] Everybody, do it. (Signal.) *Away, away.*

[17] What's the answer? (Signal.) *The mean crump went away.*

- Why did the mean crump go away? (Signal.) *Because she said, "Away, away."*

EXERCISE 6

Picture comprehension

a. Look at the picture.
b. (Ask these questions:)
   1. (Point to the crump.) Is that really a little chair? (Signal.) *No.*
   - What is it? (Signal.) *A (little, mean) crump.*
   2. What's the mean crump doing? (Signal.) *Chasing Jean.*
   3. And what is Jean doing? (The children respond.)
   4. How do you think Jean feels? (The children respond.)
   - I'd be scared if that crump was chasing me.

WORKSHEET 147

EXERCISE 7

Summary of independent activities

a. (Pass out Worksheet 147 to each child.)
b. Everybody, now you'll do your worksheet. Remember to do all parts of the worksheet and to read all the parts carefully.

END OF LESSON 147

Making Progress

	Since Lesson 1	Since Lesson 101
Word Reading	Sounds and sound combinations 816 regular words 163 irregular words Reading high frequency hard words Discriminating long and short vowel words using final *-e* rule	157 regular words 39 irregular words
Comprehension	**Picture Comprehension** Predicting what the picture will show Answering questions about the picture Answering written questions Completing picture deduction activities **Story Comprehension** Answering *who, what, when, where,* and *why* questions orally Making predictions about the story Answering questions about the story and other short passages in writing Answering review questions about stories previously read	Answering review questions about stories previously read

What to Use

Teacher	Students
Presentation Book C (pages 65–154) **Teacher's Guide** (pages 79, 82–84) **Answer Key** **Spelling Presentation Book**	**Storybook 2** (pages 107–171) **Workbook C** **Lined paper**

What's Ahead in Lessons 121–140

New Skills

- Story length increases to approximately 400 words.
- Comprehension and following directions activities are combined on Worksheets (Lesson 121).
- Children read factual information passages and answer questions about them (Lesson 132).
- Children begin working on written deductions (Lesson 123).

New Vocabulary

- *Regular words:*

  (121) flipping, human, impossible, it's, person, planner, planer, richest, stare, thud
  (122) dare, flowed, simple, spitting, true
  (123) he's, hug, hungry, instant, planning, she'd, we've
  (124) class, fingers, smarter, smartest, snapped, taking, vow
  (125) biting, life, masters, patted, ring, short, spend, vows, wiped
  (126) belong, clapped, hair, hardest, rush, taken, trained, van, vane
  (127) bringing, clock, east, hung, mate, packing, rang, rushed, spelled, stuff, too, treat, understand, vaned, west
  (128) bring, corner, dragging, rent, spelling, swell, trunk, until
  (129) drive, false, number, rented, teeth, trips, where's
  (130) chase, Jan, loaded, passing, pocket, skates
  (131) chicken, drank, dry, Ellen's, helps, wide
  (132) black, branch, Carl, chunk, crow, lay, sang, singing, slider, such, wings
  (133) cones, cons, hotter, nail, pond, shine, shining, slid, toe
  (134) cave, cheeks, coat, flame, gaped, gapped, joke, shell, slide, tears, weed
  (135) roots, sliding, snap, sneak, stool, strong, tooth
  (136) bong, sneaky, stepped, used
  (137) biter, bitter, croak, flock
  (138) chasing, fastest, lions, safe, sweet
  (139) dusty, lined, mile, owl, path, pepper, slowest, waiting
  (140) crossed, finish, happening, leaned, loudly, speed, thick

- *Irregular words:*

  (121) Marta Flores, stood
  (122) agreed, fight
  (124) knows, obey
  (125) place, yourself
  (126) Alaska, China, Japan, move, phone, they've, you've
  (127) minute, turns
  (128) dollars, phoned, rental
  (129) dental, service, trouble
  (130) already, honey, moves
  (131) feathers, turtle
  (132) caw, handsome, mice, nice
  (133) footprint, wear, world
  (136) color, light, pulled
  (137) alive, listen, watch, wolf, wolves
  (138) cookie, race, someday, watching, worker
  (139) knew, Mr.
  (140) ahead, asleep

f. (If the children make more than five errors before they reach the red 5: when they reach the 5 return to the beginning of the story and have the children reread to the 5. Do not ask comprehension questions. Repeat step *f* until firm, and then go on to step *g*.)

g. (When the children read to the red 5 without making more than five errors: read the story to the children from the beginning to the 5. Ask the specified comprehension questions. When you reach the 5, call on individual children to continue reading the story. Have each child read two or three sentences. Ask the specified comprehension questions.)

Jean Meets a Mean Crump[1]

Jean was in the land of peevish pets.[2] She was trying to remember the rule the wizard had told her about crumps. What was that rule?[3]

Jean saw an animal that looked like a frog. She said, "Are you a little crump?"[4]

The animal said, "Gump, gump."[5]

She spotted another animal. It looked like a ball of pink hair. She said, "Are you a little crump?"[6]

The animal answered, "Wup, wup."[7]

Jean asked other animals if they were crumps. But she did not find one crump. Then she said, "I think I will sit down and rest."

Just then, she saw two chairs. One chair was big and the other was little. She said, "I will sit in the little chair."[8]

Just as she was getting ready to sit down, the chair said, "Crump, crump."[9]When it said "Crump," she jumped. And she jumped just in time.⑤ The chair began to run after her.

"That little chair is a little crump," she said.[10] The crump was swinging its arms. It was trying to bite her. She ran as fast as she could go.[11]Suddenly she stopped. The wizard was standing in front of her. She said, "I don't like this place. Get me out of here."[12]

---

[1] Who will Jean meet in this story? (Signal.) *A mean crump.*

[2] Where is Jean? (Signal.) *In the land of peevish pets.*

[3] Everybody, say the rule. (Signal.) *All little crumps are mean.*

[4] What did she say? (Signal.) *Are you a little crump?*

[5] Did the animal say, "Crump, crump"? (Signal.) *No.*

• What did the animal say? (Signal.) *Gump, gump.*

[6] What did she say? (Signal.) *Are you a little crump?*

[7] Did the animal say, "Crump, crump"? (Signal.) *No.*

• What did the animal say? (Signal.) *Wup, wup.*

• Let's keep reading and see if Jean finds a crump.

[8] Where is she going to sit? (Signal.) *In the little chair.*

[9] What did the chair say? (Signal.) *Crump, crump.*

[10] What do we know about little crumps? (The children respond.) Yes, they are mean.

[11] Was the little crump mean? (Signal.) *Yes.*

[12] What did Jean tell the wizard? (Signal.) *Get me out of here.*

Look Ahead

Look Ahead

In-Program Tests
Fluency Checkouts: Rate/Accuracy

Lessons 125, 130, 135, 140

- By lesson 140, children should be reading at least 80 words per minute with 97 percent accuracy. Provide extra practice on Fluency Checkouts for those who are not at this level of mastery.

Lesson Number	Error Limit	Number of words read	Number of minutes	Words per minute
125	5	149	2	75
130	5	148	2	74
135	5	150	2	75
140	5	160	2	80

Reading Vocabulary

- As more of the new words introduced are irregular, be sure to use the spelling correction. When children misread a word, have them spell it—this helps to focus attention on the sequence of letters in the word.

Skills

	Lessons 121–140
Word Reading	155 regular words 52 irregular words
Comprehension	Reading and answering questions on factual information passages

Reading Activities

Help children develop decoding and comprehension skills by using the following activities.

Mastery Bingo (Lessons 121–140)
Make a list of 20 to 30 words with which the children had difficulty in the lessons. Write those words on small individual cards. Then make Mastery Bingo Boards by dividing 5" x 7" index cards into sixteen boxes (four boxes across and four boxes down). Randomly write the words in each box. Make a board for each child. You might want to laminate the boards. Have children play Mastery Bingo like traditional Bingo. The winner must be able to read all the covered words.

Contraction Matching (Lessons 121–140)
Select several contraction pairs to develop a matching exercise. Write a contraction and the corresponding words on separate 3" x 5" index cards. Have children match the contraction with its two-part counterpart. Check children's work by having them say each pair of words. A sample matching exercise is shown below.

Match

it's	he is
we've	she would
he's	they have
she'd	it is
they've	we have

Characters (Lessons 121–140)
Have children draw a picture of a story character in the center of a sheet of paper. Direct children to make a character web by drawing lines from the picture and listing characteristics of the character or things that the character did. An example from Lessons 133–137 is shown below.

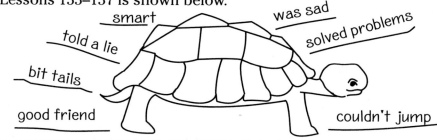

smart   was sad   told a lie   solved problems   bit tails   good friend   couldn't jump

EXERCISE 3

Children spell, then read

a. First you're going to spell each word. Then you're going to read that word the fast way.

b. (Touch the ball for **hair**.) Spell it. Get ready. (Tap under each letter as the children say:) *H-A-I-R.*

• (Return to the ball.) Read it. Get ready. (Slash.) *Hair.*

c. (Repeat step *b* for each remaining word in the column.)

d. (Repeat steps *b* and *c* until firm.)

hair

chair

place

rule

anybody

how

who

Individual test

a. (Call on individual children to read one column of words from the lesson.)

b. (Praise children who read all words with no errors.)

★ RULE REVIEW
EXERCISE 4

Rule review

a. Everybody, in the last story you learned a rule about all little crumps. Say that rule. Get ready. (Signal.) *All little crumps are mean.*

b. (Repeat until firm.)

STORY 147
EXERCISE 5

Reading—decoding

a. (Pass out Storybook 2.)

b. Everybody, open your reader to page 193.

c. Remember, if the group reads all the way to the red 5 without making more than five errors, we can go on.

d. Everybody, touch the title of the story. ✔

e. If you hear a mistake, raise your hand. Remember, children who do not have their place lose their turn. (Call on individual children to read two or three sentences. Do not ask comprehension questions. Tally all errors.)

To Correct

word-identification errors (**from,** for example)

1. That word is **from.** What word? *From.*
2. Go back to the beginning of the sentence and read the sentence again.

READING VOCABULARY

EXERCISE 1

Teacher reads the words in red

a. I'll read each word in red. Then you'll spell each word.

b. (Touch the ball for **stood.**) My turn. (Slash as you say:) Stood. What word? (Signal.) *Stood.*

c. (Return to the ball.) Spell it. Get ready. (Tap under each letter as the children say:) *S-T-O-O-D.*

• What word did you spell? (Signal.) *Stood.*

d. (Repeat steps *b* and *c* for each word in red.)

e. Your turn to read all the words in this column.

f. (Touch the ball for **stood.** Pause.) Get ready. (Slash.) *Stood.*

g. (Repeat step *f* for each remaining word in the column.)

h. (Repeat steps *f* and *g* until firm.)

stood

person

human

impossible

bub

bibby

stare

EXERCISE 2

Read the fast way

a. You're going to read all the words in this column the fast way.

b. (Touch the ball for **rich.** Pause.) Get ready. (Slash.) *Rich.*

c. (Repeat step *b* until firm.)

d. (Repeat steps *b* and *c* for each remaining word in the column.)

e. (Repeat the column until the children read all the words in order without making mistakes.)

rich

flip

woman

tried

remember

front

blanks

READING VOCABULARY

EXERCISE 1

Teacher reads the words in red

a. I'll read each word in red. Then you'll spell each word.

b. (Touch the ball for **Gump.**) My turn. (Slash as you say:) Gump. What word? (Signal.) *Gump.*

c. (Return to the ball.) Spell it. Get ready. (Tap under each letter as the children say:) *G-U-M-P.*

- What word did you spell? (Signal.) *Gump.*

d. (Repeat steps *b* and *c* for each word in red.)

e. Your turn to read all the words in this column.

f. (Touch the ball for **Gump.** Pause.) Get ready. (Slash.) *Gump.*

g. (Repeat step *f* for each remaining word in the column.)

h. (Repeat steps *f* and *g* until firm.)

Gump

Wup

brown

until

everything

Crump

coat

EXERCISE 2

Words with underlined parts

a. First you're going to read the underlined part of each word in this column. Then you're going to read the whole word.

b. (Touch the ball for **swinging.**) Read the underlined part. Get ready. (Tap the ball.) *Swing.*

- Read the whole word. (Pause.) Get ready. (Slash.) *Swinging.*

c. (Repeat step *b* until firm.)

d. (Repeat steps *b* and *c* for each remaining word in the column.)

e. (Repeat the column until children read all the words in order without making a mistake.)

swinging

lifted

mean

sixteen

sneaking

nothing

anything

EXERCISE 3

Words with underlined parts

a. First you're going to read the underlined part of each word in this column. Then you're going to read the whole word.

b. (Touch the ball for **richest**.) Read the underlined part. Get ready. (Tap the ball.) *Rich.*

• Read the whole word. (Pause.) Get ready. (Slash.) *Richest.*

c. (Repeat step *b* until firm.)

d. (Repeat steps *b* and *c* for each remaining word in the column.)

e. (Repeat the column until children read all the words in order without making a mistake.)

EXERCISE 4

Teacher introduces a name

a. Here's the name of a person you'll read about in the story. (Pause.) **Marta Flores.**

b. Your turn: What name? (Signal.) *Marta Flores.* Yes, **Marta Flores.**

• Remember that name, you'll read it in the story.

c. (Repeat exercise until all children are firm.)

richest

couldn't

closer

wonderful

flipping

called

EXERCISE 5

Read the fast way

a. You're going to read all the words in this column the fast way.

b. (Touch the ball for **formed**. Pause.) Get ready. (Slash.) *Formed.*

c. (Repeat step *b* until firm.)

d. (Repeat steps *b* and *c* for each remaining word in the column.)

e. (Repeat the column until the children read all the words in order without making mistakes.)

formed

new

few

wise

across

around

flow

Marta Flores

"What are little crumps?" Jean asked.

"That doesn't matter," the wizard answered. "Just remember the rule: All little crumps are mean."[7]

Jean said, "I'll remember that rule: All crumps are mean."[8]

"No, no," the wizard said. "All little crumps are mean."

"I've got it," Jean said. "But what and when . . . ."

The wizard was gone, and Jean was all alone in the land of peevish pets.[9]

More to come

---

[7] Everybody, what's the rule? (Signal.)
All little crumps are mean.

[8] What did Jean say about crumps? (Signal.)
All crumps are mean.

• Is that right? (Signal.) *No.* What's the rule? (Signal.) *All little crumps are mean.*
Right. All little crumps are mean.

[9] What happened to the wizard?
(The children respond.)

• Was Jean alone? (Signal.) *Yes.*

• Next time we'll read more about the crumps.

EXERCISE 6

Picture comprehension

a. What do you think you'll see in the picture?
(The children respond.)

b. Turn the page and look at the picture.

c. (Ask these questions:)

1. What is Jean doing?
(The children respond.)

2. Show me the wizard in her dream.
(The children respond.)

3. Tell me about some of the other strange things in her dream.
(The children respond.)

WORKSHEET 146

INDEPENDENT ACTIVITIES

EXERCISE 7

Reading comprehension

a. (Pass out Worksheet 146 to each child.)

b. Everybody, turn to side 2 of your worksheet. ✔

c. (Point to the story on side 2 of your worksheet.) Everybody, find this story on your worksheet. ✔

d. Today you're going to read a passage that tells about space. There's no picture for this story.

e. I'll read the passage. Everybody, follow along. (Read the passage to the children. Check that they are following along as you read.)

f. When you do your independent work, read the passage to yourself. Then answer the questions.

EXERCISE 8

Summary of independent activities

Everybody, now you'll do your worksheet. Remember to do all parts of the worksheet and to read all the parts carefully.

END OF LESSON 146

EXERCISE 6

Children spell, then read

a. First you're going to spell each word. Then you're going to read that word the fast way.

b. (Touch the ball for **close.**) Spell it. Get ready. (Tap under each letter as the children say:) *C-L-O-S-E.*

• (Return to the ball.) Read it. Get ready. (Slash.) *Close.*

c. (Repeat step *b* for each remaining word in the column.)

d. (Repeat steps *b* and *c* until firm.)

close

Thud

else

Bome

planner

planer

through

Individual test

a. (Call on individual children to read one column of words from the lesson.)

b. (Praise children who read all words with no errors.)

STORYBOOK

STORY 121
EXERCISE 7

Reading—decoding

a. (Pass out Storybook 2.)

b. Everybody, open your reader to page 107.

c. Remember, if the group reads all the way to the red 5 without making more than five errors, we can go on.

d. Everybody, touch the title of the story. ✔

e. If you hear a mistake, raise your hand. Remember, children who do not have their place lose their turn. (Call on individual children to read two or three sentences. Do not ask comprehension questions. Tally all errors.)

To Correct

word-identification errors (from, for example)

1. That word is **from.** What word? *From.*
2. Go back to the beginning of the sentence and read the sentence again.

f. (If the children make more than five errors before they reach the red 5: when they reach the 5 return to the beginning of the story and have the children reread to the 5. Do not ask comprehension questions. Repeat step *f* until firm, and then go on to step *g*.)

g. (When the children read to the red 5 without making more than five errors: read the story to the children from the beginning to the 5. Ask the specified comprehension questions. When you reach the 5, call on individual children to continue reading the story. Have each child read two or three sentences. Ask the specified comprehension questions.)

STORY 146
EXERCISE 5

Reading—decoding

a. (Pass out Storybook 2.)

b. Everybody, open your reader to page 190.

c. Remember, if the group reads all the way to the red 5 without making more than five errors, we can go on.

d. Everybody, touch the title of the story. ✔

e. If you hear a mistake, raise your hand. Remember, children who do not have their place lose their turn. (Call on individual children to read two or three sentences. Do not ask comprehension questions. Tally all errors.)

To Correct

word-identification errors (**from**, for example)
1. That word is **from**. What word? *From.*
2. Go back to the beginning of the sentence and read the sentence again.

f. (If the children make more than five errors before they reach the red 5: when they reach the 5 return to the beginning of the story and have the children reread to the 5. Do not ask comprehension questions. Repeat step *f* until firm, and then go on to step *g*.)

g. (When the children read to the red 5 without making more than five errors: read the story to the children from the beginning to the 5. Ask the specified comprehension questions. When you reach the 5, call on individual children to continue reading the story. Have each child read two or three sentences. Ask the specified comprehension questions.)

In the Land of Peevish Pets[1]

Jean was very sad. Her dad would not let her have a pet dog.[2] She said to herself, "I will go to sleep tonight. And I will sleep so hard that maybe I will go to a land that is far away. Maybe I will go to a land where I can have all the pets I want."

So Jean went to bed. She kept telling herself to sleep very hard. "Sleep hard," she said to herself.

And what do you think happened? She went to sleep and began to sleep very hard. She went into the deepest sleep there ever was. She slept and slept. And in her sleep she began to have a dream.[3] There were lots of pets in her dream, but they were not like any pets that Jean had ever seen before. There were funny green animals with big hands and red feet. ⑤ There were little bugs that talked.[4] There were strange trees that seemed to be singing. And right in the middle of her dream was an old wizard.[5] "Ho, ho," the wizard said to her. "What is your name?"

"Jean," she answered.

"Well, Jean," he said, "I hope you have a fine time here in the land of peevish pets. But you must remember this rule: All little crumps are mean."[6]

---

[1] What's the title of this story? (Signal.) *In the land of peevish pets.*

• Peevish means that they make you mad. So this story is about a land with pets that make you mad.

[2] Why was Jean sad? (Signal.) *Her dad would not let her have a pet dog.*

[3] What did Jean do in her sleep? (Signal.) *Dream.*

• Do you think she'll see pets in her dream? (The children respond.)

• Let's read and find out.

[4] Were there pets in her dream? (Signal.) *Yes.*

• Tell me about some of the strange pets. (The children respond.)

[5] Who did she meet in her dream? (Signal.) *An old wizard.* Yes, a wizard does magic.

[6] Everybody, say that rule with me. (Signal. Teacher and children say:) *All little crumps are mean.*

• (Repeat until firm.) All by yourselves. Get ready. (Signal. The children repeat the rule until firm.)

Carla Goes Home, Home, Home[1]

Carla was reading from Ott's school book. She was reading a part that told what to do if you wanted to go home. Here is what the book said:

"If you want to go home, fold your arms.[2] Then say the name of your street.[3] Then say the name of your mother.[4] Then say, 'Ib, bub, ib, bub, ib, bub, bibby. Bome, bome, bome. I want to go home, home, home.'"[5]

When Carla was through reading, she said, "Did you hear that, Ott? It told you everything you have to do to get home."

Ott said, "That is too much to remember. I can't remember all of that."

"Oh, it's not so much. Here. I'll read it again, and I'll show you the things you have to do."

Carla began to read to herself. Then she folded her arms and said, "First you say the name of my street and the name of my mother.⑤ Here I go: Oak Street . . . Marta Flores."[6]

Ott stood up and folded his arms. Then he said, "Oak Street . . . Marta Flores."

Carla said, "Here is what you say next: Ib, bub, ib, bub, ib, bub, bibby. Bome, bome, bome. I want to go home, home, home."

Suddenly, Carla was flying through the air. Thud. Now she was sitting on her front steps.[7] She was still holding the genie school book.

"Wow," Carla said, "I did that trick all by myself." She began to think of the wonderful tricks she could play just by reading the genie book.

Suddenly, Carla remembered Ott. "Oh, my," she said. "He is not here. Maybe something bad happened to him. I better call for help."[8]

Carla began flipping through the school book. She stopped at a part that told how to call for help.

More to come

[1] Is Carla going home in this story? (Signal.) *Yes.*
• How do you know? (The children respond.) Right. The title says Carla goes home, home, home.
• Let's read how it happened.
[2] What's the first thing you do? (Signal.) *Fold your arms.*
[3] What's the next thing you do? (Signal.) *Say the name of your street.*
[4] What do you do after you say the name of your street? (Signal.) *Say the name of your mother.*
[5] What's the last thing you say? (Signal.) *I want to go home, home, home.*
[6] What's the name of her street? (Signal.) *Oak.*
• And what's the name of her mother? (Signal.) *Marta Flores.* Good.
• Now she's got to say that hard stuff.
[7] Where were those front steps? (The children respond.) Yes, in front of her house.
• So did she get home? (Signal.) *Yes.*
• Did she get home by car? (Signal.) *No.*
• How did she get there? (Signal.) *By flying through the air.*
[8] What is she going to do? (Signal.) *Call for help.*
• Why does Carla want to do that? (The children respond.) Yes, Ott isn't there.

EXERCISE 8

Picture comprehension

a. Look at the picture.
b. (Ask these questions:)
  1. Where is Carla? (The children respond.) Yes, she got home.
  2. How do you know she's home? (The children respond.)
  3. What's she holding? (Signal.) The genie school book.
  4. Does she look happy? (Signal.) *Yes.*
  5. Why can't you see Ott? (The children respond.)

EXERCISE 3

Read the fast way

a. You're going to read all the words in this column the fast way.

b. (Touch the ball for **face.** Pause.) Get ready. (Slash.) *Face.*

c. (Repeat step *b* until firm.)

d. (Repeat steps *b* and *c* for each remaining word in the column.)

e. (Repeat the column until the children read all the words in order without making mistakes.)

face

space

dance

prince

time

fine

here

EXERCISE 4

Children spell, then read

a. First you're going to spell each word. Then you're going to read that word the fast way.

b. (Touch the ball for **shoes.**) Spell it. Get ready. (Tap under each letter as the children say:) *S-H-O-E-S.*

• (Return to the ball.) Read it. Get ready. (Slash.) *Shoes.*

c. (Repeat step *b* for each remaining word in the column.)

d. (Repeat steps *b* and *c* until firm.)

shoes

shirt

even

grasshopper

clothes

tried

tired

Individual test

a. (Call on individual children to read one column of words from the lesson.)

b. (Praise children who read all words with no errors.)

WORKSHEET 121

STORY ITEMS
EXERCISE 9

Following instructions

a. (Pass out Worksheet 121 to each child.)

b. (Hold up side 1 of your worksheet and point to the story-items exercise.)

c. Everybody, touch item 1. ✔

d. Everybody, touch the instructions in the box above item 1. ✔

• Those instructions tell you how to work item 1. (Call on a child.) Read the instructions in the box. *Make a line under the answer.*

e. Everybody, what are you going to do to answer item 1? (Signal.) *Make a line under the answer.*

f. Everybody, touch the instructions in the box above item 2. ✔

• Those instructions tell you how to work items 2 and 3. (Call on a child.) Read the instructions in the box. *Fill in the blanks.*

g. Everybody, are you going to circle the answers? (Signal.) *No.*

• Are you going to make a line under the answers? (Signal.) *No.*

h. What are you going to do to work items 2 and 3? (Signal.) *Fill in the blanks.*

i. Everybody, touch the instructions in the box above item 4. ✔

• Those instructions tell you how to work item 4. (Call on a child.) Read the instructions in the box. *Circle the answer.*

j. Everybody, are you going to make a line under the answer? (Signal.) *No.*

• Are you going to fill in the blanks? (Signal.) *No.*

k. What are you going to do to work item 4? (Signal.) *Circle the answer.*

l. Everybody, touch the instructions in the box above item 5. ✔

• Those instructions tell you how to work items 5 and 6. (Call on a child.) Read the instructions in the box. *Fill in the blanks.*

m. Everybody, are you going to make a line under the answers? (Signal.) *No.*

• Are you going to circle the answers? (Signal.) *No.*

n. What are you going to do to work items 5 and 6? (Signal.) *Fill in the blanks.*

o. You'll work the items later. Remember to follow the instructions that go with each item.

INDEPENDENT ACTIVITIES
EXERCISE 10

Summary of independent activities

Everybody, now you'll do your worksheet. Remember to do all parts of the worksheet and to read all the parts carefully.

END OF LESSON 121

READING VOCABULARY
EXERCISE 1

Teacher reads the words in red

a. I'll read each word in red. Then you'll spell each word.

b. (Touch the ball for **rule**.) My turn. (Slash as you say:) Rule. What word? (Signal.) *Rule.*

c. (Return to the ball.) Spell it. Get ready. (Tap under each letter as the children say:) *R-U-L-E.*

• What word did you spell? (Signal.) *Rule.*

d. (Repeat steps *b* and *c* for each word in red.)

e. Your turn to read all the words in this column.

f. (Touch the ball for **rule**. Pause.) Get ready. (Slash.) *Rule.*

g. (Repeat step *f* for each remaining word in the column.)

h. (Repeat steps *f* and *g* until firm.)

rule

crump

Jean

Peevish

wizard

dream

slept

EXERCISE 2

Words with underlined parts

a. First you're going to read the underlined part of each word in this column. Then you're going to read the whole word.

b. (Touch the ball for **these**.) Read the underlined part. Get ready. (Tap the ball.) *th.*

• Read the whole word. (Pause.) Get ready. (Slash.) *These.*

c. (Repeat step *b* until firm.)

d. (Repeat steps *b* and *c* for each remaining word in the column.)

e. (Repeat the column until children read all the words in order without making a mistake.)

these

didn't

shouldn't

deepest

herself

tonight

matter

READING VOCABULARY

EXERCISE 1

Teacher reads the words in red

a. I'll read each word in red. Then you'll spell each word.

b. (Touch the ball for **true**.) My turn. (Slash as you say:) True. What word? (Signal.) *True.*

c. (Return to the ball.) Spell it. Get ready. (Tap under each letter as the children say:) *T-R-U-E.*

• What word did you spell? (Signal.) *True.*

d. (Repeat steps *b* and *c* for each word in red.)

e. Your turn to read all the words in this column.

f. (Touch the ball for **true**. Pause.) Get ready. (Slash.) *True.*

g. (Repeat step *f* for each remaining word in the column.)

h. (Repeat steps *f* and *g* until firm.)

true

simple

spitting

agreed

right

tried

I'll

EXERCISE 2

Read the fast way

a. You're going to read all the words in this column the fast way.

b. (Touch the ball for **human**. Pause.) Get ready. (Slash.) *Human.*

c. (Repeat step *b* until firm.)

d. (Repeat steps *b* and *c* for each remaining word in the column.)

e. (Repeat the column until the children read all the words in order without making mistakes.)

human

splash

Don't

fight

water

Everybody

through

The prince was hungry. He wanted something to eat. So he went up to a man and said, "I am hungry. Give me something to eat."

But the man said, "Get out of here, you tramp."⁹

The prince was sad. He said to himself, "I didn't know how hard it is to be a tramp."

The real prince met the tramp the next day. The prince said, "You will come and live with me. You will never be a tramp again." So the prince took the tramp home.¹⁰

And years later, the prince became king.¹¹ He never forgot the day that he was a tramp. He tried to help all of the tramps in the city. He said, "The people love me because I have fine clothes. I will give the tramps nice clothes so the people will love them, too."¹²And that's what the good king did.

The end

⁹ Why are people saying that to the prince? (The children respond.)
¹⁰ What happened to the tramp? (The children respond.)
¹¹ What happened to the prince? (Signal.) *He became king.*
¹² Why did he give the tramps nice clothes? (Signal.) *So the people would love them.*

EXERCISE 6
Picture comprehension

a. Look at the picture.
b. (Ask these questions:)
   1. The prince has a purple robe. Show me the prince. (The children respond.)
   2. In this picture, what is the prince giving to the tramp? (Signal.) *The crown.*
   • What is the tramp giving to the prince? (Signal.) *A hat.*
   3. Does the tramp have shoes? (Signal.) *No.*
   4. Would you like to wear the prince's red shoes? (The children respond.)

WORKSHEET 145

INDEPENDENT ACTIVITIES
EXERCISE 7
Reading comprehension

a. (Pass out Worksheet 145 to each child.)
b. Everybody, turn to side 2 of your worksheet. ✔
c. (Point to the story on side 2 of your worksheet.) Everybody, find this story on your worksheet. ✔
d. Today you're going to read a passage that tells about how many legs insects have.
e. Everybody, touch the first picture. ✔ Does that picture show an insect? (Signal.) *Yes.*
   • Which insect does that picture show? (Signal.) *An ant.*
   • Count the legs that the ant has. (Pause.) How many legs does the ant have? (Signal.) *Six.*
   • All insects have six legs. How many legs do insects have? (Signal.) *Six.*
   • The spider is not an insect because the spider has eight legs.
f. I'll read the passage. Everybody, follow along. (Read the passage to the children. Check that they are following along as you read.)

g. When you do your independent work, read the passage to yourself. Then answer the questions.

EXERCISE 8
SUMMARY OF INDEPENDENT ACTIVITIES

Everybody, now you'll do your worksheet. Remember to do all parts of the worksheet and to read all the parts carefully.

INDIVIDUAL CHECKOUT
EXERCISE 9

2-minute individual fluency checkout: rate/accuracy

a. As you are doing your worksheet, I'll call on children one at a time to read to the star. Remember, you get two stars on the chart if you read to the star in less than two minutes and make no more than five errors.
b. (Call on each child. Tell the child:) Read to the star very carefully. Start with the title. Go. (Time the child. Tell the child any words the child misses. Stop the child as soon as the child makes the sixth error or exceeds the time limit.)
c. (If the child meets the rate-accuracy criterion, record two stars on your chart for lesson 145. Congratulate the child. Give children who do not earn two stars a chance to read to the star again before the next lesson is presented.)
160 words/**2 min** = 80 wpm **[5 errors]**

END OF LESSON 145

EXERCISE 3

Words with underlined parts

a. First you're going to read the underlined part of each word in this column. Then you're going to read the whole word.

b. (Touch the ball for **turned.**) Read the underlined part. Get ready. (Tap the ball.) *Turn.*

• Read the whole word. (Pause.) Get ready. (Slash.) *Turned.*

c. (Repeat step *b* until firm.)

d. (Repeat steps *b* and *c* for each remaining word in the column.)

e. (Repeat the column until children read all the words in order without making a mistake.)

turned

didn't

appeared

become

impossible

flowed

reading

EXERCISE 4

Read the fast way

a. You're going to read all the words in this column the fast way.

b. (Touch the ball for **where.** Pause.) Get ready. (Slash.) *Where.*

c. (Repeat step *b* until firm.)

d. (Repeat steps *b* and *c* for each remaining word in the column.)

e. (Repeat the column until the children read all the words in order without making mistakes.)

where

few

person

stood

woman

new

were

STORYBOOK

STORY 145
EXERCISE 5

Reading—decoding

a. (Pass out Storybook 2.)

b. Everybody, open your reader to page 186.

c. Remember, if the group reads all the way to the red 5 without making more than five errors, we can go on.

d. Everybody, touch the title of the story. ✔

e. If you hear a mistake, raise your hand. Remember, children who do not have their place lose their turn. (Call on individual children to read two or three sentences. Do not ask comprehension questions. Tally all errors.)

To Correct
word-identification errors (**from,** for example)
1. That word is **from.** What word? *From.*
2. Go back to the beginning of the sentence and read the sentence again.

f. (If the children make more than five errors before they reach the red 5: when they reach the 5 return to the beginning of the story and have the children reread to the 5. Do not ask comprehension questions. Repeat step *f* until firm, and then go on to step *g*.)

g. (When the children read to the red 5 without making more than five errors: read the story to the children from the beginning to the 5. Ask the specified comprehension questions. When you reach the 5, call on individual children to continue reading the story. Have each child read two or three sentences. Ask the specified comprehension questions.)

The Prince and the Tramp[1]

There once was a prince. The prince always dressed in fine clothes. He had a gold crown and a long robe and red shoes.[2] When the prince walked down the streets of the city, everybody would say, "We love the prince. He is so handsome."

When the prince was hungry, people would bring food to him. Then the prince would say to himself, "Everybody loves me."

When the prince was tired of walking, people would give him a horse to ride.[3] One day the prince met a tramp.[4] This tramp did not have a gold crown, or a long robe, or red shoes. This tramp did not have any shoes. He had an old shirt with holes in it.[5] But that tramp looked just like the prince.

The tramp said, "How strange. You look just like me."[6]

The prince said, "Let us have some fun.⑤

I will dress like you, and you will dress like ★ me."

So the prince put on the tramp's clothes, and the tramp put on the gold crown and the long robe and the red shoes. The tramp looked just like the prince.[7] The tramp left the prince and walked down the street. And what do you think happened?

All the people looked at the tramp and said, "We love the prince."

A man came up to the tramp and said, "If you are tired of walking, you may have my horse."

A lady came up to the tramp and said, "You must be hungry. Come to my house and I will give you a big meal."[8]

But the real prince did not have a good time. When he walked on the streets of the city, people said, "Get out of here, you tramp."

---

[1] Who will this story be about? (Signal.) *The prince and the tramp.*

[2] Tell me some of the fine things the prince wore. (The children respond.)

[3] Name some reasons why the prince thought everybody loved him. (The children respond.)

[4] Who did the prince meet? (Signal.) *A tramp.*

• Let's read and see if the tramp had fine clothes too.

[5] Did the tramp have fine clothes? (Signal.) *No.*

• Tell me about his clothes. (The children respond.)

[6] Who is talking? (Signal.) *The tramp.*

• Who is he talking to? (Signal.) *The prince.* Yes, they look alike.

[7] How did he get the prince's fine clothes? (The children respond.)

• So whose clothes was the prince wearing now? (Signal.) *The tramp's.*

[8] Why are people being so nice to the tramp? (The children respond.) Yes, they think he is the prince because he's wearing the prince's clothing.

EXERCISE 5

Children spell, then read

a. First you're going to spell each word. Then you're going to read that word the fast way.

b. (Touch the ball for **head**.) Spell it. Get ready. (Tap under each letter as the children say:) *H-E-A-D.*

• (Return to the ball.) Read it. Get ready. (Slash.) *Head.*

c. (Repeat step *b* for each remaining word in the column.)

d. (Repeat steps *b* and *c* until firm.)

head

stare

dare

closer

hoped

hopped

turn

Individual test

a. (Call on individual children to read one column of words from the lesson.)

b. (Praise children who read all words with no errors.)

STORYBOOK

STORY 122
EXERCISE 6

Reading—decoding

a. (Pass out Storybook 2.)

b. Everybody, open your reader to page 110.

c. Remember, if the group reads all the way to the red 5 without making more than five errors, we can go on.

d. Everybody, touch the title of the story. ✔

e. If you hear a mistake, raise your hand. Remember, children who do not have their place lose their turn. (Call on individual children to read two or three sentences. Do not ask comprehension questions. Tally all errors.)

To Correct

word-identification errors (from, for example)
1. That word is **from.** What word? *From.*
2. Go back to the beginning of the sentence and read the sentence again.

f. (If the children make more than five errors before they reach the red 5: when they reach the 5 return to the beginning of the story and have the children reread to the 5. Do not ask comprehension questions. Repeat step *f* until firm, and then go on to step *g*.)

g. (When the children read to the red 5 without making more than five errors: read the story to the children from the beginning to the 5. Ask the specified comprehension questions. When you reach the 5, call on individual children to continue reading the story. Have each child read two or three sentences. Ask the specified comprehension questions.)

EXERCISE 3

Read the fast way

a. You're going to read all the words in this column the fast way.

b. (Touch the ball for **that.** Pause.) Get ready. (Slash.) *That.*

c. (Repeat step *b* until firm.)

d. (Repeat steps *b* and *c* for each remaining word in the column.)

e. (Repeat the column until the children read all the words in order without making mistakes.)

that

those

which

tried

city

hungry

die

EXERCISE 4

Children spell, then read

a. First you're going to spell each word. Then you're going to read that word the fast way.

b. (Touch the ball for **slept.**) Spell it. Get ready. (Tap under each letter as the children say:) *S-L-E-P-T.*

• (Return to the ball.) Read it. Get ready. (Slash.) *Slept.*

c. (Repeat step *b* for each remaining word in the column.)

d. (Repeat steps *b* and *c* until firm.)

slept

thumb

later

body

hoped

what

hopped

Individual test

a. (Call on individual children to read one column of words from the lesson.)

b. (Praise children who read all words with no errors.)

Carla Calls for Help[1]

Carla was reading a genie book. The book told about many tricks. One part told how to call for help. Carla was reading that part now. She wanted to call for another genie who could help her find Ott.[2]

Carla stopped reading the part of the book that told how to call for help. Then she folded her hands and said some words. Suddenly, something appeared in the sky. It began to dive down. It was getting closer and closer. Then it stopped.[3] It was an old genie.[4] She stared at Carla. Then she said, "Don't tell me you called for help?"

"Yes, I did," Carla said. "I need help."

"But that is impossible," the old genie said. "You are a human.[5] Everybody knows that a human is not smart. Everybody knows that it is impossible for a human to do the most simple trick."⑤

"That is not so," Carla said.[6] "I don't know if I can do every trick in that book. But I called you, and I did the other trick I tried."

"That is impossible," the old genie said.[7]

"I'll show you," Carla said.

She opened the book to the part that told how to make a rock into water.[8] After she was through reading what the book said, she found a big rock. She told the old genie to hold the rock on top of her head.[9]

Suddenly, the rock turned into water. Splash. It flowed all over the old genie.[10] She began spitting water. She said, "How dare you. How dare you do a thing like that to me."[11]

Carla said, "Don't get mad at me. I called for help. I didn't call you so that we could get in a fight.[12] I need your help to find Ott."

Stop

1. I wonder who will help Carla. Let's read and find out.
2. Who does she want to help her? (Signal.) *Another genie.*
3. What do you suppose it was? (The children respond.)
- Read some more.
4. Who was it? (Signal.) *An old genie.*
5. That means she's a real person, not magic like a genie.
6. What's not so? (The children respond.) Right. She can do tricks even though she's a human.
7. What did she say? (Signal.) *That is impossible.*
- What didn't she believe? (The children respond.) Yes, the old genie didn't believe that Carla could do tricks.
8. What's she going to do? (The children respond.) Yes, turn a rock into water.
9. Oh, oh. What will happen if the rock turns into water? (The children respond.)
10. Where did all that water come from? (The children respond.)
- The rock turned into water, and there was no more rock on her head.
11. Everybody, say that. (Signal.) *How dare you do a thing like that to me.*
12. Does Carla want to fight? (Signal.) *No.*
- What does she want from the old genie? (Signal.) *Help.*
- Why? (The children respond.)
- I hope she finds Ott.

READING VOCABULARY

EXERCISE 1

Teacher reads the words in red

a. I'll read each word in red. Then you'll spell each word.

b. (Touch the ball for **wizard.**) My turn. (Slash as you say:) Wizard. What word? (Signal.) *Wizard.*

c. (Return to the ball.) Spell it. Get ready. (Tap under each letter as the children say:) *W-I-Z-A-R-D.*

• What word did you spell? (Signal.) *Wizard.*

d. (Repeat steps *b* and *c* for each word in red.)

e. Your turn to read all the words in this column.

f. (Touch the ball for **wizard.** Pause.) Get ready. (Slash.) *Wizard.*

g. (Repeat step *f* for each remaining word in the column.)

h. (Repeat steps *f* and *g* until firm.)

wizard

peevish

crown

shirt

clothes

shoe

prince

EXERCISE 2

Words with underlined parts

a. First you're going to read the underlined part of each word in this column. Then you're going to read the whole word.

b. (Touch the ball for **grasshopper.**) Read the underlined part. Get ready. (Tap the ball.) *Grass.*

• Read the whole word. (Pause.) Get ready. (Slash.) *Grasshopper.*

c. (Repeat step *b* until firm.)

d. (Repeat steps *b* and *c* for each remaining word in the column.)

e. (Repeat the column until children read all the words in order without making a mistake.)

grasshopper

handsome

dressed

Everybody

band

tramp's

forgot

WORKSHEET 122

EXERCISE 7
Picture comprehension

a. Look at the picture.
b. (Ask these questions:)
1. What's happening to the old genie? (Signal.) *She's getting wet.*
2. How did she get wet? (The children respond.)
3. Where's that rock she had on her head? (Signal.) *It turned into water.*
4. What do you think Carla is thinking? (The children respond.)
- Yes, I think she showed that old genie that she could do tricks just as good as a genie.

STORY ITEMS
EXERCISE 8
Following instructions

a. (Pass out Worksheet 122 to each child.)
b. (Hold up side 1 of your worksheet and point to the story-items exercise.)
c. Everybody, touch item 1. ✔
d. Everybody, touch the instructions in the box above item 1. ✔
- Those instructions tell you how to work item 1. (Call on a child.) Read the instructions in the box. *Circle the answer.*
e. Everybody, what are you going to do to answer item 1? (Signal.) *Circle the answer.*
f. Everybody, touch the instructions in the box above item 2. ✔
- Those instructions tell you how to work items 2, 3, 4, 5 and 6. (Call on a child.) Read the instructions in the box. *Fill in the blanks.*
g. Everybody, are you going to circle the answers? (Signal.) *No.*
- Are you going to make a line under the answers? (Signal.) *No.*
h. What are you going to do to work items 2, 3, 4, 5, and 6? (Signal.) *Fill in the blanks.*
i. Everybody, touch the instructions in the box above item 7. ✔
- Those instructions tell you how to work item 7. (Call on a child.) Read the instructions in the box. *Make a line under the answer.*
j. Everybody, are you going to fill in the blank? (Signal.) *No.*
- Are you going to circle the answer? (Signal.) *No.*

k. What are you going to do to work item 7? (Signal.) *Make a line under the answer.*
l. Everybody, touch the instructions in the box above item 8. ✔
- Those instructions tell you how to work items 8 and 9. (Call on a child.) Read the instructions in the box. *Fill in the blanks.*
m. Everybody, are you going to make a line under the answers? (Signal.) *No.*
- Are you going to circle the answers? (Signal.) *No.*
n. What are you going to do to work items 8 and 9? (Signal.) *Fill in the blanks.*
o. You'll work the items later. Remember to follow the instructions that go with each item.

INDEPENDENT ACTIVITIES
EXERCISE 9
Summary of independent activities

Everybody, now you'll do your worksheet. Remember to do all parts of the worksheet and to read all the parts carefully.

END OF LESSON 122

Mr. Hall was watching the ship go by, and he was thinking this: "If that ship doesn't pick me up, I'll never be found. I will die out here in the middle of the sea.[10]And that ship is so close I can almost reach it. If only the people could hear me."

Suddenly, Mr. Hall looked at that big dog and said, "Speak, speak."[11]

The dog lifted his head. "Woo, woo." Out came a big, deep bark. It boomed out across the sea. "Woo, woo."[12]

"Speak," Mr. Hall said again.

"Woo, woooo," the dog answered.

Now people on the deck were looking over the side of the ship. They were waving. "Hello," they were yelling. They saw Mr. Hall. Mr. Hall threw his arms around that dog and gave him a big hug.[13]

Mr. Hall still lives in a nice house. He still has a nice car and a lot of cash. But there is one thing that is not the same about him.

He shares his house with his best friend, a big, mean-looking dog. He loves that dog.[14]

The end

---

[10] What would happen if the ship didn't stop and pick up Mr. Hall? **(The children respond.)**

[11] Why does he want the dog to do that? **(The children respond.)**

[12] Did the dog have a big, deep bark? **(Signal.)** *Yes.*

- Do you think the people on the ship heard it? **(Signal.)** *Yes.* I hope so.

[13] Why did he do that? **(The children respond.)**

- Did the ship stop to pick up Mr. Hall? **(Signal.)** *Yes.*

[14] Is Mr. Hall still afraid of dogs? **(Signal.)** *No.*

- Who does he share his house with now? **(The children respond.)**

EXERCISE 6

Picture comprehension

a. Look at the picture.

b. (Ask these questions:)

1. What is the big dog doing? **(The children respond.)**

- Why is he doing that? **(The children respond.)**

2. Show me Mr. Hall. **(The children respond.)**

3. Why do you think Mr. Hall's hands are up? **(The children respond.)**

EXERCISE 7

Summary of independent activities

a. (Pass out Worksheet 144 to each child.)

b. Everybody, now you'll do your worksheet. Remember to do all parts of the worksheet and to read all the parts carefully.

END OF LESSON 144

READING VOCABULARY

EXERCISE 1

Teacher reads the words in red

a. I'll read each word in red. Then you'll spell each word.

b. (Touch the ball for **instant**.) My turn. (Slash as you say:) Instant. What word? (Signal.) *Instant.*

c. (Return to the ball.) Spell it. Get ready. (Tap under each letter as the children say:) *I-N-S-T-A-N-T.*

• What word did you spell? (Signal.) *Instant.*

d. (Repeat steps *b* and *c* for each word in red.)

e. Your turn to read all the words in this column.

f. (Touch the ball for **instant**. Pause.) Get ready. (Slash.) *Instant.*

g. (Repeat step *f* for each remaining word in the column.)

h. (Repeat steps *f* and *g* until firm.)

instant

hug

hungry

grown

our

fight

human

EXERCISE 2

Read the fast way

a. You're going to read all the words in this column the fast way.

b. (Touch the ball for **woman.** Pause.) Get ready. (Slash.) *Woman.*

c. (Repeat step *b* until firm.)

d. (Repeat steps *b* and *c* for each remaining word in the column.)

e. (Repeat the column until the children read all the words in order without making mistakes.)

woman

became

appeared

spitting

tricks

impossible

become

STORY 144
EXERCISE 5

Reading—decoding

a. (Pass out Storybook 2.)

b. Everybody, open your reader to page 182.

c. Remember, if the group reads all the way to the red 5 without making more than five errors, we can go on.

d. Everybody, touch the title of the story. ✔

e. If you hear a mistake, raise your hand. Remember, children who do not have their place lose their turn. (Call on individual children to read two or three sentences. Do not ask comprehension questions. Tally all errors.)

To Correct

word-identification errors (**from,** for example)
1. That word is **from.** What word? *From.*
2. Go back to the beginning of the sentence and read the sentence again.

f. (If the children make more than five errors before they reach the red 5: when they reach the 5 return to the beginning of the story and have the children reread to the 5. Do not ask comprehension questions. Repeat step *f* until firm, and then go on to step *g.*)

g. (When the children read to the red 5 without making more than five errors: read the story to the children from the beginning to the 5. Ask the specified comprehension questions. When you reach the 5, call on individual children to continue reading the story. Have each child read two or three sentences. Ask the specified comprehension questions.)

The Dog Saves Mr. Hall [1]

Mr. Hall was sitting on one side of the raft watching the dog. The dog was trying to get on the raft. At last he did. He shook himself and drops of water went flying. Mr. Hall did not take his eyes from the dog.[2] The dog looked at Mr. Hall. Then he sat down. He was even bigger and meaner-looking than he seemed on the ship.

Mr. Hall sat on the other side of the raft for a long time. Then Mr. Hall saw a tin of crackers floating in the sea. He reached for it. Then he opened the tin and ate one of the crackers.[3] The dog was looking at him. Mr. Hall began to think that the dog would eat him if he got hungry. So Mr. Hall tossed some crackers to the dog.[4] The dog sniffed the crackers and then looked up at Mr. Hall. ⑤

"Go on and eat them," Mr. Hall said. That was the first time he had ever talked to a dog.[5]

The dog ate the crackers.

All day, Mr. Hall sat on one side of the raft and the dog sat on the other.[6] Then, when the sun was setting, Mr. Hall saw a ship. He stood up and began to shout as loud as he could. "Here we are. Here we are," he shouted.[7] The ship came closer and closer. And Mr. Hall kept shouting, "Here we are."

Now the ship was very close. Mr. Hall could see people on the deck. He could hear the sound of a band playing. He could hear people laughing and talking, but he could not shout any more.[8] He had shouted too hard, and now he couldn't make loud sounds. "Help," he said, but nobody could hear him.[9]

[1] What's the dog going to do in this story? (Signal.) *Save Mr. Hall.*

[2] Where was the dog? (Signal.) *On the raft.*

[3] Where did Mr. Hall find the crackers? (Signal.) *Floating in the sea.*

[4] Why did Mr. Hall give the dog some crackers? (The children respond.)

• Yes, he was afraid that the dog might eat him if he got too hungry.

[5] What did Mr. Hall say to the dog? (The children respond.)

[6] Did the dog and Mr. Hall sit next to each other? (Signal.) *No.*

[7] Who is Mr. Hall shouting to? (The children respond.) Yes, he saw a ship.

[8] Was the ship close? (Signal.) *Yes.*

• How do you know? (The children respond.)

[9] Why couldn't they hear him any more? (The children respond.)

• Right. He shouted so hard, his voice was weak.

EXERCISE 3

Words with underlined parts

a. First you're going to read the underlined part of each word in this column. Then you're going to read the whole word.

b. (Touch the ball for **You're.**) Read the underlined part. Get ready. (Tap the ball.) *You.*
  • Read the whole word. (Pause.) Get ready. (Slash.) *You're.*

c. (Repeat step *b* until firm.)

d. (Repeat steps *b* and *c* for each remaining word in the column.)

e. (Repeat the column until children read all the words in order without making a mistake.)

You're

can't

He's

I'll

we've

we're

she'd

EXERCISE 4

Read the fast way

a. You're going to read all the words in this column the fast way.

b. (Touch the ball for **won't.** Pause.) Get ready. (Slash.) *Won't.*

c. (Repeat step *b* until firm.)

d. (Repeat steps *b* and *c* for each remaining word in the column.)

e. (Repeat the column until the children read all the words in order without making mistakes.)

won't

were

starting

front

simple

where

agreed

EXERCISE 3

Words with underlined parts

a. First you're going to read the underlined part of each word in this column. Then you're going to read the whole word.

b. (Touch the ball for **sniffed.**) Read the underlined part. Get ready. (Tap the ball.) *Sniff.*

• Read the whole word. (Pause.) Get ready. (Slash.) *Sniffed.*

c. (Repeat step *b* until firm.)

d. (Repeat steps *b* and *c* for each remaining word in the column.)

e. (Repeat the column until children read all the words in order without making a mistake.)

sniffed

setting

boomed

crackers

sucked

middle

faced

EXERCISE 4

Children spell, then read

a. First you're going to spell each word. Then you're going to read that word the fast way.

b. (Touch the ball for **shares.**) Spell it. Get ready. (Tap under each letter as the children say:) *S-H-A-R-E-S.*

• (Return to the ball.) Read it. Get ready. (Slash.) *Shares.*

c. (Repeat step *b* for each remaining word in the column.)

d. (Repeat steps *b* and *c* until firm.)

shares

saves

closer

waved

threw

waving

raft

Individual test

a. (Call on individual children to read one column of words from the lesson.)

b. (Praise children who read all words with no errors.)

EXERCISE 5

Children spell, then read

a. First you're going to spell each word. Then you're going to read that word the fast way.

b. (Touch the ball for **true.**) Spell it. Get ready. (Tap under each letter as the children say:) *T-R-U-E.*

• (Return to the ball.) Read it. Get ready. (Slash.) *True.*

c. (Repeat step *b* for each remaining word in the column.)

d. (Repeat steps *b* and *c* until firm.)

true

turn

planning

planing

through

right

stood

Individual test

a. (Call on individual children to read one column of words from the lesson.)

b. (Praise children who read all words with no errors.)

STORY 123
EXERCISE 6

Reading—decoding

a. (Pass out Storybook 2.)

b. Everybody, open your reader to page 113.

c. Remember, if the group reads all the way to the red 5 without making more than five errors, we can go on.

d. Everybody, touch the title of the story. ✔

e. If you hear a mistake, raise your hand. Remember, children who do not have their place lose their turn. (Call on individual children to read two or three sentences. Do not ask comprehension questions. Tally all errors.)

To Correct

word-identification errors (**from,** for example)
1. That word is **from.** What word? *From.*
2. Go back to the beginning of the sentence and read the sentence again.

f. (If the children make more than five errors before they reach the red 5: when they reach the 5 return to the beginning of the story and have the children reread to the 5. Do not ask comprehension questions. Repeat step *f* until firm, and then go on to step *g*.)

g. (When the children read to the red 5 without making more than five errors: read the story to the children from the beginning to the 5. Ask the specified comprehension questions. When you reach the 5, call on individual children to continue reading the story. Have each child read two or three sentences. Ask the specified comprehension questions.)

READING VOCABULARY
EXERCISE 1

Teacher reads the words in red

a. I'll read each word in red. Then you'll spell each word.

b. (Touch the ball for **thumb.**) My turn. (Slash as you say:) Thumb. What word? (Signal.) *Thumb.*

c. (Return to the ball.) Spell it. Get ready. (Tap under each letter as the children say:) *T-H-U-M-B.*

• What word did you spell? (Signal.) *Thumb.*

d. (Repeat steps *b* and *c* for each word in red.)

e. Your turn to read all the words in this column.

f. (Touch the ball for **thumb.** Pause.) Get ready. (Slash.) *Thumb.*

g. (Repeat step *f* for each remaining word in the column.)

h. (Repeat steps *f* and *g* until firm.)

thumb

prince

die

band

hungry

first

fourth

EXERCISE 2

Words with underlined parts

a. First you're going to read the underlined part of each word in this column. Then you're going to read the whole word.

b. (Touch the ball for **sea.**) Read the underlined part. Get ready. (Tap the ball.) *eee.*

• Read the whole word. (Pause.) Get ready. (Slash.) *Sea.*

c. (Repeat step *b* until firm.)

d. (Repeat steps *b* and *c* for each remaining word in the column.)

e. (Repeat the column until children read all the words in order without making a mistake.)

sea

Speak

shout

meaner

sinking

watched

floating

Carla Goes to Genie School[1]

Carla told the old genie that she didn't want to fight with her. She needed her help.

"I will help," the old genie said.

Then the old genie stood on one foot.[2] She said some words. "Poof." There was Ott standing next to the old genie.[3]

"You're back," Carla said. She ran over and gave Ott a big hug.

"But I'm afraid he'll have to come back to school with me," the old genie said. "He is not doing well as a genie. I will try to send another genie.[4] I will take Ott back to school with me."[5]

"No," Carla said. "I don't want another genie. I want Ott."

"But he is not fit to be a genie," the old genie said. "He can't even find his way home."

"I don't care," Carla said. "I want him for my genie. (5) He's the one who came out of the bottle when I rubbed it. And he's the genie I want."[6]

"But he must go back to school," the old genie said.

"That's all right," Carla said. "I can go to school with him."

"Oh no," the old genie said. "You can't go to our school."[7]

"Why not?" Carla asked.

"Because you are not a genie," the old genie said. "You are a human. And everybody knows that humans can't do very simple tricks."[8]

"Don't say that," Carla said, "or I will turn a thousand rocks into water and you will have to swim home."[9]

"All right, all right," the old genie said. "You can come to genie school, but I don't think you're going to like it."

"Poof."[10] In an instant, Carla and Ott were standing in front of the other children in the genie school.[11]

Stop

---

1. What's the title of this story? (Signal.) *Carla goes to genie school.*
2. What did she do first? (Signal.) *Stood on one foot.*
3. What happened after the old genie said some words? (The children respond.)
4. What does the old genie want to do? (Signal.) *Send another genie.*
5. Where does the old genie want Ott to go? (Signal.) *Back to school.*
6. Does Carla want another genie? (Signal.) *No.*
• She wants Ott even if he's not a very good genie.
7. Where does Carla want to go? (Signal.) *To genie school.*
• Does the old genie want her? (Signal.) *No.*
8. Tell me why the old genie doesn't want her. (The children respond.) Yes, she's a human, not a genie.
9. What did Carla say she would do? (Signal.) *Turn a thousand rocks into water.*
• Why did she say that? (The children respond.) Yes, she didn't want the old genie to say that humans can't do tricks.
10. Oh, oh. Something's going to happen.
11. Where were Carla and Ott and the old genie? (The children respond.)
• I wonder what the children will say about the human in genie school. We'll read more next time.

Mr. Hall opened the door to his room. He went up the stairs to the deck. People were screaming. The ship was sinking.

Mr. Hall jumped into the water. Mr. Hall looked for something to hang on to. He swam and swam.[10] Then he saw something—a big raft. He got on the raft and sat down.[11] He looked around for the ship, but the ship was gone.[12] He looked for other people, but he couldn't see anybody. He looked and looked.[13] And then, at last, he saw something swimming in the sea.[14] It was that big, mean-looking dog. "I hope he doesn't come here," Mr. Hall said to himself.[15] But the dog swam closer to the raft.

Then the dog tried to get on the raft. Mr. Hall sat on the other side of the raft. He was looking at the dog and shaking with fear.[16]

More to come

[10] Why was Mr. Hall swimming? **(The children respond.)** Yes, he's trying to find something to hang on to.

[11] Did he find something? **(Signal.)** *Yes.*

• What did he find? **(Signal.)** *A raft.*

[12] Why couldn't he see the ship? **(The children respond.)**

[13] What was he looking for? **(Signal.)** *Other people.*

• Could he see any people? **(Signal.)** *No.*

[14] What do you think he saw? **(The children respond.)**

• Let's read and find out.

[15] Who is he talking about? **(Signal.)** *The dog.*

[16] What was Mr. Hall doing? **(The children respond.)**

EXERCISE 6

Picture comprehension

a. Look at the picture.

b. (Ask these questions:)
1. Where is Mr. Hall? **(Signal.)** *On a raft.*
2. What's happening to the ship? **(The children respond.)** It's sinking.
3. How does Mr. Hall look? **(The children respond.)** Why is he shaking? **(The children respond.)**
4. What's the big dog doing? **(The children respond.)** Where does the dog want to go? **(The children respond.)**

INDEPENDENT ACTIVITIES
EXERCISE 7

Reading comprehension

a. (Pass out Worksheet 143 to each child.)

b. Everybody, turn to side 2 of your worksheet. ✔

c. (Point to the story on side 2 of your worksheet.) Everybody, find this story on your worksheet. ✔

d. Today you're going to read a passage that tells about the shape of the world.

e. Everybody, touch the first picture. ✔

• That picture shows how people once thought the world looked. They thought it was flat.

f. Everybody, touch the second picture. ✔

• That picture shows how the world really looks. Is the world flat? **(Signal.)** *No.*

• What shape is the world? **(Signal.)** *Round.*

g. I'll read the passage. Everybody, follow along. (Read the passage to the children. Check that they are following along as you read.)

h. When you do your independent work, read the passage to yourself. Then answer the questions.

EXERCISE 8

Summary of independent activities

Everybody, now you'll do your worksheet. Remember to do all parts of the worksheet and to read all the parts carefully.

END OF LESSON 143

EXERCISE 7

Picture comprehension

a. Look at the picture.

b. (Ask these questions:)

1. What's happening to Ott? (Signal.) *Carla is hugging him.* She's happy he's there.

2. Look at the old genie. What do you think she's saying? (The children respond.)

3. What are those drops on her? (Signal.) *Water.*

DEDUCTIONS

The children will need pencils.

EXERCISE 8

Written deductions

a. (Pass out Worksheet 123 to each child.)

b. (Hold up side 2 of your worksheet and touch the sentence, "Every rat thinks," in the deductions exercise.)

c. Everybody, touch this sentence on your worksheet. ✔

d. I'm going to call on different children to read a sentence. Everybody, follow along.

1. (Call on a child.) Read the sentence in the box. *Every rat thinks.*

- Everybody, what do you know about every rat? (Signal.) *It thinks.* Yes, it thinks.

2. (Call on a child.) Read the sentence next to the box. *Linda is a rat.*

- Everybody, what do you know about Linda? (Signal.) *She is a rat.*

- And what do you know about every rat? (Signal.) *It thinks.*

3. (Call on a child.) Read the sentence under the box. *What does Linda do?*

- Everybody, listen. Every rat thinks. Linda is a rat. So, what does she do? (Signal.) *She thinks.* Yes, she thinks.

e. Let's do that problem again. (Repeat the sentence reading and questions in step *d.*)

f. Everybody, write the answer in the blank. ✔

INDEPENDENT ACTIVITIES

EXERCISE 9

Summary of independent activities

Everybody, now you'll do your worksheet. Remember to do all parts of the worksheet and to read all the parts carefully.

END OF LESSON 123

STORY 143
EXERCISE 5

Reading—decoding

a. (Pass out Storybook 2.)

b. Everybody, open your reader to page 179.

c. Remember, if the group reads all the way to the red 5 without making more than five errors, we can go on.

d. Everybody, touch the title of the story. ✔

e. If you hear a mistake, raise your hand. Remember, children who do not have their place lose their turn. (Call on individual children to read two or three sentences. Do not ask comprehension questions. Tally all errors.)

To Correct

word-identification errors (**from**, for example)
1. That word is **from**. What word? *From.*
2. Go back to the beginning of the sentence and read the sentence again.

f. (If the children make more than five errors before they reach the red 5: when they reach the 5 return to the beginning of the story and have the children reread to the 5. Do not ask comprehension questions. Repeat step *f* until firm, and then go on to step *g*.)

g. (When the children read to the red 5 without making more than five errors: read the story to the children from the beginning to the five. Ask the specified comprehension questions. When you reach the 5, call on individual children to continue reading the story. Have each child read two or three sentences. Ask the specified comprehension questions.)

Mr. Hall [1]

Mr. Hall had a nice home and a nice car. He had lots of cash. Everybody said that he was a fine man. [2]

But there was something about Mr. Hall that only a few people knew. He was afraid of dogs. [3] When a dog got near him, he would begin to shake. He would start to think that the dog was going to come after him. Mr. Hall had been afraid of dogs from the time he was a little boy. [4] But he couldn't help his fear. The bigger a dog was, the more fear Mr. Hall had. [5] Mr. Hall stayed away from dogs whenever he could.

But then something strange happened. Mr. Hall was on a ship. He was on his way to Japan. [6] One day he was walking on the deck of the ship when he saw a dog. This dog was nearly as big as a horse. ⑤ [7] When Mr. Hall saw him, Mr. Hall got a chill up and down his back. Mr. Hall stopped and began to shake.

For the next three days, Mr. Hall was afraid to go on the deck of the ship. He was so afraid of the dog that he stayed in his room. [8] But he left his room on the fourth day. He was reading a book when suddenly the ship jerked. Mr. Hall fell from his chair. He tried to get up, but the ship was leaning to the side. People were yelling, "Help, help. The ship is sinking." [9]

---

[1] Who is this story about? (Signal.) *Mr. Hall.*

[2] Tell me some things about Mr. Hall. (The children respond.)

[3] What was Mr. Hall's problem? (Signal.) *He was afraid of dogs.*

[4] How long had Mr. Hall been afraid of dogs? (Signal.) *From the time he was a little boy.*

[5] Was he more afraid of big dogs or little dogs? (Signal.) *Big dogs.*

[6] Where was Mr. Hall going? (Signal.) *To Japan.*

• How was he getting there? (Signal.) *On a ship.*

[7] Where did Mr. Hall see the dog? (The children respond.)

• How big was that dog? (The children respond.) Yes, nearly as big as a horse.

• Is Mr. Hall going to get afraid? (Signal.) *Yes.*

[8] Did Mr. Hall come on deck? (Signal.) *No.*

• Why did he stay in his room? (Signal.) *He was afraid of the dog.*

[9] Did Mr. Hall leave his room? (Signal.) *Yes.*

• Why? (Signal.) *The ship was sinking.*

READING VOCABULARY

EXERCISE 1

Teacher reads the words in red

a. I'll read each word in red. Then you'll spell each word.

b. (Touch the ball for **vow.**) My turn. (Slash as you say:) Vow. What word? (Signal.) *Vow.*

c. (Return to the ball.) Spell it. Get ready. (Tap under each letter as the children say:) *V-O-W.*

• What word did you spell? (Signal.) *Vow.*

d. (Repeat steps *b* and *c* for each word in red.)

e. Your turn to read all the words in this column.

f. (Touch the ball for **vow.** Pause.) Get ready. (Slash.) *Vow.*

g. (Repeat step *f* for each remaining word in the column.)

h. (Repeat steps *f* and *g* until firm.)

vow

obey

class

fingers

snapped

anybody

won't

EXERCISE 2

Words with underlined parts

a. First you're going to read the underlined part of each word in this column. Then you're going to read the whole word.

b. (Touch the ball for **always.**) Read the underlined part. Get ready. (Tap the ball.) *All.*

• Read the whole word. (Pause.) Get ready. (Slash.) *Always.*

c. (Repeat step *b* until firm.)

d. (Repeat steps *b* and *c* for each remaining word in the column.)

e. (Repeat the column until children read all the words in order without making a mistake.)

always

Splash

smartest

smarter

When

Then

proud

EXERCISE 3

Words with underlined parts

a. First you're going to read the underlined part of each word in this column. Then you're going to read the whole word.

b. (Touch the ball for **whenever**.) Read the underlined part. Get ready. (Tap the ball.) *When.*

• Read the whole word. (Pause.) Get ready. (Slash.) *Whenever.*

c. (Repeat step *b* until firm.)

d. (Repeat steps *b* and *c* for each remaining word in the column.)

e. (Repeat the column until children read all the words in order without making a mistake.)

whenever

can't

chair

screaming

stayed

swimming

closer

EXERCISE 4

Children spell, then read

a. First you're going to spell each word. Then you're going to read that word the fast way.

b. (Touch the ball for **mice**.) Spell it. Get ready. (Tap under each letter as the children say:) *M-I-C-E.*

• (Return to the ball.) Read it. Get ready. (Slash.) *Mice.*

c. (Repeat step *b* for each remaining word in the column.)

d. (Repeat steps *b* and *c* until firm.)

mice

swam

flew

insect

world

afraid

salad

Individual test

a. (Call on individual children to read one column of words from the lesson.)

b. (Praise children who read all words with no errors.)

EXERCISE 3

Read the fast way

a. You're going to read all the words in this column the fast way.

b. (Touch the ball for **through**. Pause.) Get ready. (Slash.) *Through.*

c. (Repeat step *b* until firm.)

d. (Repeat steps *b* and *c* for each remaining word in the column.)

e. (Repeat the column until the children read all the words in order without making mistakes.)

through

hungry

become

stayed

very

Every

everybody

EXERCISE 4

Words with underlined parts

a. First you're going to read the underlined part of each word in this column. Then you're going to read the whole word.

b. (Touch the ball for **I'm**.) Read the underlined part. Get ready. (Tap the ball.) *I.*

• Read the whole word. (Pause.) Get ready. (Slash.) *I'm.*

c. (Repeat step *b* until firm.)

d. (Repeat steps *b* and *c* for each remaining word in the column.)

e. (Repeat the column until children read all the words in order without making a mistake.)

I'm

I'll

I've

we've

we're

can't

you're

READING VOCABULARY
EXERCISE 1

Teacher reads the words in red

a. I'll read each word in red. Then you'll spell each word.

b. (Touch the ball for **fourth.**) My turn. (Slash as you say:) Fourth. What word? (Signal.) *Fourth.*

c. (Return to the ball.) Spell it. Get ready. (Tap under each letter as the children say:) *F-O-U-R-T-H.*

• What word did you spell? (Signal.) *Fourth.*

d. (Repeat steps *b* and *c* for each word in red.)

e. Your turn to read all the words in this column.

f. (Touch the ball for **fourth.** Pause.) Get ready. (Slash.) *Fourth.*

g. (Repeat step *f* for each remaining word in the column.)

h. (Repeat steps *f* and *g* until firm.

fourth

sinking

raft

America

gone

strange

Japan

EXERCISE 2

Words with underlined parts

a. First you're going to read the underlined part of each word in this column. Then you're going to read the whole word.

b. (Touch the ball for **Hall.**) Read the underlined part. Get ready. (Tap the ball.) *All.*

• Read the whole word. (Pause.) Get ready. (Slash.) *Hall.*

c. (Repeat step *b* until firm.)

d. (Repeat steps *b* and *c* for each remaining word in the column.)

e. (Repeat the column until children read all the words in order without making a mistake.)

Hall

sea

shake

nearly

leaning

chill

fear

EXERCISE 5

Children spell, then read

a. First you're going to spell each word. Then you're going to read that word the fast way.

b. (Touch the ball for **few.**) Spell it. Get ready. (Tap under each letter as the children say:) *F-E-W.*

• (Return to the ball.) Read it. Get ready. (Slash.) *Few.*

c. (Repeat step *b* for each remaining word in the column.)

d. (Repeat steps *b* and *c* until firm.)

few

new

ready

taking

talking

knows

we're

Individual test

a. (Call on individual children to read one column of words from the lesson.)

b. (Praise children who read all words with no errors.)

STORYBOOK

STORY 124
EXERCISE 6

Reading—decoding

a. (Pass out Storybook 2.)

b. Everybody, open your reader to page 116.

c. Remember, if the group reads all the way to the red 5 without making more than five errors, we can go on.

d. Everybody, touch the title of the story. ✔

e. If you hear a mistake, raise your hand. Remember, children who do not have their place lose their turn. (Call on individual children to read two or three sentences. Do not ask comprehension questions. Tally all errors.)

To Correct

word-identification errors (**from,** for example)
1. That word is **from.** What word? *From.*
2. Go back to the beginning of the sentence and read the sentence again.

f. (If the children make more than five errors before they reach the red 5: when they reach the 5 return to the beginning of the story and have the children reread to the 5. Do not ask comprehension questions. Repeat step *f* until firm, and then go on to step *g*.)

g. (When the children read to the red 5 without making more than five errors: read the story to the children from the beginning to the 5. Ask the specified comprehension questions. When you reach the 5, call on individual children to continue reading the story. Have each child read two or three sentences. Ask the specified comprehension questions.)

And Casey told the fox, "Look at the thorns in the thorn bushes.[9] Hang me, or shoot me, or throw me in the lake. But please don't throw me into those thorn bushes."

The fox looked at the big thorns on the bushes. Then he said, "I will throw you into the thorn bushes." And he gave Casey a big heave.[10]

The fox said to himself, "That was a good way to get rid of that rabbit."

But suddenly, Casey began to laugh from the thorn bushes. "Ha ha, ho ho, he, he, he. I'm Casey the rabbit and you can't hurt me."[11]

Then Casey said, "I love thorn bushes, you silly fox." He jumped around in the thorns.[12]

The fox was very mad because Casey had tricked him.[13] And Casey was very happy. He laughed and said, "Ha ha, ho ho, he, he, he. I'm Casey the rabbit, and you can't hurt me."

The end

[9] Casey is pretending he's afraid of thorns. Rabbits aren't really afraid of thorn bushes.

[10] Where did the fox throw Casey? (Signal.) *Into the thorn bushes.*

• The fox thought he got rid of Casey.

[11] Everybody, read that with me. (Teacher and children read:) *"Ha ha, ho ho, he, he, he. I'm Casey the rabbit and you can't hurt me."*

[12] Did the thorns hurt Casey? (Signal.) *No.*

[13] How did Casey trick him? (The children respond.) Right. He said he didn't want to go in the thorn bushes, but he really did.

EXERCISE 6

Picture comprehension

a. Look at the picture.

b. (Ask these questions:)

  1. Show me the thorn bushes. (The children respond.)

  2. Do you think Casey looks scared? (The children respond.)

  • He looks scared of the bush. But is he really afraid of the thorn bush? (Signal.) *No.*

  3. What do you think the fox is thinking about? (The children respond.)

  4. (Point to the salad.) Why is that salad on the path? (The children respond.)

WORKSHEET 142

INDEPENDENT ACTIVITIES
EXERCISE 7

Reading comprehension

a. (Pass out Worksheet 142 to each child.)

b. Everybody, turn to side 2 of your worksheet. ✔

c. (Point to the story on side 2 of your worksheet.) Everybody, find this story on your worksheet. ✔

d. Today you're going to read a passage that tells about insects.

e. Everybody, touch the first picture. ✔

• What kind of insect is that? (Signal.) *An ant.*

• Everybody, touch the next picture. ✔

• What kind of insect is that? (Signal.) *A fly.*

• Everybody, touch the next picture. ✔

• What kind of insect is that? (Signal.) *A butterfly.*

• Everybody, touch the next picture. ✔

• That's not an insect. That's a bug. What kind of bug is that? (Signal.) *A spider.*

f. (Repeat step e until firm.)

g. The body of every insect has three parts. Everybody, touch the head of the ant. ✔

• That's the first part. Everybody, touch the middle part of the ant. ✔

• That's the second part. Everybody, touch the end of the ant. ✔

• That's the third part. How many parts does the body of an insect have? (Signal.) *Three.*

h. (Repeat step g until firm.)

i. I'll read the passage. Everybody, follow along. (Read the passage to the children. Check that they are following along as you read.)

j. When you do your independent work, read the passage to yourself. Then answer the questions.

EXERCISE 8

Summary of independent activities

Everybody, now you'll do your worksheet. Remember to do all parts of the worksheet and to read all the parts carefully.

END OF LESSON 142

Carla Is the Best in Genie School[1]

Ott and Carla and the old genie were in front of the children in the genie school. The old genie said, "This is Carla. She is going to work in this school just like the rest of you."[2]

One of the boys said, "Not here. She can't stay here. She is only a human, and everybody knows that humans can't do any tricks."[3]

Carla snapped her fingers. A rock appeared.[4] She said to the boy who had just talked, "Sit on that rock."

The boy sat on the rock. Carla folded her arms and said some words to herself.

Splash. The boy was sitting in a pool of water.[5]

"Ho, ho," the other children said. "She can do some good tricks. It will be fun to have her in school with us."

So Carla stayed in school. She worked as hard as any of the genies.⑤[6] And she was the best in the class. When the teacher told the children and Carla how to do a new trick, Carla was always the best at doing the trick.[7] Then she would help the other girls and boys work on the new trick.

Every day, Carla went to school and worked on new tricks. Every day she became smarter and better at genie tricks. Soon, she was ready to become a genie. She was very proud.[8] She was the only human in the genie school.[9] And she was better than anybody else in school. In fact, her teacher said that she was the smartest one he ever had in school.

Then the big day came. This was the day that everyone in school took a vow to be a genie.[10] After taking this vow, they became real genies and went to stay in a bottle.[11]

This was a very big day for Carla, a very big day.[12]

To be continued

1. What's the title of this story? (Signal.) *Carla is the best in genie school.*
2. What did she say she would do? (Signal.) *Work in this school just like the rest of you.*
3. Did that boy want Carla in school? (Signal.) *No.*
- Why not? (The children respond.)
- What do you think will happen? (The children respond.)
- Let's read and find out.
4. What's the first trick Carla did? (Signal.) *Made a rock appear.*
5. What's the next trick Carla did? (The children respond.) Right, she turned that rock into water.
6. How hard did Carla work? (The children respond.) Right, just as hard as any of the genies.
7. How good was she? (The children respond.) Yes, the best in the class.
8. Why was she proud? (The children respond.)
9. Were there any other humans in the genie school? (Signal.) *No.* Right, Carla was the only human.
10. A genie vow means that every one will promise to be a good genie.
11. What happens after you take the vow to be a genie? (The children respond.)
12. Do you think Carla will take her vow? (The children respond.)
- We'll find out in the next story.

STORYBOOK

STORY 142

EXERCISE 5

Reading—decoding

a. (Pass out Storybook 2.)

b. Everybody, open your reader to page 176.

c. Remember, if the group reads all the way to the red 5 without making more than five errors, we can go on.

d. Everybody, touch the title of the story. ✔

e. If you hear a mistake, raise your hand. Remember, children who do not have their place lose their turn. (Call on individual children to read two or three sentences. Do not ask comprehension questions. Tally all errors.)

To Correct

word-identification errors (**from,** for example)
1. That word is **from.** What word? *From.*
2. Go back to the beginning of the sentence and read the sentence again.

f. (If the children make more than five errors before they reach the red 5: when they reach the 5 return to the beginning of the story and have the children reread to the 5. Do not ask comprehension questions. Repeat step *f* until firm, and then go on to step *g.*)

g. (When the children read to the red 5 without making more than five errors: read the story to the children from the beginning to the 5. Ask the specified comprehension questions. When you reach the 5, call on individual children to continue reading the story. Have each child read two or three sentences. Ask the specified comprehension questions.)

Casey the Rabbit[1]

Casey was a rabbit. He was a good rabbit, but he liked to play tricks on the other animals in the woods. Most of all he liked to play tricks on a mean fox.[2]

When the fox would try to steal hens from a barn, Casey the rabbit would sneak up in back of the fox and yell, "Boo."[3] The fox would jump, and the chickens would start running around. The farmer would hear the chickens and shoot at the fox.[4]

When the fox would try to steal honey from a tree, Casey would sneak up in back of the fox and throw a rock at the bees.[5] The bees would get mad and they would chase the fox into the lake.

One day the fox said, "I must get rid of that rabbit."

So he made a trap for Casey. He put a big salad on a path in the woods. ⑤[6] When Casey stopped to eat the salad, the fox grabbed Casey.

The fox was very happy. He said, "You will never yell 'Boo' when I am stealing chickens. I am going to get rid of you."[7]

Casey said, "I don't care what you do to me, but please don't throw me into the thorn bushes."[8]

The fox said, "Why don't you want me to throw you into the thorn bushes?"

---

[1] What's the name of the rabbit in this story? (Signal.) *Casey.*

[2] Who did Casey like to play tricks on? (Signal.) *A mean fox.*

[3] What trick did Casey do when the fox tried to steal hens? (Signal.) *He'd sneak up in back of him and yell, "Boo."*

[4] What did the farmer do when he heard the chickens? (The children respond.)

[5] What did Casey do when the fox tried to steal honey? (The children respond.)

• What did those bees do? (The children respond.)

[6] Why is the fox doing that? (The children respond.) Yes, he's trying to trap Casey.

[7] What did the fox say he was going to do? (Signal.) *Get rid of Casey.*

[8] Where did Casey say he didn't want to go? (Signal.) *Into the thorn bushes.*

EXERCISE 7
Picture comprehension

a. Look at the picture.

b. (Ask these questions:)

  1. What do you think the old genie is saying to the children in the room? **(The children respond.)**

  2. Why is Ott smiling? **(The children respond.)**

  3. What could Carla be thinking here? **(The children respond.)**

  4. Can you read that writing on the chalkboard? **(The children respond.)**

DEDUCTIONS

The children will need pencils.

EXERCISE 8
Written deductions

a. (Pass out Worksheet 124 to each child.)

b. (Hold up side 2 of your worksheet and touch the sentence, "Every dog pants," in the deductions exercise.)

c. Everybody, touch this sentence on your worksheet. ✔

d. I'm going to call on different children to read a sentence. Everybody, follow along.

  1. (Call on a child.) Read the sentence in the box. *Every dog pants.*

  • Everybody, what do you know about every dog? (Signal.) *It pants.* Yes, it pants.

  2. (Call on a child.) Read the sentence next to the box. *Rob is a dog.*

  • Everybody, what do you know about Rob? (Signal.) *He is a dog.*

  • And what do you know about every dog? (Signal.) *It pants.*

  3. (Call on a child.) Read the sentence under the box. **What does Rob do?**

  • Everybody, listen. Every dog pants. Rob is a dog. So, what does he do? (Signal.) *He pants.* Yes, he pants.

e. Let's do that problem again. (Repeat the sentence reading and questions in step *d*.)

f. Everybody, write the answer in the blank. ✔

INDEPENDENT ACTIVITIES
EXERCISE 9
Summary of independent activities

Everybody, now you'll do your worksheet. Remember to do all parts of the worksheet and to read all the parts carefully.

END OF LESSON 124

EXERCISE 3

Read the fast way

a. You're going to read all the words in this column the fast way.

b. (Touch the ball for **jungle.** Pause.) Get ready. (Slash.) *Jungle.*

c. (Repeat step *b* until firm.)

d. (Repeat steps *b* and *c* for each remaining word in the column.)

e. (Repeat the column until the children read all the words in order without making mistakes.)

jungle

love

throw

body

fox

paw

kill

EXERCISE 4

Words with underlined parts

a. First you're going to read the underlined part of each word in this column. Then you're going to read the whole word.

b. (Touch the ball for **nobody.**) Read the underlined part. Get ready. (Tap the ball.) *Body.*

• Read the whole word. (Pause.) Get ready. (Slash.) *Nobody.*

c. (Repeat step *b* until firm.)

d. (Repeat steps *b* and *c* for each remaining word in the column.)

e. (Repeat the column until children read all the words in order without making a mistake.)

nobody

we've

you'll

helped

hens

jerk

plays

Individual test

a. (Call on individual children to read one column of words from the lesson.)

b. (Praise children who read all words with no errors.)

READING VOCABULARY

EXERCISE 1

Teacher reads the words in red

a. I'll read each word in red. Then you'll spell each word.

b. (Touch the ball for **short**.) My turn. (Slash as you say:) Short. What word? (Signal.) *Short.*

c. (Return to the ball.) Spell it. Get ready. (Tap under each letter as the children say:) *S-H-O-R-T.*

• What word did you spell? (Signal.) *Short.*

d. (Repeat steps *b* and *c* for each word in red.)

e. Your turn to read all the words in this column.

f. (Touch the ball for **short**. Pause.) Get ready. (Slash.) *Short.*

g. (Repeat step *f* for each remaining word in the column.)

h. (Repeat steps *f* and *g* until firm.)

short

place

fingers

obey

spend

gave

Today

EXERCISE 2

Words with underlined parts

a. First you're going to read the underlined part of each word in this column. Then you're going to read the whole word.

b. (Touch the ball for **easy**.) Read the underlined part. Get ready. (Tap the ball.) *eee.*

• Read the whole word. (Pause.) Get ready. (Slash.) *Easy.*

c. (Repeat step *b* until firm.)

d. (Repeat steps *b* and *c* for each remaining word in the column.)

e. (Repeat the column until children read all the words in order without making a mistake.)

easy

ring

snapped

these

leave

better

about

READING VOCABULARY

EXERCISE 1

Teacher reads the words in red

a. I'll read each word in red. Then you'll spell each word.

b. (Touch the ball for **Casey.**) My turn. (Slash as you say:) Casey. What word? (Signal.) Casey.

c. (Return to the ball.) Spell it. Get ready. (Tap under each letter as the children say:) C-A-S-E-Y.

• What word did you spell? (Signal.) Casey.

d. (Repeat steps b and c for each word in red.)

e. Your turn to read all the words in this column.

f. (Touch the ball for **Casey.** Pause.) Get ready. (Slash.) Casey.

g. (Repeat step f for each remaining word in the column.)

h. (Repeat steps f and g until firm.)

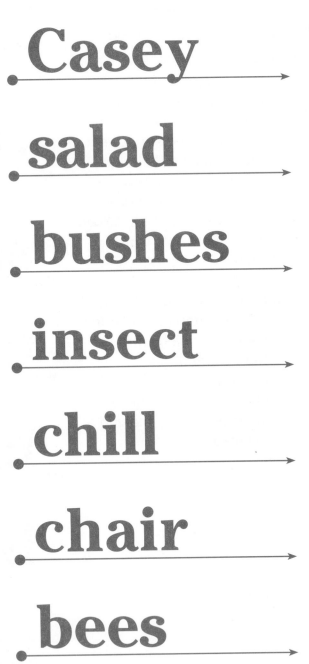

Casey

salad

bushes

insect

chill

chair

bees

EXERCISE 2

Words with underlined parts

a. First you're going to read the underlined part of each word in this column. Then you're going to read the whole word.

b. (Touch the ball for **heave.**) Read the underlined part. Get ready. (Tap the ball.) eee.

• Read the whole word. (Pause.) Get ready. (Slash.) Heave.

c. (Repeat step b until firm.)

d. (Repeat steps b and c for each remaining word in the column.)

e. (Repeat the column until children read all the words in order without making a mistake.)

heave

steal

falling

where

there

spider

mean

EXERCISE 3

Words with underlined parts

a. First you're going to read the underlined part of each word in this column. Then you're going to read the whole word.

b. (Touch the ball for **patted.**) Read the underlined part. Get ready. (Tap the ball.) *Patt.*

• Read the whole word. (Pause.) Get ready. (Slash.) *Patted.*

c. (Repeat step *b* until firm.)

d. (Repeat steps *b* and *c* for each remaining word in the column.)

e. (Repeat the column until children read all the words in order without making a mistake.)

patted

vows

showed

forget

yourself

masters

wanted

EXERCISE 4

Children spell, then read

a. First you're going to spell each word. Then you're going to read that word the fast way.

b. (Touch the ball for **class.**) Spell it. Get ready. (Tap under each letter as the children say:) *C-L-A-S-S.*

• (Return to the ball.) Read it. Get ready. (Slash.) *Class.*

c. (Repeat step *b* for each remaining word in the column.)

d. (Repeat steps *b* and *c* until firm.)

class

care

ready

bite

biting

wiped

life

Individual test

a. (Call on individual children to read one column of words from the lesson.)

b. (Praise children who read all words with no errors.)

The alligator tried to get a hold on the thorn with his teeth, but he could not. He said, "I am sorry, king lion, but I cannot get that thorn out of your paw."

The other animals tried, but none of them could get the thorn out. Then, after the other animals left, that big king lion started to cry. He said, "Ow. My paw is sore, and nobody can help me. Nobody can get that thorn out." [10]

The little mouse came up to the lion and said, "I can get that thorn out. I am little. I have little paws, so I can get a hold on that thorn." [11] And he did. He grabbed the thorn and gave it a jerk. And the thorn came out. [12]

The lion began to cry. "It feels good to get the thorn out," he said. "Little mouse, you are my best friend." [13]

So if you go to the jungle and you see a little mouse, be good to that little mouse, because he has a friend. His friend is the king of all the animals in the jungle.

This is the end.

[10] Did the other animals try to help? **(Signal.)** *Yes.*
• Could they help? **(Signal.)** *No.*
[11] Who is talking? **(Signal.)** *The mouse.*
• Why can he help? **(Signal.)**
He has little paws.
• Do you think that little mouse can help that huge lion? **(The children respond.)**
• Let's read and find out.
[12] How did the mouse get that thorn out? **(The children respond.)**
[13] Who is the lion's best friend? **(Signal.)**
The little mouse.

EXERCISE 6

Picture comprehension

a. Look at the picture.
b. (Ask these questions:)
  1. What is the mouse doing? **(Signal.)**
     Pulling the thorn from the lion's paw.
  2. Is the mouse working hard? **(Signal.)** *Yes.*
  • How do you know? **(The children respond.)**
  3. What is the lion doing? **(Signal.)** *Crying.*
  • Why is he crying? **(The children respond.)**
  4. Why does he have that crown on his head? **(Signal.)** *Because he is the king.*

EXERCISE 7

Summary of independent activities

a. (Pass out Worksheet 141 to each child.)
b. Everybody, now you'll do your worksheet. Remember to do all parts of the worksheet and to read all the parts carefully.

END OF LESSON 141

STORY 125
EXERCISE 5

Reading—decoding

a. (Pass out Storybook 2.)

b. Everybody, open your reader to page 119.

c. Remember, if the group reads all the way to the red 5 without making more than five errors, we can go on.

d. Everybody, touch the title of the story. ✔

e. If you hear a mistake, raise your hand. Remember, children who do not have their place lose their turn. (Call on individual children to read two or three sentences. Do not ask comprehension questions. Tally all errors.)

To Correct
word-identification errors (**from,** for example)
1. That word is **from.** What word? *From.*
2. Go back to the beginning of the sentence and read the sentence again.

f. (If the children make more than five errors before they reach the red 5: when they reach the 5 return to the beginning of the story and have the children reread to the 5. Do not ask comprehension questions. Repeat step *f* until firm, and then go on to step *g.*)

g. (When the children read to the red 5 without making more than five errors: read the story to the children from the beginning to the 5. Ask the specified comprehension questions. When you reach the 5, call on individual children to continue reading the story. Have each child read two or three sentences. Ask the specified comprehension questions.)

Will Carla Take the Genie Vow?[1]

The day had come for everyone in school to take a vow to be a genie. The old genie came to class that day. She had a ring for every new genie.[2]

Before she gave out the rings, she stood in front of the class and said, "Today is your last day in this school. You have worked hard and now you are ready to leave. You are ready to take your place as a genie. But before you take your vow, remember this. It is not easy to be a genie. You must forget about the things that you want to do.[3] You must think about your master. You must do only what your master wants you to do. Not all of you will have good masters. But once you take the genie vow, you must do what genies have done for ★ thousands and thousands of years. ⑤ You must obey your master at all times.[4] You must forget about yourself."

The old genie looked at Carla. Carla looked down. Then she began to cry. She felt very bad. She liked the genie school, but she didn't want to spend the rest of her life in a bottle.[5] She didn't want to forget about herself and do what her master wanted her to do.[6] She said, "I can't do it. I can't take the vow of a genie."

All of the children looked at her.[7] The old genie patted her on the back. Then the old genie said, "We don't want you to take

---

[1] What's the title? (Signal.) *Will Carla take the genie vow?*

• And what do you think she'll do? (The children respond.) Let's read and find out.

[2] What do they get when they graduate? (Signal.) *A ring.*

[3] Everybody, say that. (Signal.) *You must forget about the things that you want to do.*

[4] What do genies have to do? (The children respond.) Yes, genies must obey their masters at all times.

[5] Was Carla happy about living in a bottle? (Signal.) *No.*

• Would you want to do that? (The children respond.)

[6] Did she want to stop thinking about herself? (Signal.) *No.*

• Would you? (The children respond.)

[7] Why did they do that? (The children respond.) Yes, she didn't want to take the genie vow.

STORYBOOK

Reading—decoding

a. (Pass out Storybook 2.)

b. Everybody, open your reader to page 172.

c. Remember, if the group reads all the way to the red 5 without making more than five errors, we can go on.

d. Everybody, touch the title of the story. ✔

e. If you hear a mistake, raise your hand. Remember, children who do not have their place lose their turn. (Call on individual children to read two or three sentences. Do not ask comprehension questions. Tally all errors.)

To Correct

word-identification errors (**from,** for example)
1. That word is **from.** What word? *From.*
2. Go back to the beginning of the sentence and read the sentence again.

f. (If the children make more than five errors before they reach the red 5: when they reach the 5 return to the beginning of the story and have the children reread to the 5. Do not ask comprehension questions. Repeat step *f* until firm, and then go on to step *g.*)

g. (When the children read to the red 5 without making more than five errors: read the story to the children from the beginning to the 5. Ask the specified comprehension questions. When you reach the 5, call on individual children to continue reading the story. Have each child read two or three sentences. Ask the specified comprehension questions.)

The Lion and the Mouse[1]

There once was a lion who lived in the jungle. The lion was the king of all the animals in the jungle. He was big, and he was mean.[2] If he said, "Get out of my way," the other animals got out of his way. If he said, "Come here," the other animals came to the lion.

One day a little mouse came up to the lion. The mouse said, "I want to be your friend.[3] I am just a little mouse, but I will be a good friend."

The lion laughed. "Ha, ha," he said. "What do I need with a little friend like you?[4] What can you do for me? I am the strongest animal in the jungle. I am the best hunter. I am king of all the animals."[5]

The little mouse said, "But I will be a good friend." ⑤

The lion laughed so hard that the mouse fell down. Then the lion said, "Go away, you silly little mouse." So the mouse went away. He had a tear in his eye.[6] He wanted to be friends with the lion.

Then one day the lion got a big thorn in his paw. He roared with pain.[7] "Roooaaar." He called the other animals. He said, "Get that thorn out of my paw."[8]

The elephant tried, but he could not get a good hold on the thorn. He said, "I am sorry, king lion, but I cannot get that thorn out of your paw."[9]

---

[1] Who is this story going to be about? (Signal.) *The lion and the mouse.*

[2] Who was the king of all the animals in the jungle? (Signal.) *The lion.*

• What was he like? (Signal.) *Big and mean.*

[3] What did the mouse want? (Signal.) *To be the lion's friend.*

[4] Everybody, what question did the lion ask? (Signal.) *What do I need with a little friend like you?*

[5] Who is the strongest animal in the jungle? (Signal.) *The lion.*

• Who is the best hunter? (Signal.) *The lion.*

• That's why he doesn't think he needs the mouse for a friend.

[6] Who had a tear in his eye? (Signal.) *The mouse.*

• Why was he crying? (The children respond.)

[7] Why is the lion roaring with pain? (Signal.) *He got a big thorn in his paw.*

[8] What did he want the other animals to do? (Signal.) *Get the thorn out of his paw.*

[9] Who is speaking? (Signal.) *The elephant.*

• Could he help? (Signal.) *No.*

the vow. You are a human, and you should spend life as a human spends life. I once told you that you would not like genie school."

"But I did like it," Carla said. "I just can't take that vow."

"Carla," the old genie said, "we are very glad that you came to our school. You showed us a lot about humans.[8] We won't feel bad if you don't take the vow. This vow is for genies, not for humans."

Carla wiped her eyes. All of the children smiled. Carla could see that they were not mad at her. She felt better now.[9]

Stop

---

[8] What did the genies learn from Carla? (Signal.) *A lot about humans.*

[9] Why did she feel better? (The children respond.)

• Do you think Carla will ever see Ott again? (The children respond.) We'll finish this story next time.

EXERCISE 6

Picture comprehension

a. Look at the picture.

b. (Ask these questions:)
  1. What is Carla doing? (Signal.) *Crying.*
  2. Why is she crying? (The children respond.)
  3. What is the old genie saying to her? (The children respond.)
  4. Does that little genie look sad? (The children respond.)
  • What is he doing? (The children respond.)

DEDUCTIONS

The children will need pencils.

EXERCISE 7

Written deductions

a. (Pass out Worksheet 125 to each child.)

b. (Hold up side 2 of your worksheet and touch the sentence, "Every car has doors," in the deductions exercise.)

c. Everybody, touch this sentence on your worksheet. ✔

d. I'm going to call on individual children to read a sentence. Everybody, follow along.
  1. (Call on a child.) Read the sentence in the box. *Every car has doors.*
  • Everybody, what do you know about every car? (Signal.) *It has doors.* Yes, it has doors.
  2. (Call on a child.) Read the sentence next to the box. *Sid has a car.*
  • Everybody, what do you know about Sid? (Signal.) *He has a car.*
  • And what do you know about every car? (Signal.) *It has doors.*
  3. (Call on a child.) Read the sentence under the box. *What does Sid's car have?*
  • Everybody, listen. Every car has doors. Sid has a car. So, what does Sid's car have? (Signal.) *Doors.* Yes, Sid's car has doors.

e. Let's do that problem again. (Repeat the sentence reading and questions in step *d*.)

f. Everybody, write the answer in the blank. ✔

INDEPENDENT ACTIVITIES

EXERCISE 8

Summary of independent activities

Everybody, now you'll do your worksheet. Remember to do all parts of the worksheet and to read all the parts carefully.

INDIVIDUAL CHECKOUT

EXERCISE 9

2-minute individual fluency checkout: rate/accuracy

a. As you are doing your worksheet, I'll call on children one at a time to read to the star. Remember, you get two stars on the chart if you read to the star in less than two minutes and make no more than five errors.

b. (Call on each child. Tell the child:) Read to the star very carefully. Start with the title. Go. (Time the child. Tell the child any words the child misses. Stop the child as soon as the child makes the sixth error or exceeds the time limit.)

c. (If the child meets the rate-accuracy criterion, record two stars on your chart for lesson 125. Congratulate the child. Give children who do not earn two stars a chance to read to the star again before the next lesson is presented.)

149 words/**2 min** = 75 wpm **[5 errors]**

END OF LESSON 125

EXERCISE 3

Read the fast way

a. You're going to read all the words in this column the fast way.

b. (Touch the ball for **elephant**. Pause.) Get ready. (Slash.) *Elephant.*

c. (Repeat step *b* until firm.)

d. (Repeat steps *b* and *c* for each remaining word in the column.)

e. (Repeat the column until the children read all the words in order without making mistakes.)

elephant

started

cheer

tried

silly

eye

we've

EXERCISE 4

Children spell, then read

a. First you're going to spell each word. Then you're going to read that word the fast way.

b. (Touch the ball for **sore**.) Spell it. Get ready. (Tap under each letter as the children say:) *S-O-R-E.*

• (Return to the ball.) Read it. Get ready. (Slash.) *Sore.*

c. (Repeat step *b* for each remaining word in the column.)

d. (Repeat steps *b* and *c* until firm.)

sore

pain

Lion

sorry

pull

roared

finish

Individual test

a. (Call on individual children to read one column of words from the lesson.)

b. (Praise children who read all words with no errors.)

READING VOCABULARY

EXERCISE 1

Teacher reads the words in red

a. I'll read each word in red. Then you'll spell each word.

b. (Touch the ball for **phone.**) My turn. (Slash as you say:) Phone. What word? (Signal.) *Phone.*

c. (Return to the ball.) Spell it. Get ready. (Tap under each letter as the children say:) *P-H-O-N-E.*

• What word did you spell? (Signal.) *Phone.*

d. (Repeat steps *b* and *c* for each word in red.)

e. Your turn to read all the words in this column.

f. (Touch the ball for **phone.** Pause.) Get ready. (Slash.) *Phone.*

g. (Repeat step *f* for each remaining word in the column.)

h. (Repeat steps *f* and *g* until firm.)

phone

trained

Japan

Alaska

China

move

hair

EXERCISE 2

Words with underlined parts

a. First you're going to read the underlined part of each word in this column. Then you're going to read the whole word.

b. (Touch the ball for **passed.**) Read the underlined part. Get ready. (Tap the ball.) *Pass.*

• Read the whole word. (Pause.) Get ready. (Slash.) *Passed.*

c. (Repeat step *b* until firm.)

d. (Repeat steps *b* and *c* for each remaining word in the column.)

e. (Repeat the column until children read all the words in order without making a mistake.)

passed

belong

hardest

biggest

short

taped

tapped

READING VOCABULARY

EXERCISE 1

Teacher reads the words in red

a. I'll read each word in red. Then you'll spell each word.

b. (Touch the ball for **spider**.) My turn. (Slash as you say:) Spider. What word? (Signal.) *Spider.*

c. (Return to the ball.) Spell it. Get ready. (Tap under each letter as the children say:) S-P-I-D-E-R.

• What word did you spell? (Signal.) *Spider.*

d. (Repeat steps *b* and *c* for each word in red.)

e. Your turn to read all the words in this column.

f. (Touch the ball for **spider**. Pause.) Get ready. (Slash.) *Spider.*

g. (Repeat step *f* for each remaining word in the column.)

h. (Repeat steps *f* and *g* until firm.)

spider

jerk

jungle

bushes

paw

torn

thorn

EXERCISE 2

Words with underlined parts

a. First you're going to read the underlined part of each word in this column. Then you're going to read the whole word.

b. (Touch the ball for **hunter**.) Read the underlined part. Get ready. (Tap the ball.) *Hunt.*

• Read the whole word. (Pause.) Get ready. (Slash.) *Hunter.*

c. (Repeat step *b* until firm.)

d. (Repeat steps *b* and *c* for each remaining word in the column.)

e. (Repeat the column until children read all the words in order without making a mistake.)

hunter

something

anything

everything

anyhow

strongest

animals

EXERCISE 3

Read the fast way

a. You're going to read all the words in this column the fast way.

b. (Touch the ball for **place.** Pause.) Get ready. (Slash.) *Place.*

c. (Repeat step *b* until firm.)

d. (Repeat steps *b* and *c* for each remaining word in the column.)

e. (Repeat the column until the children read all the words in order without making mistakes.)

place

Wait

only

clapped

folded

rush

taken

EXERCISE 4

Words with underlined parts

a. First you're going to read the underlined part of each word in this column. Then you're going to read the whole word.

b. (Touch the ball for **couldn't.**) Read the underlined part. Get ready. (Tap the ball.) *Could.*

• Read the whole word. (Pause.) Get ready. (Slash.) *Couldn't.*

c. (Repeat step *b* until firm.)

d. (Repeat steps *b* and *c* for each remaining word in the column.)

e. (Repeat the column until children read all the words in order without making a mistake.)

couldn't

didn't

it's

we're

you've

he's

they've

Look Ahead

In-Program Tests
Fluency Checkouts: Rate/Accuracy

Lessons 145, 150, 155, 160

- By lesson 150, children should be reading at least 90 words per minute with 97 percent accuracy. Provide extra practice on Fluency Checkouts for those who are not at this level of mastery.

Lesson Number	Error Limit	Number of words read	Number of minutes	Words per minute
145	5	160	2	80
150	5	181	2	90
155	5	179	2	90
160	5	184	2	92

Consolidation

- The last twenty lessons of the program consolidate the skills taught and prepare children for reading in content areas, as well as later reading instruction. Children should be firm on all sounds, at applying rules for long and short vowel words, and comprehending a range of reading materials.

Reading Activities

Help children develop decoding and comprehension skills by using the following activities.

Rhyming Words (Lessons 141–160)
Choose two words with a specific word part that appears often in a lesson story. Identify the word part in each word and have children develop a list of rhyming words from that word part. An example from Lesson 146 is shown below.

-ump: crump, dump, slump, jump, pump, stump, bump, lump, hump, clump, grump, trump, plump
-eep: steep, sheep, creep, peep, keep, deep, weep, beep, sleep

Rule Review (Lessons 146–160)
Write the sixteen rules from the Peevish Pets story series on index cards with the first half of the rule on one card and the second half on another card. (See page 66 in the Teacher's Guide for a list of the rules.) An example of the first rule is shown below.

All little crumps   are mean.

New cards are presented as children learn rules from Lessons 146 to 160. After completing all the stories, mix up the cards and have children sort them.

Reading Rules (Lesson 160)
After completing Lesson 160, make up rules from the patterns found in the Peevish Pets story series. Have children read each rule and answer the deduction. Some example activities are shown below.

1. Rule: All mean girls live in the land of Bump.
   Sue is a nice girl.
   Pat is a mean girl.
   Lou is a neat girl.
   Gail is a mean girl.
   Which girls live in the land of Bump?

2. Rule: All wizards are on a dusty path.
   Don is a winner.
   Pete is a wizard.
   Joe is not a wizard.
   John is a wizard.
   Which people are on a dusty path?

EXERCISE 5

Children spell, then read

a. First you're going to spell each word. Then you're going to read that word the fast way.

b. (Touch the ball for **fine.**) Spell it. Get ready. (Tap under each letter as the children say:) *F-I-N-E.*

• (Return to the ball.) Read it. Get ready. (Slash.) *Fine.*

c. (Repeat step *b* for each remaining word in the column.)

d. (Repeat steps *b* and *c* until firm.)

fine

van

vane

biting

paper

there

where

Individual test

a. (Call on individual children to read one column of words from the lesson.)

b. (Praise children who read all words with no errors.)

STORYBOOK

STORY 126
EXERCISE 6

Reading—decoding

a. (Pass out Storybook 2.)

b. Everybody, open your reader to page 122.

c. Remember, if the group reads all the way to the red 5 without making more than five errors, we can go on.

d. Everybody, touch the title of the story. ✔

e. If you hear a mistake, raise your hand. Remember, children who do not have their place lose their turn. (Call on individual children to read two or three sentences. Do not ask comprehension questions. Tally all errors.)

To Correct

word-identification errors (**from,** for example)
1. That word is **from.** What word? *From.*
2. Go back to the beginning of the sentence and read the sentence again.

f. (If the children make more than five errors before they reach the red 5: when they reach the 5 return to the beginning of the story and have the children reread to the 5. Do not ask comprehension questions. Repeat step *f* until firm, and then go on to step *g.*)

g. (When the children read to the red 5 without making more than five errors: read the story to the children from the beginning to the 5. Ask the specified comprehension questions. When you reach the 5, call on individual children to continue reading the story. Have each child read two or three sentences. Ask the specified comprehension questions.)

Making Progress

	Since Lesson 1	Since Lesson 121
Word Reading	Sounds and sound combinations 971 regular words 215 irregular words Reading high frequency hard words Discriminating long and short vowel words using final -e rule	155 regular words 52 irregular words
Comprehension	**Picture Comprehension** Predicting what the picture will show Answering questions about the picture Answering written questions about specific pictures Completing picture deduction activities **Story Comprehension** Answering who, what, when, where, and why questions orally Making predictions about the story Answering questions about the story and other short passages in writing Answering review questions about stories previously read Reading and answering questions on factual information passages	Reading and answering questions on factual information passages

What to Use

Teacher	Students
Presentation Book C (pages 155–235) **Teacher's Guide** (pages 75–76, 80–81) **Answer Key** **Spelling Presentation Book**	**Storybook 2** (pages 172–238) **Workbook C** **Lined paper**

What's Ahead in Lessons 141–160

New Skills

- The last sixteen lessons consolidate skills learned and incorporate "rules" that the children need to remember and apply.

New Vocabulary

- *Regular words:*
  - (141) hunter, jungle, lion, pain, spider, strongest, thorn, torn
  - (142) bees, body, Casey, chair, chill, hens, insect, kill, salad
  - (143) leaning, nearly, raft, screaming, sea, sinking, whenever
  - (144) band, boomed, crackers, die, saves, shares, sniffed, speak, sucked, waving
  - (145) clothes, crown, dressed, forgot, grasshopper, later, peevish, slept, tramp's
  - (146) crump, deepest, Jean, matter, rule
  - (147) brown, sixteen, sneaking, swinging
  - (148) popped
  - (149) hadn't, hasn't, mammal, paths, remembering, rocky, tickled
  - (150) chop, grape, longest, sleepy, tallest, tries, using, vine
  - (151) eaten, filed, rules, soft, striped
  - (152) handle, muddy, red, rid
  - (153) dear, hated, stripes
  - (154) babies, trapper, wish
  - (155) angry, monkey, rather
  - (156) easiest, whale, winter
  - (157) spring, wheels
  - (158) Everest, loop, she'll, stared, taper, tapper, town
  - (159) breathe, darn, letter, squeak
  - (160) here's, licked, licking, puppy, tail, timer

- *Irregular Words:*
  - (141) animals, bushes, eye, jerk, paw, pull
  - (143) America, fourth, gone
  - (144) faced, prince, threw, thumb
  - (145) shirt, shoe, wizard
  - (146) dance, shoes, space, tonight
  - (148) dancing, forward, page
  - (149) banana
  - (150) wooden
  - (151) bananas, third
  - (152) disappeared, wonder
  - (153) eight, four
  - (155) blew, metal, warm
  - (156) anywhere, figure, they'll
  - (157) idea, mind, quick, quiet, steer, warmer
  - (158) barge, brag, large, quietly, sleek, steering, U.S.
  - (159) bay, contest, dock, finally, morning, quickly, woof
  - (160) arrows, darted, hey, motor, nap, push

Carla and Ott Are Teachers[1]

Carla had worked hard at the genie school. But she couldn't take the vow that the other genies took. She clapped as each new genie got a ring. And she clapped the hardest for Ott.[2] He was the last genie to get a ring.

Then the old genie said, "Here are your jobs. She handed each genie a folded paper. The paper told where the genie would work as a genie.[3] One genie was sent to Alaska.[4] One genie went to China.[5] One genie went to Japan.[6] And one genie went to stay in a yellow bottle that belonged to a girl named Carla.[7]

The genie who got that job was named Ott. Ott was a genie now. He could do all the genie tricks. He had passed all the tests.[8] And he had taken his vow to do what his master wants him to do.⑤

Just when Ott was reading his note, the teacher ran into the room. He told the old genie, "Five new bottles have been found. We're going to need more genies, but how are we going to train them?[9] I am the only teacher, and I will have to go to a bottle now."

Carla said, "Wait. Ott and I can train the new genies.[10] The school would have two teachers. That means the school could train more genies than it could with one teacher."

The old genie said, "That is a fine plan."

The teacher said, "Yes, that plan is good."

That's what happened.

Now lots of new genies are being trained. And the boys and girls in genie school have good teachers. Ott is a good teacher, because he remembers how hard it was for him to pick up new tricks.[11] Carla is a good teacher because she is very smart.[12]

And Ott and Carla are very, very happy.

And this is the end of the story.

1 What's the title of this story? (Signal.) *Carla and Ott are teachers.*
2 What did she do? (Signal.) *Clapped the hardest for Ott.*
• Why did she do that? (The children respond.)
3 What did the paper tell? (Signal.) *Where the genie would work as a genie.*
4 Where did one genie go? (Signal.) *To Alaska.*
5 Where was that genie sent? (Signal.) *To China.*
6 Where did he go? (Signal.) *To Japan.*
7 Who do you suppose that was? (Signal.) *Ott.*
8 So what do we know he can do? (Signal.) *Genie tricks.*
9 Why do they need more genies? (Signal.) *Because five new bottles have been found.*
• What will they have to do to the new genies? (Signal.) *Train them.* Yes, train and teach them to be genies.
10 What did she say? (Signal.) *Ott and I can train the new genies.*
11 Why is Ott a good teacher? (The children respond.)
12 Why is Carla a good teacher? (Signal.) *Because she is very smart.*

And he did. He went past the rabbit. He was getting closer and closer to the big rock.[10] A bunch of animals were waiting by the rock. When they saw the turtle coming up the side of the hill, they started to shout, "Come on, turtle. You can do it."

They yelled louder and louder as the turtle got closer and closer to the big rock. When the turtle was only a few feet from the rock, they were yelling so loud that they woke up the rabbit.

"What's this?" she said.[11] She looked around and saw the turtle near the rock. When that rabbit saw what was happening, she began to run so fast that you couldn't see her. She went so fast that the grass bent over, and the dust cloud was so thick that you couldn't see the sun.[12] She ran so fast that the other animals just looked at her with big eyes.

But she didn't win the race. The turtle stepped past the big rock just before the rabbit shot by in a cloud of dust.[13]

Now all of the animals are happy because the rabbit doesn't tell everybody how fast she is. And the rabbit is a little smarter than she was. She knows that it takes more than speed to win a race. You have to keep trying.[14]

The end

---

10 Was the turtle winning the race? (Signal.) *Yes.*
• It looks that way. What's the rabbit doing? (Signal.) *Sleeping.*
11 What woke the rabbit up? (The children respond.) Yes, the other animals were yelling so loudly.
12 What did the rabbit do after she woke up? (The children respond.)
• She sure went fast. Do you think she'll win? (The children respond.)
• Let's finish the story and find out.
13 Who won? (Signal.) *The turtle.* Did the rabbit almost win? (Signal.) *Yes.*
14 Why is the rabbit a little smarter than she was? (The children respond.)

EXERCISE 6

Picture comprehension

a. Look at the picture.
b. (Ask these questions:)
   1. What is the turtle doing? (The children respond.)
   2. Did he win the race? (Signal.) *Yes.*
   • How do you know? (The children respond.) Yes, he passed the big rock and the finish sign.
   3. What is the rabbit doing? (The children respond.)
   • Why is she running so fast? (The children respond.)
   4. What are the other animals doing? (The children respond.)

WORKSHEET 140

INDEPENDENT ACTIVITIES
EXERCISE 7

Summary of independent activities

a. (Pass out Worksheet 140 to each child.)
b. Everybody, now you'll do your worksheet. Remember to do all parts of the worksheet and to read all the parts carefully.

INDIVIDUAL CHECKOUT
EXERCISE 8

2-minute individual fluency checkout: rate/accuracy

a. As you are doing your worksheet, I'll call on children one at a time to read to the star. Remember, you get two stars on the chart if you read to the star in less than two minutes and make no more than five errors.
b. (Call on each child. Tell the child:) Read to the star very carefully. Start with the title. Go. (Time the child. Tell the child any words the child misses. Stop the child as soon as the child makes the sixth error or exceeds the time limit.)
c. (If the child meets the rate-accuracy criterion, record two stars on your chart for lesson 140. Congratulate the child. Give children who do not earn two stars a chance to read to the star again before the next lesson is presented.)
160 words/**2 min** = 80 wpm **[5 errors]**

END OF LESSON 140

EXERCISE 7

Picture comprehension

a. Look at the picture.

b. (Ask these questions:)

1. Touch the ring in the old genie's hand. (The children respond.)
2. What is Carla doing? (Signal.) *Clapping.*
3. Does she look as if she's clapping hard? (Signal.) *Yes.*
4. What do you think Ott is thinking? (The children respond.)
5. Did you like this story about Carla and Ott? **(The children respond.)**

EXERCISE 8

Summary of independent activities

a. (Pass out Worksheet 126 to each child.)

b. Everybody, now you'll do your worksheet. Remember to do all parts of the worksheet and to read all the parts carefully.

END OF LESSON 126

STORYBOOK

STORY 140
EXERCISE 5

Reading—decoding

a. (Pass out Storybook 2.)

b. Everybody, open your reader to page 168.

c. Remember, if the group reads all the way to the red 5 without making more than five errors, we can go on.

d. Everybody, touch the title of the story. ✔

e. If you hear a mistake, raise your hand. Remember, children who do not have their place lose their turn. (Call on individual children to read two or three sentences. Do not ask comprehension questions. Tally all errors.)

To Correct

word-identification errors (**from**, for example)
1. That word is **from**. What word? *From.*
2. Go back to the beginning of the sentence and read the sentence again.

f. (If the children make more than five errors before they reach the red 5: when they reach the 5 return to the beginning of the story and have the children reread to the 5. Do not ask comprehension questions. Repeat step *f* until firm, and then go on to step *g.*)

g. (When the children read to the red 5 without making more than five errors: read the story to the children from the beginning to the 5. Ask the specified comprehension questions. When you reach the 5, call on individual children to continue reading the story. Have each child read two or three sentences. Ask the specified comprehension questions.)

2

The Rabbit and the Turtle[1]

All of the other animals wanted to see the turtle beat the rabbit in a race. The rabbit had told everybody that she would stop telling how fast she was if the turtle beat her.[2] But the rabbit seemed far too fast for the turtle. The rabbit went flying over the path and over the stream. Soon she was at the hill. She stopped to look back. All she could see was a cloud of dust. "Ho, ho," she said. "That turtle must be a mile behind me. He cannot win this race."[3]

So the rabbit sat down under a tree.[4] She closed her eyes and leaned back.[5] And the first thing you know she was sound asleep.[6]

The turtle didn't stop when the rabbit got far ahead of him. The turtle kept going as fast as he could go. He just kept going and going ⑤[7] He said to himself, "I'll just keep on going, ★ and I'll beat that rabbit."[8]

After a while, the turtle came to the stream. He crossed the stream and started up the hill. He could see the big rock on the other side of the woods.[9] And he could see the rabbit. The rabbit was still sleeping under the tree.

The turtle said to himself, "I'll just keep on going."

---

[1] Which animals are in the race? (Signal.) *The rabbit and the turtle.*

[2] Why did the other animals want the turtle to win? (The children respond.)

[3] Who is talking? (Signal.) *The rabbit.*

• Why did she say that the turtle could not win? (The children respond.) Yes, the turtle must be a mile behind.

[4] Why did she do that? (The children respond.)

[5] Then what did she do? (Signal.) *Closed her eyes and leaned back.*

• What do you think she'll do next? (The children respond.)

• Let's read and find out.

[6] What did the rabbit do next? (The children respond.) Yes, she fell asleep.

[7] What did the turtle do when the rabbit got far ahead of him? (Signal.) *Kept going and going.*

[8] Everybody, what did he say? (Signal.) *I'll just keep on going and I'll beat that rabbit.*

[9] What's going to happen when he reaches the big rock? (The children respond.) Yes, he'll win the race.

READING VOCABULARY

EXERCISE 1

Teacher reads the words in red

a. I'll read each word in red. Then you'll spell each word.

b. (Touch the ball for **east.**) My turn. (Slash as you say:) East. What word? (Signal.) *East.*

c. (Return to the ball.) Spell it. Get ready. (Tap under each letter as the children say:) *E-A-S-T.*
  • What word did you spell? (Signal.) *East.*

d. (Repeat steps *b* and *c* for each word in red.)

e. Your turn to read all the words in this column.

f. (Touch the ball for **east.** Pause.) Get ready. (Slash.) *East.*

g. (Repeat step *f* for each remaining word in the column.)

h. (Repeat steps *f* and *g* until firm.)

east

minute

clock

rang

life

over

too

EXERCISE 2

Words with underlined parts

a. First you're going to read the underlined part of each word in this column. Then you're going to read the whole word.

b. (Touch the ball for **understand.**) Read the underlined part. Get ready. (Tap the ball.) *Stand.*
  • Read the whole word. (Pause.) Get ready. (Slash.) *Understand.*

c. (Repeat step *b* until firm.)

d. (Repeat steps *b* and *c* for each remaining word in the column.)

e. (Repeat the column until children read all the words in order without making a mistake.)

understand

doesn't

biggest

rushed

turns

spelled

blowing

EXERCISE 3

Words with underlined parts

a. First you're going to read the underlined part of each word in this column. Then you're going to read the whole word.

b. (Touch the ball for **loudly**.) Read the underlined part. Get ready. (Tap the ball.) *Loud.*

• Read the whole word. (Pause.) Get ready. (Slash.) *Loudly.*

c. (Repeat step *b* until firm.)

d. (Repeat steps *b* and *c* for each remaining word in the column.)

e. (Repeat the column until children read all the words in order without making a mistake.)

loudly

everybody

anybody

wanted

flying

smarter

waiting

EXERCISE 4

Words with underlined parts

a. First you're going to read the underlined part of each word in this column. Then you're going to read the whole word.

b. (Touch the ball for **robed**.) Read the underlined part. Get ready. (Tap the ball.) *Robe.*

• Read the whole word. (Pause.) Get ready. (Slash.) *Robed.*

c. (Repeat step *b* until firm.)

d. (Repeat steps *b* and *c* for each remaining word in the column.)

e. (Repeat the column until children read all the words in order without making a mistake.)

robed

asleep

ahead

robbed

crossed

happening

closer

Individual test

a. (Call on individual children to read one column of words from the lesson.)

b. (Praise children who read all words with no errors.)

EXERCISE 3

Read the fast way

a. You're going to read all the words in this column the fast way.

b. (Touch the ball for **phone.** Pause.) Get ready. (Slash.) *Phone.*

c. (Repeat step *b* until firm.)

d. (Repeat steps *b* and *c* for each remaining word in the column.)

e. (Repeat the column until the children read all the words in order without making mistakes.)

phone

hair

stuff

west

right

mate

These

EXERCISE 4

Words with underlined parts

a. First you're going to read the underlined part of each word in this column. Then you're going to read the whole word.

b. (Touch the ball for **packing.**) Read the underlined part. Get ready. (Tap the ball.) *Pack.*

• Read the whole word. (Pause.) Get ready. (Slash.) *Packing.*

c. (Repeat step *b* until firm.)

d. (Repeat steps *b* and *c* for each remaining word in the column.)

e. (Repeat the column until children read all the words in order without making a mistake.)

packing

trained

snapped

clapped

bringing

parting

treat

READING VOCABULARY

EXERCISE 1

Teacher reads the words in red

a. I'll read each word in red. Then you'll spell each word.

b. (Touch the ball for **Finish.**) My turn. (Slash as you say:) Finish. What word? (Signal.) *Finish.*

c. (Return to the ball.) Spell it. Get ready. (Tap under each letter as the children say:) *F-I-N-I-S-H.*
   • What word did you spell? (Signal.) *Finish.*

d. (Repeat steps *b* and *c* for each word in red.)

e. Your turn to read all the words in this column.

f. (Touch the ball for **Finish.** Pause.) Get ready. (Slash.) *Finish.*

g. (Repeat step *f* for each remaining word in the column.)

h. (Repeat steps *f* and *g* until firm.)

Finish

thick

pull

knew

behind

used

Mr.

EXERCISE 2

Words with underlined parts

a. First you're going to read the underlined part of each word in this column. Then you're going to read the whole word.

b. (Touch the ball for **leaned.**) Read the underlined part. Get ready. (Tap the ball.) *eee.*
   • Read the whole word. (Pause.) Get ready. (Slash.) *Leaned.*

c. (Repeat step *b* until firm.)

d. (Repeat steps *b* and *c* for each remaining word in the column.)

e. (Repeat the column until children read all the words in order without making a mistake.)

leaned

shout

there

where

while

sound

speed

EXERCISE 5

Children spell, then read

a. First you're going to spell each word. Then you're going to read that word the fast way.

b. (Touch the ball for **van.**) Spell it. Get ready. (Tap under each letter as the children say:) *V-A-N.*

• (Return to the ball.) Read it. Get ready. (Slash.) *Van.*

c. (Repeat step *b* for each remaining word in the column.)

d. (Repeat steps *b* and *c* until firm.)

van →

vanned →

vane →

vaned →

move →

hung →

carry →

Individual test

a. (Call on individual children to read one column of words from the lesson.)

b. (Praise children who read all words with no errors.)

STORYBOOK

STORY 127
EXERCISE 6

Reading—decoding

a. (Pass out Storybook 2.)

b. Everybody, open your reader to page 125.

c. Remember, if the group reads all the way to the red 5 without making more than five errors, we can go on.

d. Everybody, touch the title of the story. ✔

e. If you hear a mistake, raise your hand. Remember, children who do not have their place lose their turn. (Call on individual children to read two or three sentences. Do not ask comprehension questions. Tally all errors.)

To Correct

word-identification errors (**from,** for example)
1. That word is **from.** What word? *From.*
2. Go back to the beginning of the sentence and read the sentence again.

f. (If the children make more than five errors before they reach the red 5: when they reach the 5 return to the beginning of the story and have the children reread to the 5. Do not ask comprehension questions. Repeat step *f* until firm, and then go on to step *g*.)

g. (When the children read to the red 5 without making more than five errors: read the story to the children from the beginning to the 5. Ask the specified comprehension questions. When you reach the 5, call on individual children to continue reading the story. Have each child read two or three sentences. Ask the specified comprehension questions.)

"This will be fun," the rabbit said. "This will be an easy race for me to win."

So the animals got ready for the race. The rabbit and the turtle would have a long, long race from one side of the woods to the other.[7] They would race over the path and across the stream and over the hill. The first animal to reach the big rock on the other side of the woods would win the race.

The rabbit and the turtle lined up. Then the owl said, "Go."[8] The rabbit went down the path like a shot. She made so much dust that the turtle couldn't see. The ant and the other animals said, "It looks like the rabbit will win this race."[9]

More to come[10]

[7] Would it be a short race? (Signal.) *No.*
• Would it be a long, long race? (Signal.) *Yes.*
[8] Why did the owl say that? (The children respond.) Yes, to start the race.
[9] Everybody, what did they say? (Signal.) *It looks like the rabbit will win this race.*
• Why did they say that? (The children respond.)
[10] We'll finish the story next time. Who do you think will win? (The children respond.)

EXERCISE 6

Picture comprehension

a. Look at the picture.
b. (Ask these questions:)

1. The owl is holding a flag and a watch. Point to the owl. ✔
• Why do you think the owl has a watch? (The children respond.)
2. What do you think the owl is saying? (The children respond.) Yes, the owl could be saying, "Ready, set, go."
3. Does that rabbit look like she's going fast? (Signal.) *Yes.*
• How do you know? (The children respond.)
4. How do you think that turtle feels? (The children respond.)

WORKSHEET 139

EXERCISE 7

Summary of independent activities

a. (Pass out Worksheet 139 to each child.)
b. Everybody, now you'll do your worksheet. Remember to do all parts of the worksheet and to read all the parts carefully.

END OF LESSON 139

The Van and the Vane[1]

Kim did not spell well.[2] When she made a note, she did not spell words the right way. Here is how Kim spelled the word **made**: **mad**.[3] Here is how Kim spelled the word **van**: **vane**.[4] Here is how she spelled the word **mat**: **mate**.[5]

One day, Kim was going to leave her house and move to the other side of town. She had a lot of stuff to move. So she said, "I will call a van and have the van move my stuff to the other side of town."[6]

So Kim looked in the phone book. But she did not look under the word **van**.[7] She looked under the word **vane**.[8] She talked to a woman who made vanes. These vanes are made to show you which way the wind is blowing.[9] When the wind blows from the east, the vane turns to the east. (5) When the wind blows from the west, the vane turns to the west.

Kim said to the woman, "I want the biggest one you have. How big is your biggest one?"

The woman on the phone said, "Our biggest one is ten feet long."

"That doesn't seem very big," Kim said. "How soon could you send it to my house?"

The woman said, "I can have it at your house in five minutes."

"Good," Kim said. "Send it right over."[10]

Kim hung up the phone. Then she rushed around her house packing her things. Soon the door bell rang. Kim ran to the door. A woman was standing at the door. She was holding a big vane.

Kim said, "Where is your van?"

The woman said, "I came in a car."

Kim said, "Who is bringing the van?"

"What van?" the woman asked. "I came here with a vane."

Kim said, "What vane?"

The woman held up the vane and said, "This vane."

To be continued

[1] What will this story be about? (Signal.) *A van and a vane.* Right.

- A van is a truck. What is a van? (Signal.) *A truck.*

[2] What's Kim's problem? (Signal.) *She doesn't spell well.*

[3] Let's all spell the word made like Kim did. (Signal. Teacher and children spell:) *M-A-D.*

- She forgot the e on the end of the word made.

[4] Let's all spell the word van like Kim did. (Signal. Teacher and children spell:) *V-A-N-E.*

- Does van have an e on the end of the word? (Signal.) *No.*

[5] Is that how you spell mat? (Signal.) *No.*

- What did she do wrong? (Signal.) *She put an e at the end of the word.*

[6] Why is she calling for a van? (Signal.) *To move her stuff.*

- Why can't she use her car? (The children respond.)

[7] What word was Kim looking for in the phone book? (Signal.) *Van.*

- Did she look under the word van? (Signal.) *No.*

[8] What word did she look under? (Signal.) *Vane.*

- What word should she look under? (Signal.) *Van.*

[9] What does a vane do? (Signal.) *Show you which way the wind is blowing.*

- And what is a van? (Signal.) *A truck.*

[10] What is the woman going to send? (Signal.) *A vane.*

- Is that what Kim wants? (Signal.) *No.*

- What does she really want so that she can move her stuff? (Signal.) *A van.*

STORY 139
EXERCISE 5

Reading—decoding

a. (Pass out Storybook 2.)

b. Everybody, open your reader to page 165.

c. Remember, if the group reads all the way to the red 5 without making more than five errors, we can go on.

d. Everybody, touch the title of the story. ✔

e. If you hear a mistake, raise your hand. Remember, children who do not have their place lose their turn. (Call on individual children to read two or three sentences. Do not ask comprehension questions. Tally all errors.)

To Correct

word-identification errors (**from**, for example)
1. That word is **from.** What word? *From.*
2. Go back to the beginning of the sentence and read the sentence again.

f. (If the children make more than five errors before they reach the red 5: when they reach the 5 return to the beginning of the story and have the children reread to the 5. Do not ask comprehension questions. Repeat step *f* until firm, and then go on to step *g.*)

g. (When the children read to the red 5 without making more than five errors: read the story to the children from the beginning to the 5. Ask the specified comprehension questions. When you reach the 5, call on individual children to continue reading the story. Have each child read two or three sentences. Ask the specified comprehension questions.)

1

The Rabbit and the Turtle[1]

The rabbit was the fastest animal in the woods. She said, "Ha, ha. I am so fast that nobody can beat me in a race."[2] All of the other animals got mad at the rabbit. But none of the other animals raced with the rabbit because they knew she could beat them.[3]

One day the rabbit was jumping around and saying, "Ha, ha. I am so fast that nobody can beat me in a race." She ran around and around, making a lot of dust fly up into the air. The other animals were mad.

Then one of the animals said, "I will race with you."[4] It was the turtle, and he was the slowest animal in the woods.[5]

The rabbit laughed and laughed. "You want to race with me," she said. "That is a joke.[6] I am so fast that I could run a mile before you take one step." ⑤ The rabbit ran around the turtle a few times, making a lot of dust fly up into the air.

The turtle said, "I will race with you. And if I win the race, you will have to stop telling everybody how fast you are."

"And what if I win the race?" the rabbit said. "What will you do, Mr. Turtle?"

The turtle said, "I will ride you around the woods on my back. I will take you any place you want to go."

---

[1] Who is this story going to be about? (Signal.) *The rabbit and the turtle.*

• You'll read the first part today.

[2] Everybody, read that with me. (Signal. Teacher and children read:) *I am so fast that nobody can beat me in a race.*

[3] Who was the fastest animal in the woods? (Signal.) *The rabbit.*

• Why didn't any of the other animals race with her? (The children respond.)

[4] I wonder which animal said that. Read and find out.

[5] Who said he would race? (Signal.) *The turtle.*

• What do you know about this turtle? (Signal.) *He was the slowest animal in the woods.*

[6] Why did the rabbit think it was so funny? (The children respond.)

EXERCISE 7

Picture comprehension

a. Look at the picture.

b. (Ask these questions:)

1. What is the woman holding?
   (Signal.) *A vane.*

   • Yes, when the wind blows, the vane shows
   you which way the wind is blowing.

2. Did the woman bring a van? (Signal.) *No.*
   Why not? **(The children respond.)**

3. Does Kim look happy? (Signal.) *No.*

4. What do you think she's saying to that
   woman? **(The children respond.)**

5. What would you do with that vane?
   (The children respond.)

EXERCISE 8

Summary of independent activities

a. (Pass out Worksheet 127 to each child.)

b. Everybody, now you'll do your worksheet.
Remember to do all parts of the worksheet
and to read all the parts carefully.

END OF LESSON 127

EXERCISE 3

Words with underlined parts

a. First you're going to read the underlined part of each word in this column. Then you're going to read the whole word.

b. (Touch the ball for **he'll**.) Read the underlined part. Get ready. (Tap the ball.) *He.*

• Read the whole word. (Pause.) Get ready. (Slash.) *He'll.*

c. (Repeat step *b* until firm.)

d. (Repeat steps *b* and *c* for each remaining word in the column.)

e. (Repeat the column until children read all the words in order without making a mistake.)

he'll

you're

waiting

slowest

fastest

across

dusty

EXERCISE 4

Children spell, then read

a. First you're going to spell each word. Then you're going to read that word the fast way.

b. (Touch the ball for **place**.) Spell it. Get ready. (Tap under each letter as the children say:) *P-L-A-C-E.*

• (Return to the ball.) Read it. Get ready. (Slash.) *Place.*

c. (Repeat step *b* for each remaining word in the column.)

d. (Repeat steps *b* and *c* until firm.)

place

first

woods

path

lions

mile

Individual test

a. (Call on individual children to read one column of words from the lesson.)

b. (Praise children who read all words with no errors.)

READING VOCABULARY
EXERCISE 1
Teacher reads the words in red

a. I'll read each word in red. Then you'll spell each word.
b. (Touch the ball for **dollars.**) My turn. (Slash as you say:) Dollars. What word? (Signal.) *Dollars.*
c. (Return to the ball.) Spell it. Get ready. (Tap under each letter as the children say:) *D-O-L-L-A-R-S.*
• What word did you spell? (Signal.) *Dollars.*
d. (Repeat steps *b* and *c* for each word in red.)
e. Your turn to read all the words in this column.
f. (Touch the ball for **dollars**. Pause.) Get ready. (Slash.) *Dollars.*
g. (Repeat step *f* for each remaining word in the column.)
h. (Repeat steps *f* and *g* until firm.)

dollars

until

Trunk

truck

rent

rang

swell

EXERCISE 2
Words with underlined parts

a. First you're going to read the underlined part of each word in this column. Then you're going to read the whole word.
b. (Touch the ball for **corner.**) Read the underlined part. Get ready. (Tap the ball.) *Er.*
• Read the whole word. (Pause.) Get ready. (Slash.) *Corner.*
c. (Repeat step *b* until firm.)
d. (Repeat steps *b* and *c* for each remaining word in the column.)
e. (Repeat the column until children read all the words in order without making a mistake.)

corner

leaving

super

house

Where

bring

rush

READING VOCABULARY

EXERCISE 1

Teacher reads the words in red

a. I'll read each word in red. Then you'll spell each word.

b. (Touch the ball for **Mr.**) My turn. (Slash as you say:) Mister. What word? (Signal.) *Mister.*

c. **M-R-period** is a short way of writing **mister.** It's called an **abbreviation** of the word **mister.**

d. (Return to the ball.) Spell it. Get ready. (Tap under each letter and the period as the children say:) *M-R-period.*

- What word did you spell? (Signal.) *Mister.*

e. (Repeat steps *b* and *d* for each word in red.)

f. Your turn to read all the words in this column.

g. (Touch the ball for **Mr.** Pause.) Get ready. (Slash.) *Mister.*

h. (Repeat step *g* for each remaining word in the column.)

i. (Repeat steps *g* and *h* until firm.)

Mr.

pepper

knew

Rabbit

owl

race

animal

EXERCISE 2

Words with underlined parts

a. First you're going to read the underlined part of each word in this column. Then you're going to read the whole word.

b. (Touch the ball for **stream.**) Read the underlined part. Get ready. (Tap the ball.) *eee.*

- Read the whole word. (Pause.) Get ready. (Slash.) *Stream.*

c. (Repeat step *b* until firm.)

d. (Repeat steps *b* and *c* for each remaining word in the column.)

e. (Repeat the column until children read all the words in order without making a mistake.)

stream

there

easy

lined

why

cookie

sweet

EXERCISE 3

Read the fast way

a. You're going to read all the words in this column the fast way.

b. (Touch the ball for **clock**. Pause.) Get ready. (Slash.) *Clock.*

c. (Repeat step *b* until firm.)

d. (Repeat steps *b* and *c* for each remaining word in the column.)

e. (Repeat the column until the children read all the words in order without making mistakes.)

clock

minute

east

west

were

you're

spelling

EXERCISE 4

Words with underlined parts

a. First you're going to read the underlined part of each word in this column. Then you're going to read the whole word.

b. (Touch the ball for **you've**.) Read the underlined part. Get ready. (Tap the ball.) *You.*

• Read the whole word. (Pause.) Get ready. (Slash.) *You've.*

c. (Repeat step *b* until firm.)

d. (Repeat steps *b* and *c* for each remaining word in the column.)

e. (Repeat the column until children read all the words in order without making a mistake.)

you've

dragging

doesn't

tossed

understand

phoned

That's

The next week the boy got tired of watching sheep again.[13] So he went to town and yelled, "Wolf, wolf. A big wolf is eating the sheep." The people in town ran to the flock. But when they got there, the boy began to laugh. "Ha, ha. I played a good joke on you."[14]

Again, his father told him that someday a wolf would come, but nobody would listen to the boy when he shouted, "Wolf, wolf."

The next week, the boy was sitting on the side of the mountain when he saw something chasing a sheep. It was a big wolf.[15] "I must get the people," the boy yelled, and he ran to town as fast as he could go.

"Wolf, wolf," he yelled.[16] "A big wolf is after the sheep."

But the people did not run to save the sheep. They laughed at the boy. They said, "You can't fool us with your jokes."[17]

"I am not joking," the boy said, but the people would not believe him.

The wolf ate some sheep.[18] But after that day, the boy did his job very well. He did not get tired of watching the sheep. And he never yelled, "Wolf, wolf" when there was no wolf.[19]

This is the end.

[13] What do you think he'll do?
(The children respond.)
• Let's keep reading and see if he tries the same joke again.
[14] What was the joke? (The children respond.)
Yes, he yelled "Wolf" and there really was no wolf.
• Will people believe him if a wolf does come? (Signal.) *No.*
[15] What was chasing a sheep? (Signal.) *A big wolf.*
• Did a wolf really come this time? (Signal.) *Yes.*
[16] What did he yell? (Signal.) *Wolf, wolf.*
• Do you think the people will believe him? (The children respond.)
• Let's read and find out.
[17] Everybody, what did they say? (Signal.) *You can't fool us with your jokes.*
• Did they believe him? (Signal.) *No.*
[18] What did the wolf do? (Signal.) *Ate some sheep.*
[19] Did he ever yell "Wolf, wolf" as a joke again? (Signal.) *No.*

EXERCISE 6

Picture comprehension

a. What do you think you'll see in the picture? (The children respond.)
b. Turn the page and look at the picture.
c. (Ask these questions:)
　1. What is that wolf doing? (The children respond.) Right. The wolf is carrying off the sheep.
　2. What do you think the boy is yelling? (Signal.) *Wolf, wolf.*
　3. Could the boy use that long rod to stop the wolf? (The children respond.)

EXERCISE 7

Summary of independent activities

a. (Pass out Worksheet 138 to each child.)
b. Everybody, now you'll do your worksheet. Remember to do all parts of the worksheet and to read all the parts carefully.

END OF LESSON 138

EXERCISE 5

Children spell, then read

a. First you're going to spell each word. Then you're going to read that word the fast way.

b. (Touch the ball for **Tim.**) Spell it. Get ready. (Tap under each letter as the children say:) *T-I-M.* (Return to the ball.) Read it. Get ready. (Slash.) *Tim.*

c. (Repeat step *b* for each remaining word in the column.)

d. (Repeat steps *b* and *c* until firm.)

Tim

time

vane

van

rental

pile

ninety

Individual test

a. (Call on individual children to read one column of words from the lesson.)

b. (Praise children who read all words with no errors.)

STORYBOOK

STORY 128
EXERCISE 6

Reading—decoding

a. (Pass out Storybook 2.)

b. Everybody, open your reader to page 128.

c. Remember, if the group reads all the way to the red 5 without making more than five errors, we can go on.

d. Everybody, touch the title of the story. ✔

e. If you hear a mistake, raise your hand. Remember, children who do not have their place lose their turn. (Call on individual children to read two or three sentences. Do not ask comprehension questions. Tally all errors.)

To Correct

word-identification errors (**from,** for example)
1. That word is **from.** What word? *From.*
2. Go back to the beginning of the sentence and read the sentence again.

f. (If the children make more than five errors before they reach the red 5: when they reach the 5 return to the beginning of the story and have the children reread to the 5. Do not ask comprehension questions. Repeat step *f* until firm, and then go on to step *g*.)

g. (When the children read to the red 5 without making more than five errors: read the story to the children from the beginning to the 5. Ask the specified comprehension questions. When you reach the 5, call on individual children to continue reading the story. Have each child read two or three sentences. Ask the specified comprehension questions.)

STORY 138
EXERCISE 5

Reading—decoding

a. (Pass out Storybook 2.)

b. Everybody, open your reader to page 161.

c. Remember, if the group reads all the way to the red 5 without making more than five errors, we can go on.

d. Everybody, touch the title of the story. ✔

e. If you hear a mistake, raise your hand. Remember, children who do not have their place lose their turn. (Call on individual children to read two or three sentences. Do not ask comprehension questions. Tally all errors.)

To Correct

word-identification errors (**from,** for example)
1. That word is **from.** What word? *From.*
2. Go back to the beginning of the sentence and read the sentence again.

f. (If the children make more than five errors before they reach the red 5: when they reach the 5 return to the beginning of the story and have the children reread to the 5. Do not ask comprehension questions. Repeat step *f* until firm, and then go on to step *g.*)

g. (When the children read to the red 5 without making more than five errors: read the story to the children from the beginning to the 5. Ask the specified comprehension questions. When you reach the 5, call on individual children to continue reading the story. Have each child read two or three sentences. Ask the specified comprehension questions.)

The Boy Who Yelled "Wolf"[1]

There once was a boy who had a very big job. Every day he took a flock of sheep up the side of the mountain. His job was to watch the sheep and keep them safe.[2] He had to watch for wolves and for mountain lions.[3]

But this boy was not a hard worker. He didn't like his job.[4] One day, he said to himself, "I am tired of watching sheep. I want to have some fun." He began to think of ways to have fun. Then he smiled and said, "I think I'll run into town and play a good joke on the people.[5] I will tell them that a big wolf has come to eat the sheep.[6] They will run back here to get the wolf.[7] Then I will tell them that there is no wolf.[8] That will be a good joke." ⑤

So the boy went to town and began to shout, "Help, help. A big wolf is eating the sheep."[9]

The people ran to the flock of sheep.[10] When they got there, the boy started to laugh. "Ha, ha," he said. "I played a good joke on you. There is no wolf here."[11]

The boy's father said, "That is not a good joke. Some day a wolf will come to the flock. But nobody will believe you when you yell, 'Wolf, wolf.'"[12]

---

[1] What's this story going to be about? (Signal.) *The boy who yelled "wolf."*

• Let's read and see why he would yell wolf.

[2] What was his job? (The children respond.) Yes, to watch the sheep and keep them safe.

[3] What kinds of animals hurt sheep? (Signal.) *Wolves and mountain lions.*

[4] Was he a hard worker? (Signal.) *No.*

• Did he like his job? (Signal.) *No.*

[5] Let's read and find out what the boy thinks is a good joke.

[6] What's he going to tell them? (Signal.) *That a big wolf has come to eat the sheep.*

[7] Then what will the people do if they believe him? (Signal.) *Run back to get the wolf.*

[8] Then what will the boy tell them? (Signal.) *That there is no wolf.*

• Is that a good joke? (Signal.) *No.*

[9] Everybody, say that. (Signal.) *A big wolf is eating the sheep.*

[10] Did the people do what he thought they would do? (Signal.) *Yes.* Right, they ran to help him.

[11] And was there really a wolf there? (Signal.) *No.*

[12] Why did his father say that? (The children respond.)

The Truck and the Trunk[1]

Kim had called the woman who made vanes. That woman was at Kim's door. But Kim didn't need a big vane to tell which way the wind was blowing. Kim needed a big van so that she could take her things to the other side of town.

The woman said, "You called me and told me to bring the biggest vane I had.[2] Here it is. I will send you a bill for it."

The woman handed the vane to Kim. Then the woman left. Kim felt very mad. She tossed the big vane in the corner of the room and went back to the phone book. She said, "This time I will look up trucks. I will call for a truck."[3]

Kim looked in the phone book. But she didn't look under the word truck. She looked under the word trunk.⑤[4] She called the man and said, "I need something to take my things to the other side of town."

The man said, "I think I have just what you need. Do you have a lot of things?"

"Yes," Kim said.

"That's fine," the man said. "I'll bring you something to hold lots of things."

"Swell," Kim said. "Send it over right now.[5] I'm in a big rush."

As Kim waited for the man to come to her house, Kim piled all of her things near the door. She said, "When that truck gets here, I'll throw my stuff in it and I'll be on my way."

Soon the front door bell rang. Kim opened the door. She saw a man dragging a super big trunk.[6] Kim said, "Where's the truck?"[7]

The man said, "It's out on the street. Why do you ask?"

"What do you mean? I ask because I called for a truck."

The man looked very mad. "No," he said. "You called and asked for a trunk."

"What do I want with a trunk?" Kim said. "I need a truck, not a trunk."

"Well, you've got a trunk, because you called me and asked me to bring you a trunk. And I'm not leaving until you pay for this trunk. It sells for ninety dollars."

Kim got ninety dollars and gave it to the man.[8] Then Kim tossed her trunk in the corner with her other things. Now she had a vane and a trunk.[9]

Stop

---

[1] Name two things this story will be about. (Signal.) *A truck and a trunk.*

[2] Everybody, what did the woman say? (Signal.) *You called me and told me to bring the biggest vane I had.*

• What did Kim really want? (Signal.) *A van.*

• Why does she want a van? (The children respond.)

[3] What's she looking up in the phone book this time? (Signal.) *Trucks.*

• She doesn't spell well. I wonder if she'll get a truck.

[4] Did she look under the word truck? (Signal.) *No.*

• What word did she look under? (Signal.) *Trunk.*

• Oh, oh. A trunk is like a big suitcase.

[5] What's the man going to send? (Signal.) *A trunk.*

• And what does Kim really want from that man? (Signal.) *A truck.*

[6] What was the man doing? (Signal.) *Dragging a super big trunk.*

[7] Why is she asking that? (The children respond.)

[8] Why did she do that? (The children respond.)

[9] Name two things Kim got by mistake. (The children respond.)

• Yes, she got a vane and a trunk by mistake. What did she want instead of a vane? (Signal.) *A van.*

• What did she want instead of a trunk? (Signal.) *A truck.*

EXERCISE 3

Read the fast way

a. You're going to read all the words in this column the fast way.

b. (Touch the ball for **left.** Pause.) Get ready. (Slash.) *Left.*

c. (Repeat step *b* until firm.)

d. (Repeat steps *b* and *c* for each remaining word in the column.)

e. (Repeat the column until the children read all the words in order without making mistakes.)

left

felt

face

flock

Wolf

yelled

alive

EXERCISE 4

Children spell, then read

a. First you're going to spell each word. Then you're going to read that word the fast way.

b. (Touch the ball for **safe.**) Spell it. Get ready. (Tap under each letter as the children say:) *S-A-F-E.*

• (Return to the ball.) Read it. Get ready. (Slash.) *Safe.*

c. (Repeat step *b* for each remaining word in the column.)

d. (Repeat steps *b* and *c* until firm.)

safe

save

tired

tried

chasing

wolves

listen

Individual test

a. (Call on individual children to read one column of words from the lesson.)

b. (Praise children who read all words with no errors.)

EXERCISE 7

Picture comprehension

a. Look at the picture.

b. (Ask these questions:)

1. What's that man doing?
   (The children respond.)

2. Do you think that trunk is heavy? (Signal.)
   Yes.

 • How can you tell? (The children respond.)
   Yes, that man looks like he's
   working hard.

3. Whose truck is that in the street?
   (Signal.) *The man's.*

4. Did Kim ask for a trunk? (Signal.) *No.*
   What did she ask for? (Signal.) *A truck.*
   And what did she get? (Signal.) *A trunk.*

EXERCISE 8

Summary of independent activities

a. (Pass out Worksheet 128 to each child.)

b. Everybody, now you'll do your worksheet.
   Remember to do all parts of the worksheet
   and to read all the parts carefully.

END OF LESSON 128

READING VOCABULARY

EXERCISE 1

Teacher reads the words in red

a. I'll read each word in red. Then you'll spell each word.

b. (Touch the ball for **animal.**) My turn. (Slash as you say:) Animal. What word? (Signal.) *Animal.*

c. (Return to the ball.) Spell it. Get ready. (Tap under each letter as the children say:) *A-N-I-M-A-L.*

• What word did you spell? (Signal.) *Animal.*

d. (Repeat steps *b* and *c* for each word in red.)

e. Your turn to read all the words in this column.

f. (Touch the ball for **animal.** Pause.) Get ready. (Slash.) *Animal.*

g. (Repeat step *f* for each remaining word in the column.)

h. (Repeat steps *f* and *g* until firm.)

animal

lions

cookie

race

sweet

sheep

father

EXERCISE 2

Words with underlined parts

a. First you're going to read the underlined part of each word in this column. Then you're going to read the whole word.

b. (Touch the ball for **watching.**) Read the underlined part. Get ready. (Tap the ball.) *Watch.*

• Read the whole word. (Pause.) Get ready. (Slash.) *Watching.*

c. (Repeat step *b* until firm.)

d. (Repeat steps *b* and *c* for each remaining word in the column.)

e. (Repeat the column until children read all the words in order without making a mistake.)

watching

someday

worker

fastest

nobody

believe

mountain

READING VOCABULARY

EXERCISE 1

Teacher reads the words in red

a. I'll read each word in red. Then you'll spell each word.

b. (Touch the ball for **service.**) My turn. (Slash as you say:) Service. What word? (Signal.) *Service.*

c. (Return to the ball.) Spell it. Get ready. (Tap under each letter as the children say:) *S-E-R-V-I-C-E.*

• What word did you spell? (Signal.) *Service.*

d. (Repeat steps *b* and *c* for each word in red.)

e. Your turn to read all the words in this column.

f. (Touch the ball for **service.** Pause.) Get ready. (Slash.) *Service.*

g. (Repeat step *f* for each remaining word in the column.)

h. (Repeat steps *f* and *g* until firm.)

service

False

dental

trouble

number

loud

truck

EXERCISE 2

Words with underlined parts

a. First you're going to read the underlined part of each word in this column. Then you're going to read the whole word.

b. (Touch the ball for **rented.**) Read the underlined part. Get ready. (Tap the ball.) *Rent.*

• Read the whole word. (Pause.) Get ready. (Slash.) *Rented.*

c. (Repeat step *b* until firm.)

d. (Repeat steps *b* and *c* for each remaining word in the column.)

e. (Repeat the column until children read all the words in order without making a mistake.)

rented

answered

doesn't

today

Where's

It's

I'll

So from that day on, the frog and the turtle and the snake got along very well.[9] The frog did what frogs do. He jumped and swam and went "Croak, croak" at night. But that frog did not make fun of turtles any more.[10]

When Flame was not near the pond, she did what snakes do. She would sneak and she would eat many things. But when she was around the frog and the turtle, she was a good snake.[11]

Now the turtle felt good again. He liked to watch the frog jump and watch the snake slide along the ground. He liked the hot sun and the cool water. He liked to be alive.[12]

This is the end.

[9] Who got along? (Signal.)
The frog and the turtle and the snake.
[10] What did he stop doing? (Signal.)
Making fun of turtles.
[11] Was she sneaky around the frog and the turtle? (Signal.) *No.*
[12] Name some things that made the turtle glad to be alive. (The children respond.)

EXERCISE 6

Picture comprehension

a. Look at the picture.

b. (Ask these questions:)

1. Are the animals fighting with each other in this picture? (Signal.) *No.* Right. They're getting along with each other.
2. What is that frog doing? (Signal.) *Jumping into the water.*
3. What is Flame doing? (The children respond.)
4. What is that thing on Flame's tail? (The children respond.)
- Why is her tail bandaged? (The children respond.)
5. What's the turtle looking at? (The children respond.)

EXERCISE 7

Summary of independent activities

a. (Pass out Worksheet 137 to each child.)

b. Everybody, now you'll do your worksheet. Remember to do all parts of the worksheet and to read all the parts carefully.

END OF LESSON 137

EXERCISE 3

Read the fast way

a. You're going to read all the words in this column the fast way.

b. (Touch the ball for **bring.** Pause.) Get ready. (Slash.) *Bring.*

c. (Repeat step *b* until firm.)

d. (Repeat steps *b* and *c* for each remaining word in the column.)

e. (Repeat the column until the children read all the words in order without making mistakes.)

bring

time

Tim

stuff

Teeth

until

able

EXERCISE 4

Read the fast way

a. You're going to read all the words in this column the fast way.

b. (Touch the ball for **trips.** Pause.) Get ready. (Slash.) *Trips.*

c. (Repeat step *b* until firm.)

d. (Repeat steps *b* and *c* for each remaining word in the column.)

e. (Repeat the column until the children read all the words in order without making mistakes.)

trips

trunk

phone

strange

load

move

cap

STORYBOOK

STORY 137

EXERCISE 5

Reading—decoding

a. (Pass out Storybook 2.)

b. Everybody, open your reader to page 158.

c. Remember, if the group reads all the way to the red 5 without making more than five errors, we can go on.

d. Everybody, touch the title of the story. ✔

e. If you hear a mistake, raise your hand. Remember, children who do not have their place lose their turn. (Call on individual children to read two or three sentences. Do not ask comprehension questions. Tally all errors.)

To Correct

word-identification errors (**from,** for example)
1. That word is **from.** What word? *From.*
2. Go back to the beginning of the sentence and read the sentence again.

f. (If the children make more than five errors before they reach the red 5: when they reach the 5 return to the beginning of the story and have the children reread to the 5. Do not ask comprehension questions. Repeat step *f* until firm, and then go on to step *g.*)

g. (When the children read to the red 5 without making more than five errors: read the story to the children from the beginning to the 5. Ask the specified comprehension questions. When you reach the 5, call on individual children to continue reading the story. Have each child read two or three sentences. Ask the specified comprehension questions.)

The Frog and the Turtle and the Snake Get Along[1]

Flame the snake was sliding into the weeds.[2] She was going after the frog.

"Save me, save me," the frog yelled. "Please save me from this snake."

Suddenly, the turtle took a big bite out of the snake's tail. "Ow, ow," the snake yelled.[3] "Why did you do that?" Flame asked.[4] "I must do what snakes do."

The turtle said, "I have to do what turtles do."[5]

Then Flame called, "Frog, oh frog. Come out here."[6] The frog hopped out of the weeds. He looked scared. Flame looked at him and began to slide after him.

"Stop," the turtle called. "Stop, or I will bite your tail again."

So Flame stopped. Then the turtle said, "You can be a sneak when you are not around me or this frog. But you cannot be a sneak around us."⑤[7]

Flame said, "Can I be a sneak when I go to hunt rats near the farm?"

"Yes," the turtle said.

Flame asked, "Can I be a sneak and eat a frog?"

"No," the turtle said. "You must be good to that frog."[8]

Flame looked sad. "I will be good," she said.

---

[1] What's the title? (Signal.) *The frog and the turtle and the snake get along.*

• Yes, they will learn to live together without fighting.

[2] Why was Flame doing that? (The children respond.)

[3] Why did she do that? (The children respond.)

• Yes, the turtle bit her.

[4] Everybody, what's the question? (Signal.) *Why did you do that?*

[5] And what's the turtle's answer? (Signal.) *I have to do what turtles do.*

[6] Do you think the frog will come out? (The children respond.)

• Let's read and find out.

[7] Are snakes sneaky? (Signal.) *Yes.*

• But the frog told her not to be sneaky around there.

[8] Can Flame eat the frog? (Signal.) *No.*

• What does she have to do? (Signal.) *Be good to that frog.*

EXERCISE 5
Children spell, then read

a. First you're going to spell each word. Then you're going to read that word the fast way.

b. (Touch the ball for **dollars.**) Spell it. Get ready. (Tap under each letter as the children say:) *D-O-L-L-A-R-S.*
- (Return to the ball.) Read it. Get ready. (Slash.) *Dollars.*

c. (Repeat step *b* for each remaining word in the column.)

d. (Repeat steps *b* and *c* until firm.)

dollars
rental
face
put
drive
care
cape

Individual test

a. (Call on individual children to read one column of words from the lesson.)

b. (Praise children who read all words with no errors.)

STORYBOOK

STORY 129
EXERCISE 6
Reading—decoding

a. (Pass out Storybook 2.)

b. Everybody, open your reader to page 132.

c. Remember, if the group reads all the way to the red 5 without making more than five errors, we can go on.

d. Everybody, touch the title of the story. ✔

e. If you hear a mistake, raise your hand. Remember, children who do not have their place lose their turn. (Call on individual children to read two or three sentences. Do not ask comprehension questions. Tally all errors.)

To Correct

word-identification errors (**from,** for example)
1. That word is **from.** What word? *From.*
2. Go back to the beginning of the sentence and read the sentence again.

f. (If the children make more than five errors before they reach the red 5: when they reach the 5 return to the beginning of the story and have the children reread to the 5. Do not ask comprehension questions. Repeat step *f* until firm, and then go on to step *g*.)

g. (When the children read to the red 5 without making more than five errors: read the story to the children from the beginning to the 5. Ask the specified comprehension questions. When you reach the 5, call on individual children to continue reading the story. Have each child read two or three sentences. Ask the specified comprehension questions.)

EXERCISE 3

Read the fast way

a. You're going to read all the words in this column the fast way.

b. (Touch the ball for **stick.** Pause.) Get ready. (Slash.) *Stick.*

c. (Repeat step *b* until firm.)

d. (Repeat steps *b* and *c* for each remaining word in the column.)

e. (Repeat the column until the children read all the words in order without making mistakes.)

stick

stuck

swam

slide

light

what

many

EXERCISE 4

Children spell, then read

a. First you're going to spell each word. Then you're going to read that word the fast way.

b. (Touch the ball for **joke.**) Spell it. Get ready. (Tap under each letter as the children say:) *J-O-K-E.*

• (Return to the ball.) Read it. Get ready. (Slash.) *Joke.*

c. (Repeat step *b* for each remaining word in the column.)

d. (Repeat steps *b* and *c* until firm.)

joke

biter

bitter

from

watch

scared

color

Individual test

a. (Call on individual children to read one column of words from the lesson.)

b. (Praise children who read all words with no errors.)

A Man Brings False Teeth[1]

Kim was mad. She wanted to take her things to a house on the other side of town. But she didn't have a truck. She sent for a van, but she got a vane.[2] Then she sent for a truck and she got a trunk.[3]

Kim picked up the phone book and said, "This time I will look up a rental car.[4] I can't get all of my stuff into a rental car. But I will make two or three trips in the car. In that way, I will be able to get my stuff to the other side of town."

So Kim went through the phone book. Then she stopped to read a phone number. But she was not looking under the words rental car.[5] She was looking under the words dental care.[6] Kim was calling a man who made false teeth. ⑤[7]

When the man answered the phone, Kim said, "Hello. Do you have something I can rent today? I'll just need it for one day."

The man said, "You want to rent just for the day? That's a strange thing to do."[8]

"Do you have anything to rent?" Kim said.

"Well, yes, I do," the man said. "It may not fit, but I can bring it over."

"That will be fine," Kim said.

Soon the door bell rang. Kim opened the door. The man was standing there holding a set of false teeth.[9]

Kim said, "Where's your car?"

"It's out on the street," the man said. "And here are your false teeth. I'll let you have them for ten dollars a day."

"I don't need teeth," Kim said. "I need a car. That's why I called you. You said that you would bring me a car."

"No, I didn't," the man said. "I told you I would bring you a set of false teeth."

Kim picked up the phone book. She said, "Look at this. I'll show you that your name is under rental car." Kim opened the book.

The man said, "That doesn't say rental car. It says dental care."[10]

Now Kim had a vane and a trunk and a set of rented teeth.[11]

More next time

1. What will the man bring in this story? (Signal.) *False teeth.*
- Those are teeth the dentist gives people who don't have teeth.
2. What did she want? (Signal.) *A van.* What did she get? (Signal.) *A vane.*
3. What did she want? (Signal.) *A truck.* What did she get? (Signal.) *A trunk.*
- She's having trouble because she doesn't spell well.
4. What does she want to look up this time? (Signal.) *A rental car.* Yes, a car you can rent for a few hours.
5. Was she looking under rental car? (Signal.) *No.*
6. What words was she looking under? (Signal.) *Dental care.* Yes, she wanted rental car, but she's looking under dental care.
- She sure can't spell.
7. What did that man do? (Signal.) *Made false teeth.*
8. Right. He thinks Kim is talking about false teeth. If you need teeth, you need them all the time.
9. What did the man bring? (Signal.) *False teeth.*
10. Was the man listed under rental car? (Signal.) *No.*
- What was he listed under? (Signal.) *Dental care.*
11. Name all the things Kim has now. (The children respond.)
- You'll be surprised next time at how the story ends.

READING VOCABULARY

EXERCISE 1

Teacher reads the words in red

a. I'll read each word in red. Then you'll spell each word.

b. (Touch the ball for **flock.**) My turn. (Slash as you say:) Flock. What word? (Signal.) *Flock.*

c. (Return to the ball.) Spell it. Get ready. (Tap under each letter as the children say:) *F-L-O-C-K.*

* What word did you spell? (Signal.) *Flock.*

d. (Repeat steps *b* and *c* for each word in red.)

e. Your turn to read all the words in this column.

f. (Touch the ball for **flock.** Pause.) Get ready. (Slash.) *Flock.*

g. (Repeat step *f* for each remaining word in the column.)

h. (Repeat steps *f* and *g* until firm.)

flock

wolf

wolves

Croak

listen

alive

Along

EXERCISE 2

Words with underlined parts

a. First you're going to read the underlined part of each word in this column. Then you're going to read the whole word.

b. (Touch the ball for **sheep.**) Read the underlined part. Get ready. (Tap the ball.) *sh.*

* Read the whole word. (Pause.) Get ready. (Slash.) *Sheep.*

c. (Repeat step *b* until firm.)

d. (Repeat steps *b* and *c* for each remaining word in the column.)

e. (Repeat the column until children read all the words in order without making a mistake.)

sheep

tail

Please

Why

Than

that

sneak

WORSHEET 129

EXERCISE 7

Picture comprehension

a. Look at the picture. It shows Kim talking to the man at the dental-care place.

b. (Ask these questions:)

1. Read the words Kim is looking under. Get ready. (Signal.) *Dental care.*

• And what does she think she is looking under? (Signal.) *Rental car.*

2. What's on the table in front of the man? (Signal.) *False teeth.*

3. What do you think the man is saying? **(The children respond.)**

4. What would you do if you couldn't spell any better than Kim? **(The children respond.)**

EXERCISE 8

Summary of independent activities

a. (Pass out Worksheet 129 to each child.)

b. Everybody, now you'll do your worksheet. Remember to do all parts of the worksheet and to read all the parts carefully.

END OF LESSON 129

EXERCISE 6

Picture comprehension

a. Look at the picture.

b. (Ask these questions:)

1. What just happened to the snake?
   (The children respond.)
2. How do you know she just tried to bite
   the turtle? (The children respond.)
3. Why didn't the snake bite the turtle on
   his nose? (The children respond.)
4. What do you think the snake is saying?
   (The children respond.)
5. What do you see in the weeds? (Signal.)
   The frog.
   • What do you think he's thinking?
   (The children respond.)

INDEPENDENT ACTIVITIES
EXERCISE 7

Reading comprehension

a. (Pass out Worksheet 136 to each child.)

b. Everybody, turn to side 2 of your worksheet. ✔

c. (Point to the story on side 2 of your
   worksheet.) Everybody, find this story on
   your worksheet. ✔

d. Today you're going to read a passage that
   tells about strange animals that live in big,
   dark caves.

e. Everybody, touch the picture of the fish. ✔
   • That fish is white. Touch the eye of the fish. ✔
   • That eye cannot see. The fish is blind.

f. Everybody, can the fish see? (Signal.) *No.*
   • What color is the fish? (Signal.) *White.*

g. I'll read the passage. Everybody, follow
   along. (Read the passage to the children.
   Check that they are following along as
   you read.)

h. When you do your independent work, read
   the passage to yourself. Then answer
   the questions.

EXERCISE 8

Summary of independent activities

Everybody, now you'll do your worksheet.
Remember to do all parts of the worksheet
and to read all the parts carefully.

END OF LESSON 136

READING VOCABULARY
EXERCISE 1

Teacher reads the words in red

a. I'll read each word in red. Then you'll spell each word.

b. (Touch the ball for **honey**.) My turn. (Slash as you say:) Honey. What word? (Signal.) *Honey.*

c. (Return to the ball.) Spell it. Get ready. (Tap under each letter as the children say:) *H-O-N-E-Y.*

• What word did you spell? (Signal.) *Honey.*

d. (Repeat steps *b* and *c* for each word in red.)

e. Your turn to read all the words in this column.

f. (Touch the ball for **honey**. Pause.) Get ready. (Slash.) *Honey.*

g. (Repeat step *f* for each remaining word in the column.)

h. (Repeat steps *f* and *g* until firm.)

honey

pocket

false

service

Moves

loaded

number

EXERCISE 2

Words with underlined parts

a. First you're going to read the underlined part of each word in this column. Then you're going to read the whole word.

b. (Touch the ball for **already**.) Read the underlined part. Get ready. (Tap the ball.) *Ready.*

• Read the whole word. (Pause.) Get ready. (Slash.) *Already.*

c. (Repeat step *b* until firm.)

d. (Repeat steps *b* and *c* for each remaining word in the column.)

e. (Repeat the column until children read all the words in order without making a mistake.)

already

almost

landed

slipped

hopped

passing

we'll

STORYBOOK

STORY 136

EXERCISE 5

Reading—decoding

a. (Pass out Storybook 2.)

b. Everybody, open your reader to page 155.

c. Remember, if the group reads all the way to the red 5 without making more than five errors, we can go on.

d. Everybody, touch the title of the story. ✔

e. If you hear a mistake, raise your hand. Remember, children who do not have their place lose their turn. (Call on individual children to read two or three sentences. Do not ask comprehension questions. Tally all errors.)

To Correct

word-identification errors (**from,** for example)
1. That word is **from.** What word? *From.*
2. Go back to the beginning of the sentence and read the sentence again.

f. (If the children make more than five errors before they reach the red 5: when they reach the 5 return to the beginning of the story and have the children reread to the 5. Do not ask comprehension questions. Repeat step *f* until firm, and then go on to step *g*.)

g. (When the children read to the red 5 without making more than five errors: read the story to the children from the beginning to the 5. Ask the specified comprehension questions. When you reach the 5, call on individual children to continue reading the story. Have each child read two or three sentences. Ask the specified comprehension questions.)

A Snake Must Do What Snakes Do[1]

Flame the snake was after the turtle. Her mouth came at the turtle like a shot. The turtle was not fast like a frog, so he could not jump out of the way. The turtle pulled his head into his shell.[2] And just then —bong—the snake's mouth hit the shell.

"Ow, ow," Flame yelled.[3] "My tooth, my tooth. I think I broke my tooth on that hard shell." Flame was sliding this way and that way. "Ow, ow."

The turtle said, "That would not happen if you were a good snake. But you are a sneak."

The snake said, "You are silly. Everybody knows that snakes are sneaks. I am a snake, so I have to be sneaky."[4]

"No," the turtle said. "You do not have to be sneaky. You could be anything you want."[5]

The snake said, "You're nuts. ⑤ You can't be anything you want. Could you jump like a frog? Could you fly like a bird?"

"No," the turtle said, "I can't do those things."

Flame said, "Then why do you think I can be anything I want to be?"

The turtle said, "Maybe you are right. I can't do things that frogs do. I can only do what turtles do. You are a snake, so you must do what snakes do."[6]

"Thank you," Flame said, and smiled. "If you will get out of my way, I'll do what snakes do. I'll go into the weeds and have a frog for lunch."[7]

"Yes," the turtle said. The turtle stepped to one side and the snake began to slide into the weeds. The turtle was sad, but the turtle felt that Flame must do what snakes do.[8]

This is almost the end.[9]

---

[1] What's the title of this story? (Signal.) *A snake must do what snakes do.*

[2] What did he do? (Signal.) *Pulled his head into his shell.*

[3] Why is Flame yelling? (The children respond.)

[4] Everybody, say that. (Signal.) *I am a snake, so I have to be sneaky.*

[5] Is that true? (The children respond.)

• Let's read some more and see what Flame answers.

[6] Everybody, say that. (Signal.) *You are a snake, so you must do what snakes do.*

[7] So what's Flame going to do? (The children respond.)

[8] Why was the turtle sad? (The children respond.) Yes, he didn't want the snake to eat the frog.

[9] Is this the end of the story? (Signal.) *No.*

• The story will end next time.

EXERCISE 3

Read the fast way

a. You're going to read all the words in this column the fast way.

b. (Touch the ball for **every.** Pause.) Get ready. (Slash.) *Every.*

c. (Repeat step *b* until firm.)

d. (Repeat steps *b* and *c* for each remaining word in the column.)

e. (Repeat the column until the children read all the words in order without making mistakes.)

every

rode

rod

chase

left

Stuff

woman

EXERCISE 4

Children spell, then read

a. First you're going to spell each word. Then you're going to read that word the fast way.

b. (Touch the ball for **ready.**) Spell it. Get ready. (Tap under each letter as the children say:) *R-E-A-D-Y.*

• (Return to the ball.) Read it. Get ready. (Slash.) *Ready.*

c. (Repeat step *b* for each remaining word in the column.)

d. (Repeat steps *b* and *c* until firm.)

ready

hoped

Jan

Jane

dental

skates

trouble

Individual test

a. (Call on individual children to read one column of words from the lesson.)

b. (Praise children who read all words with no errors.)

EXERCISE 3

Read the fast way

a. You're going to read all the words in this column the fast way.

b. (Touch the ball for **light.** Pause.) Get ready. (Slash.) *Light.*

c. (Repeat step *b* until firm.)

d. (Repeat steps *b* and *c* for each remaining word in the column.)

e. (Repeat the column until the children read all the words in order without making mistakes.)

light

You're

also

sliding

would

were

stepped

EXERCISE 4

Children spell, then read

a. First you're going to spell each word. Then you're going to read that word the fast way.

b. (Touch the ball for **robed.**) Spell it. Get ready. (Tap under each letter as the children say:) *R-O-B-E-D.*
- (Return to the ball.) Read it. Get ready. (Slash.) *Robed.*

c. (Repeat step *b* for each remaining word in the column.)

d. (Repeat steps *b* and *c* until firm.)

robed

used

stool

pulled

than

they

their

Individual test

a. (Call on individual children to read one column of words from the lesson.)

b. (Praise children who read all words with no errors.)

STORY 130
EXERCISE 5

Reading—decoding

a. (Pass out Storybook 2.)

b. Everybody, open your reader to page 135.

c. Remember, if the group reads all the way to the red 5 without making more than five errors, we can go on.

d. Everybody, touch the title of the story. ✔

e. If you hear a mistake, raise your hand. Remember, children who do not have their place lose their turn. (Call on individual children to read two or three sentences. Do not ask comprehension questions. Tally all errors.)

To Correct

word-identification errors (**from,** for example)
1. That word is **from.** What word? *From.*
2. Go back to the beginning of the sentence and read the sentence again.

f. (If the children make more than five errors before they reach the red 5: when they reach the 5 return to the beginning of the story and have the children reread to the 5. Do not ask comprehension questions. Repeat step *f* until firm, and then go on to step *g*.)

g. (When the children read to the red 5 without making more than five errors: read the story to the children from the beginning to the 5. Ask the specified comprehension questions. When you reach the 5, call on individual children to continue reading the story. Have each child read two or three sentences. Ask the specified comprehension questions.)

Kim Moves Her Stuff in a Van[1]

Kim was really mad. After the man left Kim with a set of false teeth, Kim picked up the phone book and tossed it out of the window. She shouted, "That book gets me in a lot of trouble."[2]

A boy was passing by Kim's house. He stopped and picked up the phone book. He said, "Is this your book?"

"I just tossed it away," Kim said. "I can't find anything in it."

"What do you want to find?" the boy asked.[3]

"I need a van to take my things to the other side of town."

"Here," the boy said. He walked over to Kim. He had already found the right place in the phone book. "Why don't you call this number? It says that they have very fast service every day."

So Kim called the number. ⑤ She said to the ★ woman who answered the phone, "I don't want a vane. I don't need any trunks. And I have lots of teeth. I need a van. Do you have a van?"

"Yes," the woman said. "We'll send one right out to you."[4]

---

[1] What will Kim do in this story? (Signal.)
Move her stuff in a van.

[2] Everybody, say that. (Signal.)
That book gets me in a lot of trouble.

• There's nothing wrong with the book. What is Kim's problem? (Signal.) *She can't spell.*

[3] What did he ask? (Signal.)
What do you want to find?

• Who is talking to Kim? (Signal.) *A boy.*

• Do you think he can help her?
(The children respond.)

• Let's read and find out.

[4] What does that woman have? (Signal.) *A van.*

• How did Kim get the right place?
(The children respond.)

READING VOCABULARY

EXERCISE 1

Teacher reads the words in red

a. I'll read each word in red. Then you'll spell each word.

b. (Touch the ball for **color**.) My turn. (Slash as you say:) Color. What word? (Signal.) *Color.*

c. (Return to the ball.) Spell it. Get ready. (Tap under each letter as the children say:) *C-O-L-O-R.*

• What word did you spell? (Signal.) *Color.*

d. (Repeat steps *b* and *c* for each word in red.)

e. Your turn to read all the words in this column.

f. (Touch the ball for **color**. Pause.) Get ready. (Slash.) *Color.*

g. (Repeat step *f* for each remaining word in the column.)

h. (Repeat steps *f* and *g* until firm.)

color

bong

sneaky

snap

bird

lunch

strong

EXERCISE 2

Words with underlined parts

a. First you're going to read the underlined part of each word in this column. Then you're going to read the whole word.

b. (Touch the ball for **anything**.) Read the underlined part. Get ready. (Tap the ball.) *Thing.*

• Read the whole word. (Pause.) Get ready. (Slash.) *Anything.*

c. (Repeat step *b* until firm.)

d. (Repeat steps *b* and *c* for each remaining word in the column.)

e. (Repeat the column until children read all the words in order without making a mistake.)

anything

eyes

I've

robbed

roots

always

almost

And at last a van came to Kim's house. "It's about time," Kim said. And in no time Kim had loaded all of her stuff into the van. She loaded her bike and her bags and her skates and her vane and her trunk. She slipped her false teeth into her pocket. Then she got into the van.

And when she was ready to leave her house, the boy said, "I can go with you and help."

"Yes," Kim said. "You can come along and help me read the names of the streets.⁵ I am going to Jane Street.⁶ You can see to it that I don't end up on Jan Street or on Jame Street."⁷

"Okay," the boy said. He rode in the front of the van with Kim. And he told Kim when they reached Jane Street. He was a big help. When he had helped Kim take all of her stuff from the van, Kim said, "I would like to give you something for helping me."⁸ And what do you think Kim gave him?

He now has a big vane in his back yard.⁹ He is very proud of that vane.

The end of the story

⁵ How's the boy going to help Kim? (Signal.) *He'll read the names of the streets.*
⁶ Where is she going? (Signal.) *To Jane Street.*
⁷ Does she want Jan Street? (Signal.) *No.*
• Which street does she want? (Signal.) *Jane Street.*
• Does she want Jame Street? (Signal.) *No.*
⁸ Everybody, what did Kim say? (Signal.) *I would like to give you something for helping me.*
⁹ What did she give him? (Signal.) *A big vane.*

EXERCISE 6

Picture comprehension

a. Look at the picture.
b. (Ask these questions:)
   1. What is Kim giving the little boy? (Signal.) *The vane.*
   2. Does the boy look happy? (Signal.) *Yes.*
   3. What's that big truck over there? (Signal.) *A van.*
   • What did Kim use the van for? (The children respond.) Yes, to move her stuff.
   4. What's the name of the street she moved to? (Signal.) *Jane Street.*
   5. What's sticking out of Kim's back pocket? (Signal.) *The false teeth.*

WORKSHEET 130

INDEPENDENT ACTIVITIES
EXERCISE 7

Summary of independent activities

Everybody, now you'll do your worksheet. Remember to do all parts of the worksheet and to read all the parts carefully.

INDIVIDUAL CHECKOUT
EXERCISE 8

2-minute individual fluency checkout: rate/accuracy

a. As you are doing your worksheet, I'll call on children one at a time to read to the star. Remember, you get two stars on the chart if you read to the star in less than two minutes and make no more than five errors.
b. (Call on each child. Tell the child:) Read to the star very carefully. Start with the title. Go. (Time the child. Tell the child any words the child misses. Stop the child as soon as the child makes the sixth error or exceeds the time limit.)
c. (If the child meets the rate-accuracy criterion, record two stars on your chart for lesson 130. Congratulate the child. Give children who do not earn two stars a chance to read to the star again before the next lesson is presented.)
148 words/**2 min** = 74 wpm **[5 errors]**

END OF LESSON 130

WORKSHEET 135

EXERCISE 5

Picture comprehension

a. What do you think you'll see in the picture? (The children respond.)

b. Turn the page and look at the picture.

c. (Ask these questions:)
1. Show me the weeds in this picture. ✔
2. Where is the frog? (Signal.) *In the weeds.*
- What's he doing in those tall weeds? (Signal.) *Hiding.*
- Why is he hiding? (The children respond.)
3. What do you think Flame is saying? (The children respond.)
4. What do you think the turtle is saying? (The children respond.)

INDEPENDENT ACTIVITIES

EXERCISE 6

Reading comprehension

a. (Pass out Worksheet 135 to each child.)

b. Everybody, turn to side 2 of your worksheet. ✔

c. (Point to the story on side 2 of your worksheet.) Everybody, find this story on your worksheet. ✔

d. Today you're going to read a passage that tells about the roots of trees.

e. The picture shows what a tree would look like if you could see under the ground. Touch the place where the top of the ground is. ✔
- Now touch a part of the tree that is below the ground. ✔
- Those branches of the tree that grow below the ground are called roots. What are they called? (Signal.) *Roots.*

f. I'll read the passage. Everybody, follow along. (Read the passage to the children. Check that they are following along as you read.)

g. When you do your independent work, read the passage to yourself. Then answer the questions.

EXERCISE 7

Summary of independent activities

Everybody, now you'll do your worksheet. Remember to do all parts of the worksheet and to read all the parts carefully.

INDIVIDUAL CHECKOUT

EXERCISE 8

2-minute individual fluency checkout: rate/accuracy

a. As you are doing your worksheet, I'll call on children one at a time to read to the star. Remember, you get two stars on the chart if you read to the star in less than two minutes and make no more than five errors.

b. (Call on each child. Tell the child:) Read to the star very carefully. Start with the title. Go. (Time the child. Tell the child any words the child misses. Stop the child as soon as the child makes the sixth error or exceeds the time limit.)

c. (If the child meets the rate-accuracy criterion, record two stars on your chart for lesson 135. Congratulate the child. Give children who do not earn two stars a chance to read to the star again before the next lesson is presented.)

150 words/**2 min** = 75 wpm **[5 errors]**

END OF LESSON 135

READING VOCABULARY

EXERCISE 1

Teacher reads the words in red

a. I'll read each word in red. Then you'll spell each word.

b. (Touch the ball for **Eagle.**) My turn. (Slash as you say:) Eagle. What word? (Signal.) *Eagle.*

c. (Return to the ball.) Spell it. Get ready. (Tap under each letter as the children say:) *E-A-G-L-E.*

• What word did you spell? (Signal.) *Eagle.*

d. (Repeat steps *b* and *c* for each word in red.)

e. Your turn to read all the words in this column.

f. (Touch the ball for **Eagle.** Pause.) Get ready. (Slash.) *Eagle.*

g. (Repeat step *f* for each remaining word in the column.)

h. (Repeat steps *f* and *g* until firm.)

Eagle

feathers

dry

turtle

drank

drink

bottom

EXERCISE 2

Words with underlined parts

a. First you're going to read the underlined part of each word in this column. Then you're going to read the whole word.

b. (Touch the ball for **reach.**) Read the underlined part. Get ready. (Tap the ball.) *ch.*

• Read the whole word. (Pause.) Get ready. (Slash.) *Reach.*

c. (Repeat step *b* until firm.)

d. (Repeat steps *b* and *c* for each remaining word in the column.)

e. (Repeat the column until children read all the words in order without making a mistake.)

reach

cheese

smart

meal

brother

chicken

train

Flame the Snake Is a Sneak[1]

Flame the snake was looking for something to eat. The turtle said, "No, I have not seen any frogs around here."[2]

Flame smiled and started to slide back into the weeds. Then that snake stopped and said, "I will be back."

The turtle said to himself, "I don't like that snake. I think she is a sneak. I think I will leave." The turtle walked into the pond and began to swim around. Then the frog came over to him. The frog said, "What did Flame say to you?"

The turtle said, "She said that she wanted something to eat."

The frog asked, "Did she say what she wanted to eat?"

"Yes," the turtle said. "She told me that she wanted to eat a frog."

"That is bad," the frog said. "That is very, very bad."[3] The frog jumped from the pond and sat ★ on an old log. ⑤ He shook his head. "That is bad," he said again. "Flame is very strong.[4] Flame is very fast.[5] And she is a sneak.[6] She gives me a big scare."

Just then, a big mouth shot up to the log.[7] Snap. It was Flame's mouth. And it just missed the frog.[8] The frog jumped from the log, but he landed in the tall weeds. Flame smiled and began to slide into the weeds.

Flame said, "Frogs can't jump very well when they are in the weeds.[9] I think I will have my lunch now. I think my lunch is here in the weeds."

"Save me," the frog yelled. "I can't get away from that snake. Save me."

The turtle shouted, "I will save you."

The turtle began to walk as fast as he could go. Flame the snake stopped. "My, my," Flame said. "I see a walking toadstool." Flame was still smiling. "Get out of my way, you silly-looking thing, or I will eat you, too."

The turtle said, "If you don't stop sliding after that frog, I'll bite you on the nose."[10]

Flame smiled and turned away. She seemed to be going back to the log.[11] But suddenly—snap. Like a shot, her mouth came at the turtle.[12]

This story is not over.[13]

---

[1] Everybody, what is the title of this story? (Signal.) *Flame the snake is a sneak.*
- That means she's tricky. Watch out for her.

[2] Was that true? (Signal.) *No.* Right. It's a lie.

[3] What's very, very bad? (The children respond.)

[4] Tell me about Flame. (Signal.) *She's very strong.*

[5] Tell me more about Flame. (Signal.) *She's very fast.*

[6] What else is she? (Signal.) *A sneak.*

[7] Whose mouth? (Signal.) *Flame's.*

[8] Did Flame catch him? (Signal.) *No.*

[9] Why is that true? (The children respond.)

[10] Everyone, what did the turtle say? (Signal.) *If you don't stop sliding after that frog, I'll bite you on the nose.*

[11] Watch out, that snake is a sneak.

[12] Do you think Flame will get the turtle? (The children respond.)

[13] Is this the end? (Signal.) *No.* Right.

- Next time we'll read more and see what happens.

EXERCISE 3

Words with underlined parts

a. First you're going to read the underlined part of each word in this column. Then you're going to read the whole word.

b. (Touch the ball for **dropped.**) Read the underlined part. Get ready. (Tap the ball.) *Dropp.*

• Read the whole word. (Pause.) Get ready. (Slash.) *Dropped.*

c. (Repeat step *b* until firm.)

d. (Repeat steps *b* and *c* for each remaining word in the column.)

e. (Repeat the column until children read all the words in order without making a mistake.)

dropped

pocket

caned

canned

smiled

helps

Ellen's

EXERCISE 4

Children spell, then read

a. First you're going to spell each word. Then you're going to read that word the fast way.

b. (Touch the ball for **head.**) Spell it. Get ready. (Tap under each letter as the children say:) *H-E-A-D.*

• (Return to the ball.) Read it. Get ready. (Slash.) *Head.*

c. (Repeat step *b* for each remaining word in the column.)

d. (Repeat steps *b* and *c* until firm.)

head

flew

shade

chase

hole

wide

honey

Individual test

a. (Call on individual children to read one column of words from he lesson.)

b. (Praise children who read all words with no errors.)

EXERCISE 3

Children spell, then read

a. First you're going to spell each word. Then you're going to read that word the fast way.

b. (Touch the ball for **Save.**) Spell it. Get ready. (Tap under each letter as the children say:) *S-A-V-E.*

• (Return to the ball.) Read it. Get ready. (Slash.) *Save.*

c. (Repeat step *b* for each remaining word in the column.)

d. (Repeat steps *b* and *c* until firm.)

Save

chasing

here

her

bird

sliding

silly

Individual test

a. (Call on individual children to read one column of words from the lesson.)

b. (Praise children who read all words with no errors.)

STORY 135
EXERCISE 4

Reading—decoding

a. (Pass out Storybook 2.)

b. Everybody, open your reader to page 151.

c. Remember, if the group reads all the way to the red 5 without making more than five errors, we can go on.

d. Everybody, touch the title of the story. ✔

e. If you hear a mistake, raise your hand. Remember, children who do not have their place lose their turn. (Call on individual children to read two or three sentences. Do not ask comprehension questions. Tally all errors.)

To Correct

word-identification errors (**from,** for example)
1. That word is **from.** What word? *From.*
2. Go back to the beginning of the sentence and read the sentence again.

f. (If the children make more than five errors before they reach the red 5: when they reach the 5 return to the beginning of the story and have the children reread to the 5. Do not ask comprehension questions. Repeat step *f* until firm, and then go on to step *g*.)

g. (When the children read to the red 5 without making more than five errors: read the story to the children from the beginning to the 5. Ask the specified comprehension questions. When you reach the 5, call on individual children to continue reading the story. Have each child read two or three sentences. Ask the specified comprehension questions.)

STORY 131
EXERCISE 5

Reading—decoding

a. (Pass out Storybook 2.)

b. Everybody, open your reader to page 138.

c. Remember, if the group reads all the way to the red 5 without making more than five errors, we can go on.

d. Everybody, touch the title of the story. ✔

e. If you hear a mistake, raise your hand. Remember, children who do not have their place lose their turn. (Call on individual children to read two or three sentences. Do not ask comprehension questions. Tally all errors.)

To Correct

word-identification errors (**from,** for example)
1. That word is **from.** What word? *From.*
2. Go back to the beginning of the sentence and read the sentence again.

f. (If the children make more than five errors before they reach the red 5: when they reach the 5 return to the beginning of the story and have the children reread to the 5. Do not ask comprehension questions. Repeat step *f* until firm, and then go on to step *g.*)

g. (When the children read to the red 5 without making more than five errors: read the story to the children from the beginning to the 5. Ask the specified comprehension questions. When you reach the 5, call on individual children to continue reading the story. Have each child read two or three sentences. Ask the specified comprehension questions.)

Ellen the Eagle[1]

One day Ellen the eagle went on a long trip with her brother. Ellen and her brother didn't drive. They didn't go on a train. <u>They flew.</u>[2] The day was very hot and very dry.

At last her brother said, "Let's stop flying. <u>I need something to drink.</u>"[3]

So Ellen and her brother landed on the hot, dry ground. <u>But they did not see any lakes or any ponds.</u>[4] They walked around for a long time looking for water. Ellen's brother was shouting, "I need water. I can't stand this much longer."

The eagles kept looking and looking. All at once, Ellen saw a deep hole that was not very big around. She stuck her head down the hole. <u>There was water in the bottom of that hole.</u>[5] Ellen bent over as far as she could, but she could not reach the water. The hole was not very wide. ⑤ <u>So Ellen could not slide down and get the water.</u>[6]

Ellen called her brother. Her brother said, "<u>I must have water.</u>[7] I must have water." He stuck his head down the hole and tried to reach the water, but he couldn't. Then he rolled over on the ground and began to shout, "I must have water."

"Stop that," Ellen said. "If we are smart, we can find out how to get that water from the hole."

---

[1] Who is Ellen? (Signal.) *An eagle.*

[2] How did Ellen and her brother go on their trip? (Signal.) *They flew.*

[3] What did her brother need? (Signal.) *Something to drink.*

- Why? (The children respond.)

[4] How do you think they'll get water? (The children respond.)

- Let's read more and find out.

[5] Where did Ellen see water? (Signal.) *In the bottom of the hole.*

[6] Why couldn't Ellen get the water? (The children respond.)

- Right, the hole was deep and not very wide.

[7] What did her brother say? (Signal.) *I must have water.*

READING VOCABULARY

EXERCISE 1

Teacher reads the words in red

a. I'll read each word in red. Then you'll spell each word.

b. (Touch the ball for **stool.**) My turn. (Slash as you say:) Stool. What word? (Signal.) *Stool.*

c. (Return to the ball.) Spell it. Get ready. (Tap under each letter as the children say:) *S-T-O-O-L.*

- What word did you spell? (Signal.) *Stool.*

d. (Repeat steps *b* and *c* for each word in red.)

e. Your turn to read all the words in this column.

f. (Touch the ball for **stool.** Pause.) Get ready. (Slash.) *Stool.*

g. (Repeat step *f* for each remaining word in the column.)

h. (Repeat steps *f* and *g* until firm.)

stool

roots

Snap

Sneak

strong

shell

toad

EXERCISE 2

Words with underlined parts

a. First you're going to read the underlined part of each word in this column. Then you're going to read the whole word.

b. (Touch the ball for **lunch.**) Read the underlined part. Get ready. (Tap the ball.) *ch.*

- Read the whole word. (Pause.) Get ready. (Slash.) *Lunch.*

c. (Repeat step *b* until firm.)

d. (Repeat steps *b* and *c* for each remaining word in the column.)

e. (Repeat the column until children read all the words in order without making a mistake.)

lunch

where

around

these

toadstool

tooth

scare

Ellen began to think. Suddenly she jumped up. "Pick up some stones and drop them into the hole."[8]

"How will that help us?" her brother asked.[9]

"You will see," Ellen said. "Just start dropping stones into the hole."

So Ellen and her brother dropped stones into the hole. And every time a stone went to the bottom of the hole, the water moved up a little bit.[10] Up, up, up. After Ellen and her brother had dropped many stones, the water was near the top of the hole.

The eagles could reach the water now.[11] So they drank and drank and drank. Then they sat in the shade of a big tree.

Then Ellen's brother said, "Ellen, you are a smart eagle, and you are the best sister an eagle can have."[12]

The end

[8] Where are they going to drop the stones? **(Signal.)** *Into the hole.*

[9] What do you think? **(The children respond.)**

• Let's read more and find out.

[10] What happened every time a stone went to the bottom of the hole? **(Signal.)** ***The water moved up a little bit.***

[11] How did the water get high enough for them to reach? **(The children respond.)**

[12] What did Ellen do that was so smart? **(The children respond.)**

EXERCISE 6

Picture comprehension

a. Look at the picture.

b. (Ask these questions:)
   1. What do the eagles have in their mouths? **(Signal.)** *Stones.*
   2. What are Ellen and her brother doing with those stones? **(The children respond.)**
   3. Can the eagles reach the water yet? **(The children respond.)**

EXERCISE 7

Summary of independent activities

a. (Pass out Worksheet 131 to each child.)

b. Everybody, now you'll do your worksheet. Remember to do all parts of the worksheet and to read all the parts carefully.

END OF LESSON 131

"Hello," the snake said. "My name is Flame. And I need something to eat. <u>Are you good to eat?</u>"[7]

"I don't think so," the turtle said. "I don't think I'm good at anything."

"That is too bad," the snake said. "But maybe you could help me. <u>Have you seen any frogs around here?</u>"[8]

The turtle looked at the smiling snake. He looked at the snake's big mouth. Then the turtle told a lie.

"No," the turtle said, "<u>I have not seen any frogs around here.</u>"[9]

<u>To be continued</u>[10]

[7] Why did Flame ask that?
(The children respond.)
- Snakes usually eat frogs.
[8] Who is speaking? (Signal.)
Flame the snake.
[9] Was the turtle telling the truth or telling a lie? (The children respond.)
- Why did he tell that lie?
(The children respond.)
- Yes, I think he wants to save the frog.
[10] Next time we'll find out if Flame finds the frog.

EXERCISE 6

Picture comprehension

a. Look at the picture.
b. (Ask these questions:)
  1. What is that frog doing?
     (The children respond.)
     - Why is he laughing so hard?
       (The children respond.)
  2. What do you think the frog is saying?
     (The children respond.)
  3. How does the turtle feel? (Signal.)
     Very sad.
     - How do you know? (The children respond.)

WORKSHEET 134

INDEPENDENT ACTIVITIES
EXERCISE 7

Reading comprehension

a. (Pass out Worksheet 134 to each child.)
b. Everybody, turn to side 2 of your worksheet. ✔
c. (Point to the story on side 2 of your worksheet.) Everybody, find this story on your worksheet. ✔
d. Today you're going to read a passage that tells about caves.
e. Everybody, touch the first picture. ✔
  - That's a small cave.
f. Everybody, touch the second picture. ✔
  - That's the inside of a very big cave.
g. I'll read the passage. Everybody, follow along. (Read the passage to the children. Check that they are following along as you read.)
h. When you do your independent work, read the passage to yourself. Then answer the questions.

To Correct
comprehension mistakes
1. (Show the child the sentence or part of the passage that answers the question.
  - Direct the child to read that part. Then ask the child the question that was missed.)
2. (Tell the child to write the answer.)

EXERCISE 8

Summary of independent activities

Everybody, now you'll do your worksheet. Remember to do all parts of the worksheet and to read all the parts carefully.

END OF LESSON 134

READING VOCABULARY

EXERCISE 1

Teacher reads the words in red

a. I'll read each word in red. Then you'll spell each word.

b. (Touch the ball for **handsome**.) My turn. (Slash as you say:) Handsome. What word? (Signal.) *Handsome.*

c. (Return to the ball.) Spell it. Get ready. (Tap under each letter as the children say:) *H-A-N-D-S-O-M-E.*
• What word did you spell? (Signal.) *Handsome.*

d. (Repeat steps *b* and *c* for each word in red.)

e. Your turn to read all the words in this column.

f. (Touch the ball for **handsome.** Pause.) Get ready. (Slash.) *Handsome.*

g. (Repeat step *f* for each remaining word in the column.)

h. (Repeat steps *f* and *g* until firm.)

handsome

Caw

Crow

branch

nice

mice

face

EXERCISE 2

Words with underlined parts

a. First you're going to read the underlined part of each word in this column. Then you're going to read the whole word.

b. (Touch the ball for **cheese.**) Read the underlined part. Get ready. (Tap the ball.) *ch.*
• Read the whole word. (Pause.) Get ready. (Slash.) *Cheese.*

c. (Repeat step *b* until firm.)

d. (Repeat steps *b* and *c* for each remaining word in the column.)

e. (Repeat the column until children read all the words in order without making a mistake.)

cheese

chunk

such

smart

Carl

year

eagle

STORYBOOK

EXERCISE 5

Reading—decoding

a. (Pass out Storybook 2.)

b. Everybody, open your reader to page 148.

c. Remember, if the group reads all the way to the red 5 without making more than five errors, we can go on.

d. Everybody, touch the title of the story. ✔

e. If you hear a mistake, raise your hand. Remember, children who do not have their place lose their turn. (Call on individual children to read two or three sentences. Do not ask comprehension questions. Tally all errors.)

To Correct

word-identification errors (from, for example)
1. That word is **from**. What word? *From.*
2. Go back to the beginning of the sentence and read the sentence again.

f. (If the children make more than five errors before they reach the red 5: when they reach the 5 return to the beginning of the story and have the children reread to the 5. Do not ask comprehension questions. Repeat step *f* until firm, and then go on to step *g*.)

g. (When the children read to the red 5 without making more than five errors: read the story to the children from the beginning to the 5. Ask the specified comprehension questions. When you reach the 5, call on individual children to continue reading the story. Have each child read two or three sentences. Ask the specified comprehension questions.)

Flame the Snake [1]

A little turtle was very sad because he could not do things a frog did. [2] The frog could jump way up. But the turtle could not jump at all. The frog got out of the pond and yelled, "Come up here to the land. I want to take a good look at you."

So the turtle came out of the pond. He was wet all over. So the frog could not see that the turtle had tears on his cheeks.

"Ho, ho," the frog said. "You look like a big toenail. [3] You look like the foot of a horse. You look like a joke." The frog jumped up and down on the turtle's shell. "Come on," the frog said. "Take off this hard coat and let me wear it. Then I will look like a toenail." [4]

"I can't take it off," the turtle said. [5] "That hard coat is part of me."

The frog started to laugh. He laughed so hard that tears were running down his cheeks. He laughed until the ground around him was wet. [5] And then he laughed some more.

Suddenly, he stopped laughing. Suddenly, he yelled, "Get out of here. Flame the snake is coming." And then—zip—the frog jumped into the pond. [6]

Before the turtle could get into the pond, a long, fat snake came sliding out of the weeds. The snake slid up to the turtle and smiled.

---

[1] What's the name of the snake in this story? (Signal.) *Flame.*

[2] Why was he sad? (Signal.) *Because he could not do things a frog did.*

- What couldn't the turtle do? (Signal.) *Jump.*

[3] What did he say? (Signal.) *You look like a big toenail.*

- Why did the frog say that? (The children respond.)

- Yes, because of his shell.

[4] Who is speaking? (Signal.) *The frog.*

- What does he want the turtle to do? (Signal.) *Take off his shell.*

- Can the turtle do that? (Signal.) *No.*

[5] How could that happen? (The children respond.)

- Right. His tears made the ground wet.

[6] Why did he stop laughing and do that? (Signal.) *Because Flame the snake was coming.*

- Oh, oh.

EXERCISE 3

Read the fast way

a. You're going to read all the words in this column the fast way.

b. (Touch the ball for **those.** Pause.) Get ready. (Slash.) *Those.*

c. (Repeat step *b* until firm.)

d. (Repeat steps *b* and *c* for each remaining word in the column.)

e. (Repeat the column until the children read all the words in order without making mistakes.)

those

these

city

hungry

lay

black

kind

EXERCISE 4

Words with underlined parts

a. First you're going to read the underlined part of each word in this column. Then you're going to read the whole word.

b. (Touch the ball for **slider.**) Read the underlined part. Get ready. (Tap the ball.) *Slide.*

• Read the whole word. (Pause.) Get ready. (Slash.) *Slider.*

c. (Repeat step *b* until firm.)

d. (Repeat steps *b* and *c* for each remaining word in the column.)

e. (Repeat the column until children read all the words in order without making a mistake.)

<u>slid</u>er

<u>wing</u>s

<u>Trick</u>s

legs

<u>thing</u>s

<u>sing</u>ing

waved

EXERCISE 3

Read the fast way

a. You're going to read all the words in this column the fast way.

b. (Touch the ball for **world**. Pause.) Get ready. (Slash.) *World.*

c. (Repeat step *b* until firm.)

d. (Repeat steps *b* and *c* for each remaining word in the column.)

e. (Repeat the column until the children read all the words in order without making mistakes.)

world

hard

toe

Take

off

coming

ground

EXERCISE 4

Children spell, then read

a. First you're going to spell each word. Then you're going to read that word the fast way.

b. (Touch the ball for **wear**.) Spell it. Get ready. (Tap under each letter as the children say:) *W-E-A-R.*

• (Return to the ball.) Read it. Get ready. (Slash.) *Wear.*

c. (Repeat step *b* for each remaining word in the column.)

d. (Repeat steps *b* and *c* until firm.)

wear

lie

coat

cave

gaped

gapped

joke

Individual test

a. (Call on individual children to read one column of words from the lesson.)

b. (Praise children who read all words with no errors.)

EXERCISE 5

Children spell, then read

a. First you're going to spell each word. Then you're going to read that word the fast way.

b. (Touch the ball for **sing**.) Spell it. Get ready. (Tap under each letter as the children say:) *S-I-N-G*.

• (Return to the ball.) Read it. Get ready. (Slash.) *Sing*.

c. (Repeat step *b* for each remaining word in the column.)

d. (Repeat steps *b* and *c* until firm.)

sing

sang

drank

drink

feathers

dry

try

Individual test

a. (Call on individual children to read one column of words from the lesson.)

b. (Praise children who read all words with no errors.)

STORY 132
EXERCISE 6

Reading—decoding

a. (Pass out Storybook 2.)

b. Everybody, open your reader to page 141.

c. Remember, if the group reads all the way to the red 5 without making more than five errors, we can go on.

d. Everybody, touch the title of the story. ✔

e. If you hear a mistake, raise your hand. Remember, children who do not have their place lose their turn. (Call on individual children to read two or three sentences. Do not ask comprehension questions. Tally all errors.)

To Correct

word-identification errors (**from,** for example)
1. That word is **from**. What word? *From*.
2. Go back to the beginning of the sentence and read the sentence again.

f. (If the children make more than five errors before they reach the red 5: when they reach the 5 return to the beginning of the story and have the children reread to the 5. Do not ask comprehension questions. Repeat step *f* until firm, and then go on to step *g*.)

g. (When the children read to the red 5 without making more than five errors: read the story to the children from the beginning to the 5. Ask the specified comprehension questions. When you reach the 5, call on individual children to continue reading the story. Have each child read two or three sentences. Ask the specified comprehension questions.)

READING VOCABULARY
EXERCISE 1

Teacher reads the words in red

a. I'll read each word in red. Then you'll spell each word.

b. (Touch the ball for **Flame.**) My turn. (Slash as you say:) Flame. What word? (Signal.) *Flame.*

c. (Return to the ball.) Spell it. Get ready. (Tap under each letter as the children say:) *F-L-A-M-E.*

• What word did you spell? (Signal.) *Flame.*

d. (Repeat steps *b* and *c* for each word in red.)

e. Your turn to read all the words in this column.

f. (Touch the ball for **Flame.** Pause.) Get ready. (Slash.) *Flame.*

g. (Repeat step *f* for each remaining word in the column.)

h. (Repeat steps *f* and *g* until firm.)

Flame

shell

Suddenly

started

nail

slid

slide

EXERCISE 2

Words with underlined parts

a. First you're going to read the underlined part of each word in this column. Then you're going to read the whole word.

b. (Touch the ball for **tears.**) Read the underlined part. Get ready. (Tap the ball.) *Ears.*

• Read the whole word. (Pause.) Get ready. (Slash.) *Tears.*

c. (Repeat step *b* until firm.)

d. (Repeat steps *b* and *c* for each remaining word in the column.)

e. (Repeat the column until children read all the words in order without making a mistake.)

tears

cheeks

footprint

maybe

laughed

toenail

until

Carl Tricks the Crow [1]

Carl was a very smart mouse. He lived with three other mice. When the other mice played games, Carl sat. He would think and think.[2] Then he would do something smart.

One year things got very bad for the mice. There was not much food, and all the mice were very hungry.[3] They cried, and yelled, and shouted. They ran around and said, "What are we going to do?[4] What are we going to do?"

One day they came to Carl and said, "Carl, we need food. You are very smart. Can you find some food for us?"[5]

"I think so," Carl said.

Carl left the other mice and went out to find food. Soon he came to a big tree. A crow was sitting in that tree. And the crow had a very big chunk of cheese in his mouth.⑤[6] Carl said to himself, "The other mice and I could have a real meal if I could get the cheese from the crow." So Carl made up a plan for getting the cheese.[7]

Then he said, "My, you are a good-looking crow. You have such pretty wings and such big black feathers."

The crow smiled, but he did not say anything.[8] If he opened his mouth to say something, the cheese would fall from his mouth.

Carl said, "You have such big wings. I'll bet you can fly very far."

The crow smiled and held out his wings.

"Yes," Carl said. "And you have such good-looking legs. I'll bet you run fast with those legs."

The crow smiled and ran up and down the branch of the tree.

Carl said, "I'll bet you can sing well, too."

The crow shook his head no, but he didn't say a thing.[9]

"Come on," Carl said. "Just sing a little bit for me. Come on, you big handsome crow."

The crow smiled and opened his mouth.[10] "Caw, caw," he said. And as he did, the chunk of cheese fell from his mouth. Carl grabbed the cheese and waved to the crow. "You are good at singing, and you are very, very kind. Thank you for this cheese.[11] Thank you very much."

The crow started to tell Carl that he didn't mean to drop the cheese, but Carl kept talking. "I don't think I've ever seen a crow that was as handsome or as kind as you are."

The crow smiled. And Carl went home with the cheese. That night he and the other mice had a fine meal. The other mice said, "Carl, you are very smart."[12]

This story is over.

---

1. What will Carl do in this story? (Signal.) *Trick the crow.*
2. What did Carl like to do? (Signal.) *Think and think.*
3. Why were things very bad for the mice? (The children respond.)
4. Everybody, what did they say? (Signal.) *What are we going to do?*
5. What do they want Carl to do? (Signal.) *Find food for them.*
• Why do they think Carl can do it? (Signal.) *Because he's smart.*
6. Who did Carl see in the tree? (Signal.) *A crow.*
• And what did that crow have? (Signal.) *A big chunk of cheese.*
• Watch out, crow. Carl wants your cheese. Let's keep reading.
7. What do you think his plan is? (The children respond.)
8. Did he open his mouth to speak? (Signal.) *No.*
• What would happen to the cheese if the crow opened his mouth? (The children respond.)
9. Is the crow saying anything yet? (Signal.) *No.*
10. What did Carl want the crow to do? (Signal.) *Sing.*
• Let's see what happens when he sings.
11. Did Carl trick the crow and get the cheese? (Signal.) *Yes.*
12. Is that true? (Signal.) *Yes.*
• What did he do that was so smart? (The children respond.)

EXERCISE 6

Picture comprehension

a. Look at the picture.

b. (Ask these questions:)

1. What kind of animal is that? (Signal.) *A turtle.*

2. What's the turtle doing? (The children respond.) Right. He's hatching, or coming out of the egg.

3. How do you know that he's near some water? (The children respond.)

INDEPENDENT ACTIVITIES
EXERCISE 7

Reading comprehension

a. (Pass out Worksheet 133 to each child.)

b. Everybody, turn to side 2 of your worksheet. ✔

c. (Point to the story on side 2 of your worksheet.) Everybody, find this story on your worksheet. ✔

d. Today you're going to read a passage that tells about weeds.

e. Everybody, touch the picture of the first plant. ✔

• That's a weed.

f. Everybody, touch the picture of the next plant. ✔

• That's a weed.

g. Everybody, touch the picture of the next plant. ✔

• That's a rose. What is it? (Signal.) *A rose.*

h. I'll read the passage. Everybody, follow along. (Read the passage to the children. Check that they are following along as you read.)

i. When you do your independent work, read the passage to yourself. Then answer the questions.

To Correct

comprehension mistakes

1. (Show the child the sentence or part of the passage that answers the question.

• Direct the child to read that part. Then ask the child the question that was missed.)

2. (Tell the child to write the answer.)

EXERCISE 8

Summary of independent activities

Everybody, now you'll do your worksheet. Remember to do all parts of the worksheet and to read all the parts carefully.

END OF LESSON 133

EXERCISE 7

Picture comprehension

a. Look at the picture.

b. (Ask these questions:)
1. Where is the crow?
   (The children respond.)
2. (Point to the notes.) Those little things show he's singing.
3. What's that falling from the crow's mouth? (Signal.) *Cheese.*
4. What is Carl doing? (Signal.) *Catching the cheese.*
5. How does Carl look? (Signal.) *Happy.*

★ FACTUAL INFORMATION PASSAGE

EXERCISE 8

Reading comprehension

a. (Pass out Worksheet 132 to each child.)

b. Everybody, turn to side 2 of your worksheet. ✔

c. (Point to the story on side 2 of your worksheet.) Everybody, find this story on your worksheet. ✔

d. Today you're going to read a passage that tells about eggs. The pictures next to the passage show some of the animals that you'll read about.

e. Everybody, touch the chicken. ✔

f. Everybody, touch the snake. ✔

g. (Repeat step *f* for ant, turtle, fish, alligator.)

h. (Repeat steps *e*, *f*, and *g* until firm.)

i. I'll read the passage. Everybody, follow along. (Read the passage to the children. Check that they are following along as you read.)

j. When you do your independent work, read the passage to yourself. Then answer the questions.

To Correct

comprehension mistake
1. (Show the child the sentence or part of the passage that answers the question.
   • Direct the child to read that part. Then ask the child the question that was missed.)
2. (Tell the child to write the answer.)

INDEPENDENT ACTIVITIES

EXERCISE 9

Summary of independent activities

Everybody, now you'll do your worksheet. Remember to do all parts of the worksheet and to read all the parts carefully.

END OF LESSON 132

STORY 133
EXERCISE 5

Reading—decoding

a. (Pass out Storybook 2.)

b. Everybody, open your reader to page 145.

c. Remember, if the group reads all the way to the red 5 without making more than five errors, we can go on.

d. Everybody, touch the title of the story. ✔

e. If you hear a mistake, raise your hand. Remember, children who do not have their place lose their turn. (Call on individual children to read two or three sentences. Do not ask comprehension questions. Tally all errors.)

To Correct

word-identification errors (**from,** for example)

1. That word is **from.** What word? *From.*
2. Go back to the beginning of the sentence and read the sentence again.

f. (If the children make more than five errors before they reach the red 5: when they reach the 5 return to the beginning of the story and have the children reread to the 5. Do not ask comprehension questions. Repeat step *f* until firm, and then go on to step *g.*)

g. (When the children read to the red 5 without making more than five errors: read the story to the children from the beginning to the 5. Ask the specified comprehension questions. When you reach the 5, call on individual children to continue reading the story. Have each child read two or three sentences. Ask the specified comprehension questions.)

The Turtle and the Frog[1]

Once there was an egg. This egg was on the shore of a pond. It was in the sand. The sun was shining, and the egg was getting hotter and hotter.

Then one day something came out of the egg.[2] Did a chicken come out of the egg? No. Did a little duckling come out of the egg? No. What came out of the egg? A turtle.[3]

That turtle did not know that he was a turtle. He came out of the egg and looked around. Things looked good to him. The sun felt hot. That felt good. He walked to the pond. The water felt good. He went for a swim. That was fun. Then he sat on a log. He grabbed a fly and ate it.[4] That was good.[5]

Then he saw a frog. The frog got up on the log. ⑤ Then the frog said, "You are funny-looking."[6]

The turtle did not know what to say.

He had never really looked at himself. He didn't feel funny-looking. Now he felt a little sad. He said to the frog, "You look good."

"Yes," the frog said and smiled. "I am good. Watch this." The frog jumped way up and then—splash.[7] He landed in the water.

"Wow," the turtle said. "I like that. I think I'll jump way up and land in the water."

So the turtle tried to jump way up.[8] But he didn't go way up. He slid off the log and landed in the water.[9] When he came up, the frog said, "Ho, ho. You are funny. You can't even jump. Ho, ho."

The little turtle was not going "ho, ho." He was feeling very, very sad.[10] Before he met that frog, things had seemed good to him. But now the pond did not look pretty, and the sun did not feel good. Everything seemed sad.[11]

More to come[12]

---

[1] Who will this story be about? (Signal.) *The turtle and the frog.*

[2] What do you think it was? (The children respond.)

• Let's read some more and find out.

[3] What came out of the egg? (Signal.) *A turtle.*

[4] That's what turtles eat.

[5] Name some things he liked. (The children respond.)

[6] Who is talking? (Signal.) *A frog.*

• Who is he talking to? (Signal.) *The turtle.*

[7] What did the frog do? (Signal.) *Jump.* Yes, frogs are good at jumping.

[8] Do you think he can jump up high like a frog? (The children respond.)

[9] Did he make it? (Signal.) *No.*

[10] Why was he sad? (The children respond.) Yes, he didn't like being laughed at.

[11] What happened to make everything seem sad? (The children respond.)

[12] We'll read more about the turtle next time.

READING VOCABULARY

EXERCISE 1

Teacher reads the words in red

a. I'll read each word in red. Then you'll spell each word.

b. (Touch the ball for **world.**) My turn. (Slash as you say:) World. What word? (Signal.) *World.*

c. (Return to the ball.) Spell it. Get ready. (Tap under each letter as the children say:) *W-O-R-L-D.*

• What word did you spell? (Signal.) *World.*

d. (Repeat steps *b* and *c* for each word in red.)

e. Your turn to read all the words in this column.

f. (Touch the ball for **world.** Pause.) Get ready. (Slash.) *World.*

g. (Repeat step *f* for each remaining word in the column.)

h. (Repeat steps *f* and *g* until firm.)

world

wear

toe

turtle

footprint

duckling

nail

slid

EXERCISE 2

Read the fast way

a. You're going to read all the words in this column the fast way.

b. (Touch the ball for **branch.** Pause.) Get ready. (Slash.) *Branch.*

c. (Repeat step *b* until firm.)

d. (Repeat steps *b* and *c* for each remaining word in the column.)

e. (Repeat the column until the children read all the words in order without making mistakes.)

branch

pond

nice

place

handsome

crow

know

EXERCISE 3

Read the fast way

a. You're going to read all the words in this column the fast way.

b. (Touch the ball for **water.** Pause.) Get ready. (Slash.) *Water.*

c. (Repeat step *b* until firm.)

d. (Repeat steps *b* and *c* for each remaining word in the column.)

e. (Repeat the column until the children read all the words in order without making mistakes.)

water

frog

Splash

weed

chicken

hotter

didn't

EXERCISE 4

Children spell, then read

a. First you're going to spell each word. Then you're going to read that word the fast way.

b. (Touch the ball for **snake.**) Spell it. Get ready. (Tap under each letter as the children say:) *S-N-A-K-E.*

• (Return to the ball.) Read it. Get ready. (Slash.) *Snake.*

c. (Repeat step *b* for each remaining word in the column.)

d. (Repeat steps *b* and *c* until firm.)

snake

cons

cones

shine

felt

shore

shining

Individual test

a. (Call on individual children to read one column of words from the lesson.)

b. (Praise children who read all words with no errors.)

Grade 1 Reading Curriculum Map

Reading Mastery Signature Edition, Grade 1

Key: (for Teachers)   √= informal assessment   Numbers = exercise numbers   Bold face type = first appearance

		Lesson 1	Lesson 2	Lesson 3	Lesson 4	Lesson 5
Phonemic Awareness		Segmentation review: 16	Segmentation: 18	Segmentation: 6	Segmentation: 6	
Print Awareness						
Letter Sound Correspondence		Introduction: 4 (ar) Review: 1 (ă, ŭ, th, ĕ, wh, d, ŏ, h, ĭ); 5, 7, 8 (ar) √: 1, 4, 5, 7, 8	Review: 1 (ŭ, th, ĕ, wh, ŏ, h, ĭ, sh, er, ĭ); 7, 8, 9, 10, 11 (ar) √: 1, 7, 8 ,9, 10	Review:1 (ĕ, ĭ, wh, ŭ, sh, th, ă, ŏ, m, ch) √: 1	Review: 1 (ŏ, ŏ, th, wh, ch , sh, ĕ, ĭ, ă, er, ĕ, g, l, s) √: 1	Review: 1 (ŭ, ĕ, ch, ĭ, ă, d, ŏ, m, sh, b, f, r) √: 1
		Review: 15, 16	Review: 17, 18	Review: 7, 11	Review: 7, 11	Review: 18
Phonics and Word Recognition	*Irregular*			**of:** 4 √	**do:** 4 √	**walk, talk, walking:** 4 **talking:** 5 √: 4, 5
	Regular	Blending sounds into words: 2 **(lift)**, 3 **(clap)**, 5 **(far)**, 9 **(road, sitting, went, every, this, that, the, then)** Reading words: 5 **(far)**, 6 **(are)**, 7 **(bar)**, 8 **(car)**, 9 **(road, sitting, went, every, this, that, the, then)** √	Blending sounds into words: 2 **(paint)**, 3 **(mail)**, 4 **(kissed, when)**, 5 **(where)**, 6 **(there)** √: 2, 3, 4, 5, 6 Reading words: 2 **(paint)**, 3 **(mail)**, 4 **(kissed, when)**, 5 **(where)**, 6 **(there)**, 8, 9 **(farm)**, 10 **(charm)**, 11 **(cart)** √: 2, 3, 4, 5, 6, 8, 9, 10, 11	Reading words: 2, 4 **(them, her, here, didn't, don't, for, she, ate, barn, why)**, 5 √: 2, 4, 5	Reading words: 2, 4 **(he, were, at, they, these, those, even, very, did, yard)** √: 2, 4	Blending sounds into words: 2, 3, 4, 6 **(stop)**, 7, 9, 10 Reading words: 2, 3, 4 **(live)**, 5 **(girls, going)**, 6, 7, 8 **(arm)**, 9, 10, 11
		Reading words: 10 Connected text: 11, 12 √: 11, 12	Reading words: 12 Connected text: 13, 14 √: 13, 14			Reading words: 13 Connected text:14, 15 √: 14, 15
		Reading words review: 14, 16	Reading words review: 16, 18	Reading words review: 6, 8		Reading words review: 17, 18
Fluency		Reading words: 2, 3, 5, 6, 7, 8, 9 √: 2, 3, 5, 6, 7, 8, 9	Reading words: 2, 3, 4, 5, 6, 8, 9, 10, 11 √: 2, 3, 4, 5, 6, 8, 9, 10, 11	Repeated reading: 5 √	Repeated reading: 5 √	Reading words: 2–10 √: 2–10
		Repeated reading: 12 √	Repeated reading: 14 √			Repeated reading: 15 √
						Individual Checkout (I.C.): 19
Comprehension				Following directions: 3	Following directions: 3	Following directions: 12
		Note details: 12, 13 Visualize: 13 Determine character emotions: 13 Make judgments: 12 Make deductions: 12 Drawing inferences:13 Predictions: 13	Note details: 14, 15 Visualize: 15 Make deductions: 14 Drawing inferences: 14 Predictions: 15 Cause/effect: 14			Note details: 15, 16 Predictions: 15 Make judgments: 15, 16 Drawing inferences: 15, 16 Cause/effect: 15 Determine character emotions: 16
		Note details: 14, 16	Note details: 16, 18 Determine character emotions: 18	Note details: 6, 10	Note details: 6, 10 Determine character emotions: 6	Note details: 17, 18
Spelling		Phonograms review: 1–5 Segmentation review: 2–5	Phonograms review: 1–3 Segmentation review: 2, 3	Phonograms review: 1–3 Segmentation review: 2, 3	Phonograms review: 1–5 Segmentation review: 2–5	Phonograms review: 1–3 Segmentation review: 2, 3
		Writing sounds: 1 Writing words: 2–5	Writing sounds: 1 Writing words: 2, 3	Writing sounds: 1 Writing words: 2, 3	Writing sounds: 1 Writing words: 2–5	Writing sounds: 1 Writing words: 2, 3

Key: (for Teachers)   √= informal assessment   Numbers = exercise numbers   Bold face type = first appearance

		Lesson 6	Lesson 7	Lesson 8	Lesson 9	Lesson 10
Phonemic Awareness						
Print Awareness						
Letter Sound Correspondence		Review: 1 (ĭ, ĭ, r, l, ĕ, ĕ, s, ŏ, h, ŭ, x, t) √: 1	Review: 1 (ĕ, ĕ, b, h, d, ā, ŏ, l, ĭ, t, ŭ, c), 5 (ar), 6 (ar), 7 (ar) √: 1, 5, 6, 7	Review: 1 (ŏ, ā, ĕ, ĭ, ŏ, ŭ, l, m, r, s, t, w) √ 1	Review: 1 (ĕ, ĭ, ŏ, ŭ, t, m, n, w, s, ā, ĭ, ŏ, th) √ 1	Review: 1 (ĕ, ĕ, b, d, ŏ, ŏ, n, m, ŭ, w, s, r), 8 (ar) √: 1, 8
		Review: 19, 20	Review: 18, 19, 20	Review: 7, 8, 9	Review: 7, 8, 9	Review: 17
Phonics and Word Recognition	**Irregular**	3– **away** √				Blending sounds into words: 5 (**other**), 6 (**book**), 7 (**another**) √: 5, 6, 7 Reading words: : 5 (**other**), 6 (**book**), 7 (**another**) √: 5, 6, 7
	Regular	Blending sounds into words: 2, 3 (**can**), 6 (**yarn**), 7 (**start**), 8, 9 (**lived**) √: 2, 6, 7, 8, 9 Reading words: 2, 3 (**can**), 4 (**dig, dog, big, dug, cop, hole**), 5, 6 (**yarn**), 7 (**start**), 8, 9 (**lived**), 10 √: 2 – 9	Blending sounds into words: 2, 3 (**came**), 4 (**made**), 5 (**art**), 6 (**tart**), 7, 9 (**never**) √: 2, 3, 4, 5, 6, 7 Reading words: : 2, 3 (**came**), 4 (**made**), 5 (**art**), 6 (**tart**), 7, 8 (**starting, yes, liked**), 9 (**never**), 10 √: 2–9	Reading words: 2, 4 √: 2, 4	Reading words: 2, 4 √: 2, 4	Blending sounds into words: 2 (**like**), 3 (**with, bath, help, helped, happy, then, when, where, played**) , 9 (**shark**) √: 2, 3, 9 Reading words: 2 (**like**), 3 (**with, bath, help, helped, happy, then, when, where, played**) , 4 (**swim**), 5 (**other**), 6 (**book**), 7 (**another**), 8 (**ark**), 9 (**shark**), 10 (**arf, bark, barked**) √: 2–10 Onset rime: 4 (**swim**) √
		Reading words: 12 Connected text: 13, 14 √: 13, 14	Reading words: 12 Connected text: 13, 14 √: 13, 14			Reading words: 11 Connected text: 12, 13 √: 12, 13
		Reading words review: 16, 18, 20	Reading words review: 16, 18, 20	Reading words review: 5, 7, 9	Reading words review: 5, 7, 9	Reading words review: 15, 16
Fluency		Reading words: 2–10 √: 2–9	Reading words: 2–10 √: 2–9	Reading words:4 √	Reading words: 4 √	Reading words: 2–10 √: 2–10
		Repeated reading: 14 √	Repeated reading: 14 √			Repeated reading: 13 √
						Individual Checkout (I.C.): 18
Comprehension		Following directions: 11	Following directions: 11	Following directions: 3	Following directions: 3	
		Making judgments: 14, 15 Noting details: 14, 15 Making deductions: 14 Determining character emotions: 14 Making connections: 15	Noting details: 14, 15 Drawing inferences: 14 Making connections: 15			Noting details: 13, 14 Making predictions: 13 Drawing conclusions: 13, 14 Determining character emotions: 14 Making connections: 14
		Noting details: 16, 18	Noting details: 16, 18	Noting details: 7 Determining character emotions: 7	Noting details: 7 Determining character emotions: 7	Noting details: 15, 16, 17
Spelling		Phonograms review: 1–3 Segmentation review: 2, 3	Phonograms review: 1, 2 Segmentation review: 2	Phonograms review: 1, 2 Segmentation review: 2	Phonograms review: 1–3 Segmentation review: 2, 3	Phonograms review: 1–3 Segmentation review: 2, 3
		Writing sounds: 1 Writing words: 2, 3	Writing sounds: 1 Writing words: 2	Writing sounds: 1 Writing words: 2	Writing sounds: 1 Writing words: 2, 3	Writing sounds: 1 Writing words: 2, 3

Reading Mastery Signature Edition, Grade 1

		Lesson 11	Lesson 12	Lesson 13	Lesson 14	Lesson 15
Phonemic Awareness						
Print Awareness						
Letter Sound Correspondence		Review: 1 (er, ĕ, ā, ē, th, wh, ch, sh, short-y, g, h, p), 4, 5, 6 (ar) √: 1, 4, 5, 6	Review: 1 (ŏ, ē, ŏ, ĕ, h, z, g, p, short-y, w), 4, 6 (ar) √: 1, 4, 6	Review: 1 (ī, ŏ, Ī, ŏ, th, wh, c, v, g, m, r, n) √: 1	Review: 1 (f, h, z, k, short-y, long-y, r, p, ī, ă, ī, ā) √: 1	Review: 1 (short-y, long-y, ă, ŏ, ā, ŏ, v, p, d, f, m, k) √: 1
		Review: 19, 20, 22	Review: 17, 18, 23, 24	Review: 9, 10	Review: 18, 19	Review: 16
Phonics and Word Recognition	**Irregular**	Blending sounds into words: 11, 12 (**took**) √: 11, 12 Reading words: 13 (**looked, cooked**) √: 13	Blending sounds into words: 10 (**books**) Reading words: 11 (**looks**) √: 10, 11		Blending sounds into words: 4 (**boy**), 9 (**touch**) √	
	Regular	Blending sounds into words: 2, 3, 6, 7, 9 (**after, yelled, swimming**) √: 2, 3, 6, 7, 9 Reading words: 2, 3, 5, 6, 7, 8, 9 (**after, yelled, swimming**), 10 (**funny**) √: 2, 3, 5, 6, 7, 8, 9, 10 Onset rime: 8 (**swam**) √	Blending sounds into words: 2 (**swims**), 3 (**plays**), 4, 6, 7 (**better**), 8, 10 (**horse**) √: 2, 3, 4, 6, 7, 8, 10 Reading words: 2 (**swims**), 3 (**plays**), 4, 5, 6, 7 (**better**), 8, 9, 10 (**horse**), 11 √: 2–11	Reading words: 4 √: 4	Blending sounds into words: 2 (**ride**), 3 (**fast**), 4 (**cow, stopped**) 5 (**try**), 6 (**fly**) √: 2–6 Reading words: 2 (**ride**), 3 (**fast**), 4 (**cow, stopped**) 5 (**try**), 6 (**fly**), 7, 8, 9, 10 √: 2–9 Onset rime: 8 (**creek**) √	Blending sounds into words: 2, 3, 4 (**rode, let's faster, next**), 6, 7, 8 (**stream**), 9 (**splash**) √: 2, 3, 4, 6, 7, 8, 9 Reading words: 2, 3, 4 (**rode, let's faster, next**), 5, 6, 7, 8 (**stream**), 9 (**splash**), 10 √: 2–10
		Reading words: 14 Connected text: 15, 16 √: 15, 16	Reading words: 12 Connected text: 13, 14 √: 13, 14		Reading words: 12 Connected text: 13, 14 √: 13, 14	Reading words: 12 Connected text: 13, 14 √: 13, 14
		Reading words review: 18, 19, 21, 22	Reading words review: 16, 17, 19, 20	Reading words review: 5		
Fluency		Reading words: 2, 3, 5, 6, 7, 8, 9, 10, 11, 12, 13 √: 2, 3, 5, 6, 7, 8, 9, 10, 11, 12, 13	Reading words: 2–11 √: 2–11	Reading words: 4 √: 4	Reading words: 2–10 √: 2–9	Reading words: 2–10 √: 2–9
		Repeated reading: 16√	Repeated reading: 14 √		Repeated reading: 14 √	Repeated reading: 14 √
		Sentence copying: 25	Sentence copying: 17	Sentence copying: 10	Sentence copying: 18	Sentence copying: 16
						IC: 17
Comprehension				Following directions: 3	Following directions: 11	Following directions: 11
		Noting details: 16, 17 Determining character emotions: 16 Making connections: 17	Noting details: 14, 15 Making predictions: 14 Drawing conclusions: 15 Making connections: 15		Noting details: 14, 15 Making connections: 14, 15 Making predictions: 14, 15 Determining character emotions: 15	Noting details: 14, 15 Making predictions: 14, 15 Making connections: 15
		Noting details: 22, 24, 27	Noting details: 16, 19, 20, 22, 25	Noting details: 5, 7, 8 Determining character emotions: 8	Noting details: 17, 20, 21	Noting details: 16
Spelling		Phonograms review: 1–4 Segmentation review: 3, 4	Phonograms review: 1–5 Segmentation review: 2, 3, 5	Phonograms review: 1–4 Segmentation review: 3, 4	Phonograms review: 1–4 Segmentation review: 3, 4	Phonograms review: 1–5 Segmentation review: 3, 4
						Writing sounds: 1, 2 Writing words: 3, 4, 5
		Writing sounds: 1, 2 Writing words: 3, 4	Writing sounds: 1, 4 Writing words: 2, 3, 5	Writing sounds: 1, 2 Writing words: 3, 4	Writing sounds: 1, 2 Writing words: 3, 4	

Reading Mastery Signature Edition, Grade 1

	Lesson 16	Lesson 17	Lesson 18	Lesson 19	Lesson 20
Phonemic Awareness					
Print Awareness	Sentence copying: 17	Sentence copying: 18	Sentence copying: 9	Sentence copying: 18	Sentence copying: 16
Letter Sound Correspondence	Review: 1 (ŏ, ŭ, ō, b, y, f, t, h, n, y, s, v), 8 (ar) √: 1, 8	Review: 1 (b, ĕ, h, t, k y, m, z, n, y) √: 1	Review: 1 (th, wh, ch, ī, ĭ, d, x, k, r, z, s,ŭ, w) √: 1	Review: 1 (ŏ, x, ch, qu, ing, z, er, w, sh, c, n, y, s), 6 (ar)	Review: 1 (qu, x, ing, er, sh, c, h, z, j, ĕ, ē, ĭ)
	Review: 17, 18	Review: 18, 19	Review: 9, 10	Review: 18, 20	Review: 16
Phonics and Word Recognition — *Irregular*	Blending sounds into words: 4 (**come, some**), 6 (**what**)	Blending sounds into words: 5 (**water**), 9 (**circle**) √: 5, 9		Reading words: 7 (**girl**) √	Blending sounds into words: 5 (**good**) √: 5 Reading words: 2 (**mother, brother**)
Phonics and Word Recognition — *Regular*	Blending sounds into words: 2, 3, 4 (**best, same, over**), 7 (**bank**), 8 √:2, 3, 4, 7, 8 Reading words: : 2, 3, 4 (**best, same, over**), 5, 7 (**bank**), 8, 9	Blending sounds into words: 2, 3 (**real**), 4 (**jumping**), 6, 8 √: 2, 3, 4, 6, 8 Reading words: 2, 3 (**real**), 4 (**jumping**), 6, 7, 8, 10 √: 2, 3, 4, 6, 7, 8	Reading words: 2, 4 √: 4	Blending sounds into words: 2 (**story**), 3, 4 (**tried, cry, cried**), 5, 6 √: 2–6 Reading words: : 2 (**story**), 3, 4 (**tried, cry, cried**), 5, 6, 7, 8 √: 2–7	Blending sounds into words: 3 (**self**), 4 (**ask**), 5 (**reading, really, rabbit**), 6, 7 (**read**), 8 (**play**) √: 3–8 Reading words: 2, 3 (**self**), 4 (**ask**), 5 (**reading, really, rabbit**), 6, 7 (**read**), 8 (**play**), 9 √: 2–8
	Reading words: 11 Connected text: 12, 13 √: 12, 13	Reading words: 12 Connected text: 13, 14 √: 13, 14		Reading words: 10 Connected text:11, 12 √: 11, 12	Reading words: 11 Connected text: 12, 13 √: 12, 13
			Reading words review: 5	Reading words review: 14	Reading words review: 15
Fluency	Reading words: 2–9 √: 2–8	Reading words: 2–10 √: 2–9	Reading words: 4 √: 4	Reading words: 2–8 √: 2–7	Reading words: 2–9 √: 2–8
	Repeated reading: 13	Repeated reading: 14		Repeated reading: 12 √	Repeated reading: 13 √
					IC: 17
Comprehension	Following directions: 10	Following directions: 11	Following directions: 3	Following directions: 9	Following directions: 10
	Noting details: 13, 14 Determining character emotions: 14	Noting details: 14 Making predictions: 14 Cause/effect: 14, 15 Determining character emotions: 15 Making connections: 15		Noting details: 12 Making predictions: 13 Making connections: 13	Noting details: 12, 13 Accessing prior knowledge: 12, 13 Making connections: 14
	Noting details: 16, 19, 20	Noting details: 17, 20, 21	Following directions: 5 Noting details: 7, 8 Determining character emotions: 8	Following directions: 14 Noting details: 16, 17, 19	Following directions: 15 Noting details: 16
					Lesson 20 Curriculum-Based Assessment
Spelling	Phonograms review: 1–3 Segmentation review: 3	Phonograms review: 1–4 Segmentation review: 3, 4	Phonograms review: 1–4 Segmentation review: 3, 4	Phonograms review:1–4 Segmentation review: 3, 4	Phonograms review: 1–4 Segmentation review: 3, 4
	Writing sounds: 1, 2 Writing words: 3, 4	Writing sounds: 1, 2 Writing words: 4, 5	Writing sounds: 1, 2 Writing words: 3–5	Writing sounds: 1, 2 Writing words: 3–5	Writing sounds: 1, 2 Writing words: 3–5

Reading Mastery Signature Edition, Grade 1

		Lesson 21	Lesson 22	Lesson 23	Lesson 24	Lesson 25
Spelling		Writing sounds: 1 Writing words: 2–4 Writing sentences: 5 Phonograms review: 1–3 Segmentation review: 2, 3	Writing sounds: 1 Writing words: 2, 3 Writing sentences: 4 Phonograms review: 1, 2 Segmentation review: 2	Writing sounds: 1, 2 Writing words: 3, 4 Writing sentences: 5 Phonograms review: 1, 2, 3 Segmentation review: 3	Writing sounds: 1, 2 Writing words: 3–6 Writing sentences: 7 Phonograms review: 1–5 Segmentation review: 3–5	Writing sounds: 1, 2 Writing words: 3–6 Writing sentences: 7 Phonograms review: 1–5 Segmentation review: 3–5
Comprehension		Following directions: 11 Noting details: 13, 14, 15 Making connections: 15 Making predictions: 15 Determining character emotions: 19 Noting details: 17, 19, 21 Following directions: 18	Following directions: 10 Noting details: 12, 13, 14 Cause/effect: 13 Noting details: 16, 18, 20 Following directions: 17	Following directions: 12 Noting details: 14, 15 Drawing conclusions: 15 Making connections: 15 Noting details: 18, 20, 22 Following directions: 19	Following directions: 8 Noting details: 10, 11, 12 Cause/effect: 11 Drawing conclusions: 11 Making connections: 12 Noting details: 14, 16, 18 Following directions: 15	Following directions: 15 Noting details: 17, 18 Making predictions: 18, 19 Cause/effect: 18, 19 Making connections: 19 Determining character emotions: 19 Noting details: 20 Following directions: 20 IC: 21
Fluency		Reading words: 2–10 √: 2–9 Repeated reading: 14 √ Sentence copying: 21	Reading words: 2–9 √: 2–8 Repeated reading: 13 Sentence copying: 19	Reading words: 2–11 √: 2–10 Repeated reading: 15 √ Sentence copying: 21	Reading words: 2–7 √: 2–6 Repeated reading: 11 √ Sentence copying: 17	Reading words: 2–14 √: 2–13 Repeated reading: 18 √ Sentence copying: 20
Phonics and Word Recognition	Regular	Blending sounds into words: 2 (bake), 3, 4 (bakes, cake), 5, 6 (asked), 7 (kind), 8 (hard), 9 (card), 10 √: 2–6 Reading words: 3, 4, 5 (bakes, cake), 5, 6 (asked), 7 (kind), 8 (hard), 9 (card), 10 √: 2–9 Connected text: 13, 14 Reading words: 12 √: 13, 14	Blending sounds into words: 2 (hates), 3, 4, 5 (baked, eagle, bones), 7 (spot), 8 (smelled), 9 √: 2, 3, 4, 5, 7, 8 Reading words: 2 (hates), 3, 4, 5 (baked, eagle, bones), 7 (spot), 8 (smelled), 9 √: 2–8 Connected text: 12, 13 Reading words: 11 √: 12, 13	Blending sounds into words: 3 (getting), 4 (fine), 5 (leave), 6 (side), 7 (pay, meal, well), 8, 9, 10, 11 (street) √: 3, 4, 5, 6, 7, 8 Reading words: 3 (getting), 4 (fine), 5 (leave), 6 (side), 7 (pay, meal, well), 8, 9, 10, 11 (street) √: 2–10 Onset rime: 9 (broom) √ Connected text: 14, 15 Reading words: 13 √: 14, 15	Blending sounds into words: 2 (room), 3, 4 (still) √: 2–4 Reading words: 2 (room), 3, 4 (still), 5, 6 (note, my, pad), 7 √: 2–6 Connected text: 10, 11 Reading words: 9 √: 10, 11	Blending sounds into words: 2 (white), 3 (steps), 4 (must), 5, 9, 11 (told) √: 2, 3, 4, 5, 11 Reading words: 2 (white), 3 (steps), 4 (must), 5, 6, 7, 8, 9, 10, 11 (told), 12, 14 √: 2–12 Onset rime: 12 (brush) √ Connected text: 17, 18 Reading words: 16 √: 17, 18
	Irregular			Reading words: 2 (look) √	Reading words: 6 (walked)	Blending sounds into words: 6 (who), 13 (answered) √: 6, 13 Reading words: 8 (doing) √
Letter Sound Correspondence		Review: 20, 22 Review: 1 (u, m, n, g, u, ing, sh, f, p, r, h, j), 8 (ar) √: 1, 8	Review: 19, 21 Review: 1 (i, r, o, b, t, c, n, f, w, x, l, p) √: 1	Review: 21, 23 Review: 1 (sh, b, d, f, ā, g, w, j, z, k, l) √: 1	Review: 17, 19 Review: 1 (ī, ā, z, wh, n, d, l, h, ō, ī, m, v), 5 (ar) √: 1, 5	Review: 20 Review: 1 (ā, ī, th, n, s, er, ū, ō, j, k, t, y), 7 (ar) √: 1, 7
Print Awareness						
Phonemic Awareness						

Key: (for Teachers)   √= informal assessment   Numbers = exercise numbers   Bold face type = first appearance

Key: (for Teachers)   √ = informal assessment   Numbers = exercise numbers   Bold face type = first appearance

		Lesson 26	Lesson 27	Lesson 28	Lesson 29	Lesson 30
Phonemic Awareness			Onset rime: 10			
Print Awareness		Sentence copying: 19	Sentence copying: 23	Sentence copying: 19	Sentence copying: 21	Sentence copying: 20
Letter Sound Correspondence		Review: 1 (ĕ, ŏ, ch, f, j, th,wh, m, s, ing) √	Review: 1 (ĭ, ā, th, wh, ch, qu, l, p, r, x, sh, h), 13 (ar) √: 1, 13	Review: 1 (v, ă, er, w, sh, k, b, n, g, ŏ, ĕ, j), 6 (ar), 7 (ar) √: 1, 6, 7	Review: 1 (ŭ, ĭ, ĕ, th, ing, h, sh, f, p, j, ŏ), 10 (ar) √: 1, 10	Review: 1 (j, ōāĭ, th, wh, n, t, qu, b, d, h), 7 (ar), 11 (al), 12 (al) √: 1, 7, 11
		Review: 19	Review: 23	Review: 19	Review: 21	Review: 20
Phonics and Word Recognition	**Irregular**	Blending sounds into words: 7 (**from**) √	Blending sounds into words: 7 (**bird**), 8 (**money**), 12 (**because**) √: 7, 8, 12	Blending sounds into words: 4 (**brothers, love**), 8 (**want**), 9 (**buttons**)	Blending sounds into words: 5 (**buy**)	Reading words: 10 (**wanted, one**)
	Regular	Blending sounds into words: 2, 3 (**sore**), 4 (**blow**), 5 (**legs**), 6 (**painted, Don's, old, horn**), 8 (**drop**) √: 2–6, 8 Reading words: 2, 3 (**sore**), 4 (**blow**), 5 (**legs**), 6 (**painted, Don's, old, horn**), 8 (**drop**), 9 (**hold, each, dropped**), 10 √: 2–9	Blending sounds into words: 2, 3, 4, 5 (**held**), 6, 9 (**rob, store, robbers, toot**) √: 2–6, 9 Reading words: 2, 3, 4, 5 (**held**), 6, 9 (**rob, store, robbers, toot**), 11 (**dropping, bags**), 13, 14 √: 2–6, 9, 11, 13	Blending sounds into words: 2, 3, 4 (**cannot, jumps, sky**) √: 2–4 Reading words: 2, 3, 4 (**cannot, jumps, sky**), 5 (**grabbed, six, than**), 6, 7, 10 √: 2–7, 10	Blending sounds into words: 2 (**more**), 3 (**pants**), 4, 6 (**think, pink, bag**), 7 (**off**), 8, 10 (**farmer**), 11 √: 2, 3, 4, 6, 8, 10, 11 Reading words: : 2 (**more**), 3 (**pants**), 4, 6 (**think, pink, bag**), 7 (**off**), 8, 9 (**gold, sold**), 10 (**farmer**), 11, 12 √: 2, 3, 4, 6–11	Blending sounds into words: 2, 3 (**lady**), 4 (**yellow**), 5, 6 (**three**), 8 (**trip**), 9, 13 (**selling**) √: 2–5, 6, 8, 9, 13 Reading words: 2, 3 (**lady**), 4 (**yellow**), 5, 6 (**three**),7, 8 (**trip**), 9, 10 (**cold, kept**), 12 (**ball**), 13 (**selling**), 14 √: 2–10, 12, 13
		Reading words: 12 Connected text: 13, 14 √: 13, 14	Reading words: 16 Connected text: 17, 18 √: 17, 18	Reading words: 12 Connected text: 13, 14 √: 13, 14	Reading words: 14 Connected text: 15, 16 √: 15, 16	Reading words: 16 Connected text: 17, 18 √: 17, 18
Fluency		Reading words: 2–10 √: 2–9	Reading words: 2–14 √: 2–13	Reading words: 2–10 √: 2–9	Reading words: 2–12 √: 2–11	Reading words: 2–10, 12, 13, 14 √: 2–10, 13
		Repeated reading: 14 √	Repeated reading: 18 √	Repeated reading: 14	Repeated reading: 16 √	Repeated reading: 18 √
						IC: 21
Comprehension		Following directions: 11	Following directions: 15	Following directions: 11	Following directions: 13	Following directions: 15
		Accessing prior knowledge: 13, 14 Noting details: 13, 14, 15 Making deductions: 13 Making connections: 15	Noting details: 17, 18, 19 Cause/effect: 18 Determining character emotions: 19 Making deductions: 19	Noting details: 13, 14, 15 Activating prior knowledge: 15 Making connections: 15	Noting details: 16, 17 Making predictions: 16 Cause/effect: 16 Drawing inferences: 17	Accessing prior knowledge: 17 Making judgments: 17 Noting details: 17, 18 Making predictions: 18
		Noting details: 17, 20 Following directions: 18	Noting details: 21, 24 Following directions: 22	Noting details: 17, 20 Following directions: 18	Noting details: 19, 22 Following directions: 20	Noting details: 20 Following directions: 20
Spelling		Phonograms review: 1–4 Segmentation review: 3, 4	Phonograms review: 1–4 Segmentation review: 3, 4	Phonograms review: 1–3 Segmentation review: 3	Phonograms review: 1–4 Segmentation review: 3, 4	Phonograms review: 1–3 Segmentation review: 3
						Writing sounds: 1, 2 Writing words: 3, 4 Writing sentences: 5
		Writing sounds: 1, 2 Writing words: 3–5 Writing sentences: 6	Writing sounds: 1, 2 Writing words: 3–5 Writing sentences: 6	Writing sounds: 1, 2 Writing words: 3, 4 Writing sentences: 5	Writing sounds: 1, 2 Writing words: 3–5 Writing sentences: 6	

Reading Mastery Signature Edition, Grade 1

		Lesson 31	Lesson 32	Lesson 33	Lesson 34	Lesson 35
Phonemic Awareness				Onset rime: 11 **(small)** √: 11		Onset rime: 12 **(sleep)**, 18, 19 √: 12, 18, 19
Print Awareness		Sentence copying: 21	Sentence copying: 9	Sentence copying: 22	Sentence copying: 29	Sentence copying: 26
Letter Sound Correspondence		Review: 1 (s, ĕ, ŏ, ā, ĭ, ū, ch, b, c, d, g, m), 7–10 (al) √:1, 7–10	Review: 1 (p, b, d, t, h, k, m, ă, ĭ, ā, ŏ, r) √: 1	Review: 1 (ē, ū, ĕ, ŏ, th, ch, ing, j, sh, b, d, g), 8–9 (al) √: 1, 8, 9	Review: 1 (h, k, ĭ, ĭ, r, wh, qu, er, ŭ, c, f, n), 2 (ar, al), 14 (ar), 15 (al), 17 (al) √: 1, 2, 14, 15, 17	Review: 1 (ē, j, ō, g, n, w, l, ĕ, s, z, v, ŏ, short y), 2 (ar, al), 13 (ar), 14 (al), 15 (al), 16 (al)
		Review: 21	Review: 9	Review: 22	Review: 29	Review: 26
Phonics and Word Recognition	**Irregular**				Blending sounds into words: 12 **(saw)** √	Blending sounds into words: 5 **(oh)** √
	Regular	Blending sounds into words: 2 **(rip)**, 4, 5 **(miles)**, 6 √: 2, 4, 5, 6 Reading words: 2 **(rip)**, 3 **(dim)**, 4, 5 **(miles)**, 6, 8 **(fall)**, 9 **(hall)**, 10 **(ball)**, 11**(all)**, 12 √: 2–6, 8–11	Reading words: 2, 4, 6 √: 2, 4, 6	Blending sounds into words: 2, 3 **(left)**, 4, 6, 7 **(playing)** √: 2, 3, 4, 6, 7 Reading words: : 2, 3 **(left)**, 4, 5 **(fat)**, 6, 7 **(playing)**, 9, 10 **(call)**, 11 **(small)**, 12 √: 2–7, 9–11	Blending sounds into words: 3 **(bent)**, 4 **(bug)**, 5, 6, 7 **(last)**, 8, 9 **(lick)**, 11 **(floor)**, 13 **(spotted)** √: 3–9, 11, 13 Reading words: 3 **(bent)**, 4 **(bug)**, 5, 6, 7 **(last)**, 8, 9 **(lick)**, 10 **(mole, box, I'll)**, 11 **(floor)**, 13 **(spotted)**, 14, 15 **(mall)**, 16, 17 **(salt)**, 18 **(tall, stall)**, 19 √: 3–11, 13–18	Blending sounds into words: 3, 4 **(hope)**, 6 **(dream)**, 8 **(picked)**, 9, 10, 11, 13 **(party)** √: 3, 4, 6, 8, 9, 10, 11, 13 Reading words: 3, 4 **(hope)**, 6 **(dream)**, 7 **(dreaming, goes, meets)**, 8 **(picked)**, 9, 10, 11, 12, 13 **(party)**, 14, 15, 16, 17, 18, 19, 20 √: 3, 4, 6–19
		Reading words: 14 Connected text: 15, 16 √: 15, 16		Reading words: 14 Connected text: 15, 16 √: 15, 16	Reading words: 21 Connected text: 22, 23 √: 22, 23	Reading words: 22 Connected text: 23, 24 √: 23, 24
Fluency		Reading words: 2–6, 8–12 √: 2–6, 8–11	Reading words: 2, 4, 6 √: 2, 4, 6	Reading words: 2–7, 9–12 √: 2–7, 9–11	Reading words: 3–19 √: 3– 18	Reading words: 3–20 √: 3–19
		Repeated reading: 16 √		Repeated reading: 16 √	Repeated reading: 23 √	Repeated reading: 24 √
						IC: 27
Comprehension		Following directions: 13	Following directions: 3, 5	Following directions: 13	Following directions: 20	Following directions: 21
		Noting details: 15, 16, 17 Drawing inferences: 16 Accessing prior knowledge: 17		Noting details: 16, 17 Accessing prior knowledge: 16 Drawing inferences: 17	Noting details: 23, 24 Making predictions: 24 Drawing conclusions: 24 Determining character emotions: 24	Noting details: 24, 25 Cause/effect: 24, 25 Making connections: 24, 25 Determining character emotions: 25
		Noting details: 19, 22 Following directions: 20	Noting details: 8 Following directions: 10	Noting details: 19, 21 Following directions: 20	Noting details: 26, 28 Following directions: 27	Noting details: 26 Following directions: 26
Spelling		Phonograms review: 1–3 Segmentation review: 3	Phonograms review: 1–4 Segmentation review: 3, 4	Phonograms review: 1–5 Segmentation review: 3–5	Phonograms review: 1, 2 Segmentation review: 2	Phonograms review: 1–3 Segmentation review: 2, 3
						Writing sounds: 1 Writing words: 2–4 Writing sentences: 5
		Writing sounds: 1, 2 Writing words: 3, 4 Writing sentences: 5	Writing sounds: 1, 2 Writing words: 3–5 Writing sentences: 6	Writing sounds: 1, 2 Writing words: 3–6 Writing sentences: 7	Writing sounds: 1 Writing words: 2, 3 Writing sentences: 4	

Reading Mastery Signature Edition, Grade 1

Key: (for Teachers)   √ = informal assessment   Numbers = exercise numbers   Bold face type = first appearance

		Lesson 36	Lesson 37	Lesson 38	Lesson 39	Lesson 40
Phonemic Awareness						
Print Awareness						
Letter Sound Correspondence		Review: 1 (ĕ, ĭ, ŭ, ă, ĕ, ĭ, ŏ, ŭ, th, wh, ch, qu, d, b, c), 2 (al, ar), 12 (ar), 16 (al) √: 1, 2, 12, 16	Review: 1 (ŏ, ō, ĕ, wh, qu, d, sh, b, r, c, l, f, n, g, j), 15 (ar), 16 (al), 17 (al) √: 1, 15–17	Review: 1 (ă, ĕ, ĭ, ō, ŭ, ă, ĕ, ĭ, ō), 3 (ar), 13 (al), 14 (al) √: 1, 13, 14	Review: 1 (ā, ĕ, ĭ, ō, ă, ĕ, ĭ, ō, ŭ), 12 (ar)	Introduction: 1, 2 (vowel letter names) √ Review: 13 (al), 15 (ar) √: 13, 15
		Review: 28	Review: 28	Review: 25	Review: 26	Review: 23
Phonics and Word Recognition	**Irregular**	Blending sounds into words: 9 (would), 15 (please)	Blending sounds into words: 12 (should) √ Reading words: 4 (football) √	Blending sounds into words: 8 (your), 11 (could) √: 8, 11 Reading words: 10 (touching) √	Blending sounds into words: 2 (head), 8 (word), 9 (put), 11 elephant	Blending sounds into words: 11 (any)
	Regular	Blending sounds into words: 3 (can't), 4 (silly), 5, 10 (sing), 11, 12, 16 √: 3, 4, 6, 10–12, 16 Reading words: 3 (can't), 4 (silly), 5, 6, (inside), 7, 8, 10 (sing), 11, 12, 13, 14 (stand), 16, 17, 18 √: 3–8, 10–14, 16, 17 Two-part words: 6 (inside), 7, 8 √: 6–8 Onset rime: 14 (stand) √	Blending sounds into words: 5, 6, 7, 8, 9 (much), 11 (bet), 13 (chunks), 14, 15 (part), 16, 17 (taller) √: 5–9, 11, 13–17 Reading words: 2 (smiled), 3, 5, 6, 7, 8, 9 (much), 10, 11 (bet), 13 (chunks), 14, 15 (part), 16, 17 (taller), 18 √: 2, 3, 5–9, 11, 13–17 Onset rime: 2 (smiled) √ Two-part words: 3, 4 (football) √: 3, 4	Blending sounds into words: 2, 3, 9 (week, win), 12, 14 √: 2, 3, 9, 12, 14 Reading words: 2, 3, 4, 5, 6 (always), 7 (also), 9 (week, win), 10, 12, 13, 14, 15 √: 2–7, 9, 10, 12–14 Two-part words: 4, 5, 6 (always), 7 (also) √: 4–7	Blending sounds into words: 3, 4, 5, 7 (glasses), 10, 12, 15 √: 3, 4, 5, 7, 10, 12, 15 Reading words: 3, 4, 5, 6 (falls, piles), 7 (glasses), 10, 12, 13, 14, 15, 16 √: 3–7, 10, 12–15 Two-part words: 13, 14 √: 13, 14	Blending sounds into words: 3, 4, 5 (table), 6, 8 (rod), 9, 10, 12, 13, 15, 16 √: 3–6, 8–10, 12, 13, 15, 16 Reading words: 3, 4, 5 (table), 6, 7, 8 (rod), 9, 10, 12, 13, 14, 15, 16, 17 √: 3–10, 12–17
		Reading words: 20 Connected text: 21, 22 √: 21, 22	Reading words: 20 Connected text: 21, 22 √: 21, 22	Reading words: 17 Connected text: 18, 19 √: 18, 19	Reading words: 18 Connected text: 19, 20 √: 19, 20	Reading words: 18 Connected text: 19, 20
						Reading words review: 22
Fluency		Reading words: 3–18 √: 3–17	Reading words: 2–18 √: 2–17	Reading words: 2–15 √: 2–14	Reading words: 3–16 √: 3–15	Reading words: 3–17 √: 3–17
		Repeated reading: 22 √	Repeated reading: 22 √	Repeated reading: 19	Repeated reading: 20 √	Repeated reading: 20 √
		Sentence copying: 28	Sentence copying: 28	Sentence copying: 25	Sentence copying: 26	Sentence copying: 23
						IC: 24
Comprehension		Following directions: 19	Following directions: 19	Following directions: 16	Following directions: 17	
		Noting details: 22, 23 Drawing conclusions: 22, 23 Making predictions: 22 Accessing prior knowledge: 23	Noting details: 22, 23 Making deductions: 22, 23 Making predictions: 23	Noting details: 19, 20 Drawing inferences: 19 Making predictions: 19 Determining character emotions: 20	Noting details: 20, 21 Making deductions: 20 Making connections: 20, 21 Making predictions: 21 Accessing prior knowledge: 21	Noting details: 20, 21 Making deductions: 20 Making connections: 20, 21 Determining character emotions: 21
		Noting details: 25, 27 Following directions: 26	Noting details: 25, 27 Following directions: 26	Noting details: 22, 24 Following directions: 23	Noting details: 23, 25 Determining character emotions: 23 Following directions: 24	Following directions: 22, 23 Noting details: 23
						Lesson 40 Curriculum-Based Assessment
Spelling		Phonograms review: 1 Segmentation review: 1	Phonograms review: 1 Segmentation review: 1	Phonograms review: 1 Segmentation review: 1	Phonograms review: 1, 2 Segmentation review: 1, 2	Phonograms review: 1–3 Segmentation review: 1–3
		Writing words: 1, 2 Writing sentences: 3	Writing words: 1, 2 Writing sentences: 3	Writing words: 1, 2 Writing sentences: 3	Writing words: 1–3 Writing sentences: 4	Writing words: 1–4 Writing sentences: 5

Reading Mastery Signature Edition, Grade 1

Key: (for Teachers)	√= informal assessment	Numbers = exercise numbers	Bold face type = first appearance

		Lesson 41	Lesson 42	Lesson 43	Lesson 44	Lesson 45
Phonemic Awareness						
Print Awareness						
Letter Sound Correspondence		Review: 1 (vowel letter names), 12 (al), 13 (al) √: 1, 12, 13	Review: 1 (al, ar), 2 (vowel letter names), 7 (ar), 9 (al) √ 1, 2, 7, 9	Review: 1 (vowel letter names), 8 (ar), 9 (al) √: 1, 8, 9	Review: 1 (ar, al), 2 (vowel letter names), 11 (al), 12 (ar) √: 1, 2, 11, 12	Introduction: 6, 7, 8, 9, 10 (ou) Review: 1 (al, ar), 2 (vowel letter names), 4 (al), 5 (ar) √: 1, 4, 5, 6, 7, 8, 9, 10
		Review: 24	Review: 14	Review: 14	Review: 17	Review: 19
Phonics and Word Recognition	**Irregular**	Blending sounds into words: 5 (loved) Reading words: 14 (wouldn't, couldn't)	Reading words: 6 (shouldn't) √	Reading words: 7 (ready) √		
	Regular	Blending sounds into words: 3, 4, 6, 12, 13 (Walter) √: 3, 4, 6, 12, 13 Reading words: 3, 4, 6, 7 (felt, dinner), 8, 9, 10, 11, 12, 13 √: 3, 4, 6-13 Two-part words: 8, 9 (himself), 10 √: 8-10 Onset rime: 11 (score) √	Blending sounds into words: 3 (not), 4, 8, 9 √: 3, 4, 8, 9 Reading words: 3 (not), 4, 5 (team, cheer, cheered, cheering), 6 (game, scored), 7 (cars), 8, 9	Blending sounds into words: 2 (fin), 3, 4 (Walter's, scores, kick) √: 2, 3, 4 Reading words: 2 (fin), 3, 4 (Walter's, scores, kick), 5, 6, 7 (player, falling), 8, 9, (balls) √: 2, 3, 4, 5, 6, 7, 8, 9 Two-part words: 5, 6 √: 5, 6	Blending sounds into words: 3, 4 (hop), 5, 9 √: 3, 4, 5, 9 Reading words: 3, 4 (hop), 5, 6, 7, 8 (runner), 9, 10, 11, 12 √: 3, 4, 5, 6, 7, 8, 9, 10, 11, 12 Two-part words: 7, 8 (runner) √: 7, 8	Blending sounds into words: 4 (wall), 5, 11, 12 √: 4, 5, 11, 12 Reading words: 3 (just, needed, shot, past, time), 4 (wall), 5, 7 (out), 8 (shout), 9 (loud), 10 (cloud), 11, 12, 13, 14 (almost) √: 3, 4, 5, 7, 8, 9, 10, 11, 12, 13, 14 Two-part words: 13, 14 (almost) √: 13, 14
		Reading words: 15 Connected text: 16. 17 √: 16, 17	Reading words: 10 Connected text: 11, 12 √: 11, 12	Reading words: 10 Connected text: 11, 12 √: 11, 12	Reading words: 13 Connected text: 14, 15 √: 14, 15	Reading words: 15 Connected text: 16, 17 √: 16, 17
Fluency		Reading words: 3-14 √: 3-14	Reading words: 3-9 √	Reading words: 2, 3, 4, 5, 6, 7, 8, 9 √	Reading words: 3, 4, 5, 6, 7, 8, 9, 10, 11, 12√	Reading words: 3, 4, 5, 7, 8, 9, 10, 11, 12, 13, 14 √: 3, 4, 5, 7, 8, 9, 10, 11, 12, 13, 14
		Repeated reading: 17 √	Repeated reading: 12 √	Repeated reading: 12 √	Repeated reading: 15	Repeated reading: 17 √
		Sentence copying: 24	Sentence copying: 14	Sentence copying: 14	Sentence copying: 17	Sentence copying: 19
						Individual Checkout: 20
Comprehension		Noting details: 17 Determining character emotions: 17, 18 Making predictions: 18 Drawing inferences: 18 Making connections: 18	Noting details: 12, 13 Identifying literal cause/effect: 12 Activating prior knowledge: 12 Determining character emotions: 13 Making connections: 13	Making predictions: 12 Noting details: 12 Inferring cause/effect: 12 Identifying literal cause/effect: 12 Inferring story details/events: 13 Interpreting character emotions: 13	Making predictions: 15 Identifying literal cause/effect: 15 Noting details: 15, 16 Inferring story details/events: 16 Making connections: 16	Making predictions: 17 Noting details: 17, 18 Inferring cause/effect: 17 Interpreting a character's emotions: 17, 18 Inferring story details/events: 18
		Recalling details: 21 Following directions: 22 Noting details: 23	Recalling details: 14 Following directions: 14 Noting details: 14	Recalling details: 14 Following directions: 14 Noting details: 14	Recalling details: 17 Following directions: 17 Noting details: 17	Recalling details: 19 Following directions: 19 Noting details: 19
Spelling		Segmentation review: 1	Segmentation review: 1	Segmentation review: 1	Segmentation review: 1, 2	Segmentation review: 1, 2
						Word writing: 1, 2, 3 Sentence writing: 4
		Word writing: 1, 2 Sentence writing: 3	Word writing: 1, 2 Sentence writing: 3	Word writing: 1, 2 Sentence writing: 3	Word writing: 1, 2, 3 Sentence writing: 4	

Key: (for Teachers) √= informal assessment   Numbers = exercise numbers   Bold face type = first appearance

		Lesson 46	Lesson 47	Lesson 48	Lesson 49	Lesson 50
Phonemic Awareness						
Print Awareness						
Letter Sound Correspondence		Review: 1 (al, ar), 2 (vowel letter names), 9 (al), 10 (ar), 11 (ou), 12 (ou), 13 (ou) √: 1, 2, 9–13	Review: 1 (vowel letter names) √	Review: 1 (ou, al), 2 (vowel letter names), 11–13 (ou) √: 1, 2, 11–13	Review: 1 (ou, ar), 2 (vowel letter names), 9–13 (ou) √: 1, 2, 9–13	Review: 1 (vowel letter names), 13 (ou), 14 (ou)
		Review: 23		Review: 23		
Phonics and Word Recognition	**Irregular**	Reading words: 8 (**wants**) √		Reading words: 14 (**about**) √		Blending sounds into words: 5 (**afraid**), 11 (**once**), 12 (**mountain**) √: 5, 11, 12 Reading words: 15 (**around**) √
	Regular	Blending sounds into words: 3, 4, 5, 7, 10 (**star**) √: 3–5, 7, 10 Reading words: 3, 4, 5, 6, 7, 8 (**pick**), 9, 10 (**star**), 12, 13 (**bout**), 14 √: 3–10, 12–14 Two-part word: 6 √	Reading words: 2, 4, 6 √: 6	Blending sounds into words: 3, 4 (**mad**), 6 (**children**), 10 (**moo, petted, how**), 11 (**our**) √: 3, 4, 6, 10, 11 Reading words: 3, 4 (**mad**), 5, 6 (**children**), 7 (**Carmen**), 8, 9 (**teacher**), 10 (**moo, petted, how**), 11 (**our**), 12 (**mouse**), 13 (**house**), 14 √: 3–14 Two-part words: 7 (**Carmen**), 8 √: 7, 8 Introduction of final–e rule: 5	Blending sounds into words: 3, 4, 6, 7 (**saved, grass**), 12 (**shouted**), 13 (**sounds**) √: 3, 4, 6, 7, 12, 13 Reading words: 2, 3, 4, 5, 6, 7 (**saved, grass**), 8 (**mooing, glad**), 9, 10, 11, 12 (**shouted**), 13 (**sounds**) √: 3–13 Final–e rule: 5	Blending sounds into words: 2, 3, 10 (**piled, screamed**), 13 (**hound**), 14 (**pound**) √: 2, 3, 10, 13, 14 Reading words: 2, 3, 4, 6, 7, 8, 9, 10 (**piled, screamed**), 13 (**hound**), 14 (**pound**), 15 (**clouds**) √: 2, 3, 4, 6–10, 13–15 Two-part words: 7, 8, 9 √: 7–9 Final–e rule: 4
		Reading words: 15 Connected text: 16, 17 √: 16, 17		Reading words: 15 Connected text: 16, 17 √: 16, 17	Reading words: 14 Connected text: 15, 16 √: 15, 16	Reading words: 16 Connected text: 17, 18 √: 17, 18
Fluency		Reading words: 3–10, 12–14 √: 3–10, 12–14	Reading words: 2, 4, 6 √: 6	Reading words: 3–14 √: 3–14	Reading words: 3–13 √: 3–13	Reading words: 2–15 √: 2–15
		Repeated reading: 17 √		Repeated reading: 17	Repeated reading: 16 √	Repeated reading: 18 √
		Sentence copying: 23		Sentence copying: 23		
						IC: 21
Comprehension			Following directions: 3, 5			
		Making predictions: 17 Noting details: 17, 18 Accessing prior knowledge: 17 Inferring story details/events: 17 Interpreting character emotions: 17, 18 Making connections: 18		Noting details: 17, 18 Identifying literal cause/effect: 17 Making predictions: 17, 18 Inferring story details/events: 18 Recalling details: 18 Accessing prior knowledge: 18 Determining character emotions: 18	Making predictions: 15 Recalling details: 15, 17 Identifying literal cause/effect: 16 Noting details: 16, 17 Interpreting character emotions: 16 Inferring story details/events: 17	Making predictions: 18 Noting details: 18, 19 Inferring cause/effect: 18, 19 Interpreting character emotions: 18 Making connections: 19
		Recalling details: 20 Following directions: 21 Noting details: 22	Noting details: 7 Inferring story details/events: 8 Following directions: 9, 11	Recalling details: 20 Following directions: 21 Noting details: 22	Recalling details: 19 Following directions: 20, 22 Noting details: 21	Recalling details: 20 Following directions: 20 Interpreting character emotions: 20
Spelling		Phonograms review: 1 Segmentation review: 1	Phonograms review: 1 Segmentation review: 1	Phonograms review: 1 Segmentation review: 1	Phonograms review: 1 Segmentation review: 1	Phonograms review: 1, 2 Segmentation review: 2
						Writing sounds: 1 Writing words: 2, 3 Writing sentences: 4
		Writing words: 1, 2 Writing sentences: 3	Writing words: 1, 2 Writing sentences: 3	Writing words: 1, 2 Writing sentences: 3	Writing words: 1, 2 Writing sentences: 3	

Reading Mastery Signature Edition, Grade 1

	Lesson 51	Lesson 52	Lesson 53	Lesson 54	Lesson 55
Spelling	Writing sounds: 1 Writing words: 2–4 Writing sentences: 5	Writing sounds: 1 Writing words: 2–4 Writing sentences: 5	Writing sounds: 1 Writing words: 2–4 Writing sentences: 5	Writing sounds: 1 Writing words: 2–4 Writing sentences: 5	Writing words: 1, 2 Writing sentences: 3
	Phonograms review: 1–3 Segmentation review: 2, 3	Phonograms review: 1–3 Segmentation review: 2, 3	Phonograms review: 1–3 Segmentation review: 2, 3	Phonograms review: 1–3 Segmentation review: 2, 3	Phonograms review: 1 Segmentation review: 1
Comprehension	Noting details: 17 Identifying literal cause/effect: 17 Making predictions: 17, 18 Drawing inferences: 18 Recalling details: 20 Following directions: 21, 23 Noting details: 22	Recalling details: 16 Identifying literal cause/effect: 17, 18 Making predictions: 18 Recalling details: 20 Following directions: 21, 23 Noting details: 22	Recalling details: 12 Noting details: 13 Interpreting character emotions: 14 Recalling details: 16 Following directions: 17, 19 Noting details: 18	Recalling details: 13 Noting details: 14 Making predictions: 14, 15 Inferring cause/effect: 15 Recalling details: 17 Following directions: 18, 20 Noting details: 19	Recalling details: 13 Noting details: 14, 15 Identifying literal cause/effect: 14, 15 Making connections: 14 Sequencing: 14 Interpreting character motives: 14 Making judgments: 15 Recalling details: 16 Following directions: 16 Noting details: 16
Fluency	Reading words: 2–14 √: 2–14 Repeated reading: 17 √	Reading words: 3–14 √: 3–14 Repeated reading: 17 √	Reading words: 1–10 √: 1–10 Repeated reading: 13	Reading words: 3–11 √: 3–11 Repeated reading: 14 √	Reading words: 1–11 √: 1–11 Repeated reading: 14 √ IC: 17
Phonics and Word Recognition — Regular	Blending sounds into words: 2 (rat), 3 (rate), 8, 11 √: 2, 3, 8, 11 Reading words: 2 (rat), 3 (rate), 4, 7 (steep), 8, 11 √: 2, 3, 4, 7, 8, 10–14 Final-e rule: 4 (rat, rate) √ Two-part word: 10 (herself) Reading words: 15 Connected text: 16, 17 √: 16, 17	Blending sounds into words: 3 (rest), 4 (open), 5 (before), 6, 7, 8 (slammed), 9, 10, 11 (hanging, only) 12, 13 (ouch), 14 (hounds) √: 1, 3–14 Final-e rule: 6 Reading words: 15 Connected text: 16, 17 √: 16, 17	Blending sounds into words: 6, 7, 8 (door), 9 (thousand), 10 (found) Reading words: 3 (rest), 4 (behind), 5 (slowly, opened), 6, 7, 8 (thousand), 9 (thousand), 10 (found) √: 1, 3–10 Final-e rule: 1 Reading words: 11 Connected text: 12, 13 √: 12, 13	Blending sounds into words: 10 (elf), 11 (cross) √: 6–10 Reading words: 3 (careful), 4 (bigger), 5, 6, 7, 8, 9, 10 (elf), 11 (cross) √: 3–11 Two-part word: 3 (careful), 4 (bigger) √: 3, 4 Final-e rule: 5 Reading words: 12 Connected text: 13, 14 √: 13, 14	Blending sounds into words: 1 (reached), 2 (tired), 3 (woke), 4 (lie) √: 1–4 Reading words: 1 (reached), 2 (tired), 3 (woke), 4 (lie), 5 (cane), 6 (site), 7 (sit), 8, 9, 10, 11 √: 1–11 Final-e rule: 5 (cane) Two-part word: 10 (setting) Reading words: 12 Connected text: 13, 14 √: 13, 14
Phonics and Word Recognition — Irregular	Blending sounds into words: 5 (magic), 6 (eyes), 9 (father) √: 5, 6, 9	Blending sounds into words: 10 (coming)	Two-part word: 2 (anyone) √ Reading words: 5 (touched) √	Blending sounds into words: 2 (full) Reading words: 9 (many) √	Blending sounds into words: 9 (been) √
Letter Sound Correspondence	Review: 1 (vowel letter names), 11 (ou), 12 (al), 13 (ar) √: 1, 12, 13	Review: 1 (vowel letter names), 2 (al, ou), 12–14 (ou) √: 1,2, 12–14	Review: 9–10 (ou) √: 9, 10	Review: 1 (ar, ou)	
Print Awareness					
Phonemic Awareness					

Reading Mastery Signature Edition, Grade 1

		Lesson 56	Lesson 57	Lesson 58	Lesson 59	Lesson 60
Phonemic Awareness						
Print Awareness						
Letter Sound Correspondence		Review: 17 (ou) √	Review: 2 (al, ou, ar), 7 (ou) √: 2, 7		Review: 2 (al), 3 (ou), 4 (ar) √: 2–4	Review: 1 (ar), 2, (al), 3 (ou) √: 1–3
Phonics and Word Recognition	**Irregular**	Blending sounds into words: 12 (**dirty**), 13 (**does**) √: 12, 13 Two-part words: 15 (**into**), 16 (**something**) √: 15, 16		Blending sounds into words: 6 (**work**) √		
	Regular	Blending sounds into words: 1, 2, 3, 4 (**rich**), 5, 10, 11 (**clean**),17 (**round**) √: 1–5, 10, 11, 17 Reading words: 1, 2, 3, 4 (**rich**), 5, 6, 7, 8 (**cam**), 9 (**hide, hid**), 10, 11 (**clean**), 14 (**rubbed**), 17 (**round**) √: 1–11, 14, 17 Final–e rule: 6 √	Blending sounds into words: 7, 8 (**stayed**), 9, 10 √: 7–10 Reading words: 1 (**holding**), 3, 4 (**pan**), 5 (**pane**), 6, 7, 8 (**stayed**), 9, 10, 11, 12 (**lake**), 13 √: 1, 3–13 Final–e rule review: 3, 9, 10, 11, 12 (**lake**), 13 √: 3, 9–13	Blending sounds into words: 7 √ Reading words: 1 (**keep**), 2, 3, 4, 5, 7, 8 (**take**), 9, 10 √: 1–5, 7–10 Final–e rule review: 2, 5, 8 (**take**) Two-part word: 9, 10 √: 9, 10	Blending sounds into words: 1, 3, 4, 10 (**fix**), 12 √: 1, 3, 4, 10, 12 Reading words: 1, 2, 3, 4, 5 (**pine, pin**), 6, 7, 8, 9 (**smile**), 10 (**fix**), 11, 12 √: 1–12 Final–e rule review: 5 (**pine, pin**), 8, 9 (**smile**), 12 √: 8, 9, 12	Blending sounds into words: 1 (**park**), 10, 12 (**kite**), 13 (**kit**), 14 (**steal**) √: 1, 10, 12–14 Reading words: 1 (**park**), 2, 3, 4, 5, 6, 7, 8 (**robber**), 9 (**running**), 10, 11, 12 (**kite**), 13 (**kit**), 14 (**steal**), 15 √: 1–15 Final–e rule review: 4, 7, 10, 12 (**kite**) √: 4, 7, 10, 12 Two-part words: 8 (**robber**), 9 (**running**) √: 8, 9
		Reading words: 18 Connected text: 19, 20 √: 19, 20	Reading words: 14 Connected text: 15, 16 √: 15, 16	Reading words: 11 Connected text: 12, 13 √: 12, 13	Reading words: 13 Connected text: 14, 15 √: 14, 15	Reading words: 16 Connected text: 17, 18 √: 17, 18
Fluency		Reading words: 1–17 √: 1–17	Reading words: 1, 3–13 √: 1, 3–13	Reading words: 1–10 √: 1–10	Reading words: 1–12 √: 1–12	Reading words: 1–15 √: 1–15
		Repeated reading: 20 √	Repeated reading: 16 √	Repeated reading: 13 √	Repeated reading: 15 √	Repeated reading: 18 √
						IC: 21
Comprehension		Identifying literal cause/effect: 20 Noting details: 20, 21 Inferring cause and effect: 20, 21 Inferring story details/events: 20 Determining character emotions: 21 Making connections: 21	Recalling details: 15, 16 Inferring story details/events: 16, 17 Noting details: 16, 17 Inferring cause/effect: 16 Interpreting character actions: 16, 17 Making predictions: 16, 17 Determining/interpreting character emotions: 17	Recalling details: 12, 13 Noting details: 13, 14 Inferring cause/effect: 13, 14 Interpreting character motives: 13 Determining character emotions: 14 Making connections: 14	Noting details: 15, 16 Interpreting character actions: 15 Activating prior knowledge: 15 Interpreting character actions: 16	Noting details: 18, 19 Interpreting character motives/ actions: 18, 19 Inferring story details/events: 18 Inferring cause/effect: 18 Making predictions: 18
		Recalling details: 23 Following directions: 24, 26 Noting details: 25	Recalling details: 19 Following directions: 20, 22 Noting details: 21 Inferring cause/effect: 21	Recalling details: 16 Following directions: 17, 19 Noting details: 18 Drawing inferences: 18	Recalling details: 18 Following directions: 19, 20 Noting details: 20 Inferring cause/effect: 20	Recalling details: 20 Following directions: 20 Noting details: 20
						Lesson 60 Curriculum-Based Assessment
Spelling		Phonograms review: 1, 2 Segmentation review: 2	Phonograms review: 1, 2, 3 Segmentation review: 2, 3	Phonograms review: 1, 2 Segmentation review: 2	Phonograms review: 1, 2 Segmentation review: 2	Phonograms review: 1, 2, 3 Segmentation review: 2, 3
		Writing sounds: 1 Writing words: 2, 3 Writing sentences: 4	Writing sounds: 1 Writing words: 2, 3, 4 Writing sentences: 5	Writing sounds: 1 Writing words: 2, 3 Writing sentences: 4	Writing sounds: 1 Writing words: 2, 3 Writing sentences: 4	Writing sounds: 1 Writing words: 2, 3, 4 Writing sentences: 5

Reading Mastery Signature Edition, Grade 1

		Lesson 61	Lesson 62	Lesson 63	Lesson 64	Lesson 65
Phonemic Awareness						
Print Awareness						
Letter Sound Correspondence		Review: 9 (ar), 10 (al) √: 9–10	Review: 1 (al, ou, ar), 9 (ar), 10 (ou), 11 (al) √: 9–11	Review: 1 (ar, ou, al), 8 (ou), 9 (ar) √: 1, 8, 9	Review: 1 (ar, ou, al), 6 (ou), 7 (ar), 10 (al) √: 1, 6, 7, 10	Review: 1 (ou, al, ar), 11 (al), 15 (ar), 16 (ou) √: 1, 11, 15, 16
Phonics and Word Recognition	**Irregular**		Reading words: 14 (**wood, you'll**) √	Blending sounds into words: 6 (**know**), 7 (**again**) √: 6, 7	Blending sounds into words: 4 (**pretty**), 11 (**two**) √: 4, 11	Two-part words: 6 (**someone**), 7 (**today**) √: 6, 7
	Regular	Blending sounds into words: 2, 3 (**bending**), 4, 9 (**sharp**), 10, 11 √: 2–4, 9–11 Reading words: 1, 2, 3 (**bending**), 4,5, 6 (**bit**), 7 (**bite**), 8, 9 (**sharp**), 10, 11, 12, 13 (**save**), 14, 15 (**hugged**) √: 1–15 Final –e rule review: 5, 11, 12, 13 (**save**) √: 5, 11–13 Two-part words: 14 √	Blending sounds into words: 2, 3, 4 (**string**), 9 (**starts**) √: 2–4, 9 Reading words: 2, 3, 4 (**string**), 5 (**fate**), 6, 7, 8 (**wind**), 9 (**starts**), 10, 11, 12, 13 (**kites**), 14 (**paper, we'll**) √: 2–13 Final –e rule review: 12 √ Two-part words: 13 (**kites**) √	Blending sounds into words: 8, 9, 10, 11 (**lifted**) √: 8–11 Reading words: 2, 3 (**five**), 4 5 (**no, go, shake, shaking**), 8, 9, 10, 11 (**lifted**), 12 (**landed**), 13, 14, 15 (**won't**) √: 2–5, 8–15 Final –e rule review: 3 (**five**), 4 √: 3–4 Two-part words: 12 (**landed**), 13, 14 √: 12–14	Blending sounds into words: 3, 5 (**happened**), 6 (**proud**), 7 (**darker**), 9 (**thunder**) √: 3, 5, 6, 7, 9 Reading words: 2 (**Tim**), 3, 5 (**happened**), 6 (**proud**), 7 (**darker**), 8 (**began, grow**), 9 (**thunder**), 10, 12 (**makes**), 13, 14 (**blowing, maker, making**) √: 2, 3, 5–10, 12–14 Final –e rule review: 13 √ Two-part words: 12 (**makes**) √	Blending sounds into words: 9 (**sadder**), 12 (**trapped**), 13, 14 (**float**), 15 √: 9, 12–15 Reading words: 2 (**Sam**), 3 (**fire**), 4 (**while**), 5 (**makes**), 8 (**forest**), 9 (**sadder**), 10, 11, 12 (**trapped**), 13, 14 (**float**), 15, 16 √: 2–5, 8–16 Final –e rule review: 3 (**fire**), 4 (**while**) √: 3, 4 Two-part words: 8 (**forest**) √: 8
		Reading words: 16 Connected text: 17, 18 √: 17, 18	Reading words: 15 Connected text: 16, 17 √: 16, 17	Reading words: 16 Connected text: 17, 18 √: 17, 18	Reading words: 15 Connected text: 16, 17 √: 16, 17	Reading words: 17 Connected text: 18, 19 √: 18, 19
Fluency		Reading words: 1–15 √: 1–15	Reading words: 2–14 √: 2–14	Reading words: 2–15 √: 2–15	Reading words: 2–14 √: 2–14	Reading words: 2–16 √: 2–16
		Repeated reading: 18 √	Repeated reading: 17 √	Repeated reading: 18 √	Repeated reading: 17 √	Repeated reading: 19 √
						IC: 65
Comprehension		Predicting narrative outcomes: 18, 19 Answering literal questions about a text: 18 Interpreting a character's feelings: 19 Inferring causes and effects: 18 Noting details: 18, 19 Drawing inferences: 19	Predicting narrative outcomes: 17 Answering literal questions about a text: 17 Interpreting a character's motives: 17 Noting details: 17, 18 Following directions: 18	Answering literal questions about a text: 18 Interpreting a character's feelings: 18, 19 Inferring causes and effects: 18 Inferring story details and events: 18, 19 Noting details: 19 Drawing inferences:18	Predicting narrative outcomes: 17, 18 Answering literal questions about a text: 17, 18 Interpreting a character's feelings: 17, 18 Inferring causes and effects: 18 Inferring story details and events: 17 Noting details: 18 Drawing inferences: 17	Predicting narrative outcomes: 19 Answering literal questions about a text: 19, 20 Interpreting a character's feelings: 20 Inferring causes and effects: 19 Inferring story details and events: 19, 20 Noting details: 20
		Recalling details: 23 Interpreting a character's feelings: 21 Following written directions: 20 Answering literal questions about a text: 24	Recalling details: 21 Noting details: 19 Following written directions: 22 Answering literal questions about a text: 23	Recalling details: 21 Noting details: 23 Following written directions: 22 Answering literal questions about a text: 24	Recalling details: 20 Noting details: 22 Following written directions: 21 Answering literal questions about a text: 23	Recalling details: 21 Following written directions: 21 Answering literal questions about a text: 21
Spelling		Phonogram review: 1, 2, 3 Segmentation review: 2, 3	Phonogram review: 1, 2, 3 Segmentation review: 2, 3	Phonogram review: 1, 2, 3, 4 Segmentation review: 2, 3, 4	Phonogram review: 1, 2 Segmentation review: 1, 2	Phonogram review: 1 Segmentation review: 1
						Writing words: 1, 2 Writing sentences: 3
		Writing sounds: 1 Writing words: 2, 3, 4 Writing sentences: 5	Writing sounds: 1 Writing words: 2, 3, 4 Writing sentences: 5	Writing sounds: 1 Writing words: 2, 3, 4, 5 Writing sentences: 6	Writing words: 1, 2, 3 Writing sentences: 4	

Reading Mastery Signature Edition, Grade 1

Key: (for Teachers) √ = informal assessment   Numbers = exercise numbers   Bold face type = first appearance

		Lesson 66	Lesson 67	Lesson 68	Lesson 69	Lesson 70
Phonemic Awareness						
Print Awareness						
Letter Sound Correspondence		Review: 1 (ar. al. ou), 3 (al), 4 (ou), 5 (ar) √: 1, 3, 4, 5	Review: 11 (th) √: 11	Review: 3 (ou), 9 (th) √: 3, 9	Review: 7 (ar), 8 (ou) √: 7, 8	
Phonics and Word Recognition	**Irregular**	Blending sounds into words: 6 (**first**), 7 (**water**), 13 (**woman**) √: 6, 7, 13 Reading words: 9 (**shook**), 17 (**tv**) √: 9, 17	Blending sounds into words: 1 (**school**) √: 1 Two-part words: 12 (**anything**) √: 12	Blending sounds into words: 8 (**front**) √: 8		
	Regular	Blending sounds into words: 8 (**floated**) √: 8 Reading words: 2 (**hat, hate**), 3, 4, 5, 8 (**floated**), 9 (**plane, soaked**), 10, 11 (**fires**), 12 (**became**), 14 (**scare**), 15 (**wade**), 16 (**wading, or**) √: 2–5, 8, 10–12, 14–16 Final –e rule review: 15 (**wade**) √: 15 Two-part words: 10, 11 (**fires**), 12 (**became**) √: 10–12 Onset rime: 14 (**scare**) √: 14	Blending sounds into words: 4 (**bear**), 5 (**train**), 6 (**hundred**), 7 (**beans, meat, fifty, hunting**) √: 4–7 Reading words: 2 (**gave**), 3, 4 (**bear**), 5 (**train**), 6 (**hundred**), 7 (**beans, meat, fifty, hunting**), 8 (**pile**), 9, 10, 11 √: 2–11 Final –e rule review: 2 (**gave**) √: 2 Two-part words: 9, 10 √: 9, 10	Blending sounds into words: 3 (**counted**) √: 3 Reading words: 1 (**everything**), 2, 3 (**counted**), 4 (**counter**), 5, 6 (**home, nine, standing, tracks**), 7 (**missing, sandy**), 9 √: 1–7, 9 Two-part words: 1 (**everything**), 2, 4 (**counter**) √: 1, 2, 4	Blending sounds into words: 7 (**parked**), 11 √: 7, 11 Reading words: 1 (**Sid**), 2, 3, 4, 5, 6 (**ninety**), 7 (**parked**), 8, 9, 10, 11, 12 √: 1–12 Final –e rule review: 5 √: 5 Two-part words: 2, 3, 4 √: 2, 3, 4	Blending sounds into words: 8 (**rail**) √: 8 Reading words: 1, 2, 3, 4 (**followed, shed, sets**), 5, 6, 7, 8 (**rail**) √: 1–8 Two-part words: 5, 6 √: 5, 6 Onset rime: 7 √: 7
		Reading words: 18 Connected text: 19, 20 √: 19, 20	Reading words: 13 Connected text: 14, 15 √: 14, 15	Reading words: 10 Connected text: 11, 12 √: 11, 12	Reading words: 13 Connected text: 14, 15 √: 14, 15	Reading words: 9 Connected text: 10, 11 √: 10, 11
Fluency		Reading words: 2–17 √: 2–17	Reading words: 1–12 √: 1–12	Reading words: 1–9 √: 1–9	Reading words: 1–12 √: 1–12	Reading words: 1–8 √: 1–8
		Repeated reading: 20 √	Repeated reading: 15 √	Repeated reading: 12 √	Repeated reading: 15 √	Repeated reading: 11 √
						IC: 70
Comprehension		Answering literal questions about a text: 20, 21 Predicting narrative outcomes: 20 Inferring story details and events: 20 Interpreting a character's feelings: 21 Inferring causes and effects: 20, 21 Interpreting a character's motives: 20 Recalling details: 20, 21 Noting details: 20	Answering literal questions about a text: 15 Predicting narrative outcomes: 15, 16 Inferring story details and events: 15 Interpreting a character's feelings: 15 Interpreting a character's motives: 15 Recalling details: 16 Noting details: 16	Answering literal questions about a text: 12,13 Following directions: 13 Predicting narrative outcomes: 13 Inferring story details and events: 13 Activating prior knowledge: 12 Recalling details: 13 Drawing inferences: 12	Answering literal questions about a text: 14, 15 Inferring story details and events: 15, 16 Recalling details: 14, 15, 16 Noting details: 16	Answering literal questions about a text: 11 Following directions: 11 Predicting narrative outcomes: 11, 12 Inferring story details and events: 11 Interpreting a character's feelings: 11 Inferring causes and effects: 12 Noting details: 12
		Recalling details: 23 Following written directions: 24 Noting details: 26 Answering literal questions about a text: 25	Recalling details: 18 Following written directions: 19 Noting details: 20 Answering literal questions about a text: 20, 21	Recalling details: 15 Following written directions: 16 Noting details: 17 Answering literal questions about a text: 18	Recalling details: 18 Following written directions: 19 Noting details: 20 Answering literal questions about a text: 21	Recalling details: 13 Following written directions: 13 Noting details: 13 Answering literal questions about a text: 13
Spelling		Phonogram review: 1, 2 Segmentation review: 2	Phonogram review: 1, 2, 3 Segmentation review: 2, 3	Phonogram review: 1, 2, 3 Segmentation review: 2, 3	Phonogram review: 1, 2, 3 Segmentation review: 2, 3	Phonogram review: 1, 2, 3 Segmentation review: 2, 3
						Writing sounds: 1 Writing words: 2, 3, 4 Writing sentences: 5
		Writing sounds: 1 Writing words: 2, 3 Writing sentences: 4	Writing sounds: 1 Writing words: 2, 3, 4 Writing sentences: 5	Writing sounds: 1 Writing words: 2, 3, 4 Writing sentences: 5	Writing sounds: 1 Writing words: 2, 3, 4 Writing sentences: 5	

Reading Mastery Signature Edition, Grade 1

	Lesson 71	Lesson 72	Lesson 73	Lesson 74	Lesson 75
Spelling	Writing sounds: 1 Writing words: 2, 3 Writing sentences: 4 Phonogram review: 1, 2 Segmentation review: 2	Writing sounds: 1 Writing words: 2, 3 Writing sentences: 4 Phonogram review: 1, 2 Segmentation review: 2	Writing sounds: 1 Writing words: 2, 3 Writing sentences: 4 Phonogram review: 1, 2 Segmentation review: 2	Writing words: 1, 2 Writing sentences: 3 Phonogram review: 1 Segmentation review: 1	Writing words: 1, 2 Writing sentences: 3 Phonogram review: 1 Segmentation review: 1
Comprehension	Answering literal questions about a text: 11, 12 Inferring story details and events: 11, 12 Interpreting a character's feelings: 12 Interpreting a character's motives: 11 Inferring causes and effects: 11 Activating prior knowledge: 11 Noting details: 13 Recalling details: 14 Following written directions: 15 Noting details: 16 Answering literal questions about a text: 17	Answering literal questions about a text: 11 Inferring story details and events: 12, 13 Recalling details: 13 Noting details: 13 Recalling details: 15 Following written directions: 16 Noting details: 17 Answering literal questions about a text: 18	Answering literal questions about a text: 10 Following directions: 11 Inferring story details and events: 11 Interpreting a character's motives: 10 Noting details: 10 Recalling details: 12 Following written directions: 12 Noting details: 12 Answering literal questions about a text: 12	Answering literal questions about a text: 13 Following directions: 13 Predicting narrative outcomes: 14 Inferring story details and events: 13, 14 Interpreting a character's thoughts/feelings: 14 Interpreting a character's motives: 13 Recalling details: 13 Noting details: 14 Recalling details: 16 Following written directions: 16 Noting details: 16 Answering literal questions about a text: 16	Answering literal questions about a text: 10 Inferring story details and events: 10, 11 Predicting narrative outcomes: 11 Noting details: 11 Interpreting a character's motives: 10 Noting details: 11 Activating prior knowledge: 10 Drawing inferences: 10 Recalling details: 12 Following written directions: 12 Noting details: 12 Answering literal questions about a text: 12 IC: 75
Fluency	Reading words: 1–8 √: 1–8 Repeated reading: 11 √	Reading words: 1–9 √: 1–9 Repeated reading: 12 √	Reading words: 1–7 √: 1–7 Repeated reading: 10 √	Reading words: 1–10 √: 1–10 Repeated reading: 13 √	Reading words: 1–7 √: 1–7 Repeated reading: 10 √
Phonics and Word Recognition — Regular	Blending sounds into words: 5 (truck), 6 (waited), 7 √: 5, 6, 7 Reading words: 1, 2, 3, 4, 5 (truck), 6 (waited), √: 1–8 Two-part words: 2, 3, 4 √: 2, 3, 4 Reading words: 9 Connected text: 10, 11 √: 10, 11	Blending sounds into words: 2, 3 (sorry), 4 (lied), 5 √: 2–5 Reading words: 1, 2, 3 (sorry), 4 (lied), 5, 6, 7 (okay) √: 1–9 Two-part words: 6, 7 (scared) √: 6, 7 Reading words: 10 Connected text: 11, 12 √: 11, 12	Blending sounds into words: 4 (easy), 5 (check) √: 4, 5 Reading words: 1 (dish, wishing), 2, 3 (that's), 4, 5 (easy), 6, 7 (tar) √: 1–7 Reading words: 8 Connected text: 9, 10 √: 9, 10	Blending sounds into words: 3, 4 (lying), 5 (loading) √: 3–5 Reading words: 1 (shop, she's), 3, 4 (lying), 5 (loading), 6, 7, 8, 9, 10 (mean, mark, near) √: 3–10 Two-part words: 8, 9 √: 8, 9 Reading words: 11 Connected text: 12, 13 √: 12, 13	Blending sounds into words: 1, 2, 3, 4 (showed), 5 (gift, finding, leaving, I've), 6, 7 √: 1–7 Reading words: 1, 2, 3, 4 (showed) 5 (gift, finding, leaving, I've), 6, 7 √: 1–3, 6 Reading words: 8 Connected text: 9, 10
Phonics and Word Recognition — Irregular	Reading words: 8 (crooks) √: 8		Reading words: 3 (says) √: 3	Blending sounds into words: 2 (their) √: 2 Reading words: 10 (what's) √: 10	
Letter Sound Correspondence		Review: 1 (sh) √: 1	Review: 1 (sh), 6 (al), 7 (ar) √: 1, 6, 7	Review: 1 (sh), 6 (ou), 7 (al) √: 1, 6, 7	
Print Awareness					
Phonemic Awareness					

Key: (for Teachers)   √= informal assessment   Numbers = exercise numbers   Bold face type = first appearance

Reading Mastery Signature Edition, Grade 1

Key: (for Teachers)   √ = informal assessment   Numbers = exercise numbers   Bold face type = first appearance

		Lesson 76	Lesson 77	Lesson 78	Lesson 79	Lesson 80
Phonemic Awareness						
Print Awareness						
Letter Sound Correspondence		Review: 2 (ing), 3 (ar) √: 2, 3	Review: 1 (ing), 7 (ar) √: 1, 7	Review: 8 (ing), 9 (ar) √: 8–9		Review: 6 (al), 7 (ar), 8 (ou), 9 (ou) √: 6–9
Phonics and Word Recognition	Irregular		Reading words: 9 (worked) √: 9	Blending sounds into words: 7 (done) √: 7		Blending sounds into words: 4 (ice), 11 (close) √: 4, 11 Reading words: 12 (closed) √: 12
	Regular	Blending sounds into words: 1, 3 (parts) √: 1, 3 Reading words: 1, 2, 3 (parts), 4, 5 (else), 6 √: 1–6 Final –e rule review: 4 √: 4	Blending sounds into words: 2 (tent), 3, 4, 5 (mixed), 6 (job), 7 √: 2–7 Reading words: 1, 2 (tent), 3, 4, 5 (mixed), 6 (job), 7, 8 (care), 9 √: 1–9	Blending sounds into words: 2, 3, 4, 5 √: 2–5 Reading words: 1, 2, 3, 4, 5, 6 (passed), 8 (thing), 9, 10, 11 √: 1–6, 8–11 Two-part word: 11 (everybody) √: 11	Blending sounds into words: 1 (stuck), 2, 3 (colder, snow) √: 1–3 Reading words: 1 (stuck), 2, 3 (colder, snow), 4, 5, 6, 7 (slipped), 8, 9, 10 (ears, window, show, deep) √: 1–10 Two-part words: 5, 6, 7 (slipped), 8, 9 √: 5–9	Blending sounds into words: 1 (drink), 2 (sly), 5 (cream), 6, 7, 8 (mouth) √: 1, 2, 5–8 Reading words: 1 (drink), 2 (sly), 3 (con, cone), 5 (cream), 6, 7, 8 (mouth), 9, 10, 12 (giving, conned, cool) √: 1–3, 5–10, 12
		Reading words: 7 Connected text: 8, 9 √: 8, 9	Reading words: 10 Connected text: 11, 12 √: 11, 12	Reading words: 12 Connected text: 13, 14 √: 13, 14	Reading words: 11 Connected text: 12, 13 √: 12, 13	Reading words: 13 Connected text: 14, 15 √: 14, 15
Fluency		Reading words: 1–6	Reading words: 1–9	Reading words: 1–11 √: 1–11	Reading words: 1–10 √: 1–10	Reading words: 1–12 √: 1–12
		Repeated reading: 9 √: 9	Repeated reading: 12 √	Repeated reading: 14 √	Repeated reading: 13 √	Repeated reading: 15 √
						IC: 80
Comprehension		Answering literal questions about text: 9 Predicting narrative outcomes: 9 Inferring story details and events: 9, 10 Inferring causes and effects: 9 Interpreting a character's motives: 10 Activating prior knowledge: 9 Following directions: 9 Noting details: 10	Answering literal questions about text: 12 Predicting narrative outcomes: 12 Inferring story details and events: 12 Interpreting a character's feelings: 12 Following directions: 13 Noting details: 13	Answering literal questions about text: 14 Predicting narrative outcomes: 15 Inferring story details and events: 14, 15 Recalling details: 14 Noting details: 15	Answering literal questions about text: 13 Inferring story details and events: 13 Interpreting a character's feelings: 13 Inferring causes and effects: 13 Activating prior knowledge: 14 Following directions: 13 Noting details: 14 Recalling details: 14	Answering literal questions about text: 15 Predicting narrative outcomes: 15 Interpreting a character's feelings: 16 Inferring causes and effects: 15 Interpreting a character's motives: 15 Following directions: 15 Noting details: 16
		Recalling details: 12 Following written directions: 13 Noting details: 14 Answering literal questions about text: 15	Recalling details: 15 Following written directions: 16 Noting details: 17 Answering literal questions about text: 18	Recalling details:17 Following written directions: 18 Noting details: 19 Answering literal questions about text: 20	Recalling details: 16 Following written directions: 17 Noting details: 18 Answering literal questions about text: 19	Recalling details: 17 Following written directions: 17 Noting details: 17 Answering literal questions about text: 17
						Lesson 80 Curriculum-Based Assessment
Spelling		Phonogram review: 1 Segmentation review: 1	Phonogram review: 1, 2 Segmentation review: 2	Phonogram review: 1, 2, 3 Segmentation review: 2, 3	Phonogram review: 1, 2, 3 Segmentation review: 2, 3	Phonogram review: 1, 2, 3 Segmentation review: 2, 3
		Writing words: 1, 2 Writing sentences: 3	Writing sounds: 1 Writing words: 2, 3 Writing sentences: 4	Writing sounds: 1 Writing words: 2, 3, 4 Writing sentences: 5	Writing sounds: 1 Writing words: 2, 3, 4 Writing sentences: 5	Writing sounds: 1 Writing words: 2, 3 Writing sentences: 4

Reading Mastery Signature Edition, Grade 1

Key: (for Teachers) √ = informal assessment | Numbers = exercise numbers | Bold face type = first appearance

Category		Lesson 81	Lesson 82	Lesson 83	Lesson 84	Lesson 85
Spelling		Writing sounds: 1 Writing words: 2, 3 Writing sentences: 4	Writing sounds: 1 Writing words: 2, 3 Writing sentences: 4	Writing sounds: 1 Writing word families: 2 Writing sentences: 4	Writing sounds: 1 Writing words: 2, 3 Writing sentences: 4	Writing words: 3 Writing sentences: 4
		Phonogram review: 1, 2, 3 Segmentation review: 2, 3	Phonogram review: 1, 2 Segmentation review: 2	Word families: 2 Segmentation review: 2	Phonogram review: 1, 2 Segmentation review: 2	Grapheme recognition: 1 √ Phoneme-grapheme correspondence: 2 √
Comprehension		Following directions: 9 Answering literal questions about a text: 11, 12 Identifying literal cause and effect: 11 Recalling details and events: 11 Predicting narrative outcomes: 11, 12 Activating prior knowledge: 11 Interpreting a character's motives: 11 Noting details: 12 Recalling details: 13 Following written directions: 13 Answering literal questions about a text: 13 Noting details: 13	Following directions: 9 Answering literal questions about a text: 11, 12 Identifying literal cause and effect: 11 Recalling details and events: 11 Predicting narrative outcomes: 12 Following written directions: 13 Answering literal questions about a text: 13 Recalling details: 13	Following directions: 10 Answering literal questions about a text: 12 Recalling details and events: 12 Predicting narrative outcomes: 12, 13 Following directions: 13 Following written directions: 14 Answering literal questions about a text: 14 Recalling details: 14	Following directions: 9 Answering literal questions about a text: 10, 11 Identifying literal cause and effect: 10, 11 Recalling details and events: 10, 11 Predicting narrative outcomes: 10, 11 Activating prior knowledge: 11 Following written directions: 12 Answering literal questions about a text: 12 Recalling details: 12 Interpreting a character's feelings: 12	Following directions: 10 Answering literal questions about a text: 11, 12 Identifying literal cause and effect: 11, 12 Recalling details and events: 11, 12 Predicting narrative outcomes: 11, 12 Drawing inferences: 12 Recalling details: 12 Noting details: 13 Following written directions: 13 Answering literal questions about a text: 13 Interpreting a character's feelings: 13
Fluency		Repeated reading: 11 √ Reading words: 2–7 √: 2–7	Repeated reading: 11 √ Reading words: 2–7 √: 2–7	Repeated reading: 12 √ Reading words: 4–8 √: 2–7	Reading words: 3–7 √: 4–8	IC: 85 Reading words: 5–8 √: 5–8
Phonics and Word Recognition	**Regular**	Blending sounds into words: 6 (got) √: 6 Reading words: 2, 3, 4, 5 (super, plan, trick), 6 (got, fox), 7 (mope) √: 2–7 Underlined parts of words: 4 √: 4 Reading words: 8 Connected text: 10, 11 √: 10, 11	Blending sounds into words: 4 (gas) √: 4 Reading words: 2 (shoot), 3 (stairs, saying), 4 (gas), 5 (mopped, mopper), 6 (day), 7 (mop) √: 2–7 Underlined parts of words: 2, 5 (mopped) √: 2, 5 Reading words: 8 Connected text: 10, 11 √: 10, 11	Reading words: 4 (dark), 5 (tape, mess), 6 (tap), 7 (broke, holes, dimes), 8 (times) Underlined parts of words: 4 (dark), 6 (mopping, handed, tapped) √: 4, 6 Reading words: 9 Connected text: 11, 12 √: 11, 12	Reading words: 3, 4 (tape, mess), 5 (smiles, hopped), 7 (pow) √: 3–7 Underlined parts of words: 3, 6 (smiles, hopped) √: 3, 6 Reading words: 8 Connected text: 10 √: 10	Reading words: 5 (crash, walls), 6 (heave, having), 7 (dive), 8 (crashed) √: 5–8 Underlined parts of words: 5 (crash, walls), 8 (crashed) √: 5, 8 Reading words: 9 Connected text: 11 √: 11
	Irregular	Reading words: 5 (buying, woods, somebody) √: 5	Reading words: 3 (continued), 5 (talked) √: 3, 5 Underlined parts of words: 5 (talked) √: 5	Reading words: 8 (answer) √: 8		
Letter Sound Correspondence		Introduction: 4 (ea) Review: 4 (th, wh, ar, ou) √: 4	Review: 2 (ea, oo, er, wh, ou) √: 2	Introduction: 4 (ee) Review: 4 (wh, ar, al, th, ea) √: 4	Review: 3 (th, wh, al, ou, ar) √: 3	Review: 5 (sh, ou, wh, ar, al) √: 5
Print Awareness		Grapheme recognition: 6 (g)		Introduction to letter names: 1 (a – z) √: 2	Review letter names: 1 (a-z) √: 2	Review letter names: 1 (a-z), 3 (a-z) √: 2, 4
Phonemic Awareness						

Reading Mastery Signature Edition, Grade 1

	Lesson 86	Lesson 87	Lesson 88	Lesson 89	Lesson 90
Phonemic Awareness					
Print Awareness	Review letter names: 1 (a-z) √: 2	Introduction to capital letters: 1 (P, C, Y, F, W, K, I, Z, O, J, S, M, N, T, V, X, U)	Review capital letters: 1 (O, I, Z, V, P, J, N, T, C, U, M, F, Y, K, X, S, W)	Introduction to capital letters: 2 (A, R, D, E, Q) Review capital letters: 1 (T, K, N, J, Z, W, U, S, Y, C, P, I, F, X, O, V, M)	Review capital letters: 1 (R, E, A, D, Q)
Letter Sound Correspondence		Review: 4 (ea, al, ar, ch, oo) √: 4	Review: 4 (al, ea, th, wh, ou) √: 4	Review: 7 (ar, ing, er, ou, ee, wh) √: 7	Review: 6 (sh, ou, th) √: 6
Phonics and Word Recognition — Irregular	Reading words: 4 (said, nothing) √: 4 Spell by letter name: 4 (said, nothing) √: 4		Reading words: 3A (you), 5 (anybody) √: 3A, 5 Spell by letter name: 3B (you) √: 3B Underlined parts of words: 5 (anybody) √: 5		Reading words: 2 (words) √: 2
Phonics and Word Recognition — Regular	Reading words: 3, 4, 5 (throw, men), 6 √: 3, 4, 5, 6 Spell by letter name: 3, 4 √: 3, 4 Underlined parts of words: 6 (throw, men) √: 6	Reading words: 2, 3 (long), 4 (cheek, tear), 5 (longer, nobody) √: 2, 3, 4, 5, 5 Spell by letter name: 2, 3 (long) √: 2, 3 Underlined parts of words: 4 (cheek, tear), 5 (longer, nobody) √: 4, 5	Reading words: 2 (fixed, carry, baby), 3A (moping), 3B (moping), 4, 5 (thanked) √: 2, 3, 4, 5 Spell by letter name: 2 (fixed, carry), 3B (moping) √: 2, 3B Underlined parts of words: 4, 5 (thanked) √: 4, 5	Reading words: 3 (nailed, most), 4A/B (diner), 5, 6 (moped), 7 (need) √: 3, 4, 5, 6, 7 Spell by letter name: 3 (nailed), 4B (taped, diner) √: 3, 4 Underlined parts of words: 6 (moped), 7 (need) √: 6, 7	Reading words: 2 (plants, boss, key), 3A/B (pinned, pined, send, sent), 4, 5 (plant, seed), 6 (sticks, packed) √: 2, 3, 4, 5, 6 Spell by letter names: 2 (plants, boss, key), 3B (pinned, pined, send, sent) √: 2, 3B Underlined parts of words: 6 (sticks, packed) √: 6
Phonics and Word Recognition — Regular (cont.)	Reading words: 7 Connected text: 9 √: 9	Reading words: 6 Connected text: 8 √: 8	Reading words: 6 Connected text: 8 √: 8	Reading words: 8 Connected text: 10 √: 10	Reading words: 7 Connected text: 9 √: 9
Fluency	Reading words: 3, 4, 5, 6 √: 3, 4, 5, 6	Reading words: 2, 3, 4, 5, 5 √: 2, 3, 4, 5, 5	Reading words: 2, 3, 4, 5 √: 2, 3, 4, 5	Reading words: 3, 4, 5, 6, 7 √: 3, 4, 5, 6, 7	Reading words: 2, 3, 4, 5, 6 √: 2, 3, 4, 5, 6 Individual Checkout: 90
Comprehension	Following directions: 8	Following directions: 7	Following directions: 7	Following directions: 9	Following directions: 8
	Answering literal questions about a text: 9, 10 Identifying literal cause and effect: 9 Recalling details and events: 9 Predicting narrative outcomes: 9 Interpreting a character's feelings: 9 Following directions: 9 Drawing inferences: 9, 10	Answering literal questions about a text: 8 Identifying literal cause and effect: 8 Recalling details and events: 8 Predicting narrative outcomes: 8 Interpreting a character's feelings: 8, 9 Drawing inferences: 8, 9	Answering literal questions about a text: 8 Identifying literal cause and effect: 8 Recalling details and events: 9 Predicting narrative outcomes: 8 Drawing inferences: 9	Answering literal questions about a text: 10 Identifying literal cause and effect: 10 Recalling details and events: 11 Predicting narrative outcomes: 10, 11 Drawing inferences: 10	Answering literal questions about a text: 9, 10 Identifying literal cause and effect: 9 Recalling details and events: 10 Predicting narrative outcomes: 9 Interpreting a character's feelings: 9 Following directions: 10 Drawing inferences: 9 Activating prior knowledge: 9
	Recalling details: 11 Following written directions: 11 Answering literal questions about a text: 11 Noting details: 11 Interpreting a character's feelings: 11	Recalling details: 10 Following written directions: 10 Answering literal questions about a text: 10 Noting details: 10 Interpreting a character's feelings: 10	Recalling details: 10 Following written directions: 10 Answering literal questions about a text: 10 Noting details: 10 Interpreting a character's feelings: 10	Recalling details: 12 Following written directions: 12 Answering literal questions about a text: 12 Noting details: 12 Interpreting a character's feelings: 12	Recalling details: 11 Following written directions: 11 Answering literal questions about a text: 11 Noting details: 11
Spelling	Grapheme recognition: 1 √ Phoneme-grapheme correspondence: 2 √ Phonogram review: 3 Segmentation review: 3	Grapheme recognition: 1 √ Phoneme-grapheme correspondence: 2 √	Grapheme recognition: 1 √ Phoneme-grapheme correspondence: 2 √	Grapheme recognition: 1 √ Phoneme-grapheme correspondence: 2 √	Grapheme recognition: 1 √ Phoneme-grapheme correspondence: 2 √ Writing words: 3 Writing sentences: 4
	Writing words: 3 Writing sentences: 4	Writing words: 3 Writing sentences: 4	Writing words: 3 Writing sentences: 4	Writing words: 3 Writing sentences: 4	

Reading Mastery Signature Edition, Grade 1

	Lesson 91	Lesson 92	Lesson 93	Lesson 94	Lesson 95
Phonemic Awareness					
Print Awareness	Review capital letters: 1 (E, D, R, Q, A) Introduction to capital letters: 2 (B, L, H, G)	Review capital letters: 1 (H, L, G, B)	Review capital letters: 1 (D, B, H, L, R, Q, G, A, E)	Review capital letters: 1 (Q, G, R, E, B, L, A, H, D)	
Letter Sound Correspondence	Review: 7 (ou, al, er, wh, ing, ea) √: 7	Review: 6 (ou, ing, th, ar, wh, ou) √: 6	Review: 5 (ing, er, th, wh, ou) √: 5	Review: 3 (ea, ar, ou, ch, oo) √: 3	Review: 2 (al, ea, ou, ar, th, oo), 3 (al) √: 2, 3
Phonics and Word Recognition — Irregular		Reading words: 3 (**right**) √: 3 Spell by letter name: 3 (**right**) √: 3			Reading words: 1 (**early**), 2 (**schools**) √: 1, 2 Spell by letter name: 1 (**early**) √: 1 Underlined parts of words: 2 (**schools**) √: 2
Phonics and Word Recognition — Regular	Reading words: 3 (**Now**), 4 (**oak, jail, jailer**), 5 (**cane**), 6 (**notes, canned, caned, seems**), 7 √: 3, 4, 5, 6, 7 Spell by letter name: 3 (**Now**), 4 (**oak, jail, jailer**) √: 3, 4 Underlined parts of words: 6 (**notes, canned, caned, seems**), 7 √: 6, 7	Reading words: 2 (**As, Have**), 3 (**slope**), 4A/B (**slop**), 5 (**noted, planted, dumped**), 6 (**swing, tossed**) √: 2, 3, 4, 5, 6 Spell by letter name: 2 (**As, Have**), 3 √: 2, 3 Underlined parts of words: 5 (**noted, planted, dumped**), 6 (**swing, tossed**) √: 5, 6	Reading words: 2 (**Let**), 3 (**swung**), 4 (**yelling**), 5 (**planting**) √: 2, 3, 4, 5 Spell by letter name: 2 (**Let**), 3 (**swung**) √: 2, 3 Underlined parts of words: 4 (**yelling**), 5 (**planting**) √: 4, 5	Reading words: 2 (**If, And**), 3 (**cheese, fool, leaves**), 4 (**hoped, canner**), 5 (**fixes, spent**), 6A (**tapping**), 6B (**teaches**) √: 2, 3, 4, 5, 6A, 6B Spell by letter name: 2 (**If, And**), 6B (**tapping, teaches**) √: 2, 6B Underlined parts of words: 3 (**cheese, fool, leaves**), 4 (**hoped, canner**) √: 3, 4	Reading words: 1 (**Ann, Dan, lucky**), 2 (**smart**), 3 4 (**spell**) √: 1, 2, 3, 4 Spell by letter name: 1 (**Ann, Dan, lucky**), 4 (**spell**) √: 1, 4 Underlined parts of words: 2 (**smart**), 3 √: 2, 3
	Reading words: 8 Connected text: 10 √: 10	Reading words: 7 Connected text: 9 √: 9	Reading words:6 Connected text: 8 √: 8	Reading words: 7 Connected text: 9 √: 9	Connected text: 5 √: 5
Fluency	Reading words: 3, 4, 5, 6, 7 √: 3, 4, 5, 6, 7	Reading words: 2, 3, 4, 5, 6 √: 2, 3, 4, 5, 6	Reading words: 2, 3, 4, 5 √: 2, 3, 4, 5	Reading words: 2, 3, 4, 5, 6A, 6B √: 2, 3, 4, 5, 6A, 6B	Reading words: 1, 2, 3, 4 √: 1, 2, 3, 4
					Individual Checkout: 95
Comprehension	Following directions: 9	Following directions:8	Following directions:7	Following directions: 8	
	Answering literal questions about a text: 10, 11 Identifying literal cause and effect: 10 Recalling details and events: 10 Predicting narrative outcomes: 10, 11 Following directions: 11 Drawing inferences: 10	Answering literal questions about a text: 9, 10 Identifying literal cause and effect: 10 Recalling details and events: 9, 10 Predicting narrative outcomes: 9 Interpreting a character's feelings: 9 Following directions: 10 Activating prior knowledge: 9	Answering literal questions about a text: 8, 9 Identifying literal cause and effect: 8 Recalling details and events: 8 Predicting narrative outcomes: 8, 9 Interpreting a character's feelings: 9 Drawing inferences: 8	Answering literal questions about a text: 9 Identifying literal cause and effect: 9 Recalling details and events: 9 Interpreting a character's feelings: 10 Following directions: 10 Drawing inferences: 9, 10	Answering literal questions about a text: 5, 6 Recalling details and events: 5, 6 Predicting narrative outcomes: 5 Following directions: 6 Drawing inferences: 5, 6
	Recalling details: 12 Following written directions: 12 Answering literal questions about a text: 12 Noting details: 12	Recalling details: 11 Following written directions: 11 Answering literal questions about a text: 11 Noting details: 11	Recalling details: 10 Following written directions: 10 Answering literal questions about a text: 10 Noting details: 10 Interpreting a character's feelings: 10	Recalling details: 11 Following written directions: 11 Answering literal questions about a text: 11 Noting details: 11 Interpreting a character's feelings: 11	Recalling details: 8 Following written directions: 8 Answering literal questions about a text: 8 Using rules to classify objects: 7
Spelling	Phoneme-grapheme correspondence: 1 √ Phonemic segmentation: 2 √: 2 Spelling words: 3 √	Phoneme-grapheme correspondence: 1 Phonemic segmentation: 2 √: 2 Spelling words: 3 √	Phoneme-grapheme correspondence: 1 Phonemic segmentation: 2 √: 2 Spelling words: 3 √	Answering literal questions about a text: 5, 6 Recalling details and events: 5, 6 Predicting narrative outcomes: 5 Following directions: 6 Drawing inferences: 5, 6	Spelling words: 2 , 3 √: 2
					Word copying: 1 Phoneme-grapheme correspondence: 1 Writing words: 3
	Writing sentences: 4	Word copying: 1 Phoneme-grapheme correspondence: 1 Writing sentences: 4	Word copying: 1 Phoneme-grapheme correspondence: 1 Writing sentences: 4	Phoneme-grapheme correspondence: 1 Writing sentences: 4	

Key: (for Teachers)	√= informal assessment	Numbers = exercise numbers	Bold face type = first appearance

		Lesson 96	Lesson 97	Lesson 98	Lesson 99	Lesson 100
Phonemic Awareness						
Print Awareness						
Letter Sound Correspondence			Review: 2 (ing, sh, ch, ar) √: 2	Review: 2 (sh, al, th, ea, oo), 3 (ing) √: 2, 3	Review: 2 (ea, wh, th, al, er) √: 2	
Phonics and Word Recognition	Irregular			Reading words: 1 (question), 3 (You're) √: 1, 3 Spell by letter name: 1 (question) √: 1 Underlined parts of words: 3 (you're) √: 3	Reading words: 1 (grew) √: 1 Spell by letter name: 1 (grew) √: 1	Reading words: 1 (None, friend, swan), 3 (become) √: 1, 3 Spell by letter name: 1 (None, friend, swan) √: 1
	Regular	Reading words: 1 (Helper), 2 (hopping, wagged, boys), 3 (begin, tone, tame), 4 (tiger, seat) √: 1, 2, 3, 4 Spell by letter name: 1 (Helper), 4 (tiger, seat) √: 1, 4 Underlined parts of words: 2 (hopping, wagged, boys) √: 2	Reading words: 1 (wait), 2 (stones, cash), 3, 4 (hoping) √: 1, 2, 3, 4 Spell by letter name: 1 (wait), 4 (hoping) √: 1, 4 Underlined parts of words: 2 (stones, cash) √: 2	Reading words: 1, 2, 3, 4, 5 √: 1, 2, 3, 4, 5 Spell by letter name: 5 √: 5 Underlined parts of words: 2, 3 √: 2, 3	Reading words: 1 (hatched), 2 (leap, which), 3, 4 (wig) √: 1, 2, 3, 4 Spell by letter name: 1 (hatched), 4 (wig) √: 1, 4 Underlined parts of words: 2 (leap, which), 3 √: 2, 3	Reading words: 1 (Title, Ugly, grown), 2 (names, duckling), 3 (hello, egg), 4 √: 1, 2, 3, 4 Spell by letter name: 1 (Title, Ugly, grown), 4 (pals) √: 1, 4 Underlined parts of words: 2 (names, duckling) √: 2
		Connected text: 5 √: 5	Connected text: 5 √: 5	Connected text: 6 √: 6	Connected text: 5 √: 5	Connected text: 5 √: 5
Fluency		Reading words: 1, 2, 3, 4 √: 1, 2, 3, 4	Reading words: 1, 2, 3, 4 √: 1, 2, 3, 4	Reading words: 1, 2, 3, 4, 5 √: 1, 2, 3, 4, 5	Reading words: 1, 2, 3, 4 √: 1, 2, 3, 4	Reading words: 1, 2, 3, 4 √: 1, 2, 3, 4
						Individual Checkout: 100
Comprehension		Answering literal questions about a text: 5, 6 Identifying literal cause and effect: 5 Interpreting a character's feelings: 5, 6 Drawing inferences: 5	Answering literal questions about a text: 5, 6 Recalling details and events: 5 Predicting narrative outcomes: 5, 6 Following directions: 6 Drawing inferences: 5, 6 Activating prior knowledge: 5	Answering literal questions about a text: 6, 7 Recalling details and events: 6 Predicting narrative outcomes: 6	Answering literal questions about a text: 5, 6 Identifying literal cause and effect: 5 Predicting narrative outcomes: 5, 6 Interpreting a character's feelings: 5, 6 Drawing inferences: 5, 6 Activating prior knowledge: 5	Answering literal questions about a text: 5, 6 Identifying literal cause and effect: 5 Recalling details and events: 5 Predicting narrative outcomes: 5, 6 Interpreting a character's feelings: 5 Following directions: 6 Drawing inferences: 5, 6 Activating prior knowledge: 5
		Recalling details: 8 Following written directions: 8 Answering literal questions about a text: 8 Interpreting a character's feelings: 8 Using rules to classify objects: 7	Recalling details: 8 Following written directions: 8 Answering literal questions about a text: 8 Noting details: 8 Using rules to classify objects: 7	Recalling details: 9 Following written directions: 9 Answering literal questions about a text: 9 Using rules to classify objects: 8	Recalling details: 8 Following written directions: 8 Answering literal questions about a text: 8 Using rules to classify objects: 7	Recalling details: 7 Following written directions: 7 Answering literal questions about a text: 7 Using rules to classify objects: 7 Lesson 100 Curriculum-Based Assessment
Spelling		Phonemic segmentation: 1 √: 1 Spelling words: 2, 3 √: 3	Spelling words: 2, 3	Phonemic segmentation: 1 √: 1 Spelling words: 2, 3	Identifying spelled words: 1 Spelling words: 2, 3	Identifying spelled words: 1 Spelling words: 2, 3
		Writing words: 3	Word copying: 1 Phoneme-grapheme correspondence: 1 Sentence copying: 2 Writing words: 3	Writing words: 3	Sentence copying: 2 Phoneme-grapheme correspondence: 2 Writing words: 3	Sentence copying: 2 Phoneme-grapheme correspondence: 2 Writing words: 3

	Lesson 101	Lesson 102	Lesson 103	Lesson 104	Lesson 105
Spelling	Sentence copying: 2 Phoneme-grapheme correspondence: 2 Writing words: 3 Identifying spelled words: 1 Spelling words: 2, 3	Writing sentences: 2 Writing words: 3 Patterns: 1 √ Spelling words: 1, 3	Writing words: 3 Patterns: 1 √ Spelling words: 1, 2, 3	Writing words: 3 Identifying spelled words: 1 Spelling words: 1, 2, 3	Word copying: 1 Phoneme-grapheme correspondence: 1 Writing words: 3 Spelling words: 2, 3
Comprehension	Answering literal questions about a text: 5, 6 Identifying literal cause and effect: 5 Recalling details and events: 5 Interpreting a character's feelings: 5, 6 Drawing inferences: 5, 6 Recalling details: 7, 8 Following written directions: 8 Answering literal questions about a text: 8 Interpreting a character's feelings: 8 Using rules to classify objects: 8	Answering literal questions about a text: 5, 6 Recalling details and events: 5 Predicting narrative outcomes: 5 Interpreting a character's motives: 6 Interpreting a character's feelings: 6 Drawing inferences: 5, 6 Recalling details: 7, 8 Following written directions: 8 Answering literal questions about a text: 8 Using rules to classify objects: 8	Answering literal questions about a text: 5, 6 Recalling details and events: 5 Predicting narrative outcomes: 5 Following directions: 6 Drawing inferences: 5, 6 Recalling details: 7 Following written directions: 7 Using rules to classify objects: 7	Answering literal questions about a text: 6, 7 Recalling details and events: 6 Predicting narrative outcomes: 6 Interpreting a character's motives: 6 Activating prior knowledge: 6 Recalling details: 8 Following written directions: 8 Using rules to classify objects: 8	Answering literal questions about a text: 5, 6 Identifying literal cause and effect: 5 Recalling details and events: 5 Interpreting a character's feelings: 6 Drawing inferences: 5, 6 Activating prior knowledge: 5 Recalling details: 7 Following written directions: 7 Answering literal questions about a text: 7 Using rules to classify objects: 7
Fluency	Reading words: 1–4 √: 1–4	Reading words: 1–4 √: 1–4	Reading words: 1–4 √: 1–4	Reading words: 1–5 √: 1–5	Reading words: 1–4 √: 1–4 IC: 105
Phonics and Word Recognition — Regular	Reading words: 1 (nest, lunch, bowl, kitten), 2 (reach), 3 (eat, needs, wet), 4 √: 1–4 Spell by letter name: 1 (nest, lunch, bowl, kitten), 4 √: 1–4 Underlined parts of words: 2 (reach) √: 2 Connected text: 5 √: 5	Reading words: 1 (milk, king, sheep), 2 (bald, bean), 3 (homes), 4 (arms, kitten) Spell by letter name: 1 (milk, king, sheep), 3 (homes) √: 1, 3 Underlined parts of words: 2 (bald, bean), 4 (arms, kittens) √: 2, 4 Connected text: 5 √: 5	Reading words: 1 (Boo), 2 (horses, tricks), 3 (heap), 4 (games) Spell by letter name: 1 (Boo), 4 (games) √: 1–5 Underlined parts of words: 2 (horses, tricks) √: 2 Connected text: 5 √: 5	Reading words: 1 (cast, castle, monster, green, frog), 2 (biggest, planning), 3, 4, 5 Spell by letter name: 1 (cast, castle, monster, shopping), 5 √: 1–5 Underlined parts of words: 3 √: 3 Connected text: 6 √: 6	Reading words: 1 (tickle, toad, howling), 2 (bead), 3 (stays), 4 (robed, robbed) Spell by letter name: 1 (tickle, toad, howling), 4 (robed, robbed) √: 1–4 Underlined parts of words: 3 (stays) √: 3 Connected text: 5 √: 5
Phonics and Word Recognition — Irregular	Reading words: 1 (new) Spell by letter name: 1 (new) √: 1	Reading words: 1 (people, ghost, laugh) Spell by letter name: 1 (people, ghost, laugh) √: 1	Reading words: 2 (sometimes), 4 (night) Spell by letter name: 1 (night) √: 2, 4 Underlined parts of words: 2 (sometimes) √: 2	Reading words: 2 (turned, watched), 4 (laughing) Spell by letter name: 1 (turned, watched) √: 1, 2	Reading words: 1 (animal, turn) Spell by letter name: 1 (animal) √: 1
Letter Sound Correspondence	Review: 2 (ar, ou, wh, ch, ing, ea) √: 2	Review: 2 (al, ar, ou, ea, wh), 4 (ea) √: 2, 4	Review: 2 (ea) √: 2	Review: 3 (wh, th, ea, ou, ing) √: 3	Review: 3 (al, ing) √: 3
Print Awareness					
Phonemic Awareness					

Reading Mastery Signature Edition, Grade 1

Key: (for Teachers) √ = informal assessment Numbers = exercise numbers Bold face type = first appearance

		Lesson 106	Lesson 107	Lesson 108	Lesson 109	Lesson 110
Phonemic Awareness						
Print Awareness						
Letter Sound Correspondence			Review: 2 (al, ou, ea, ing) √: 2	Review: 2 (sh, ou, ing, ar, ea) √: 2	Review: 2 (ing) √: 2	Review: 2 (ar, al, ee, ea, ou) √: 2
Phonics and Word Recognition	Irregular	Reading words: 2 (laughed) √: 2 Underlined parts of words: 2 (laughed) √: 2	Reading words: 1 (knock) √: 1 Spell by letter name: 1 (knock) √: 1	Reading words: 1 (along, flew), 3 (knocked) √: 1, 3 Spell by letter name: 1 (along, flew) √: 1 Underlined parts of words: 3 (knocked) √: 3	Reading words: 1 (anyhow), 3 (doesn't) √: 1, 3 Spell by letter name: 1 (anyhow) √: 1	Reading words: 1 (might) √: 1 Spell by letter name: 1 (might) √: 1
	Regular	Reading words: 1 (dress, bode, leaf), 2 (dresses, myself), 3 (fear), 4 √: 1–4 Spell by letter name: 1 (dress, bode), 4 √: 1, 4 Underlined parts of words: 2 (dresses, myself) √: 2	Reading words: 1, 2 (lead, eating, themselves), 3 (meaner), 4 (caped, capped) √: 1–4 Spell by letter name: 4 (caped, capped) √: 4 Underlined parts of words: 2 (lead, eating, themselves) √: 2	Reading words: 1 (plate), 2 (flash, telling, dart, he'll), 3 (rammed, spells, floating, heaved), 4 (bites) √: 1–4 Spell by letter name: 1 (plate), 4 (bites) √: 1–4 Underlined parts of words: 2 (flash, telling, dart, he'll), 3 (rammed, spells, floating, heaved), √: 2, 3	Reading words: 1 (bin, flower, scream), 2, 3, 4 (cope, hopper) √: 1–4 Spell by letter name: 1 (bin, flower), 4 (cope, hopper) √: 1, 4 Underlined parts of words: 2 √: 2	Reading words: 1 (snake, shy, smiling), 2 (feel), 3 (we, casts), 4 (panes, pans, sip) √: 1–4 Spell by letter name: 1 (snake, shy, smiling), 4 (panes, pans, sip) √: 1, 4 Underlined parts of words: 2 (feel) √: 2
		Connected text: 5 √: 5	Connected text: 5 √: 5	Connected text: 5 √: 5	Connected text: 5 √: 5	Connected text: 5 √: 5
Fluency		Reading words: 1–4 √: 1–4	Reading words: 1–4 √: 1–4	Reading words: 1–4 √: 1–4	Reading words: 1–4 √: 1–4	Reading words: 1–4 √: 1–4
						IC: 110
Comprehension		Answering literal questions about a text: 5, 6 Identifying literal cause and effect: 5 Predicting narrative outcomes: 5 Interpreting a character's feelings: 6 Interpreting a character's motives: 5 Drawing inferences: 5	Answering literal questions about a text: 5, 6 Recalling details and events: 5 Predicting narrative outcomes: 5, 6 Interpreting a character's motives: 5 Drawing inferences: 5, 6	Answering literal questions about a text: 5, 6 Recalling details and events: 5 Predicting narrative outcomes: 5 Interpreting a character's motives: 5 Drawing inferences: 5, 6	Answering literal questions about a text: 5, 6 Identifying literal cause and effect: 6 Recalling details and events: 5, 6 Predicting narrative outcomes: 6 Interpreting a character's feelings: 6 Drawing inferences: 5, 6	Answering literal questions about a text: 5, 6 Recalling details and events: 5 Predicting narrative outcomes: 5, 6 Drawing inferences: 5, 6
		Recalling details: 7 Following written directions: 7 Answering literal questions about a text: 7 Using rules to classify objects: 7	Recalling details: 7 Following written directions: 7 Answering literal questions about a text: 7 Using rules to classify objects: 7	Recalling details: 7 Following written directions: 7 Answering literal questions about a text: 7 Using rules to classify objects: 7	Recalling details: 7 Following written directions: 7 Answering literal questions about a text: 7 Using rules to classify objects: 7	Recalling details: 7 Following written directions: 7 Answering literal questions about a text: 7 Using rules to classify objects: 7
Spelling		Phonemic segmentation: 1 √: 1 Spelling words: 2, 3	Identifying spelled words: 1 Patterns: 2 √ Spelling words: 2, 3	Identifying spelled words: 1 Patterns: 2 √ Spelling words: 2, 3	Spelling words: 2, 3	Phonemic segmentation: 1 √: 1 Patterns: 2 √ Spelling words: 2, 3
						Writing words: 3
		Writing words: 3	Writing words: 3	Writing words: 3	Word copying: 1 Phoneme–grapheme correspondence: 1 Writing words: 3	

Key: (for Teachers)   √ = informal assessment   Numbers = exercise numbers   Bold face type = first appearance

		Lesson 111	Lesson 112	Lesson 113	Lesson 114	Lesson 115
Phonemic Awareness						
Print Awareness						
Letter Sound Correspondence		Review: 2 (er, ou, ee, sh) √: 2	Review: 2 (ee, sh, er, wh, ou) √: 2		Review: 2 (ing), 3 (ea, sh, oo, I) √: 2, 3	Review: 2 (ing, ea, oo, ou, ch) √: 2
Phonics and Word Recognition	Irregular	Reading words: 1 (**genie**), 2 (**appear**) √: 1, 2 Spell by letter name: 1 (**genie**) √: 1 Underlined parts of words: 2 (**appear**) √: 2	Reading words: 1 (**strange, disappear**) √: 1 Spell by letter name: 1 (**strange, disappear**) √: 1	Reading words: 2 (**genies**) √: 2 Underlined parts of words: 2 (**genies**) √: 2	Reading words: 1 (**Carla**), 2 (**alone, icebox**) √: 1, 2 Spell by letter name: 1 (**Carla**) √: 1 Underlined parts of words: 2 (**alone, icebox**) √: 2	Reading words: 1 (city), 4 (**appears**) √: 1, 4 Spell by letter name: 1 (city), 4 (**appears**) √: 1, 4
	Regular	Reading words: 1 (**bumpy, master, rolled, shore, storm**), 2 (**year, peek, wishes**), 3, 4 (**maybe**) √: 1–4 Spell by letter name: 1 (**bumpy, master, rolled, shore, storm**), 4 (**maybe**) √: 1, 4 Underlined parts of words: 2 (**year, peek, wishes**) √: 2	Reading words: 1 (**puff, Ott, alligator, apple, bottles**), 2, 3 (**rubs**), 4 (**smoke**) √: 1–4 Spell by letter name: 1 (**puff, Ott, alligator, apple, bottles**), 4 (**smoke**) √: 1, 4 Underlined parts of words: 2 √: 2	Reading words: 1 (**Test, suddenly, beach, peach, peaches, heel**), 2 (**dimmer**), 3, 4 (**takes, dimmed**) √: 1–4 Spell by letter name: 1 (**Test, suddenly, beach**), 4 (**takes, dimmed**) √: 1, 4 Underlined parts of words: 2 (**dimmer**) √: 2	Reading words: 1 (**bust, bunch, junk, melt, step**), 2 (**lies**), 3 (**beat, smash**), 4 (**Bide, coned, flies**) √: 1–4 Spell by letter name: 1 (**bust, bunch, junk, melt**), 4 (**Bide, coned, flies**) √: 1, 4 Underlined parts of words: 2 (**lies**), 3 (**beat, smash**) √: 2, 3	Reading words: 1 (**remember, forgot, Rome, middle, banking**), 2 (**spanking, sounded, thousands**), 3 (**folded**), 4 (**waved, able**) √: 1–4 Spell by letter name: 1 (**remember, forgot, Rome, middle, banking**), 4 (**waved, able**) √: 1, 4 Underlined parts of words: 2 (**spanking, sounded, thousands**) √: 2
		Connected text: 5 √: 5	Connected text: 5 √: 5	Connected text: 5 √: 5	Connected text: 5 √: 5	Connected text: 5 √: 5
Fluency		Reading words: 1–4 √: 1–4	Reading words: 1–4 √: 1–4	Reading words: 1–4 √: 1–4	Reading words: 1–4 √: 1–4	Reading words: 1–4 √: 1–4
						IC: 115
Comprehension		Answering literal questions about a text: 5, 6 Identifying literal cause and effect: Recalling details and events: Predicting narrative outcomes: Interpreting a character's feelings: 5, 6 Interpreting a character's motives: 5 Drawing inferences: 5, 6 Activating prior knowledge: 5	Answering literal questions about a text: 5, 6 Identifying literal cause and effect: 5 Recalling details and events: Interpreting a character's feelings: 6 Drawing inferences: 5 Following directions: 6 Activating prior knowledge: 5	Answering literal questions about a text: 5, 6 Recalling details and events: 5 Interpreting a character's feelings: 6 Interpreting a character's motives: 5 Drawing inferences: 5, 6 Following directions: 6 Activating prior knowledge: 6	Answering literal questions about a text: 5, 6 Identifying literal cause and effect: 5 Recalling details and events: 5 Predicting narrative outcomes: 5 Interpreting a character's feelings: 6 Interpreting a character's motives: 5 Drawing inferences: 5, 6	Answering literal questions about a text: 5 Recalling details and events: 5, 6 Predicting narrative outcomes: 5 Drawing inferences: 5, 6 Activating prior knowledge: 5
		Recalling details: 7 Following written directions: 7 Answering literal questions about a text: 7 Using rules to classify objects: 7	Recalling details: 7 Following written directions: 7 Answering literal questions about a text: 7 Using rules to classify objects: 7	Recalling details: 7 Following written directions: 7 Answering literal questions about a text: 7 Using rules to classify objects: 7	Recalling details: 7 Following written directions: 7 Answering literal questions about a text: 7 Using rules to classify objects: 7	Recalling details: 7 Following written directions: 7 Answering literal questions about a text: 7 Using rules to classify objects: 7
Spelling		Identifying spelled words: 1 Patterns: 2 √ Spelling words: 2, 3	Patterns: 2 √ Spelling words: 2	Phonemic segmentation: 1 √: 1 Spelling words: 2	Spelling words: 1, 2, 3 Patterns: 2	Spelling words: 1 Phonemic segmentation: 2 √: 2
						Writing sentences: 3
		Writing words: 3	Word copying: 1 Phoneme–grapheme correspondence: 1 Writing sentences: 3	Writing sentences: 3	Sentence copying: 1 Writing words: 2, 3	

Key: (for Teachers)   √ = informal assessment   Numbers = exercise numbers   Bold face type = first appearance

		Lesson 116	Lesson 117	Lesson 118	Lesson 119	Lesson 120
Phonemic Awareness						
Print Awareness						
Letter Sound Correspondence		Review: 2 (er) √: 2	Review: 2 (wh, ea, ou, sh, ing) √: 2	Review: 2 (ing, ea) √: 2	Review: 2 (ar, er, ch, ing, th, ea) √: 2	
Phonics and Word Recognition	**Irregular**	Reading words: 1 (face) √: 1 Spell by letter name: 1 (face) √: 1	Reading words: 3 (appeared), 4 √: 3, 4 Underlined parts of words: 3 (appeared) √: 3	Reading words: 1 (through, across), 3 (disappears), 4 (believe) √: 1, 3, 4 Spell by letter name: 1 (through, across), 4 (believes) √: 1, 4	Reading words: 1 (believed) √: 1 Spell by letter name: 1 (believed) √: 1	Reading words: 1 (few, wonderful) √: 1 Spell by letter name: 1 (few, wonderful) √: 1
	Regular	Reading words: 1 (air, blushed, spin, poorest), 2 (being, hatter), 3 (hater, poof), 4 √: 1–4 Spell by letter name: 1 (air, blushed, spin, poorest), 4 √: 1, 4 Underlined parts of words: 2 (being, hatter) √: 2	Reading words: 1 (filled, we're, haven't), 2 (streaming, wished) √: 1–4 Spell by letter name: 1 (filled), 4 √: 1–4 Underlined parts of words: 2 (streaming, wished), 3 √: 2, 3	Reading words: 1 (fact, wise), 2 (closer, resting), 3, 4 (splat, formed, flow, copper) √: 1–4 Spell by letter name: 1 (fact, wise), 4 (splat, formed, flow) √: 1, 4 Underlined parts of words: 2 (closer, resting) √: 2	Reading words: 1 (broken, cans, canes), 2, 3 (spank, stick, glass), 4 (windows), 5 √: 1–5 Spell by letter name: 1 (broken, cans, canes) √: 1 Underlined parts of words: 2, 4 (windows) √: 2, 4	Reading words: 1 (blanks, flip), 2 (flipped, parting), 3 (yet), 4 (shade, planned, planed) √: 1–4 Spell by letter name: 1 (blanks), 4 (shade, planned, planed) √: 1, 4 Underlined parts of words: 2 (flipped, parting) √: 2
		Connected text: 5 √: 5	Connected text: 5 √: 5	Connected text: 5 √: 5	Connected text: 6 √: 6	Connected text: 5 √: 5
Fluency		Reading words: 1–4 √: 1–4	Reading words: 1–4 √: 1–4	Reading words: 1–4 √: 1–4	Reading words: 1–5 √: 1–5	Reading words: 1–4 √: 1–4
						IC: 120
Comprehension		Answering literal questions about a text: 5, 6 Identifying literal cause and effect: 5 Recalling details and events: 5 Predicting narrative outcomes: 5 Interpreting a character's feelings: 5, 6 Drawing inferences: 5 Following directions: 6	Answering literal questions about a text: 5, 6 Identifying literal cause and effect: 5 Recalling details and events: 5 Predicting narrative outcomes: 6 Interpreting a character's motives: 6 Drawing inferences: 5, 6 Activating prior knowledge: 5	Answering literal questions about a text: 5, 6 Identifying literal cause and effect: 5 Recalling details and events: 5, 6 Predicting narrative outcomes: 6 Interpreting a character's feelings: 6 Interpreting a character's motives: 5 Drawing inferences: 5	Answering literal questions about a text: 6, 7 Identifying literal cause and effect: 6 Recalling details and events: 7 Predicting narrative outcomes: 6, 7 Interpreting a character's motives: 6, 7 Drawing inferences: 6, 7	Answering literal questions about a text: 5, 6 Recalling details and events: 5 Predicting narrative outcomes: 5 Interpreting a character's feelings: 6 Interpreting a character's motives: 5 Drawing inferences: 5
		Recalling details: 7 Following written directions: 7 Answering literal questions about a text: 7 Using rules to classify objects: 7	Recalling details: 7 Following written directions: 7 Answering literal questions about a text: 7 Using rules to classify objects: 7	Recalling details: 7 Following written directions: 7 Answering literal questions about a text: 7 Using rules to classify objects: 7	Recalling details: 8 Following written directions: 8 Answering literal questions about a text: 8 Using rules to classify objects: 8	Recalling details: 7 Following written directions: 7 Answering literal questions about a text: 7 Using rules to classify objects: 7
						Lesson 120 Curriculum-Based Assessment
Spelling		Spelling words: 1 Identifying spelled words: 2 √: 2	Spelling words: 1, 2, 3	Spelling words: 1, 2, 3	Spelling words: 1 Identifying spelled words: 2 √: 2	Spelling words: 1 Phonemic segmentation: 2 √: 2
		Sentence copying: 1 Phoneme–grapheme correspondence: 1 Writing sentences: 3	Sentence copying: 1 Phoneme–grapheme correspondence: 1 Writing words: 3	Sentence copying: 1 Phoneme–grapheme correspondence: 1 Writing words: 3	Sentence copying: 1 Phoneme–grapheme correspondence: 1 Writing sentences: 3	Sentence copying: 1 Phoneme–grapheme correspondence: 1 Writing sentences: 3

		Lesson 121	Lesson 122	Lesson 123	Lesson 124	Lesson 125
Phonemic Awareness						
Print Awareness						
Letter Sound Correspondence				Review: 3 (I) √: 3	Review: 2 (al, sh, ar, er, wh, th, ou), 4 (I) √: 2, 4	Review: 2 (ea, ing, th, er, ou) √: 2
Phonics and Word Recognition	Irregular	Reading words: 1 (**stood**), 4 (**Marta Flores**) √: 1, 4 Spell by letter name: 1 (**stood**) √: 1	Reading words: 1 (**agreed**), 2 (**fight**) √: 1, 2 Spell by letter name: 1 (**agreed**) √: 1		Reading words: 1 (**obey**), 5 (**knows**) √: 1, 5 Spell by letter name: 1 (**obey**), 5 (**knows**) √: 1, 5	Reading words: 1 (**place**), 3 (**yourself**) √: 1, 3 Spell by letter name: 1 (**place**) √: 1 Underlined parts of words: 3 (**yourself**) √: 3
	Regular	Reading words: 1 (**person, human, impossible, stare**), 2, 3 (**richest, flipping**), 5, 6 (**planner, planer**) √: 1–3, 5–6 Spell by letter name: 1 (**person, human, impossible, stare**), 6 (**planner, planer**) √: 1, 6 Underlined parts of words: 3 (**richest, flipping**) √: 3	Reading words: 1 (**true, simple, spitting**), 2, 3 (**flowed**), 4, 5 (**dare**) √: 1–5 Spell by letter name: 1 (**true, simple, spitting**), 5 (**dare**) √: 1, 5 Underlined parts of words: 3 (**flowed**) √: 3	Reading words: 1 (**instant, hug, hungry**), 2, 3 (**he's we've, she'd**), 4, 5 (**planing**) √: 1–5 Spell by letter name: 1 (**instant, hug, hungry**), 5 (**planing**) √: 1, 5 Underlined parts of words: 3 (**he's, we've, she'd**) √: 3	Reading words: 1 (**vow, class, fingers, snapped**), 2 (**smartest, smarter**), 3, 4, 5 (**taking**) √: 1–5 Spell by letter name: 1 (**vow, class, fingers, snapped**), 5 (**taking**) √: 1, 5 Underlined parts of words: 2 (**smartest, smarter**), 4 √: 2, 4	Reading words: 1 (**short, spend**), 2 (**ring**), 3 (**patted, vows, masters**), 4 (**biting, wiped, life**) √: 1–4 Spell by letter name: 1 (**short, spend**), 4 (**biting, wiped, life**) √: 1, 4 Underlined parts of words: 2 (**ring**), 3 (**patted, vows, masters**) √: 2, 3
		Connected text: 7 √: 7	Connected text: 6 √: 6	Connected text: 6 √: 6	Connected text: 6 √: 6	Connected text: 5 √: 5
Fluency		Reading words: 1–6 √: 1–6	Reading words: 1–5 √: 1–5	Reading words: 1–5 √: 1–5	Reading words: 1–5 √: 1–5	Reading words: 1–4 √: 1–4
						IC: 125
Comprehension		Answering literal questions about a text: 7, 8 Recalling details and events: 7, 8 Interpreting a character's feelings: 8 Interpreting a character's motives: 7 Drawing inferences: 7, 8	Answering literal questions about a text: 6, 7 Recalling details and events: 7 Predicting narrative outcomes: 6 Drawing inferences: 6	Answering literal questions about a text: 6, 7 Identifying literal cause and effect: 6 Predicting narrative outcomes: 6 Interpreting a character's motives: 6 Drawing inferences: 7	Answering literal questions about a text: 6, 7 Recalling details and events: 6 Predicting narrative outcomes: 6 Interpreting a character's feelings: 7 Interpreting a character's motives: 6 Drawing inferences: 6	Answering literal questions about a text: 5, 6 Recalling details and events: 5 Predicting narrative outcomes: 5 Interpreting a character's feelings: 5 Interpreting a character's motives: 5 Drawing inferences: 5, 6
		Recalling details: 10 Following written directions: 9, 10 Answering literal questions about a text: 10 Using rules to classify objects: 10	Recalling details: 9 Following written directions: 8, 9 Answering literal questions about a text: 9 Using rules to classify objects: 9	Written deductions: 8 Recalling details: 8 Following written directions: 9 Answering literal questions about a text: 9 Using rules to classify objects: 9	Written deductions: 8 Recalling details: 9 Following written directions: 9 Answering literal questions about a text: 9 Using rules to classify objects: 9	Written deductions: 7 Recalling details: 8 Following written directions: 8 Answering literal questions about a text: 8 Using rules to classify objects: 8
Spelling		Spelling words: 2, 3 √: 3	Identifying spelled words: 1 √: 1 Spelling words: 2, 3	Identifying spelled words: 1 Phonemic segmentation: 2 √: 2 Spelling words: 1, 3	Phonemic segmentation: 1 √: 1 Spelling words: 2, 3	Phonemic segmentation: 1 √: 1 Spelling words: 2, 3
		Writing sentences: 1	Writing words: 3	Writing words: 3	Writing words: 3	

Reading Mastery Signature Edition, Grade 1

Key: (for Teachers)	√= informal assessment	Numbers = exercise numbers	Bold face type = first appearance

		Lesson 126	Lesson 127	Lesson 128	Lesson 129	Lesson 130
Phonemic Awareness						
Print Awareness						
Letter Sound Correspondence		Review: 2 (or) √: 2	Review: 4 (ea) √: 4	Review: 2 (er, ea, ou, wh, ing, sh) √: 2	Review: 2 (l) √: 2	
Phonics and Word Recognition	Irregular	Reading words: 1 (**phone, Japan, Alaska, China, move**), 4 (**you've, they've**) √: 1, 4 Spell by letter name: 1 (**phone, Japan, Alaska, China, move**) √: 1 Underlined parts of words: 4 (**you've, they've**) √: 4	Reading words: 1 (**minute**), 2 (**turns**) √: 1, 2 Spell by letter name: 1 (**minute**) √: 1 Underlined parts of words: 2 (**turns**) √: 2	Reading words: 1 (**dollars**), 4 (**phoned**), 5 (**rental**) √: 1, 4, 5 Spell by letter name: 1 (**dollars**), 5 (**rental**) √: 1, 5 Underlined parts of words: 4 (**phoned**) √: 4	Reading words: 1 (**service, dental, trouble**) √: 1 Spell by letter name: 1 (**service, dental, trouble**) √: 1	Reading words: 1 (**honey, moves**), 2 (**already**) √: 1, 2 Spell by letter name: 1 (**honey**) √: 1 Underlined parts of words: 2 (**already**) √: 2
	Regular	Reading words: 1 (**trained, hair**), 2 (**belong, hardest**), 3 (**chapped, rush, taken**), 4, 5 (**van, vane**) √: 1–5 Spell by letter name: 1 (**trained, hair**), 5 (**van, vane**) √: 1, 5 Underlined parts of words: 2 (**belong, hardest**), 4 √: 2, 4	Reading words: 1 (**east, clock, rang, too**), 2 (**understand, rushed, spelled**), 3 (**stuff, west, mate**), 4 (**packing, bringing, treat**), 5 (**vaned, hung**) √: 1–5 Spell by letter name: 1 (**east, clock, rang**), 5 (**vaned, hung**) √: 1, 5 Underlined parts of words: 2 (**understand, rushed, spelled**), 4 (**packing, bringing, treat**) √: 2, 4	Reading words: 1 (**until, Trunk, rent, swell**), 2 (**corner, bring**), 3 (**spelling**), 4 (**dragging**), 5 √: 1–5 Spell by letter name: 1 (**until, Trunk**) √: 1 Underlined parts of words: 2 (**corner, bring**), 4 (**dragging**) √: 2, 4	Reading words: 1 (**False, number**), 2 (**rented, where's**), 3 (**teeth**), 4 (**trips**), 5 (**drive**) √: 1–5 Spell by letter name: 1 (**False, number**), 5 (**drive**) √: 1, 5 Underlined parts of words: 2 (**rented, where's**) √: 2	Reading words: 1 (**pocket, loaded**), 2 (**passing**), 3 (**chase**), 4 (**Jan, skates**) √: 1–4 Spell by letter name: 1 (**pocket**), 4 (**Jan, skates**) √: 1, 4 Underlined parts of words: 2 (**passing**) √: 2
		Connected text: 6 √: 6	Connected text: 6 √: 6	Connected text: 6 √: 6	Connected text: 6 √: 6	Connected text: 5 √: 5
Fluency		Reading words: 1–5 √: 1–5	Reading words: 1–5 √: 1–5	Reading words: 1–5 √: 1–5	Reading words: 1–5 √: 1–5	Reading words: 1–4 √: 1–4
						IC: 130
Comprehension		Answering literal questions about a text: 6, 7 Recalling details and events: 6 Interpreting a character's feelings: 7 Drawing inferences: 6, 7	Answering literal questions about a text: 6, 7 Recalling details and events: 6, 7 Predicting narrative outcomes: 6 Interpreting a character's feelings: 7 Interpreting a character's motives: 6 Drawing inferences: 6 Following directions: 6 Activating prior knowledge: 6	Answering literal questions about a text: 6, 7 Recalling details and events: 6, 7 Predicting narrative outcomes: 6 Interpreting a character's motives: 6 Drawing inferences: 6, 7	Answering literal questions about a text: 6, 7 Recalling details and events: 6, 7 Predicting narrative outcomes: 6, 7 Drawing inferences: 7	Answering literal questions about a text: 5, 6 Recalling details and events: 5, 6 Predicting narrative outcomes: 5 Interpreting a character's feelings: 6 Drawing inferences: 5
		Written deductions: 8 Recalling details: 8 Following written directions: 8 Answering literal questions about a text: 8 Using rules to classify objects: 8	Written deductions: 8 Recalling details: 8 Following written directions: 8 Answering literal questions about a text: 8 Using rules to classify objects: 8	Written deductions: 8 Recalling details: 8 Following written directions: 8 Answering literal questions about a text: 8 Using rules to classify objects: 8	Written deductions: 8 Recalling details: 8 Following written directions: 8 Answering literal questions about a text: 8 Using rules to classify objects: 8	Written deductions: 7 Recalling details: 7 Following written directions: 7 Answering literal questions about a text: 7 Using rules to classify objects: 7
Spelling		Patterns: 2	Patterns: 2	Identifying spelled words: 1 Spelling words: 1, 2, 3	Phonemic segmentation: 1 √: 1 Spelling words: 2, 3	Spelling words: 2
						Word copying: 1 Phoneme–grapheme correspondence: 1 Writing sentences: 3
		Word parts (Affixes): 1 Writing sentences: 3	Word copying: 1 Word parts (Affixes): 1 Writing words: 2 Writing sentences: 3	Writing words: 3	Writing words: 3	

Reading Mastery Signature Edition, Grade 1

		Lesson 131	Lesson 132	Lesson 133	Lesson 134	Lesson 135
Phonemic Awareness						
Print Awareness						
Letter Sound Correspondence		Review: 2 (ch, ee, ar, ea, er) √: 2	Review: 2 (ch, ar, ea) √: 2			Review: 2 (ch, wh, ou, th, oo) √: 2
Phonics and Word Recognition	**Irregular**	Reading words: 1 **(feathers, turtle)** √: 1 Spell by letter name: 1 **(feathers, turtle)** √: 1	Reading words: 1 **(handsome, Caw, nice, mice)** √: 1 Spell by letter name: 1 **(handsome, Caw, nice)** √: 1	Reading words: 1 **(world, wear, footprint)** √: 1 Spell by letter name: 1 **(world, wear, footprint)** √: 1		
	Regular	Reading words: 1 **(dry, drank)**, 2 **(chicken)**, 3 **(helps, Ellen's)**, 4 **(wide)** √: 1–4 Spell by letter name: 1 **(dry, drank)**, 4 **(wide)** √: 1, 4 Underlined parts of words: 2 **(chicken)**, 3 **(helps, Ellen's)** √: 2, 3	Reading words: 1 **(Crow, branch)**, 2 **(chunk, such, Carl)**, 3 **(lay, black)**, 4 **(slider, wings, singing)**, 5 **(sang)** √: 1–5 Spell by letter name: 1 **(Crow, branch)**, 5 **(sang)** √: 1, 5 Underlined parts of words: 2 **(chunk, such, Carl)**, 4 **(slider, wings, singing)** √: 2, 4	Reading words: 1 **(toe, nail, slid)**, 2 **(pond)**, 3 **(weed, hotter)**, 4 **(cons, cones, shine, shining)** √: 1–4 Spell by letter name: 1 **(toe)**, 4 **(cons, cones, shine, shining)** √: 1, 4	Reading words: 1 **(Flame, shell, slide)**, 2 **(tears, cheeks)**, 3, 4 **(coat, cave, gaped, gapped, joke)** √: 1–4 Spell by letter name: 1 **(Flame, shell)**, 4 **(coat, cave, gaped, gapped, joke)** √: 1, 4 Underlined parts of words: 2 **(tears, cheeks)** √: 2	Reading words: 1 **(stool, roots, snap, sneak, strong)**, 2 **(tooth)**, 3 **(sliding)** √: 1–3 Spell by letter name: 1 **(stool, roots, snap, sneak, strong)**, 3 **(sliding)** √: 1, 3 Underlined parts of words: 2 **(tooth)** √: 2
		Connected text: 5 √: 5	Connected text: 6 √: 6	Connected text: 5 √: 5	Connected text: 5 √: 5	Connected text: 4 √: 4
Fluency		Reading words: 1–4 √: 1–4	Reading words: 1–5 √: 1–5	Reading words: 1–4 √: 1–4	Reading words: 1–4 √: 1–4	Reading words: 1–3 √: 1–3 IC: 135
Comprehension		Answering literal questions about a text: 5, 6 Identifying literal cause and effect: 5 Recalling details and events: 5, 6 Predicting narrative outcomes: 5 Drawing inferences: 5	Answering literal questions about a text: 6, 7 Identifying literal cause and effect: 6 Recalling details and events: 6 Predicting narrative outcomes: 6 Interpreting a character's feelings: 7 Drawing inferences: 6	Answering literal questions about a text: 5, 6 Recalling details and events: 5 Predicting narrative outcomes: 5 Drawing inferences: 5, 6	Answering literal questions about a text: 5, 6 Recalling details and events: 5 Interpreting a character's feelings: 6 Interpreting a character's motives: 5 Drawing inferences: 5, 6	Answering literal questions about a text: 4, 5 Recalling details and events: 4 Predicting narrative outcomes: 4, 5 Interpreting a character's motives: 5 Drawing inferences: 4 Following directions: 5
		Written deductions: 7 Recalling details: 7 Following written directions: 7 Answering literal questions about a text: 7 Using rules to classify objects: 7	Written deductions: 9 Recalling details: 9 Following directions: 8 Answering literal questions about a text: 9 Using rules to classify objects: 9	Written deductions: 8 Recalling details: 8 Following directions: 7, 8 Answering literal questions about a text: 8 Using rules to classify objects: 8	Written deductions: 8 Recalling details: 8 Following directions: 7, 8 Answering literal questions about a text: 8 Using rules to classify objects: 8	Written deductions: 7 Recalling details: 7 Following directions: 6, 7 Answering literal questions about a text: 7 Using rules to classify objects: 7
Spelling		Spelling words: 1, 2 Word families: 2	Spelling words: 1, 2, 3 Word families: 2	Spelling words: 1, 2, 3	Spelling words: 1, 2, 3	Spelling words: 1 Phonemic segmentation: 2 √: 2 Sentence copying: 1 Phoneme–grapheme correspondence: 1 Writing sentences: 3
		Sentence copying: 1 Writing sentences: 3	Writing words: 3	Sentence copying: 1 Phoneme–grapheme correspondence: 1 Writing words: 3	Sentence copying: 1 Phoneme–grapheme correspondence: 1	

Key: (for Teachers)   √= informal assessment   Numbers = exercise numbers   Bold face type = first appearance

		Lesson 136	Lesson 137	Lesson 138	Lesson 139	Lesson 140
Phonemic Awareness						
Print Awareness						
Letter Sound Correspondence		Review: 2 (l, al) √: 2	Review: 2 (sh, ai, ea, wh, th) √: 2	Review: 2 (er, ou) √: 2	Review: 2 (ea, th, wh, ee) √: 2	Review: 2 (ea, sh, th, wh, ou, ee) √: 2
Phonics and Word Recognition	Irregular	Reading words: 1 (**color**), 3 (**light**), 4 (**pulled**) √: 1, 3, 4 Spell by letter name: 1 (**color**), 4 (**pulled**) √: 1, 4	Reading words: 1 (**wolf, wolves, listen, alive**), 4 (**watch**) √: 1, 4 Spell by letter name: 1 (**wolf, wolves, listen, alive**), 4 (**watch**) √: 1, 4	Reading words: 1 (**cookie, race**), 2 (**watching, someday, worker**) √: 1, 2 Spell by letter name: 1 (**cookie, race**) √: 1 Underlined parts of words: 2 (**watching, someday, worker**) √: 2	Reading words: 1 (**Mr., knew**) √: 1 Spell by letter name: 1 (**Mr., knew**) √: 1	Reading words: 4 (**asleep, ahead**) √: 4 Underlined parts of words: 4 (**asleep, ahead**) √: 4
	Regular	Reading words: 1 (**bong, sneaky**), 2, 3 (**stepped**), 4 (**used**) √: 1–4 Spell by letter name: 1 (**bong**), 4 (**used**) √: 1, 4 Underlined parts of words: 2 √: 2	Reading words: 1 (**flock, Croak**), 2, 3, 4 (**biter, bitter**) √: 1–4 Spell by letter name: 1 (**flock, Croak**), 4 (**biter, bitter**) √: 1, 4 Underlined parts of words: 2 √: 2	Reading words: 1 (**lions, sweet**), 2 (**fastest**), 3, 4 (**safe, chasing**) √: 1–4 Spell by letter name: 1 (**lions, sweet**), 4 (**safe, chasing**) √: 1, 4 Underlined parts of words: 2 (**fastest**) √: 2	Reading words: 1 (**pepper, owl**), 2 (**lined**), 3 (**waiting, slowest, dusty**), 4 (**path, mile**) √: 1–4 Spell by letter name: 1 (**pepper**), 4 (**path, mile**) √: 1, 4 Underlined parts of words: 2 (**lined**), 3 (**waiting, slowest, dusty**) √: 2, 3	Reading words: 1 (**Finish, thick**), 2 (**leaned, speed**), 3 (**loudly**), 4 (**crossed, happening**) √: 1–4 Spell by letter name: 1 (**Finish, thick**) √: 1 Underlined parts of words: 2 (**leaned, speed**), 3 (**loudly**), 4 (**crossed, happening**) √: 2–4
		Connected text: 5 √: 5	Connected text: 5 √: 5	Connected text: 5 √: 5	Connected text: 5 √: 5	Connected text: 5 √: 5
Fluency		Reading words: 1–4 √: 1–4	Reading words: 1–4 √: 1–4	Reading words: 1–4 √: 1–4	Reading words: 1–4 √: 1–4	Reading words: 1–4 √: 1–4 IC: 140
Comprehension		Answering literal questions about a text: 5, 6 Recalling details and events: 5, 6 Interpreting a character's feelings: 5 Interpreting a character's motives: 6 Drawing inferences: 5, 6	Answering literal questions about a text: 5, 6 Recalling details and events: 5 Predicting narrative outcomes: 5 Interpreting a character's motives: 5 Drawing inferences: 5, 6	Answering literal questions about a text: 5, 6 Recalling details and events: 5 Predicting narrative outcomes: 5, 6 Interpreting a character's motives: 5 Drawing inferences: 5	Answering literal questions about a text: 5 Identifying literal cause and effect: 5 Predicting narrative outcomes: 5 Interpreting a character's feelings: 6 Interpreting a character's motives: 5 Drawing inferences: 5, 6 Following directions: 6	Answering literal questions about a text: 5, 6 Identifying literal cause and effect: 5 Recalling details and events: 5 Predicting narrative outcomes: 5 Interpreting a character's motives: 5 Drawing inferences: 5, 6
		Written deductions: 8 Recalling details: 7 Following directions: 7, 8 Answering literal questions about a text: 7, 8 Using rules to classify objects: 8	Written deductions: 7 Recalling details: 7 Following written directions: 7 Answering literal questions about a text: 7 Using rules to classify objects: 7	Written deductions: 7 Recalling details: 7 Following written directions: 7 Answering literal questions about a text: 7 Using rules to classify objects: 7	Written deductions: 7 Recalling details: 7 Following written directions: 7 Answering literal questions about a text: 7 Using rules to classify objects: 7	Written deductions: 7 Recalling details: 7 Following written directions: 7 Answering literal questions about a text: 7 Using rules to classify objects: 7
						Lesson 140 Curriculum-Based Assessment
Spelling		Spelling words: 1, 2, 3 Identifying spelled words: 2		Phonemic segmentation: 1 √: 1 Spelling words: 3 √	Spelling words: 1	Identifying spelled words: 2 Spelling words: 2
		Sentence copying: 1 Phoneme–grapheme correspondence: 1 Writing words: 3	Sentence writing: 1, 3 Word parts (Affixes): 2	Word copying: 2 Word parts (Affixes): 2	Word copying: 2 Word parts (Affixes): 2 Writing sentences: 3	Word copying: 1 Phoneme–grapheme correspondence: 1 Writing sentences: 3

	Lesson 141	Lesson 142	Lesson 143	Lesson 144	Lesson 145
Spelling	Patterns: 1 / Spelling words: 1, 2 / Writing sentences: 3	Patterns: 1 / Spelling words: 1, 2 / Writing sentences: 3	Patterns: 1 / Spelling words: 1, 3 √: 2 / Phonemic segmentation 2 √: 2 / Writing sentences: 3	Spelling words: 2 / Identifying spelled words: 2 / Writing words: 3	Patterns: 1 / Spelling words: 1, 2, 3 √: 1 / Writing words: 3
Comprehension	Using rules to classify objects: 7 / Answering literal questions about a text: 7 / Following written directions: 7 / Recalling details: 7 / Written deductions: 7 / Predicting narrative outcomes: 5 / Drawing inferences: 5, 6 / Answering literal questions about a text: 5, 6	Using rules to classify objects: 8 / Answering literal questions about a text: 7, 8 / Following directions: 6 / Recalling details: 8 / Written deductions: 8 / Interpreting a character's feelings: 6 / Predicting narrative outcomes: 5, 6 / Drawing inferences: 5, 6 / Answering literal questions about a text: 5, 6	Using rules to classify objects: 8 / Answering literal questions about a text: 8 / Following directions: 7 / Recalling details: 8 / Written deductions: 8 / Drawing inferences: 5, 6 / Interpreting a character's feelings: 5, 6 / Predicting narrative outcomes: 5 / Identifying literal cause and effect: 5 / Recalling details and events: 5, 6 / Answering literal questions about a text: 5, 6	Using rules to classify objects: 7 / Answering literal questions about a text: 7 / Following written directions: 7 / Recalling details: 7 / Written deductions: 7 / Drawing inferences: 5, 6 / Interpreting a character's motives: 6 / Interpreting a character's feelings: 5 / Answering literal questions about a text: 5, 6	Using rules to classify objects: 8 / Answering literal questions about a text: 8 / Following directions: 8 / Recalling details: 8 / Written deductions: 8 / Drawing inferences: 5, 6 / Interpreting a character's feelings: 5 / Interpreting a character's motives: 5 / Predicting narrative outcomes: 5 / Identifying literal cause and effect: 5 / Answering literal questions about a text: 5, 6
Fluency	Reading words: 1–4 √: 1–4	Reading words: 1–4 √: 1–4	Reading words: 1–4 √: 1–4	Reading words: 1–4 √: 1–4	Reading words: 1–4 √: 1–4 / IC: 145
Phonics and Word Recognition — Regular	Connected text: 5 √: 5 / Reading words: 1 (**spider**, **jungle**, **torn**, **thorn**), 2 (**hunter**, **strongest**), 3 (**eye**), 4 (**pain**, **lion**) √: 1–4 / Spell by letter name: 1 (**spider**, **jungle**), 4 (**pain**, **lion**) √: 1–4 / Underlined parts of words: 2 (**hunter**, **strongest**) √: 2	Connected text: 5 √: 5 / Reading words: 1 (**Casey**, **salad**, **insect**, **chill**, **chair**, **bees**), 2, 3 (**body**, **kill**), 4 (**hens**) √: 1–4 / Spell by letter name: 1 (**Casey**, **salad**, **insect**, **chill**, **chair**, **bees**) √: 1–4 / Underlined parts of words: 2, 4 (**hens**) √: 2, 4	Connected text: 5 √: 5 / Reading words: 1 (**sinking**, **raft**), 2 (**sea**, **nearly**, **leaning**), 3 (**whenever**, **screaming**), 4 √: 1–4 / Spell by letter name: 1 (**sinking**, **raft**), 4 √: 1–4 / Underlined parts of words: 2 (**sea**, **nearly**, **leaning**), 3 (**whenever**, **screaming**) √: 2, 3	Connected text: 5 √: 5 / Reading words: 1 (**die**, **band**), 2 (**speak**), 3 (**sniffed**, **boomed**, **crackers**, **sucked**), 4 (**shares**, **saves**, **waving**) √: 1–4 / Spell by letter name: 1 (**die**, **band**), 4 (**shares**, **saves**, **waving**) √: 1–4 / Underlined parts of words: 2 (**speak**), 3 (**sniffed**, **boomed**, **crackers**, **sucked**) √: 2, 3	Connected text: 5 √: 5 / Reading words: 1 (**peevish**, **crown**, **clothes**), 2 (**grasshopper**, **dressed**, **tramp's**, **forgot**), 3, 4 (**slept**, **later**) √: 1 / Spell by letter name: 1 (**peevish**, **crown**, **clothes**), 4 (**slept**, **later**) √: 1, 4 / Underlined parts of words: 2 (**grasshopper**, **dressed**, **tramp's**, **forgot**) √: 2
Phonics and Word Recognition — Irregular	Reading words: 1 (**jerk**, **bushes**, **paw**), 2 (**pull**) √: 1, 2, 4 / Spell by letter name: 1 (**jerk**, **bushes**, **paw**), 4 (**pull**) √: 1, 4 / Underlined parts of words: 2 (**animals**) √: 2		Reading words: 1 (**fourth**, **America**, **gone**) √: 1 / Spell by letter name: 1 (**fourth**, **America**, **gone**) √: 1	Reading words: 1 (**thumb**, **prince**), 3 (**faced**) √: 1, 2, 4 (**threw**) / Spell by letter name: 1 (**thumb**, **prince**), 4 (**threw**) √: 1, 3, 4 / Underlined parts of words: 3 (**faced**) √: 3	Reading words: 1 (**wizard**, **shirt**, **shoe**) √: 1 / Spell by letter name: 1 (**wizard**, **shirt**, **shoe**) √: 1
Letter Sound Correspondence			Review: 2 (al, ea, wh, th, er) √: 2	Review: 2 (al, ea, sh, ch) √: 2	Review: 2 (ea, ou, er, ing, ch) √: 2
Print Awareness					
Phonemic Awareness					

Reading Mastery Signature Edition, Grade 1

Key: (for Teachers) √ = informal assessment Numbers = exercise numbers Bold face type = first appearance

		Lesson 146	Lesson 147	Lesson 148	Lesson 149	Lesson 150
Phonemic Awareness						
Print Awareness						
Letter Sound Correspondence		Review: 2 (th) √: 2	Review: 2 (ea) √: 2	Review: 2 (ea, al, ch) √: 2	Review: 2 (ea, ou, ar, ch) √: 2	
Phonics and Word Recognition	Irregular	Reading words: 2 **(tonight)**, 3 **(space, dance)**, 4 **(shoes)** √: 2, 3, 4 Spell by letter name: 4 **(shoes)** √: 4 Underlined parts of words: 2 **(tonight)** √: 2		Reading words: 1 **(page, forward)**, 3 **(dancing)** √: 1, 3 Spell by letter name: 1 **(page, forward)**, 3 **(dancing)** √: 1, 3	Reading words: 1 **(banana)** √: 1 Spell by letter name: 1 **(banana)** √: 1	Reading words: 2 **(wooden)** √: 2 Underlined parts of words: 2 **(wooden)** √: 2
	Regular	Reading words: 1 **(rule, crump, Jean)**, 2 **(deepest, matter)**, 3, 4 √: 1–4 Spell by letter name: 1 **(rule, crump, Jean)**, 4 √: 1, 4 Underlined parts of words: 2 **(deepest, matter)** √: 2	Reading words: 1 **(brown)**, 2 **(swinging, sixteen, sneaking)**, 3 √: 1–3 Spell by letter name: 1 **(brown)**, 3 √: 1, 3 Underlined parts of words: 2 **(swinging, sixteen, sneaking)** √: 2	Reading words: 1, 2 **(popped)**, 3 √: 1–3 Spell by letter name: 1, 3 √: 1, 3 Underlined parts of words: 2 **(popped)** √: 2	Reading words: 1 **(mammal, tickled, rocky)**, 2 **(remembering)**, 3 **(paths, hasn't, hadn't)** √: 1–3 Spell by letter name: 1 **(mammal)** √: 1 Underlined parts of words: 2 **(remembering)**, 3 **(paths, hasn't, hadn't)** √: 2, 3	Reading words: 1 **(vine, grape, Chop, sleepy)**, 2 **(tallest, longest)**, 3 **(tries)**, 4 **(using)** √: 1–4 Spell by letter name: 1 **(vine, grape, Chop)**, 4 **(using)** √: 1, 4 Underlined parts of words: 2 **(tallest, longest)** √: 2
		Connected text: 5 √: 5	Connected text: 5 √: 5	Connected text: 5 √: 5	Connected text: 5 √: 5	Connected text: 6 √: 6
Fluency		Reading words: 1–4 √: 1–4	Reading words: 1–3 √: 1–3	Reading words: 1–3 √: 1–3	Reading words: 1–3 √: 1–3	Reading words: 1–4 √: 1–4 IC: 150
Comprehension		Rule introduction: 5 Answering literal questions about a text: 5, 6 Predicting narrative outcomes: 5, 6 Recalling details and events: 5 Interpreting a character's feelings: 5 Drawing inferences: 5 Following directions: 6	Rule introduction: 5 Rule review: 4, 5 Applying rules: 5 Answering literal questions about a text: 5, 6 Recalling details and events: 5 Predicting narrative outcomes: 5 Interpreting a character's feelings: 6 Drawing inferences: 6 Activating prior knowledge:	Rule introduction: 5 Rule review: 4, 5 Applying rules: 5 Answering literal questions about a text: 5, 6 Identifying literal cause and effect: 5 Recalling details and events: 6 Predicting narrative outcomes: 5 Interpreting a character's feelings: 6 Drawing inferences: 5, 6	Rule introduction: 5 Rule review: 4, 5 Applying rules: 5 Answering literal questions about a text: 5, 6 Identifying literal cause and effect: 5 Recalling details and events: 6 Predicting narrative outcomes: Drawing inferences: 5 Following directions: 6	Rule introduction: 6 Rule review: 5 Applying rules: 6, 7 Answering literal questions about a text: 6, 7 Identifying literal cause and effect: 6 Interpreting a character's motives: 7 Drawing inferences: 6
		Written deductions: 8 Recalling details: 8 Following written directions: 8 Answering literal questions about a text: 8 Using rules to classify objects: 8 Rule review: 8	Written deductions: 7 Recalling details: 7 Following written directions: 7 Answering literal questions about a text: 7 Using rules to classify objects: 7 Rule review: 7 Applying rules: 7	Written deductions: 7 Recalling details: 8 Following written directions: 8 Answering literal questions about a text: 8 Applying rules: 8	Written deductions: 7, 8 Recalling details: 8 Following written directions: 8 Answering literal questions about a text: 8 Rule review: 8	Written deductions: 8, 10 Recalling details: 10 Following written directions: 10 Answering literal questions about a text: 10 Rule review: 10
Spelling		Patterns: 1 Spelling words: 1 √: 1 Phonemic segmentation: 2 √: 2	Patterns: 1 Spelling words: 1, 3	Patterns: 1 Spelling words: 1, 3	Spelling words: 1	Phonemic segmentation: 1 √: 1 Identifying spelled words: 2 Spelling words: 2, 3
						Writing words: 3
		Writing sentences: 3	Word parts (Affixes): 2 Writing words: 2	Word copying: 2 Word parts (Affixes): 2 Writing words: 3	Word copying: 2 Word parts (Affixes): 2 Writing sentences: 3	

Reading Mastery Signature Edition, Grade 1

Key: (for Teachers) √= informal assessment   Numbers = exercise numbers   Bold face type = first appearance

	Lesson 151	Lesson 152	Lesson 153	Lesson 154	Lesson 155
Phonemic Awareness					
Print Awareness					
Letter Sound Correspondence	Review: 2 (ou, ea, ch, ing) √: 2	Review: √:		Review: 3 (al, sh, wh, ee, er) √: 3	Review: 2 (l, ing) √: 2
Phonics and Word Recognition — Irregular	Reading words: 1 (**third**), 3 (**bananas**) √: 1, 3 Spell by letter name: 1 (**third**) √: 1	Reading words: 1 (**wonder, disappeared**) √: 1 Spell by letter name: 1 (**wonder**) √: 1	Reading words: 1 (**eight**), 4 (**four**) √: 1, 4 Spell by letter name: 1 (**eight**), 4 (**four**) √: 1, 4		Reading words: 1 (**metal, warm, blew**) √: 1 Spell by letter name: 1 (**metal, warm**) √: 1
Phonics and Word Recognition — Regular	Reading words: 1 (**soft**), 2 (**eaten**), 3 (**rules**), 4 (**filed, striped**) √: 1–4 Spell by letter name: 1 (**soft**) √: 1 Underlined parts of words: 2 (**eaten**), 4 (**filed, striped**) √: 2, 4	Reading words: 1 (**handle**), 2 (**muddy**), 3 (**rid, red**), 4 √: 1–4 Spell by letter name: 1 (**handle**), 4 √: 1, 4 Underlined parts of words: 2 (**muddy**) √: 2	Reading words: 1, 2 (**hated**) 3 (**dear**), 4 (**stripes**) √: 1–4 Spell by letter name: 1, 4 (**stripes**) √: 1, 4 Underlined parts of words: 2 (**hated**) √: 2	Reading words: 1 (**babies**), 2, 3 (**wish, trapper**) √: 1–3 Spell by letter name: 1 (**babies**) √: 1 Underlined parts of words: 2, 3 (**wish, trapper**) √: 2, 3	Reading words: 1 (**monkey, rather, angry**), 2, 3, 4 √: 1–4 Spell by letter name: 1 (**monkey, rather, angry**), 4 √: 1, 4 Underlined parts of words: 2 √: 2
	Connected text: 6 √: 6	Connected text: 6 √: 6	Connected text: 6 √: 6	Connected text: 5 √: 5	Connected text: 6 √: 6
Fluency	Reading words: 1–4 √: 1–4	Reading words: 1–4 √: 1–4	Reading words: 1–4 √: 1–4	Reading words: 1–3 √: 1–3	Reading words: 1–4 √: 1–4
					IC: 155
Comprehension	Rule introduction: 6 Rule review: 5, 6 Answering literal questions about a text: 6, 7 Predicting narrative outcomes: 6 Recalling details and events: 6 Interpreting a character's feelings: 7 Following directions: 7	Rule introduction: 6 Rule review: 5, 6 Answering literal questions about a text: 6, 7 Recalling details and events: 6, 7 Interpreting a character's motives: 7 Drawing inferences: 6 Following directions: 7	Rule introduction: 6 Rule review: 5, 6 Answering literal questions about a text: 6, 7 Predicting narrative outcomes: 6, 7 Recalling details and events: 6 Interpreting a character's feelings: 7 Drawing inferences: 6, 7	Rule introduction: 5 Rule review: 4, 5 Answering literal questions about a text: 5, 6 Predicting narrative outcomes: 5, 6 Recalling details and events: 5 Interpreting a character's feelings: 5, 6 Drawing inferences: 5, 6 Applying rules: 5	Rule introduction: 6 Rule review: 5, 6 Answering literal questions about a text: 6, 7 Predicting narrative outcomes: 6 Recalling details and events: 6, 7 Interpreting a character's feelings: 7 Drawing inferences: 6, 7 Applying rules: 6
	Written deductions: 9 Recalling details: 9 Following written directions: 9 Answering literal questions about a text: 9 Rule review: 9 Interpreting a character's feelings: 9	Written deductions: 9 Recalling details: 9 Following written directions: 9 Answering literal questions about a text: 9 Rule review: 9	Written deductions: 9 Recalling details: 9 Following written directions: 9 Answering literal questions about a text: 9 Rule review: 9 Applying rules: 9	Written deductions: 8 Recalling details: 8 Following written directions: 8 Answering literal questions about a text: 8 Rule review: 8 Applying rules: 8	Written deductions: 8 Recalling details: 8 Following written directions: 8 Answering literal questions about a text: 8 Rule review: 8
Spelling	Phonemic segmentation: 1 √: 1 Spelling words: 2	Identifying spelled words: 1 Spelling words: 1, 2	Spelling words: 2	Phonemic segmentation: 1 √: 1 Spelling words: 2, 3	Identifying spelled words: 1 Spelling words: 1, 2, 3
					Writing words: 3
	Writing sentences: 3	Writing sentences: 3	Word copying: 1 Phoneme–grapheme correspondence: 1 Writing sentences: 3	Writing words: 3	

Reading Mastery Signature Edition, Grade 1

		Lesson 156	Lesson 157	Lesson 158	Lesson 159	Lesson 160
Phonemic Awareness						
Print Awareness						
Letter Sound Correspondence			Review: 4 (wh, al, ea, th, er) √: 4		Review: 2 (ea, ing) √: 2	Review: 2 (ea) √: 2
Phonics and Word Recognition	Irregular	Reading words: 1 (**figure, easiest**), 2 (**they'll**), 4 (**anywhere**) √: 1, 2, 4 Spell by letter name: 1 (**figure, easiest**), 4 (**anywhere**) √: 1, 4 Underlined parts of words: 2 (**they'll**) √: 2	Reading words: 1 (**idea**), 2 (**warmer**) √: 1, 2 Spell by letter name: 1 (**idea**) √: 1 Underlined parts of words: 2 (**warmer**) √: 2	Reading words: 1 (**U.S.**) √: 1 Spell by letter name: 1 (**U.S.**) √: 1	Reading words: 3 (**Woof**) √: 3 Spell by letter name: 3 (**Woof**) √: 3	Reading words: 1 (**arrows**) √: 1 Spell by letter name: 1 (**arrows**) √: 1
	Regular	Reading words: 1 (**whale, winter**), 2, 3, 4 √: 1–4 Spell by letter name: 1 (**whale, winter**), 4 √: 1, 4 Underlined parts of words: 2 √: 2	Reading words: 1 (**spring**), 2, 3, 4 (**wheels**) √: 1–4 Spell by letter name: 1 (**spring**), 4 (**wheels**) √: 1, 4 Underlined parts of words: 2 √: 2	Reading words: 1 (**town**), 2 (**Everest, she'll**), 3, 4 (**taper, tapper, loop, stared**) √: 1–4 Spell by letter name: 4 (**taper, tapper, loop, stared**) √: 4 Underlined parts of words: 2 (**Everest, she'll**) √: 2	Reading words: 1 (**Darn, Squeak, breathe, letter**), 2, 3 √: 1–3 Spell by letter name: 1 (**Darn, Squeak, breathe, letter**), 3 √: 1, 3 Underlined parts of words: 2 √: 2	Reading words: 1 (**puppy, Here's**), 2, 3 (**tail**), 4 (**timer**) √: 1–4 Spell by letter name: 1, 4 (**timer**) √: 1, 4 Underlined parts of words: 2 (**licked, licking**) √: 2
		Connected text: 6 √: 6	Connected text: 6 √: 6	Connected text: 6 √: 6	Connected text: 5 √: 5	Connected text: 6 √: 6
Fluency		Reading words: 1–4 √: 1–4	Reading words: 1–4 √: 1–4	Reading words: 1–4 √: 1–4	Reading words: 1–3 √: 1–3	Reading words: 1–4 √: 1–4
						IC: 160
Comprehension		Rule introduction: 6 Rule review: 5, 6 Answering literal questions about a text: 6, 7 Predicting narrative outcomes: 6 Recalling details and events: 6 Drawing inferences: 6, 7	Rule introduction: 6 Rule review: 5, 6 Answering literal questions about a text: 6, 7 Predicting narrative outcomes: 6 Recalling details and events: 6 Drawing inferences: 7	Rule introduction: 6 Rule review: 5, 6 Answering literal questions about a text: 6, 7 Predicting narrative outcomes: 6 Recalling details and events: 6 Interpreting a character's feelings: 7 Drawing inferences: 6, 7	Rule introduction: 5 Rule review: 4, 5 Answering literal questions about a text: 5, 6 Recalling details and events: 5 Interpreting a character's feelings: 6 Drawing inferences: 6	Rule introduction: 6 Rule review: 5 Answering literal questions about a text: 6, 7 Predicting narrative outcomes: 6 Recalling details and events: 6, 7 Interpreting a character's feelings: 7 Interpreting a character's motives: 6 Drawing inferences: 6
		Written deductions: 9 Recalling details: 9 Following written directions: 9 Answering literal questions about a text: 9 Rule review: 9	Written deductions: 9 Recalling details: 9 Following written directions: 9 Answering literal questions about a text: 9 Rule review: 9	Written deductions: 9 Recalling details: 9 Following written directions: 9 Answering literal questions about a text: 9 Rule review: 9	Written deductions: 8 Recalling details: 8 Following written directions: 8 Answering literal questions about a text: 8 Rule review: 8	Written deductions: 9 Recalling details: 9 Following written directions: 9 Answering literal questions about a text: 9 Rule review: 9 Interpreting a character's feelings: 9
						Lesson 160 Curriculum-Based Assessment
Spelling		Spelling words: 2, 3	Phonemic segmentation: 1 √: 1 Spelling words: 2	Identifying spelled words: 1 Spelling words: 1, 2	Spelling words: 2, 3	Spelling words: 1
		Word copying: 1 Phoneme–grapheme correspondence: 1 Writing words: 3	Writing sentences: 3	Writing sentences: 3	Word copying: 1 Phoneme–grapheme correspondence: 1 Writing words: 3	Writing words: 1 Writing sentences: 2